YOU DECIDE! 2012

Current Debates in American Politics

JOHN T. ROURKE

University of Connecticut

PEARSON

Boston Columbus Indianapolis New York San Francisco Upper Saddle River
Amsterdam Cape Town Dubai London Madrid Milan Munich Paris Montreal Toronto
Delhi Mexico City Sao Paulo Sydney Hong Kong Seoul Singapore Taipei Tokyo

Executive Editor: Reid Hester
Editorial Assistant: Emily Sauerhoff
Executive Marketing Manager: Wendy Gordon
Production Manager: Savoula Amanatidis
Project Coordination, Text Design, and Electronic Page Makeup: Lorraine Patsco
Cover Design Manager: John Callahan
Cover Photo: Courtesy of Getty Images, Inc.
Senior Manufacturing Buyer: Roy L. Pickering, Jr.
Printer and Binder: R. R. Donnelley and Sons Company–Crawfordsville
Cover Printer: R. R. Donnelley and Sons Company–Crawfordsville

For permission to use copyrighted material, grateful acknowledgment is made to the copyright holders on pp. 284–285, which are hereby made part of this copyright page.

Cataloging-in-Publication Data on file at the Library of Congress

10 9 8 7 6 5 4 3—DOC—14 13 12

www.pearsonhighered.com   ISBN-10: 0-205-86542-9
ISBN-13: 978-0-205-86542-0

CONTENTS

PREFACE   xiv

1. CONSTITUTION   2

THE MANDATE THAT INDIVIDUALS BUY HEALTH INSURANCE:
NECESSARY AND PROPER *OR* UNCONSTITUTIONAL REQUIREMENT?

The Mandate That Individuals Buy Health Insurance: Necessary and Proper

ADVOCATE: John Kroger, Attorney General of Oregon

SOURCE: Testimony during hearings on "The Constitutionality of the Affordable Care Act," before the U.S. Senate, Committee on the Judiciary, February 2, 2011

The Mandate That Individuals Buy Health Insurance: Unconstitutional Requirement

ADVOCATE: Kenneth T. Cuccinelli, II, Attorney General of Virginia

SOURCE: Testimony during hearings on "The Constitutionality of the Individual Mandate," before the U.S. House of Representatives, Committee on the Judiciary, February 16, 2011

Also suitable for chapters on Congress, Courts, Health Care Policy

2. FEDERALISM   16

ARIZONA'S LAW ENCOURAGING CITIZEN IDENTITY CHECKS BY POLICE:
STATE INTRUSION INTO NATIONAL POLICY *OR* PERMISSIBLE STATE ACTION?

Arizona's Law Encouraging Citizen Identity Checks by Police: State Intrusion into National Policy

ADVOCATE: Attorneys representing the U.S. government seeking to enjoin the enforcement of Arizona's S.B. 1070

SOURCE: *The United States of America, Plaintiff, v. The State of Arizona; and Janice K. Brewer, Governor of the State of Arizona, in her Official Capacity, Defendants,* Case 2:10-cv-01413, U.S. District Court for the District of Arizona, July 6, 2010

Arizona's Law Encouraging Citizen Identity Checks by Police: Permissible State Action

ADVOCATE: Attorneys representing Arizona and its governor, Janice K. Brewer, seeking to block a petition by the U.S. government to enjoin the enforcement of Arizona's S.B. 1070

SOURCE: *The United States of America, Plaintiff, v. The State of Arizona; and Janice K. Brewer, Governor of the State of Arizona, in her Official Capacity, Defendants,* Case 2:10-cv-01413, U.S. District Court for the District of Arizona, July 20, 2010

Also suitable for chapters on Civil Rights, Courts, Constitution, Criminal Justice

3. CIVIL LIBERTIES   38

THE PHRASE "UNDER GOD" IN THE PLEDGE OF ALLEGIENCE: VIOLATION OF THE FIRST AMENDMENT *OR* ACCEPTABLE TRADITIONAL EXPRESSION?

The Phrase "Under God" in the Pledge of Allegiance: Violation of the First Amendment

ADVOCATE: Douglas Laycock, Professor, School of Law, University of Texas; and Counsel of Record for 32 Christian and Jewish clergy filing an amicus curiae brief with the Supreme Court in *Elk Gove School District v. Newdow*

SOURCE: A discussion of the topic "Under God? Pledge of Allegiance Constitutionality," sponsored by the Pew Forum on Religion and Public Life and held before the National Press Club, Washington, D.C., March 19, 2004

The Phrase "Under God" in the Pledge of Allegiance: Acceptable Traditional Expression

ADVOCATE: Jay Alan Sekulow, Chief Counsel, American Center for Law and Justice; and Counsel of Record for 76 members of Congress and the Committee to Protect the Pledge filing an amicus curiae brief with the Supreme Court in *Elk Gove School District v. Newdow*

SOURCE: A discussion of the topic "Under God? Pledge of Allegiance Constitutionality," sponsored by the Pew Forum on Religion and Public Life and held before the National Press Club, Washington, D.C., March 19, 2004

Also suitable for chapters on Courts, Political Culture (role of religion in politics)

4. CIVIL RIGHTS   54

CALIFORNIA'S PROPOSITION 8 BARRING GAY MARRIAGES: EQUAL RIGHTS VIOLATION OF THE U.S. CONSTITUTION *OR* VALID STATE LAW?

California's Proposition 8 Barring Gay Marriages: Equal Rights Violation of the U.S. Constitution

ADVOCATE: Attorneys representing plaintiffs Kristen M. Perry, et al. and the City of San Francisco seeking to have California's constitutional clause barring gay marriage declared a violation of the U.S. Constitution

SOURCE: *Kristin M. Perry, et al., Plaintiffs, and the City and County of San Francisco, Plaintiff-Intervenor, v. Arnold Schwarzenegger, et al., Defendants, and Proposition 8 Official Proponents Dennis Hollingsworth, et al., Defendant-Intervenors*; Case 3:09-cv-02292-VRW; U.S. District Court for the Northern District of California; Responses to Court's Questions for Closing Arguments, June 15, 2010

California's Proposition 8 Barring Gay Marriages: Valid State Law

ADVOCATE: Attorneys representing Proposition 8 official proponents Dennis Hollingsworth, et al., seeking to have California's constitutional clause barring gay marriage upheld

SOURCE: *Kristin M. Perry, et al., Plaintiffs, and the City and County of San Francisco, Plaintiff-Intervenor, v. Arnold Schwarzenegger, et al., Defendants, and Proposition 8 Official Proponents Dennis Hollingsworth, et al., Defendant-Intervenors;* Case 3:09-cv-02292-VRW; U.S. District Court for the Northern District of California; Responses to Court's Questions for Closing Arguments, June 15, 2010

Also suitable for chapters on the Constitution, Federalism, Political Culture, the Courts

5. AMERICAN PEOPLE/POLITICAL CULTURE   76

THE CULTURAL ASSIMILATION OF IMMIGRANTS:
THE MELTING POT IS BROKEN *OR* BLENDING SATISFACTORILY?

The Cultural Assimilation of Immigrants: The Melting Pot Is Broken

ADVOCATE: John Fonte, Director, Center for American Common Culture, Hudson Institute

SOURCE: Testimony during hearings on "Comprehensive Immigration Reform: Becoming Americans—U.S. Immigrant Integration" before the U.S. House of Representatives, Committee on the Judiciary, Subcommittee on Immigration Citizenship, Refugees, Border Security, and International Law, May 16, 2007

The Cultural Assimilation of Immigrants: Blending Satisfactorily

ADVOCATE: Gary Gerstle, James Stahlman Professor, Department of History, Vanderbilt University

SOURCE: Testimony during hearings on "Comprehensive Immigration Reform: Becoming Americans—U.S. Immigrant Integration" before the U.S. House of Representatives, Committee on the Judiciary, Subcommittee on Immigration Citizenship, Refugees, Border Security, and International Law, May 16, 2007

Also suitable for chapters on Social Policy

6. PARTICIPATION   94

REQUIRING PHOTO IDENTIFICATION TO VOTE:
PROTECTING THE INTEGRITY OF ELECTIONS *OR* SUPPRESSING VOTER TURNOUT?

Requiring Photo Identification to Vote: Protecting the Integrity of Elections

ADVOCATE: Hans von Spakovsky, Senior Legal Fellow, Center for Legal & Judicial Studies, Heritage Foundation

SOURCE: "Voter Photo Identification: Protecting the Security of Elections," Legal Memorandum #70, Heritage Foundation, July 13, 2011

Requiring Photo Identification to Vote: Suppressing Voter Turnout

ADVOCATE: Shirley Jackson Lee, Democrat, U.S. House of Representatives, Texas

SOURCE: "Voter Suppression and Voter ID," remarks to the U.S. House of Representatives, *Congressional Record*, July 19, 2011

Also suitable for chapters on Civil Liberties, Elections

7. MEDIA   108

THE FUTURE OF QUALITY JOURNALISM:
IMPERILED *OR* SECURE?

The Future of Quality Journalism: Imperiled

ADVOCATE: David Simon, creator and executive producer of the HBO television series *The Wire*

SOURCE: Testimony during hearings on Senate Subcommittee on "The Future of Journalism" before the U.S. Senate, Committee on Commerce, Science, and Transportation; Subcommittee on Communications, Technology, and the Internet, May 6, 2009

The Future of Quality Journalism: Secure

ADVOCATE: Arianna Huffington, founder of the *Huffington Post*

SOURCE: Testimony during hearings on "The Future of Journalism" before the U.S. Senate, Committee on Commerce, Science, and Transportation; Subcommittee on Communications, Technology, and the Internet, May 6, 2009

Also suitable for chapters on Civil Liberties, Social Policy

8. INTEREST GROUPS   120

PERMITTING CORPORATIONS TO PARTICIPATE IN ELECTION
CAMPAIGNS:
A BLOW TO DEMOCRACY *OR* CONSTITUTIONALLY APPROPRIATE?

Permitting Corporations to Participate in Election Campaigns: A Blow to Democracy

ADVOCATES: Monica Youn, Counsel at the Brennan Center for Justice at the New York University School of Law

SOURCE: Testimony during hearings on the "First Amendment and Campaign Finance Reform After *Citizens United*," before the Committee on the Judiciary, U.S. House of Representatives, February 3, 2010

Permitting Corporations to Participate in Election Campaigns: Constitutionally Appropriate

ADVOCATE: M. Todd Henderson, Assistant Professor of Law, University of Chicago Law School

SOURCE: "*Citizens United*: A Defense," Faculty Blog, University of Chicago Law School, March 12, 2010

Also suitable for chapters on Elections

9. POLITICAL PARTIES   134

TEA PARTY MEMBERS:
IRRESPONSIBLE ZEALOTS *OR* RESPONSIBLY DISSENTING CITIZENS?

Tea Party Members: Irresponsible Zealots

ADVOCATE: Frank Lautenberg, Member, U.S. Senate, Democrat, New Jersey

SOURCE: "Toxic Tea," remarks to the U.S. Senate, *Congressional Record*, March 10, 2011

Tea Party Members: Responsibly Dissenting Citizens
ADVOCATE: Mitch McConnell, Minority Leader, U.S. Senate, Republican, Kentucky
SOURCE: "Tea Party," remarks to the U.S. Senate, *Congressional Record*, March 31, 2011

Also suitable for chapters on Political Behavior/Thought, Elections

10. VOTING/CAMPAIGNS/ELECTIONS   142

ELECTING THE PRESIDENT:
ADOPT THE NATIONAL POPULAR VOTE PLAN *OR* PRESERVE ELECTORAL COLLEGE?

Electing the President: Adopt the National Popular Vote Plan
ADVOCATE: National Popular Vote, an advocacy organization
SOURCE: "Agreement Among the States to Elect the President by National Popular Vote" from the Web site of National Popular Vote, April 29, 2009

Electing the President: Preserve the Electoral College
ADVOCATE: John Samples, Director, Center for Representative Government, Cato Institute
SOURCE: "A Critique of the National Popular Vote Plan for Electing the President," *Policy Analysis*, October 13, 2008

Also suitable for chapters on Presidency, Federalism

11. CONGRESS   164

SENATE FILIBUSTERS:
BLOCKING MAJORITY RULE *OR* PREVENTING MAJORITY TYRANNY?

Senate Filibusters: Blocking Majority Rule
ADVOCATE: Thomas E. Mann, W. Averell Harriman Chair and Senior Fellow, Brookings Institution
SOURCE: Testimony during hearings on "Examining the Filibuster: Legislative Proposals to Change Senate Procedures" before the Committee on Rules and Administration, U.S. Senate, June 23, 2010

Senate Filibusters: Preventing Majority Tyranny
ADVOCATE: Lee Rawls Faculty Member, National War College and Adjunct Professor, College of William and Mary
SOURCE: Testimony during hearings on "Examining the Filibuster: Legislative Proposals to Change Senate Procedures" before the Committee on Rules and Administration, U.S. Senate, June 23, 2010

Also suitable for chapters on Courts, Democracy

12. PRESIDENCY   176

BARACK OBAMA'S USE OF THE PRESIDENT'S WAR POWERS: REASONABLE *OR* EXCESSIVE?

Barack Obama's Use of the President's War Powers: Reasonable

ADVOCATE: Hongju Koh, Legal Adviser, U.S. Department of State

SOURCE: Testimony during hearings on "Libya and War Powers," before the U.S. Senate, Committee on Foreign Relations, June 28, 2011

Barack Obama's Use of the President's War Powers: Excessive

ADVOCATE: Louis Fisher, Scholar in Residence, Constitution Project

SOURCE: Testimony during hearings on "Libya and War Powers," before the U.S. Senate, Committee on Foreign Relations, June 28, 2011

Also suitable for chapters on Constitution, Congress, Foreign/National Security Policy

13. BUREAUCRACY   192

THE NEW CONSUMER FINANCIAL PROTECTION BUREAU: CONSUMER GUARDIAN *OR* DANGEROUS BUREAUCRACY?

The New Consumer Financial Protection Bureau: Consumer Guardian

ADVOCATE: Elizabeth Warren, Special Advisor to the Secretary of the Treasury for the Consumer Financial Protection Bureau

SOURCE: Testimony during hearings on "The Rulemaking Process and Unitary Executive Theory" before the U.S. House of Representatives, Committee on the Judiciary, Subcommittee on Commercial and Administrative Law, May 6, 2008

The New Consumer Financial Protection Bureau: Dangerous Bureaucracy

ADVOCATE: Todd Zywicki, Foundation Professor of Law, George Mason University

SOURCE: Testimony during hearings on "Who's Watching the Watchmen? Oversight of the Consumer Financial Protection Bureau" before the U.S. House of Representatives, Committee on Oversight and Government Relations, Subcommittee on TARP, Financial Services, and Bailouts of Public and Private Programs, May 24, 2011

Also suitable for chapters on Presidency, Environmental Policy

14. JUDICIARY   208

DECIDING ON THE CONSTITUTION'S MEANING: RELY ON THE ORIGNAL AUTHORS *OR* INTERPRET IN LIGHT OF MODERN CIRCUMSTANCES?

Deciding the Constitution's Meaning: Rely on the Original Authors

ADVOCATE: Keith E. Whittington, William Nelson Cromwell Professor of Politics, Princeton University

SOURCE: "Originalism Within the Living Constitution," *Advance: The Journal of the American Constitution Society Issues Groups*, Fall 2007

Deciding the Meaning of the Constitution: Interpret in Light of Modern Circumstances
ADVOCATE: Erwin Chemerinsky, Alston & Bird Professor of Law and Political Science, Duke University
SOURCE: "Constitutional Interpretation for the Twenty-first Century," *Advance: The Journal of the American Constitution Society Issues Groups*, Fall 2007

Also suitable for chapters on Courts, Civil Liberties, Civil Rights

15. STATE AND LOCAL GOVERNMENT   222

ALLOWING STATES TO COLLECT SALES TAXES ON INTERSTATE COMMERCE:
LEVELING THE PLAYING FIELD *OR* A THREAT TO ELECTRONIC COMMERCE?

Allowing States to Collect Sales Taxes on Interstate Commerce: Leveling the Playing Field
ADVOCATE: Steven Rauschenberger, past President, National Conference of State Legislatures
SOURCE: Testimony during hearings on "H.R. 3396—The Sales Tax Fairness and Simplification Act" before the House of Representatives, Committee on the Judiciary, Subcommittee on Administrative and Commercial Law, December 6, 2007

Allowing States to Collect Sales Taxes on Interstate Commerce: A Threat to Electronic Commerce
ADVOCATE: George S. Isaacson, Tax Counsel for the Direct Marketing Association
SOURCE: Testimony during hearings on "H.R. 3396—The Sales Tax Fairness and Simplification Act" before the House of Representatives, Committee on the Judiciary, Subcommittee on Administrative and Commercial Law, December 6, 2007

Also suitable for chapters on Constitution, Federalism, Economic Policy

16. BUDGETARY POLICY   252

ADDING A BALANCED BUDGET AMENDMENT TO THE CONSTITUTION:
FISCAL IMPERATIVE *OR* UNNECESSARY AND UNWISE

Adding a Balanced Budget Amendment to the Constitution: Fiscal Imperative
ADVOCATE: Andrew Moylan, Vice President of Government Affairs, National Taxpayers Union
SOURCE: Testimony during hearings on "Should the Constitution Be Amended to Address the Federal Deficit" held before U.S. House of Representatives, Committee on the Judiciary, Subcommittee on the Constitution, May 13, 2011

Adding a Balanced Budget Amendment to the Constitution: Unnecessary and Unwise
ADVOCATE: Robert Greenstein, President, Center on Budget and Policy Priorities

SOURCE: Testimony during hearings on "Should the Constitution Be Amended to Address the Federal Deficit" held before U.S. House of Representatives, Committee on the Judiciary, Subcommittee on the Constitution, May 13, 2011

Also suitable for chapters on Congress, Economic Policy

---

17. NATIONAL SECURITY POLICY   270

TRYING THOSE ACCUSED OF TERRORISM: USE CIVILIAN COURTS *OR* USE MILITARY COMMISSIONS?

Trying Those Accused of Terrorism: Use Civilian Courts

ADVOCATE: Stephen A. Saltzburg, Wallace and Beverley Woodbury University Professor, George Washington University Law School

SOURCE: Testimony during hearings on "Justice for America: Using Military Commissions to Try the 9/11 Conspirators" before the U.S. House of Representatives, Committee on the Judiciary, Subcommittee on Crime, Terrorism and Homeland Security, April 5, 2011

Trying Those Accused of Terrorism: Use Military Commissions

ADVOCATE: Stephanie Hessler, Adjunct Fellow, Manhattan Institute for Policy Studies

SOURCE: Testimony during hearings on "Justice for America: Using Military Commissions to Try the 9/11 Conspirators" before the U.S. House of Representatives, Committee on the Judiciary, Subcommittee on Crime, Terrorism and Homeland Security, April 5, 2011

Also suitable for chapters on Civil Liberties, Courts, Foreign Policy

---

CREDITS   284

EXTENDED CONTENTS

WEB ISSUES

The following topics are available on the Web at:
www.pearsonhighered.com/rourke2012.

18. ENVIRONMENTAL POLICY

FEDERAL POLICY REGARDING GLOBAL WARMING:
TAKE STRONGER ACTION NOW *OR* PROCEED CAUTIOUSLY AT BEST?

Federal Policy Regarding Global Warming: Take Stronger Action Now
ADVOCATE: Kerry A. Emanuel, Breene M. Kerr Professor of Atmospheric Science, Massachusetts Institute of Technology
SOURCE: Testimony on "Climate Change: Examining the Processes Used to Create Science and Policy" during hearings before the U.S. House of Representatives, Committee on Science, Space, and Technology, March 31, 2011

Federal Policy Regarding Global Warming: Proceed Cautiously at Best
ADVOCATE: W. David Montgomery, Economist and Consultant specializing in environmental issues
SOURCE: Testimony on "Climate Change: Examining the Processes Used to Create Science and Policy" during hearings before the U.S. House of Representatives, Committee on Science, Space, and Technology, March 31, 2011

Also suitable for chapters on Environments, Policymaking

19. CRIMINAL JUSTICE POLICY

THE DEATH PENALTY:
FATALLY FLAWED *OR* DEFENSIBLE?

The Death Penalty: Fatally Flawed
ADVOCATE: Stephen B. Bright. Director, Southern Center for Human Rights, Atlanta, Georgia; Visiting Lecturer in Law, Harvard and Yale Law Schools
SOURCE: Testimony during hearings on "An Examination of the Death Penalty in the United States" before the U.S. Senate, Committee on the Judiciary, Subcommittee on the Constitution, February 1, 2006

The Death Penalty: Defensible
ADVOCATE: John McAdams, Professor of Political Science, Marquette University
SOURCE: Testimony during hearings on "An Examination of the Death Penalty in the United States" before the U.S. Senate, Committee on the Judiciary, Subcommittee on the Constitution, February 1, 2006

Also suitable for chapters on Civil Rights

20. SOCIAL WELFARE POLICY

POVERTY IN AMERICA:
BAD AND GETTING WORSE *OR* NOT BAD AND GETTING BETTER?

Poverty in America: Bad and Getting Worse

ADVOCATE: John Podesta, President, Center for American Progress

SOURCE: Testimony during hearings on "Economic Opportunity and Poverty in America" before U.S. House of Representatives, Committee on Ways & Means, Subcommittee on Income Security and Family Support, April 26, 2007

Poverty in America: Not Bad and Getting Better

ADVOCATE: Robert Rector, Senior Policy Analyst, The Heritage Foundation

SOURCE: Testimony during hearings on "Economic Opportunity and Poverty in America" before U.S. House of Representatives, Committee on Ways & Means, Subcommittee on Income Security and Family Support, April 26, 2007

Also suitable for chapters on Introduction, Policymaking, Economic Policy

21. WOMEN'S RIGHTS POLICY

ACHIEVING GENDER PAY EQUITY:
TOUGHER LAWS NEEDED *OR* CURRENT LAW SATISFACTORY?

Achieving Gender Pay Equity: Tougher Laws Needed

ADVOCATE: Marcia D. Greenberger, Co-President, National Women's Law Center

SOURCE: Testimony during hearings on the "Paycheck Fairness Act" before the U.S. House of Representatives, Committee on Education and Labor, Subcommittee on Workforce Protection, July 11, 2007

Achieving Gender Pay Equity: Current Law Satisfactory

ADVOCATE: Barbara Berish Brown, Chair, Washington, D.C. office of Paul, Hastings, Janofsky & Walker and Vice-Chair, Labor & Employment Law Section, American Bar Association

SOURCE: Testimony during hearings on the "Paycheck Fairness Act" before the U.S. Senate, Committee on Health, Education, Labor & Pensions, April 12, 2007

Also suitable for chapters on Economic Policy, Women and Politics, Civil Rights

22. EDUCATION POLICY

ASSIGNING STUDENTS TO SCHOOLS BASED ON RACE:
JUSTIFIED *OR* UNACCEPTABLE?

Assigning Students to Schools Based on Race: Justified

ADVOCATE: National Education Association, et al.

SOURCE: Amicus Curiae brief to the U.S. Supreme Court in *Parents Involved in Community Schools v. Seattle School District No. 1* (2007)

Assigning Students to Schools Based on Race: Unacceptable

ADVOCATE: Asian American Legal Foundation

SOURCE: Amicus Curiae brief to the U.S. Supreme Court in *Parents Involved in Community Schools v. Seattle School District No. 1* (2007)

Also suitable for chapters on Constitution, Civil Rights

PREFACE

To the Students

This book is founded on two firm convictions. The first is that each of you who reads this book is profoundly affected by politics, probably in more ways than you know. The second "truth" is that it is important that everyone be attentive to and active in politics.

WHAT IS NEW IN THIS EDITION

The following debates are new to this edition:

- The Mandate that Individuals Buy Health Insurance: Necessary and Proper *or* Unconstitutional Requirement?
- Requiring Photo Identification to Vote: Protecting the Integrity of Elections *or* Suppressing Voter Turnout?
- Tea Party Members: Irresponsible Zealots *or* Responsibly Dissenting Citizens?
- Barack Obama's Use of the President's War Powers: Reasonable *or* Excessive?
- The New Consumer Financial Protection Bureau: Consumer Guardian *or* Dangerous Bureaucracy?
- Adding a Balanced Budget Amendment to the Constitution: Fiscal Imperative *or* Unnecessary and Unwise
- Trying Those Accused of Terrorism: Use Civilian Courts *or* Use Military Commissions
- Federal Policy Regarding Global Warming: Take Stronger Action Now or Proceed Cautiously at Best?

POLITICS AFFECTS YOU

The outcome of many of the 17 debates in this printed volume and the 5 supplemental debates on the Web will impact your life directly. If you are a woman, for example, the controversy over gender pay equity laws in **Debate 21** has, and will help, determine whether your pay will be equal to that of men doing the same work with the same experience. College-age students are most likely to be sent to (and to die in) wars, and for young adults, even more than most Americans, the question of who should decide when U.S. forces go into combat, the focus of **Debate 12**, has potential life-altering importance.

On the domestic front, freedom of religion is one of Americans' most cherished rights and is protected by the First Amendment. But the application of the First Amendment is something of a double-edged sword. There is widespread agreement that people should have the right to whatever religious belief they may hold. What is controversial and presented in **Debate 3** is whether even such traditional references to God, such as the words "under God" in the Pledge of Allegiance, violate the separation of church and state principle in the First Amendment.

YOU CAN, AND SHOULD, AFFECT POLITICS

The second thing this volume strongly suggests is that you can, and should, take part in politics. One necessity to be involved is to know what is happening, and for that Americans necessarily rely heavily on the press. However, one of the traditional pillars of the news media—newspapers—are in huge financial trouble. There are also complaints that the most widely followed of the news media, television, is sacrificing solid news content for infotainment in order to hold its audience, and, by extension, its ad revenues. **Debate 7** takes up the implications of these media woes. If participation in politics is good, then we should be wary of anything that limits participation. **Debate 6** addresses one proposed barrier to voting, the need to present a photo ID to vote. Are the gains from instituting such a proposal worth the costs? **Debate 10** also arguably involves a limitation on participation, given the argument by those who would abolish the Electoral College that it tends to suppress voting in the majority of states that are safe bets for one or the other presidential candidate. Whether they are for or against the candidate who clearly wins in their state, many people ask themselves: Why bother to vote? It may be, though, that more participation by all "persons" is *not* desirable. **Debate 8** takes up the wisdom of the Supreme Court's ruling in *Citizens United v. FEC* (2010) that a law barring corporations from sponsoring independent "electioneering communications" close to elections violated the First Amendment free speech rights of corporations because they are considered legal "persons" under Supreme Court decisions to the early 1800s.

POLITICS SHOULD NOT ALWAYS AFFECT YOU

It is true that politics affects us all and that we should try to affect politics, but it is also a cornerstone of democracy that many aspects of our lives should be shielded from political control. This principle is the basis of, among other things, the Bill of Rights. Many of the debates in this volume address the line between where the government can make policy and where it is violating our political and civil rights.

For example, **Debate 22** takes up how far the government can go to achieve racial integration in the country's schools. This debate focuses on the policy of the Seattle schools to try to achieve balance in the racial composition of the district's schools by sometimes busing students.

PAY ATTENTION TO THE POLICY PROCESS

Process may seem less interesting than policy to many people, but you do not have to study politics very long to learn that *who* decides something very often determines *what* the policy will be. Process does not always determine which policy is adopted, but it plays a large role. Therefore, there are a number of debates in this volume whose outcome does not directly affect a specific policy, but which could have a profound impact on the policy process. For example, **Debate 2**, on Federalism, debates how far in the federal system Arizona can go in passing laws affecting immigration, an area of regulation generally dominated by the national government. Federalism is also a key component of the dispute in **Debate 15** over whether states should be allowed to levy a sales tax on goods ordered from another state on the Internet or other form of remote commerce.

There is little doubt that the president is the most powerful actor in the political process, and **Debate 12** examines one aspect of that authority: the extent of the president's ability as commander in chief to unilaterally use U.S. military power. Yet another matter of process, the use of filibusters to defeat or force modification of legislation in the U.S. Senate is the subject of **Debate 11**. Both sides agree that filibusters contravene the principle of majority rule but disagree on whether that is a good or bad thing.

WHO SERVES INFLUENCES POLICY

Policy is a reflection, in part, of who serves and the process by which they come to and remain in office. **Debates 9** and **10** both focus on that issue. **Debate 9** takes up the newest phenomenon in electoral politics, the Tea Party movement, and its impact on elections and subsequent policy making in Washington, D.C. and across the country. Then **Debate 10** takes up the complex procedure by which Americans elect their presidents, and debates a plan to abolish the Electoral College and have the president be decided by a national popular vote.

The vast government bureaucracy is also part of the policy process. The newest major federal bureaucratic actor is the Consumer Financial Protection Bureau, and the controversy over its authority, the concentration of that authority in its director, and its insulation from congressional oversight is at the center of **Debate 13**.

It is also important to realize that the courts, especially the U.S. Supreme Court, are very much part of the policy process. That is evident in **Debate 1**, in which the advocates disagree on the constitutionality of the requirement in the recently enacted health care bill that everyone without health insurance has to buy a policy or be fined. If the courts rule the mandate unconstitutional, then the financing for the new health care system and perhaps the system itself will be unworkable. Along somewhat similar lines, **Debate 14** addresses the question of whether the meaning of the Constitution should be judged solely in terms of what those who wrote its provisions meant or more broadly in terms of contemporary circumstances and values.

STATE AND LOCAL GOVERNMENTS ARE IMPORTANT, TOO

The federal government is just one of the more than 80,000 different governments in the United States. Each of the state and local governments has the power to pass laws, establish regulations, and tax and spend. For example, state and local governments now collect over $1.2 trillion a year in taxes. About a quarter of this revenue comes from sales taxes, and **Debate 15** takes up whether to add to these receipts by allowing states to tax interstate commerce.

THERE ARE OFTEN MORE THAN TWO SIDES TO A QUESTION

Often public policy questions are put in terms of "pro and con," "favor or oppose," or some other such stark choice. This approach is sometimes called a Manichean approach, a reference to Manicheanism, a religion founded by the Persian prophet Mani (c. 216–276). It taught "dualism," the idea that the universe is divided into opposite, struggling, and equally powerful realities, light (good) and darkness (evil).

The view here is that many policy issues are more a matter of degree, and that the opinion of people is better represented as a place along a range of possibilities, rather than a black-or-white Manichean choice. Numerous issues are like that. For example, virtually all Americans favor doing something to begin to narrow the federal government's massive budget deficits and to eventually balance the budget. **Debate 16** presents something of a yes–no debate regarding whether to amend the Constitution to require a balanced budget, but the core of reforming the budget will be very complex. What would you spend less on, and how much? Taxes may be even more complex. Whose taxes should get increased and by how much? Should entirely new taxes, like a national sales tax, be instituted? Would it be advisable to end some tax breaks, like homeowners deducting their mortgage interest and real estate taxes from their income taxes? Another such issue that many people would say extends beyond a simple yes–no dichotomy is the question of how to imprison, try, and otherwise deal with captured foreign terrorists. President Obama has been criticized by both the left and right about his policies, and **Debate 17** struggles with how to balance the imperative of providing just trials for alleged terrorists on the one hand, and on the other meeting the national security interests of the United States.

MANY ISSUES CANNOT BE DECIDED BY RATIONALITY ALONE

Values are an important aspect of many debates. For most Americans, the death penalty, the focus of **Debate 19**, is a matter of what is just or moral. Some people believe that no reason is great enough to execute someone. Other people believe with equal fervor that murderers and some other types of criminals forfeit their right to life, and justice is served by their execution. This does not mean that there are no objective, rational aspects to the death penalty debate, or that everyone is absolutely convinced one way or the other. Indeed, while a large majority of Americans favor the death penalty, surveys also show that people are troubled by a range of possible injustices, such as the relationship of wealth to the ability to mount a top-notch defense, the ability to execute people for crimes committed while a juvenile, and claims of racial injustice. What is just is also at the heart of **Debate 4**, which considers whether state laws barring same-sex marriages are a violation of equal rights under the U.S. Constitution.

The discussion in **Debate 5** about how well recent immigrants are melding into the larger American culture also has multiple aspects, including both facts and values. At the objective level, the question is the degree of the immigrants' acculturation. How much of their old culture have immigrants and their families kept, and how "Americanized" have they become, especially after an extended time and into the second and third generations? Irrespective of the answer, there is also a question of values. How much should these newcomers and their families become homogenized? **Debate 20**, on poverty, also includes both objective and subjective aspects. How objectively do we determine who is poor? You will see that the formula for measuring poverty is very controversial. There is also the question of what and how much to do about poverty. To a degree, your views probably depend in part on whether you think an individual's success in life is the product of that person's abilities and effort or the product of society.

SOME CONCLUDING THOUGHTS

The points with which we began are important enough to reiterate. Whether you care about politics or not, it affects you every day in many ways. As the legendary heavyweight boxer Joe Louis put it after knocking out Billy Conn, a more agile but less powerful opponent, in their 1941 championship fight, "You can run, but you can't hide."

Simply paying attention is a good start, but action is even better. Everyone should be politically active, at least to the level of voting. Doing so is in your self-interest because decisions made by the federal, state, and local governments in the U.S. political system provide each of us with both tangible benefits (such as roads and schools) and intangible benefits (such as civil liberties and security). Also, for good or ill, the government takes things away from each of us (such as taxes) and restricts our actions (such as speed limits). It is also the case in politics, as the old saying goes, that squeaky wheels get the grease. Those who participate actively are more likely to be influential. Those who do not, and young adults are by far the age group least likely to even vote, are consigned to grumbling impotently on the sideline.

As an absolute last thought (really!), let me encourage you to contact me with questions or comments. My e-mail address is john.rourke@uconn.edu. Compliments are always great, but if you disagree with anything I have written or my choice of topics and readings, or if you have a suggestion for the next edition, let me know.

To the Faculty

Having plied the podium, so to speak, for three decades, I have some well-formed ideas of what a good reader should do. It is from that perspective that I have organized this reader to work for the students who read it and the faculty members who adopt it for use in their classes. Below is what I look for in a reader and how I have constructed this one to meet those standards.

PROVOKE CLASS DISCUSSION

The classes I have enjoyed the most over the years have been the ones that have been the liveliest, with students participating enthusiastically in a give-and-take among themselves and with me. Many of the debates herein have been selected to engender such participation in your classes by focusing on hot-button topics that provoke heated debate even among those who are not heavily involved in politics and who do not have a lot of background on the topic. Just a few of the other hot-button topics are: use of the phrase "under God" in the Pledge of Allegiance (**Debate 3**), the death penalty (**Debate 20**), school busing (**Debate 22**), and gay marriage (**Debate 4**). I hope they rev up your classes as much as they have energized mine.

Another point about class discussion that I highlight in the preface section "To the Students" is that, while the debate titles imply two sides, many policy topics are not a Manichean choice between yes and no. Instead, I have tried to include many issues on which opinion ranges along a scale. From that perspective, I often urge students to try to formulate a policy that can gain majority support, if not a consensus. You will also find that many of the issues herein are multifaceted, and I try to point that out to the students. For instance, the debate about the mandate to buy health insurance is about more than that requirement as such; it is also about how we interpret and apply the Constitution.

BE CURRENT

An important factor in engaging the students is being current. Discussing the interstate commerce clause is important, but it is brought to life when considering, as **Debate 1** does, whether Congress' authority to regulate interstate commerce means that federal law can require all adults without health insurance to buy a policy. Therefore, I vigorously update each edition. Even though *You Decide!* appears annually, almost a third of the topics in *You Decide! 2012* are wholly new or are revised from *You Decide! 2011*. Additionally, some of the introductory material, and especially the "Continuing Debate" sections of the issues are updated.

PROVIDE A GOOD RANGE OF TOPICS

I always look for a reader that "covers the waterfront" and have tried to put together this reader to do that. There are numerous debates on specific policy issues and others on process. All the major institutions are covered in one or more debates, and there are also debates touching on such "input" elements as parties, campaigns, interest groups, and the media. The primary focus of this book is on the national government, but federalism receives attention in **Debate 2**, and state and local government issues are taken up in **Debate 15** on taxing interstate commerce. I have also included several debates that are at the intersection of domestic and foreign affairs, including **Debate 17** (trying foreign terrorists) and **Debate 18** (global warming policy).

My sense of a good range of topics has meant balancing hot-button topics with others that, while they will draw less of an emotional response, are important to debate because they give insight about how the system works and how it might work differently. One example is **Debate 11** on the use of filibusters in the Senate: Does their use subvert or protect democracy? In another example, **Debate 4** relates to the hot-button topic of gay marriage, but as noted, its also touches on the issue of democracy and when, in a government that is supposed to respond to the public, are the courts justified in overturning a law that was not just enacted, but done so by a majority of a state's people voting in a referendum. How does that square with democracy?

GIVE THE STUDENTS SOME BACKGROUND FOR THE READING

Readers that work well provide students with some background material that is located just before the reading. This debate volume follows that scheme. There is a two-page introduction to each debate that establishes the context of the debate. As part of this setup, each introduction provides the students with several "points to ponder" as they read the debates.

Moreover, the introductions do more than just address the topic per se. Instead, they try to connect it to the chapter for which it is designed. For example, the introduction to **Debate 9** on the Tea Party begins with a discussion of the role of third parties in American history and the circumstances under which important third parties are most likely to come to the fore.

PROVIDE FOLLOW-UP POSSIBILITIES

One of the rewards of our profession is seeing students get excited about a field that intrigues us, and the reader provides a "Continuing Debate" section after each of the two readings. This section has three parts. "What Is New" provides an update of what has occurred since the date(s) of the two articles. "Where to Find More" points students to places to explore the topic further. I have particularly emphasized resources that can be accessed on the Internet on the theory that students are more likely to pursue a topic if they can do so via computer than by walking to the library. Needless to say, however, I think libraries are great and students should have to use them, so there are also numerous references to books and academic journals. Finally, the continuing debate section has a "What More to Do" part. This segment presents topics for discussion, suggests projects, and advises how to get active on a topic.

FIT WITH THE COURSE

I favor readers that fit the course I am teaching. I prefer a book with readings that supplement all or most of the major topics on my syllabus and that also allows me to spread the reading out, so that it is evenly distributed throughout the semester. To that end, this book is organized to parallel the outline of the major introduction to American politics texts in use today. For those who favor the foundations-politics-institutions-policy approach, the table of contents of this volume should match almost exactly with their text and syllabus. For those who use a foundations-institutions-politics-policy scheme, a little, but not much, adjustment will synchronize the debates herein with your plans. Moreover, to help with that, I have labeled each debate in the table of contents with the syllabus topic that fits with the debate. Additionally, for the 17 debates in the printed edition, I have indicated an alternative syllabus topic for each, and I have also made suggestions about how each of the 5 debates on the Web might fit with various text chapters and syllabus topics.

FLEXIBILITY

While there is a fair amount of similarity in the organization of the major introduction to American politics texts, I suspect that the syllabi of faculty members are a good deal more individualistic. With that in mind, I have provided flexibility in the reader. First, there are 17 debates in the printed edition, each of which is related to a topic, but each of which has suggestions in the table of contents for alternative assignments. Then there are 5 additional readings on the Pearson Web site associated with *You Decide!* Each of these also has multiple uses and my suggestions about how to work each one into your syllabus. Thus, you can use all 22 debates or many fewer; you can substitute some on the Web for some in the printed edition; you can follow the order in the book fairly closely with most texts; or you can rearrange the order at will. As the Burger King slogan goes, "Have it Your Way!"

As a final note, let me solicit your feedback. Every text and reader that anticipates future editions should be a work in progress. *You Decide!* certainly is. Of course, I will be pleased to hear about the things you like, but I and the next edition of the text will surely benefit more from hearing how I could have done better and what topics (and/or readings) would be good in the next edition. Thanks!

— John T. Rourke

1   CONSTITUTION

THE MANDATE THAT INDIVIDUALS BUY HEALTH INSURANCE:
Necessary and Proper *or* Unconstitutional Requirement?

NECESSARY AND PROPER

ADVOCATE: John Kroger, Attorney General of Oregon

SOURCE: Testimony during hearings on "The Constitutionality of the Affordable Care Act," before the U.S. Senate, Committee on the Judiciary, February 2, 2011

UNCONSTITUTIONAL REQUIREMENT

ADVOCATE: Kenneth T. Cuccinelli, II, Attorney General of Virginia

SOURCE: Testimony during hearings on "The Constitutionality of the Individual Mandate," before the U.S. House of Representatives, Committee on the Judiciary, February 16, 2011

Shortly after World War II, Harry Truman became the first of several presidents to call for a health system to cover all Americans, but that goal was not realized until March 2010 when Congress passed the Patient Protection and Affordable Care Act (PPACA) after a bruising battle, and President Barack Obama signed the measure into law. The battle was not over though. When the 112th Congress convened in January 2011, the Republicans launched numerous efforts to repeal or eviscerate "Obamacare." The attack on the PPACA has been waged not only in Congress, but in the courts as well. The opponents have focused on the PPACAs requirement that everyone who does not have health insurance is required purchase an individual policy.

The extension of the political battle over health care into the courts is a traditional tactic in American politics. As French political observer Alexis de Tocqueville noted sagely in his *Democracy in America* (1835), "There is hardly a political question in the United States which does not sooner or later turn into a judicial one." One reason this occurs is the Constitution itself. This document governs what is arguably the most massive and complex organization in world history: the United States with its more than 311 million residents, more than 3.7 million square miles of territory, a nearly $15 trillion national economy, and a nearly $4 trillion national budget. Yet the Constitution is very short compared to other national constitutions or even U.S. state constitutions. This brevity leaves much of what the Constitution says vague and therefore open to interpretation. Moreover, the historical record of creating the Constitution is limited. No verbatim record was kept of the debates in 1787 at the Constitutional Convention, the closest approximation, James Madison's *Notes* of the proceedings, provides only selective insights, and the widely quoted *Federalist Papers* written by Madison, Alexander Hamilton, and John Jay, were attempts to ease concerns in the country about the new constitution and, as such, do not always accurately reflect the intent of the framers.

The frequent lack of clarity about what one or another clause of the Constitution means has sparked an ongoing dispute about how the courts should interpret it. That issue is taken up at a theoretical level in Debate 14. Here by contrast we will look at a specific issue to illustrate the ongoing importance of the Constitution and how it is interpreted. Two clauses, both in Article I, Section 8, are of particular importance to this debate. One of them is clause 3, the "interstate commerce clause," which gives Congress the authority to "regulate commerce…among the several states." Also important is clause 18. It empowers Congress to make laws that are "necessary and proper" to exercise its specific powers, including regulating interstate commerce.

The PPACA requires that anyone who is otherwise without health insurance and whose income is above the poverty level purchase a policy with certain prescribed level of coverage from a private or governmental source that will cost up to 8 percent of the individual's monthly income. Those who do not comply will be fined $695 a year or 2.5 percent of their annual income, whichever is higher. In the following two articles, two state attorneys general take up the constitutionality of this "individual mandate." John Kroger of Oregon contends that providing health care and health care insurance are matters of interstate commerce and, therefore, subject to legislation by Congress. Virginia's Kenneth Cuccinelli, II, disagrees, arguing that the mandate that individuals buy something or be fined distorts the intent of the interstate commerce clause and has worrisome implications for Americans' freedoms.

POINTS TO PONDER

➤ Given the reality that the U.S. economy has become highly integrated and virtually all financial transactions have at least some interstate connections, what if any are the boundaries of "interstate commerce"?

➤ When you read Debate 2 on federalism, think about what the implications of the expansive view of the interstate commerce clause are for the separation of powers between the state governments and the federal government in the federal system.

➤ Whether or not you favor national health care, are you comfortable with the implications of individual mandates for the future privacy of Americans vis-à-vis the government?

The Mandate That Individuals Buy Health Insurance: Necessary and Proper

JOHN KROGER

Distinguished Members of the Committee—thank you for your invitation to address the Committee and for giving me the opportunity to discuss my views as Oregon Attorney General on the importance and constitutionality of the Affordable Care Act.

I. INTRODUCTION

As a sovereign state, Oregon is charged with protecting and promoting the health and welfare of its citizens. Citizen access to affordable medical care is necessary for our state to promote health, prevent disease, and heal the sick. In our modern system of advanced yet costly medical care, comprehensive health insurance coverage is critical to achieving that end. It is well documented that a lack of health insurance coverage leads to increased morbidity, mortality, and individual financial burdens.

In connection with our duties to protect and promote the health and welfare of our citizens, Oregon and many other states have engaged in varied, creative, and determined efforts to expand and improve health insurance coverage and to contain health care costs. Despite some successes, these state-by-state efforts have fallen short. As a consequence, we believe that a national solution is necessary.

Oregon's predicament illustrates the problem that states now face. Despite a variety of legislative efforts to increase access to insurance coverage, 21.8% of Oregonians lack health insurance. Absent health care reform, Oregon expects that figure to rise to approximately 27.4% in the next ten years.

In 2009, Oregon spent approximately $2.6 billion on Medicaid and CHIP [Children's Health Insurance Program]. Absent health care reform, that figure is expected to grow to approximately $5.5 billion by 2019.

The situation that states now face is unsustainable. And without national reform, state-level health care costs will rise dramatically over the next ten years. Even as states are forced to spend more to keep up with skyrocketing health care costs, the number of individuals without insurance will continue to rise if we do not implement national health care reform.

The Patient Protection and Affordable Care Act (ACA) is a national solution that will help us fulfill our duty to protect and promote the health and welfare of our citizens. The law strikes an appropriate balance between national requirements that promote the goal of expanding access to health care in a cost-effective manner and state flexibility in designing programs to achieve that goal. As at least two different U.S. District Courts have concluded, the ACA achieves these goals without running afoul of any constitutional limits on federal government authority.

II. BACKGROUND

As Congress recognized, the nation's health cares system is in a state of crisis. As of 2008, 43.8 million people in the United States had no health insurance coverage and thus no or little access to health care. Indeed, Congress found that "62 percent of all personal bankruptcies are caused in part by medical expenses." And state-level health care costs will only continue to rise.

These increases threaten to overwhelm already overburdened state budgets. Without a national solution to the health care crisis, states would be forced for the foreseeable future to spend more and more on health care and yet still slide further and further away from their goal of protecting the health and well-being of their citizens.

The ACA will allow states to expand and improve health insurance coverage. The ACA achieves coverage increases through a variety of mechanisms, including the implementation of a minimum coverage provision that requires most residents of the United States, starting in 2014, to obtain health insurance or pay a tax. Among other exceptions, the minimum coverage provision does not apply to those whose income falls below a specified level or to those who can demonstrate that purchasing insurance would pose a hardship. In other words, the minimum coverage provision targets those who, while they can afford it, choose not to purchase insurance and choose instead to "self insure," relying on luck, their own financial reserves, and the health care social safety net of emergency rooms and public insurance programs to catch them when they fall ill.

Some of the opponents of the ACA claim that the individual coverage provision exceeds Congress's Commerce Clause power. As they frame their argument, the Commerce Clause empowers Congress to regulate only activity and not, as they characterize it, the "inactivity" of refusing to purchase health insurance. But these arguments ignore the effect on interstate commerce of refusing to comply with the minimum coverage provision and thus mischaracterize the conduct as "inactivity." Moreover, they lose sight of the principal concern that animates the Supreme Court's Commerce Clause jurisprudence, namely, ensuring a meaningful distinction between what is truly national and what is truly local. For the reasons explained below, the minimum coverage provision fits easily within Congress's Commerce Clause authority.

III. THE ACA'S MINIMUM COVERAGE PROVISION IS CONSTITUTIONAL

A. The minimum coverage provision is necessary for the success of health care reform and the overall stability of the nation's health insurance markets.

Any fair review of Congress's authority under the Commerce Clause to enact the minimum coverage provision must be conducted in the context of examining why the minimum coverage provision is crucial to national health care reform. One of the primary goals of the ACA is to increase the number of Americans who have access to health insurance coverage. Insurance is a system of shared risk. But in a system where purchasing insurance is purely voluntary, people with higher than average health risks will disproportionately enroll in insurance plans, as those individuals are more likely to purchase insurance when they expect to require health care services. This phenomenon is commonly referred to as "adverse selection."

Adverse selection raises the cost of insurance premiums for two reasons: first, because adverse selection tends to create insurance pools with higher than average risks and premiums that reflect the average cost of providing care for the members of the pool, the overall cost is higher. Second, because insurers fear the potentially substantial costs associated with individuals with non-obvious high health risks disproportionately enrolling in their insurance plans, insurers will often add an extra loading fee to their premiums, particularly in the small group and individual markets. An individual mandate addresses both of these problems. First, the law moves low-risk people into the risk pool and thus drives down average costs. Second, by lessening the probability that a given individual is purchasing insurance solely because he or she knows something the insurer does not know about his or her health status, the law reduces insurer hedging and the fees associated with adverse selection.

Another consequence of adverse selection is that insurers enact a variety of policies designed to keep high-cost individuals out of their plans and limit the financial cost to the plan if those individuals enroll—such as limiting coverage for preexisting conditions, denying coverage, charging higher premiums for those with actual or anticipated health problems, and imposing benefit caps. The ACA seeks to eliminate many of these adverse selection avoidant practices by outlawing preexisting condition exclusions and requiring insurers to issue policies to anyone who applies.

These reforms are, of course, designed to increase access to insurance. However, the reality is that "[i]nsurance pools cannot be stable over time, nor can insurers remain financially viable, if people enroll only when their costs are expected to be high...[a]nd research leaves no doubt that without an individual mandate, many people will remain uninsured" until they get sick.

Young Americans are especially inclined to forgo purchasing health insurance in favor of other purchases. If pre-existing conditions are eliminated with no requirement that one purchase insurance, these people would have an incentive to forgo coverage until they get sick—and the high-risk pool would collapse from inadequate funding. A minimum coverage requirement that requires everyone to pay into the risk pool will dramatically reduce adverse selection, and make it financially practical to insist upon coverage for individuals with pre-existing conditions.

B. The minimum coverage provision fits within Congress's authority under the Commerce Clause and the Necessary and Proper Clause.

1. Congress has broad authority to regulate activities that substantially affect interstate commerce.

The United States Constitution empowers Congress to "make all Laws which shall be necessary and proper" to "regulate Commerce...among the several States." [According to the Supreme Court,] Commerce Clause power includes the authority to "regulate those activities having a substantial relation to interstate commerce,... *i.e.*, those activities that substantially affect interstate commerce."

The Supreme Court has long understood the Commerce Clause to be an exceptionally wide grant of authority. In that regard, three important principles have emerged from the Court's cases that are relevant here. First, an activity will be deemed to have a "substantial effect" on interstate commerce if the activity, when aggregated with the similar activity of many others similarly situated, will substantially affect interstate commerce. Second, local, non-economic activities will be held to affect interstate commerce substantially if regulation of the activity is an integral or essential part of a comprehensive regulation of interstate economic activity, and if failure to regulate that activity would undercut the general regulatory scheme. Third, in determining whether a regulated activity substantially affects interstate commerce within the meaning of the Commerce Clause, the Court [has held that it] "need not determine whether...[the regulated activities] taken in the aggregate, substantially affect interstate commerce in fact, *but only whether a 'rational basis' exists for so concluding.*" Congress's judgment that an activity would undermine the statutory scheme "is entitled to a strong presumption of validity."

Although the Commerce Clause authority to regulate interstate commerce is thus broad, it is not without limits. Courts will not "pile inference upon inference" to find that a local, noncommercial activity that is not part of a comprehensive regulatory scheme nonetheless substantially affects interstate commerce. In *U.S. v Lopez* (1995), the Court struck down the federal Gun-Free School Zones Act that prohibited carrying a gun within 1,000 feet of a school. In finding the statute outside of the authority of the Commerce Clause, the Court observed that the act at issue was a criminal statute that had "nothing to do with 'commerce' or any sort of economic enterprise" and was "not an essential part of a larger regulation of economic activity, in which the regulatory scheme could be undercut unless the intrastate activity were regulated." In *United States v. Morrison* (2000), [the Court] also sustained a Commerce Clause challenge to [a] statutory provision creating federal civil remedy for victims of gender-motivated violence.

Lopez and *Morrison* notwithstanding, the Supreme Court's more recent cases have reaffirmed the broad reach of Congress's commerce clause authority. In *Gonzalez v. Raich* (2005), for example, the Court upheld federal power to prohibit the wholly intrastate cultivation and possession of small amounts of marijuana for medical purposes, despite express state policy to the contrary. Expressly reaffirming its holding in *Wickard v. Filburn* (1942), the *Raich* Court concluded that Congress had a rational basis for concluding that marijuana cultivation is an "economic activity" that, in the aggregate, has a substantial effect on interstate commerce. *Raich* also makes clear that Congress may "regulate activities that form part of a larger regulation of economic activity." In other words, Congress can regulate wholly intrastate activity to make effective a comprehensive regulation of an interstate market. [As the Court held,] even if an activity is "local and though it may not be regarded as commerce, it may still, *whatever its nature*, be reached by Congress if it exerts a substantial economic effect on interstate commerce."

Congress's broad commerce power is also rooted in the Necessary and Proper Clause. That clause authorizes the federal government to enact regulations that, while not within the specifically enumerated powers of the federal government, are nonetheless "necessary and proper for carrying [out] the powers vested by the Constitution in the government of the United States." In other words, the Necessary and Proper clause permits Congress to enact regulations that are necessary or convenient to the regulation of commerce. In *U.S. v. Comstock* (2010), the Supreme Court recently explained that the Necessary and Proper clause provides federal regulatory authority where "the means chosen are reasonably adapted to the attainment of a legitimate end under the commerce power or under other powers that the Constitution grants Congress the authority to implement."

2. The minimum coverage provision is constitutional because it regulates activity that substantially affects interstate commerce and because it is an essential part of comprehensive regulation of interstate economic activity.

a. The minimum coverage provision regulates activity that substantially affects interstate commerce.
In the ACA, Congress specifically found that the minimum coverage requirement is "commercial and economic in nature, and substantially affects interstate commerce." Congress certainly had a rational basis for reaching that conclusion. An individual's decision to not purchase health insurance, when aggregated with the purchasing decisions of thousands of other individuals who choose not to maintain health insurance—because they cannot afford it or for some other reason—has a powerful and generally adverse impact on the health insurance and health care markets. In the aggregate, these econom-

ic decisions regarding how to pay for health care services—including, in particular, decisions to forgo coverage, pay later, and if need be, to depend on free care—have a substantial effect on the interstate health care market. As the Supreme Court recognized in *Raich* and in *Wickard*, the Commerce Clause empowers Congress to regulate these direct and aggregate effects. When individuals choose not to purchase health insurance, they are still participants in the interstate health care marketplace. When the uninsured get sick, they seek medical attention within the health care system. The medical care provided to the uninsured costs a substantial amount of money.

Approximately one third of the cost of that care is covered by the uninsured themselves. The remaining two thirds of the cost are passed on to other public and private actors in the interstate health care and health insurance system, including the state and federal governments, multi-state private insurance companies, and large multi-state employers. Although researchers disagree as to the price tag for uncompensated care, it is generally agreed that the cost is substantial—billions of dollars each year.

Oregon's experience illustrates the financial impact of the uninsured on the health care market. Because the uninsured are often unable to pay their medical bills, providers shift those costs onto the insured. Experts have estimated that this so-called "hidden tax" amounts to $225 per privately insured Oregonian, accounting for approximately 9% of a commercial premium. Hospitals foot this bill as well. In 2009, Oregon hospitals spent a combined $1.1 billion—an average 7.8% of gross patient revenue—on uncompensated care. To put this number in perspective, Oregon hospitals had a combined net income of $255 million in 2009.

The cost of the uncompensated care provided to the uninsured is magnified by the fact that the uninsured frequently delay seeking care. By the time they are treated, their medical problems are often more costly to treat than they would have been had they sought care earlier. Furthermore, because emergency rooms are required by federal law to screen everybody who walks through their doors and to provide stabilizing treatment to those with an emergency medical condition, much of the care for the uninsured is delivered in this costly and inefficient setting. Indeed, treatment in an emergency room costs approximately three times as much as a visit to a primary care physician, at a cost of approximately $4.4 billion across the United States.

In addition to the direct impact on the health care and health insurance systems, individuals who choose to forgo insurance affect the national economy in other ways, including lost productivity due to poor health and personal bankruptcies due to health care costs, and some of the limited health care resources are shifted to emergency departments, rather than to preventative care.

In the aggregate, economic decisions regarding how to pay for health care services, particularly decisions to forgo coverage, have a substantial effect on the interstate health care market, because the costs of providing care to the uninsured are passed on to everyone else through higher premiums, on average, over $1,000 a year, and higher health care costs.

b. The minimum coverage provision is an essential part of comprehensive regulation of interstate economic activity.

The Commerce Clause challenge to the minimum coverage provision also fails because it is an essential part of comprehensive regulation of the health care and health insurance industries. Health insurance and health care are both economic activities in interstate commerce that are indisputably within Congress's Commerce Clause power to regulate. Seventeen percent of the United States economy is devoted to health care.

The federal government has for decades been deeply involved in health care regulation, including, among other programs Medicare, Medicaid, and CHIP. As the Supreme Court recently recognized [*in Comstock*], such a longstanding history helps to illustrate "the reasonableness of the relation between the new statute and pre-existing federal interests."

The minimum coverage provision is an essential component of creating an affordable, accessible, and robust insurance market that all Americans can rely on—the central goal of the ACA. As explained above, Congress's purpose in including the minimum coverage provision was to combat the problem of adverse selection. It does that by incorporating healthy people into the risk pool, thus driving down average costs. Moreover, without a minimum coverage provision, it would be impossible to prohibit insurers from excluding from coverage individuals with pre-existing conditions. In short, the minimum coverage provision is an integral part of the ACA's comprehensive framework for regulating health care, the absence of which would severely undercut Congress's regulatory scheme. It is therefore constitutional under *Raich*. ("Congress can…regulate purely intrastate activity that is not itself 'commercial,'…if it concludes that failure to regulate that class of activity would undercut the regulation of the interstate market in that commodity."

For the same reasons, the minimum coverage provision is a means "reasonably adapted" to achieving "a legitimate end under the commerce power." There can be no dispute that creating an affordable and accessible health insurance market is a legitimate congressional goal, and one well within the scope of its Commerce Clause authority. The minimum coverage provision is a reasonably adapted means to that end. The provision is therefore a "necessary and proper" regulation that Congress is empowered to enact.

The Mandate That Individuals Buy Health Insurance: Unconstitutional Requirement

KENNETH T. CUCCINELLI, II

Distinguished members of the Committee: Thank you for inviting me to testify today. I am Kenneth T. Cuccinelli, II, and I currently serve as the Attorney General of the Commonwealth of Virginia. As you know, the Commonwealth is engaged in litigation with the federal government over the constitutionality of the Patient Protection and Affordable Care Act of 2010. I appreciate this opportunity to discuss the arguments and ideas that underpin Virginia's suit.

Despite all of the attention it has received, it should be noted that Virginia's challenge to the Patient Protection and Affordable Care Act is modest. We do not seek to overturn any prior decisions of the United Sates Supreme Court or develop any new doctrine. Rather, within the boundaries of constitutional text and precedent, we simply seek a determination that, in passing the individual mandate and penalty as part of the Patient Protection and Affordable Care Act, Congress exceeded the powers granted it by the Constitution.

Resolving such a suit is and has been one of the primary functions of the federal courts since the inception of the nation. As [Supreme Court] Justice [Sandra Day] O'Connor noted in *New York v. United States* (1992), a State which seeks the aid of the federal courts in resolving competing claims of state and federal power acts in accordance with the foundational and traditional function of those courts:

> In 1788, in the course of explaining to the citizens of New York why the recently drafted Constitution provided for federal courts, Alexander Hamilton observed [in Federalist No. 82]: "The erection of a new government, whatever care or wisdom may distinguish the work, cannot fail to originate questions of intricacy and nicety; and these may, in a particular manner, be expected to flow from the establishment of a constitution founded upon the total or partial incorporation of a number of distinct sovereignties." Hamilton's prediction has proved quite accurate. While no one disputes the proposition that the Constitution created a Federal Government of limited powers, and while the Tenth Amendment makes explicit that "the powers not delegated to the United States by the Constitution, nor prohibited by it to the States, are reserved to the States respectively, or to the people"; the task of ascertaining the constitutional line between federal and state power has given rise to many of the Court's most difficult and celebrated cases. At least as far back as *Martin v. Hunter's Lessee* (1816), the Court has resolved questions "of great importance and delicacy" in determining whether particular sovereign powers have been granted by the Constitution to the Federal Government or have been retained by the States.

Turning to the merits of Virginia's suit, the central issue is tied to the Commerce Clause. As you know, in the act itself, Congress asserted that the Commerce Clause empowered it to order private citizens, who were not presently engaged in commercial activity, to purchase insurance from private vendors or pay a penalty to the government. Such a use of the Commerce Clause is literally unprecedented. As [a recent report by] the Congressional Research service noted when the Senate Finance Committee inquired as to the constitutionality of the mandate:

Whether such a requirement would be constitutional under the Commerce Clause is perhaps the most challenging question posed by such a proposal, as it is a novel issue whether Congress may use this clause to require an individual to purchase a good or a service.

While not dispositive, the mere fact that no Congress had ever attempted to use the Commerce Clause in this way casts grave doubt at to whether Congress has such a power. As the Supreme Court noted in *Printz v. United States* (1997), the fact that Congress has not asserted a particular power or practice for 200 years "tends to negate the existence of the congressional power…" claimed.

The gravamen of Virginia's suit is that the claimed power exceeds Congress's enumerated powers because it lacks any principled limit and is tantamount to a national police power—that is, the power to legislate on matters of health, safety and welfare that was considered part of the reserve powers retained by the states at the time of the founding.

Since *Wickard v. Filburn* (1942), the United States Supreme Court has reached no further than to hold that Congress can regulate (1) the "use of the channels of interstate commerce," (2) "the instrumentalities of interstate commerce, or persons and things in interstate commerce," and (3) "*activities* that substantially affect interstate commerce." The Patient Protection and Affordable Care Act seeks to regulate *inactivity* affecting interstate commerce, a claimed power well in excess of the affirmative outer limits of the Commerce Clause, even as executed by the Necessary and Proper Clause. This claimed power also violates the negative outer limits of the Commerce Clause identified in *Lopez* and in *United States v. Morrison* (2000). As was so clearly stated by the Court in *Morrison*: "We *always* have rejected readings of the Commerce Clause and the scope of federal power that would permit Congress to exercise a police power."

In the face of these problems with the Commerce Clause argument, the federal government has adopted a fallback position in the various cases challenging the Patient Protection and Affordable Care Act. Despite no indication from Congress that it thought it was doing anything other than attempting to use its Commerce Clause powers, and despite the protests of the President that the individual mandate and penalty were most definitely not taxes, the federal government now claims that the mandate and penalty are merely an exercise of Congress's taxing power.

While the Commerce Clause argument advanced by the federal government is unprecedented, the taxing power argument is simply radical.

At the outset, it is important to note that the taxing power argument is inconsistent with the very words chosen by Congress. What lawyers from the Justice Department now call a "tax" was not called a tax by Congress; it is identified in the Patient Protection and Affordable Care Act as a "penalty." Accordingly, the first flaw in the taxing power argument is that it, by necessity, ignores the words that Congress chose to use.

Even if the Justice Department could overcome the fact that Congress chose to explicitly impose a penalty as opposed to levying a tax, the taxing power argument would still fail. The United States Supreme Court has long recognized that "taxes" and "penalties" are separate and distinct, stating that "[a] tax is an enforced contribution to provide for the support of government; a penalty, as the word is here used, is an exaction imposed by statute as punishment for an unlawful act." As the *La Franca* court held [in *United States v. La Franca* (1931)], the word "tax" and the word "penalty" are not interchangeable, one for the other. No mere exercise of the art of lexicography can alter the essential nature of an act or a thing; and if an exaction be clearly a penalty it cannot be converted into a tax by the simple expedient of calling it such. That the exaction here in question is not a true tax, but a penalty involving the idea of punishment for infraction of the law is settled. To prevail, the federal government's taxing power argument requires that courts ignore Congress's express decision to denominate the penalty a "penalty" and it has to "alter the essential nature" of the penalty by ignoring its function so that it can be called a tax.

The Justice Department has tried to avoid the Supreme Court's consistent view, that, substantively, a penalty is an imposition for failing to obey a command of government, by resorting to idiosyncratic definitions. It has staked out the position that unlawful acts are limited to criminal violations, so that penalties for violating non-criminal statutes are not penalties at all. This is simply not the law.

The idea that it is only unlawful to violate criminal statutes as opposed to civil statutes is incorrect as a simple matter of definition. *Black's Law Dictionary* defines "unlawful" as:

> That which is contrary to, prohibited, or unauthorized by law. That which is not lawful. The acting contrary to, or in defiance of the law; disobeying or disregarding the law. Term is equivalent to without excuse or justification. While necessarily not implying the element of criminality, it is broad enough to include it.

Clearly, "unlawful" comprehends the violation of any law, whether civil or criminal.

This plain-meaning, common-sense definition finds firm support in precedents of the Supreme Court. For instance, in *Dep't. of Rev. of Mont. v. Kurth Ranch* (1994), the Court explicitly recognizes "civil penalties" as being distinct from "taxes," noting that "tax statutes serve a purpose quite different from civil penalties...."

Additionally, the Justice Department has argued that the penalty must be a tax because it "is codified in the Internal Revenue Code in a subtitle labeled 'Miscellaneous Excise Taxes.'" This formalistic argument is not likely to prevail because it is foreclosed by both statutory and Supreme Court authority. A provision of the Internal Revenue Code provides that "[n]o inference, implication, or presumption of legislative construction shall be drawn or made by reason of the location or grouping of any particular section or provision of this title...." Furthermore, the United States Supreme Court [has found in finding] that an exaction that Congress had denominated a "tax," located in a section of the Internal Revenue Code titled "Miscellaneous Excise Taxes," was actually a penalty and not a tax, stated that "[n]o inference of legislative construction should be drawn from the placement of a provision in the Internal Revenue Code."

Even if it could be assumed that the penalty was a tax, it would still need to pass muster under an enumerated power other than the taxing power so long as it is being used for regulation. While some have suggested that courts can ignore these decisions, the Supreme Court has not overruled them. In fact, the relevant rationale of the 1922 *Child Labor Tax Case* was cited with approval by the Supreme Court in 1994, when the Court wrote:

> Yet we have also recognized that "there comes a time in the extension of the penalizing features of the so-called tax when it loses its character as such and becomes a mere penalty with the characteristics of regulation and punishment."

Given that the Supreme Court as recently as 1994 cited the *Child Labor Tax Case* for the very proposition for which the Commonwealth offers it, it cannot be demonstrated that it is no longer good law. Furthermore, the holdings of these cases are perfectly consistent with the overarching principle found in *Morrison*, that the Court has "*always*...rejected readings of...the scope of federal power that would permit Congress to exercise a police power."

Comparisons to Social Security taxes and the inheritance tax do not aid the Justice Department's case, but rather, underscore why it fails. It is true that in 1937 the Court upheld the Social Security tax, but it did so because it was a valid excise on a voluntary activity/transaction—the employment relationship. Nothing in that opinion suggests that Congress has the power to impose an employment excise tax on workers who are not working or on businesses that do not currently exist. Similarly, the Court upheld the estate tax [in 1900] as an excise tax or duty; it was upheld not as a tax on a person or even a person's death, but rather, as a tax on a commercial event—the transfer of property.

Like the Commerce Clause argument, the taxing power argument ultimately fails because it is not bounded by any principled limits, and therefore, arrogates to the federal government a national police power denied to it by the Constitution. As the Justice Department has summarized its position, anything that "imposes involuntary pecuniary burdens for a public purpose...is an exercise of the taxing power...," and therefore, is constitutional. This radical position has already been rejected by the Supreme Court in *Morrison* as quoted above.

Faced with these legal obstacles, supporters of the Patient Protection and Affordable Care Act often make arguments that are not based on the Constitution or on decisions of the Supreme Court, but rather, are nothing more than appeals to address a pressing national problem. The argument is that there is a serious problem that must be fixed, and thus, the Patient Protection and Affordable Care Act must be constitutional because it is an attempt to solve that problem.

In a society based on the rule of law, such an argument cannot be credited. As the Supreme Court held in *New York v. United States* (1992):

> Some truths are so basic that, like the air around us, they are easily overlooked. Much of the Constitution is concerned with setting forth the form of our government, and the courts have traditionally invalidated measures deviating from that form. The result may appear "formalistic" in a given case to partisans of the measure at issue, because such measures are typically the product of the era's perceived necessity. But the Constitution protects us from our own best intentions: It divides power among sovereigns and among branches of government precisely so that we may resist the temptation to concentrate power in one location as an expedient solution to the crisis of the day.... [Something may be a] pressing national problem, but a judiciary that licensed extraconstitutional government with each issue of comparable gravity would, in the long run, be far worse.

THE CONTINUING DEBATE:
The Mandate That Individuals Buy Health Insurance

What Is New

With the Democrats in control of the Senate and with President Barack Obama in the White House, there no possibility that the Republican attacks on the PPACA in Congress will succeed during the 112th Congress (2011–2012). Instead, the Republican effort is meant to set the stage for the presidential and congressional elections in November 2012. How the issue will impact those elections is unclear, with a January 2011 Gallup poll finding 46%of Americans in favor of repealing the health care law, 40% opposed, and 14% unsure. As for the legal challenges, their success has been mixed. In an initial round of suits filed in federal district courts, the judges in three found the law constitutional, and two found it unconstitutional. All these decisions were appealed to the U.S. Court of Appeals. The first two rulings were a split decision, with individual mandate held to be constitutional by the Cincinnati-based 6th Circuit in June 2011 and unconstitutional by the Atlanta-based 11th Circuit in August. Further rulings on other appeals are expected from the Richmond-based 4th Circuit and the Circuit for the District of Columbia by the end of 2011, but the split between the 6th and 11th Circuits also certainly means that the issue will go to the Supreme Court.

Where to Find More

Little has yet been published in the journals on the debate over the individual mandate. Three articles that have appeared are Ryan C. Patterson, "'Are You Serious?': Examining the Constitutionality of an Individual Mandate for Health Insurance," *Notre Dame Law Review* (2010); Elizabeth J. Bondurant and Steven D. Henry, "Constitutional Challenges to the Patient Protection and Affordable Care Act," *Defense Counsel Journal* (2011), and Stephen H. Gorin, "The Affordable Care Act: Background and Analysis," *Health and Social Work* (2011). For up-to-date information the legal contest, there are several good law blogs, with SCOTUSblog (www.scotusblog.com/) focusing on the high court.

What More to Do

Hold a debate/discussion in class on the principle of an individual mandate by the government to purchase something from a private source with no way to opt out. Clearly, the government can tax people to support government-supplied insurance like Medicare. Also, the government can make people buy insurance to operate a government-licensed vehicle, but it is possible to not own one. But the individual mandate to buy health care insurance is a first in that if you exist, you must comply. Avoid linking your opinion to your position on the general idea of universal health care and debate the principle in isolation from a specific use. Think of other possible individual mandates and consider your view on those.

FEDERALISM

ARIZONA'S LAW ENCOURAGING CITIZEN IDENTITY CHECKS BY POLICE:
State Intrusion into National Policy *or* Permissible State Action?

STATE INTRUSION INTO NATIONAL POLICY

ADVOCATE: Attorneys representing the U.S. government seeking to enjoin the enforcement of Arizona's S.B. 1070

SOURCE: *The United States of America, Plaintiff, v. The State of Arizona; and Janice K. Brewer, Governor of the State of Arizona, in her Official Capacity, Defendants*, Case 2:10-cv-01413, U.S. District Court for the District of Arizona, July 6, 2010

PERMISSIBLE STATE ACTION

ADVOCATE: Attorneys representing Arizona and its governor, Janice K. Brewer, seeking to block a petition by the U.S. government to enjoin the enforcement of Arizona's S.B. 1070

SOURCE: *The United States of America, Plaintiff, v. The State of Arizona; and Janice K. Brewer, Governor of the State of Arizona, in her Official Capacity, Defendants*, Case 2:10-cv-01413, U.S. District Court for the District of Arizona, July 20, 2010

Immigration has become a hot-button topic in the United States. According to the U.S. Census Bureau, there are about 38 million U.S. residents who are foreign-born. Of these, about 26 million have entered the country in accordance with U.S. immigration laws. These 26 million individuals can be further divided into the approximately 16 million who have become naturalized U.S. citizens and another 9 million or so who have "green cards" and are on the path to citizenship. Additionally, there are nearly 12 million residents who have entered the United States in contravention of its laws. Members of this group are often called "illegal," "undocumented," or, as the Census Bureau calls them, "unauthorized" immigrants. Something like two-thirds of all unauthorized immigrants are from Mexico, with Central America the origin of another 20% or so of the unauthorized immigrants.

Public concern over what to do about unauthorized immigration, including how to deal with those unauthorized immigrants who have been in the United States, has risen and fallen over the years, but has been on an upsurge in recent years. President George W. Bush offered a comprehensive reform plan to Congress, including increased border security and an accelerated path to permanent residency for unauthorized immigrants already in the country. However, Bush's initiative failed. Subsequently, there have been some steps to increase border security, but these have only somewhat slowed unauthorized immigrations.

Surveys taken in 2010 show that American attitudes toward all, not just unauthorized immigrants have become negative. Asked about recent immigrants, 62% of Americans said they add to the crime problem, 69% said they burden U.S. taxpayers, and 59% believe that immigrants take jobs away from Americans. Not surprisingly, such attitudes have resulted in 74% of Americans saying they were angry about or dissatisfied with the number of unauthorized immigrants in the country. Moreover, 77% say that the federal government was not doing enough to keep authorized immigrants out of the country.

The impact of unauthorized immigration is strongest in the states along the border with Mexico, and in April 2010 Arizona enacted a law commonly called S.B. 1070 (after Senate Bill 1070). It makes it a misdemeanor for non-citizens to fail to carry their immigration status papers as required under federal law, authorizes Arizona police to check the papers of anyone whom they reasonably suspect of being an illegal immigrant, and authorizes police to detain those without proper identification.

The new Arizona law immediately came under attack on two fronts, with several cases filed in federal court to halt the law from going into effect. Some suits charge is that the law is racist because it causes police to profile Latinos, and therefore violates their civil rights. The second charge, and the one that is the focus here, is that S.B. 1070 violates the division of powers in the federal system. In the first reading, lawyers in the U.S. Department of Justice ask a federal district court to block S.B. 1070 from going into effect because it impinges on what the U.S. government says are its exclusive powers: to regulate immigration, to conduct foreign policy, and to regulate interstate commerce. The second reading urges the court to dismiss the suit, arguing that S.B. 1070 is on sound constitutional grounds and does not violate the federal division of powers.

POINTS TO PONDER

➢ Does S.B. 1070 create new immigration law or merely supplement and enforce federal law?
➢ In the federal system, there are some areas of policy controlled exclusively by the federal government, a few controlled exclusively by the states, and many more that are "concurrent" areas of control by both the federal and state governments. Where should immigration law fall?
➢ Numerous state and local governments have passed laws assisting unauthorized immigrants. Are these different constitutionally from S.B. 1070, are they all constitutional, or are they all unconstitutional?

Arizona's Law Encouraging Citizen Identity Checks by Police: State Intrusion into National Policy

ATTORNEYS REPRESENTING THE U.S. GOVERNMENT

In this action, the United States seeks to declare invalid and preliminarily and permanently enjoin the enforcement of S.B. 1070, as amended and enacted by the State of Arizona, because S.B. 1070 is preempted by federal law and therefore violates the Supremacy Clause of the U.S. Constitution. In our constitutional system, the federal government has preeminent authority to regulate immigration matters. This authority derives from the U.S. Constitution and numerous acts of Congress. The nation's immigration laws reflect a careful and considered balance of national law enforcement, foreign relations, and humanitarian interests. Congress has assigned to the U.S. Department of Homeland Security [DHS], Department of Justice [DOJ], and Department of State [DOS], along with other federal agencies, the task of enforcing and administering these immigration-related laws. In administering these laws, the federal agencies balance the complex—and often competing—objectives that animate federal immigration law and policy. Although states may exercise their police power in a manner that has an incidental or indirect effect on aliens, a state may *not* establish its own immigration policy or enforce state laws in a manner that interferes with the federal immigration laws. The Constitution and the federal immigration laws do not permit the development of a patchwork of state and local immigration policies throughout the country.

Despite the preeminent federal authority and responsibility over immigration, the State of Arizona recently enacted S.B. 1070, a sweeping set of provisions that are designed to "work together to discourage and deter the unlawful entry and presence of aliens" by making "attrition through enforcement the public policy of all state and local government agencies in Arizona."

S.B. 1070 pursues only one goal—"attrition"—and ignores the many other objectives that Congress has established for the federal immigration system. And even in pursuing attrition, S.B. 1070 disrupts federal enforcement priorities and resources that focus on aliens who pose a threat to national security or public safety. If allowed to go into effect, S.B. 1070's mandatory enforcement scheme will conflict with and undermine the federal government's careful balance of immigration enforcement priorities and objectives.

The United States understands Arizona's legitimate concerns about illegal immigration and has undertaken significant efforts to secure our nation's borders. The federal government, moreover, welcomes cooperative efforts by states and localities to aid in the enforcement of the nation's immigration laws. But the U.S. Constitution forbids Arizona from supplanting the federal government's immigration regime with its own state-specific immigration policy—a policy that, in purpose and effect, interferes with the numerous interests the federal government must balance when enforcing and administering the immigration laws and disrupts the balance actually established by the federal government. Accordingly, S.B. 1070 is invalid under the Supremacy Clause of the U.S. Constitution and must be struck down.

FEDERAL AUTHORITY AND LAW GOVERNING IMMIGRATION AND STATUS OF ALIENS

The Supremacy Clause of the Constitution mandates that "[t]his Constitution, and the Laws of the United States which shall be made in Pursuance thereof…shall be the supreme Law of the Land." The Constitution [also] affords the federal government the power to "establish an uniform Rule of Naturalization," and to "regulate Commerce with foreign Nations." Further, the federal government has broad authority to establish the terms and conditions for entry and continued presence in the United States, and to regulate the status of aliens within the boundaries of the United States. The Constitution [additionally] affords the President of the United States the authority to "take Care that the Laws be faithfully executed." Further, the President has broad authority over foreign affairs. Immigration law, policy, and enforcement priorities are affected by and have impacts on U.S. foreign policy, and are themselves the subject of diplomatic arrangements.

Congress has exercised its authority to make laws governing immigration and the status of aliens within the United States by enacting the various provisions of the INA [Immigration and Nationalization Act of 1952] and other laws regulating immigration. Through the INA, Congress set forth the framework by which the federal government determines which aliens may be eligible to enter and reside in the United States, which aliens may be removed from the United States, the consequences for unlawful presence, the penalties on persons who violate the procedures established for entry, conditions of residence, and employment of aliens, as well as the process by which certain aliens may ultimately become naturalized citizens of the United States. The INA also vests the executive branch with considerable discretion in enforcing the provisions of the federal immigration laws, generally allowing federal agencies to ultimately decide whether particular immigration remedies are appropriate in individual cases.

In exercising its significant enforcement discretion, the federal government prioritizes for arrest, detention, prosecution, and removal those aliens who pose a danger to national security or a risk to public safety. Consistent with these enforcement priorities, the federal government principally targets aliens engaged in or suspected of terrorism or espionage; aliens convicted of crimes, with a particular emphasis on violent criminals, felons, and repeat offenders; certain gang members; aliens subject to outstanding criminal warrants; and fugitive aliens, especially those with criminal records.

In crafting federal immigration law and policy, Congress has necessarily taken into account multiple and often competing national interests. Assuring effective enforcement of the provisions against illegal migration and unlawful presence is a highly important interest, but it is not the singular goal of the federal immigration laws. The laws also take into account other uniquely national interests, including facilitating trade and commerce; welcoming those foreign nationals who visit or immigrate lawfully and ensuring their fair and equitable treatment wherever they may reside; responding to humanitarian concerns at the global and individual levels; and otherwise ensuring that the treatment of aliens present in our nation does not harm our foreign relations with the countries from which they come or jeopardize the treatment of U.S. citizens abroad. Because immigration control and management is [according to the Supreme Court] "a field where flexibility and the adaptation of the congressional policy to infinitely variable conditions constitute the essence of the program," Congress vested substantial discretion in the President and the administering federal agencies to adjust the balance of these multiple interests as appropriate.

Congress has tasked DHS and DOJ with overseeing significant portions of the United States' immigration interests, and has provided each with specific powers to promote the various goals of the federal immigration scheme and to enforce the federal immigration authority under the INA. The Department of State is also empowered by the INA to administer aspects of the federal immigration laws, including visa programs. DHS may generally order an alien immediately removed where the alien either fails to present the appropriate documentation or commits fraud at the time of the alien's inspection. DHS may also place an alien into removal proceedings, and may ultimately remove an alien who entered the United States unlawfully or violated the conditions of his admission. DOJ may order an alien removed for many reasons, including if the alien has stayed in the United States longer than permitted or has engaged in certain unlawful conduct. In addition to removal, the statute authorizes DHS and DOJ to employ civil and criminal sanctions against an alien for immigration violations, such as unlawful entry, failing to appropriately register with the federal government, and document fraud. However, in the exercise of discretion, the administering agencies may decide not to apply a specific sanction and may, among other steps, permit the alien to depart the country voluntarily at his or her own expense and may even decide not to pursue removal of the alien if deferred federal enforcement will help pursue some other goal of the immigration system.

Under federal law, both DHS and DOJ may, for humanitarian or other reasons, decline to exercise certain immigration sanctions or grant an otherwise unlawfully present or removable [could be deported] alien an immigration benefit—and potentially adjust that alien's immigration status—if the alien meets certain conditions. DHS may also refrain from enforcement actions, in appropriate circumstances, against persons unlawfully present in the United States. Decisions to forego removal or criminal penalties result not only from resource constraints, but also from affirmative policy considerations—including humanitarian and foreign policy interests—established by Congress and balanced by the executive branch.

Congress, which holds exclusive authority for establishing alien status categories and setting the conditions of aliens' entry and continued presence, has affirmatively decided that unlawful presence—standing alone—should not subject an alien to criminal penalties and incarceration although unlawful presence may subject the alien to the civil remedy of removal. However, unlawful presence becomes an element of a criminal offense when an alien is found in the United States after having been previously removed or after voluntarily departing from the United States while a removal order was pending. Congress specifically authorized federal immigration officers to patrol the United States border, as well as search vehicles and lands near the border, to prevent aliens from unlawfully entering the United States, and it empowered these officers to arrest an alien who is seen attempting unlawful entry at the border or who the officer has reason to believe has unlawfully entered the county and is likely to escape before a warrant can be obtained.

Congress has created a comprehensive alien registration system for monitoring the entry and movement of aliens within the United States. As part of this federal alien registration system, Congress has specified the content of the registration forms, what special circumstances may require deviation, and the confidential nature of registration information. Aliens who are 18 years and older are required to carry in their possession their certificate of alien registration or alien registration receipt card. The INA provides that any alien who fails to comply with this requirement may be fined and imprisoned not more than 30 days.

However, there are several circumstances in which an alien would not be provided with evidence of registration notwithstanding the federal government's knowledge of the alien's presence. Federal law provides a variety of humanitarian options for aliens including unlawfully present aliens who have been victimized or fear persecution or violence. To qualify for such programs an alien needs to apply and satisfy the criteria that the program at issue requires. [While the application being reviewed], an alien may not have evidence of registration even though the federal government is aware of the alien's presence, has decided against removing the alien, and certainly has no interest in prosecuting the alien for a crime. It would therefore violate federal policy to prosecute or detain these types of aliens on the basis of their immigration status.

Congress has further exercised its authority over the entry and movement of aliens by criminalizing the smuggling of unlawful aliens into the country, as well as the facilitation of unlawful immigration within the nation's borders. Specifically, federal law prohibits the knowing attempt to bring an alien into the United States "at a place other than a designated port of entry or place other than as designated by the [Secretary of Homeland Security]," and imposes criminal penalties on a person who, "knowing or in reckless disregard" of the fact that an alien has unlawfully entered or remained in the United States, attempts to "transport or move" the alien within the United States "in furtherance of such violation of law." These criminal sanctions are directed at the smuggler and are not meant to serve as a criminal sanction for the unlawfully present alien or for incidental transportation. Congress chose not to penalize an unlawfully present alien's mere movement within the country or across state lines unless other factors are present, nor do the federal immigration laws penalize the provision of transportation services in such situations.

Federal law also imposes criminal penalties on a person who, "conceals, harbors, or shields from detection," an alien in "knowing or in reckless disregard" of the fact that the alien has unlawfully entered or remained in the United States. Similarly, it is unlawful to "encourage or induce an alien to come to, enter, or reside in the United States, knowing or in reckless disregard of the fact that" such entry or residence will be in violation of the law. Federal law does not, as a general matter, restrict the movement of aliens—whether lawfully or unlawfully present—between different states.

Congress has further exercised its authority over immigration and the status of aliens by prohibiting the hiring of aliens not authorized to work in the United States. In addition, Congress established civil penalties for immigration-related document fraud, such as the presentation of fraudulent documents to demonstrate work eligibility. In enacting penalties on employers of unlawful aliens, as well as on unlawful aliens who engage in document fraud, Congress chose not to impose criminal penalties on aliens for solely seeking or obtaining employment in the United States without authorization and in fact decided that criminal sanctions for seeking or obtaining employment would run counter to the purposes of the immigration system. Although unlawfully present aliens may be subject to removal, no criminal penalty attaches simply because an alien has solicited or performed work without proper authorization.

DHS is primarily charged with administering and enforcing the INA and other laws relating to immigration, which it accomplishes mainly through its components, U.S.

Immigration and Customs Enforcement ("ICE"), U.S. Customs and Border Protection ("CBP"), and U.S. Citizenship and Immigration Services ("USCIS"). DHS also receives state and local cooperation in its enforcement efforts. In addition, Congress prescribed by statute a number of ways in which states may assist the federal government in its enforcement of the immigration laws.

Through a variety of programs, DHS works cooperatively with states and localities to accomplish its mission to enforce the federal immigration laws. Among these efforts is the Law Enforcement Agency Response program ("LEAR"), an Arizona-specific program for responding to calls from state and local law enforcement officers seeking assistance from ICE regarding suspected unlawfully present aliens. But the opportunity that federal law provides for participation by state and local officials does not mean that states can enact their own immigration policies to rival the national immigration policy; the formulation of immigration policy and balancing of immigration enforcement priorities is a matter reserved for the federal government. Such regulations do not fall within the state's traditional police powers and remain the exclusive province of the federal government.

ARIZONA'S S.B. 1070

On April 23, 2010, [Arizona's] Governor [Janet] Brewer signed into law S.B. 1070, which [among other things] includes a provision that requires, in the context of a lawful stop, detention, or arrest, the verification of an individual's immigration status when practicable where there is "reasonable suspicion" that the individual is unlawfully present in the United States.

On the same day that she signed S.B. 1070 into law, Governor Brewer issued an executive order requiring law enforcement training to "provide clear guidance to law enforcement officials regarding what constitutes reasonable suspicion," and to "make clear that an individual's race, color or national origin alone cannot be grounds for reasonable suspicion to believe any law has been violated." One week after S.B. 1070 was signed into law, the Arizona Legislature passed, and Governor Brewer signed, H.B. 2162, which amended S.B. 1070 for the purpose of responding to those who [according to Governor Brewer] "expressed fears that the original law would somehow allow or lead to racial profiling."

S.B. 1070 (as amended) attempts to second guess federal policies and re-order federal priorities in the area of immigration enforcement and to directly regulate immigration and the conditions of an alien's entry and presence in the United States despite the fact that those subjects are federal domains and do not involve any legitimate state interest. Arizona's adoption of a maximal "attrition through enforcement" policy disrupts the national enforcement regime set forth in the INA and reflected in federal immigration enforcement policy and practice, including the federal government's prioritization of enforcement against dangerous aliens.

S.B. 1070 implements Arizona's stated immigration policy through a novel and comprehensive immigration regime that, among other things, creates a series of state immigration crimes relating to the presence, employment, and transportation of aliens, expands the opportunities for Arizona police to push aliens toward incarceration for those crimes by enforcing a mandatory immigration status verification system, and allows for arrests based on crimes with no nexus to Arizona. [As such], S.B. 1070 conflicts with and otherwise stands as an obstacle to Congress's demand that federal immigration policy accommodate the competing interests of immigration control, national security and public safety, humanitarian concerns, and foreign relations—a balance implemented through the policies of the President and various executive officers with the discretion to enforce the federal immigration laws. Enforcement of S.B. 1070 would also effectively create state crimes and sanctions for unlawful presence despite Congress's considered judgment to not criminalize such status. S.B. 1070 would thus interfere with federal policy and prerogatives in the enforcement of the U.S. immigration laws.

Because S.B. 1070, in both its singularly stated purpose and necessary operation, conflicts with the federal government's balance of competing objectives in the enforcement of the federal immigration laws, its passage already has had foreign policy implications for U.S. diplomatic relations with other countries, including Mexico and many others. S.B. 1070 has also had foreign policy implications concerning specific national interests regarding national security, drug enforcement, tourism, trade, and a variety of other issues. S.B. 1070 has subjected the United States to direct criticism by other countries and international organizations and has resulted in a breakdown in certain planned bilateral and multilateral arrangements on issues such as border security and disaster management. S.B. 1070 has in these ways undermined several aspects of U.S. foreign policy related to immigration issues and other national concerns that are unrelated to immigration.

Numerous other states are contemplating passing legislation similar to S.B. 1070. The development of various conflicting state immigration enforcement policies would result in further and significant damage to (1) U.S. foreign relations, (2) the United States' ability to fairly and consistently enforce the federal immigration laws and provide immigration-related humanitarian relief, and (3) the United States' ability to exercise the discretion vested in the executive branch under the INA, and would result in the non-uniform treatment of aliens across the United States.

Section 2 of S.B. 1070

Section 2 of S.B. 1070 mandates that for any lawful "stop, detention or arrest made by a law enforcement official" (or agency) in the enforcement of any state or local law, including civil ordinances, where reasonable suspicion exists that an individual is an alien and is "unlawfully present" in the United States, the officer must make a reasonable attempt to determine the individual's immigration status when practicable, and to verify it with the federal government. Section 2 also requires that "[a]ny person who is arrested shall have the person's immigration status determined before the person is released."

Section 2 provides that any legal resident of Arizona may bring a civil action in an Arizona court to challenge any official or agency that "adopts or implements a policy that limits or restricts the enforcement of federal immigration laws...to less than the full extent permitted by federal law." Whereas Arizona police (like federal officers and police in other states) formerly had the discretion to decide whether to verify immigration status during the course of a lawful stop, the combination of the verification requirement and the threat of private lawsuits now removes such discretion and mandates verification. This provision also mandates the enforcement of the remaining provisions of S.B. 1070.

The mandatory nature of Section 2, in tandem with S.B. 1070's new or amended state immigration crimes, directs officers to seek maximum scrutiny of a person's immigration status, and mandates the imposition of state criminal penalties for what is effectively unlawful presence, even in circumstances where the federal government has decided not to impose such penalties because of federal enforcement priorities or humanitarian, foreign policy, or other federal interests. In addition, the mandatory nature of this alien inspection scheme will necessarily result in countless inspections and detentions of individuals who are lawfully present in the United States. Verification is mandated for all cases where an Arizona police officer has a "reasonable suspicion" that a person in a lawful stop is unlawfully present and it is practicable to do so. But a "reasonable suspicion" is not definitive proof, and will often result in the verification requirement being applied—wholly unnecessarily—to lawfully present aliens and U.S. citizens. Further, because the federal authorities may not be able to immediately verify lawful presence—and may rarely have information related to stopped U.S. citizens—Section 2 will result in the prolonged detention of lawfully present aliens and U.S. citizens. Section 2 of S.B. 1070 will therefore impose burdens on lawful immigrants and U.S. citizens alike who are stopped, questioned, or detained and cannot readily prove their immigration or citizenship status, including those individuals who may not have an accepted form of identification because, for example, they are legal minors without a driver's license. Arizona's alien inspection scheme therefore will subject lawful aliens to the possibility of inquisitorial practices and police surveillance a form of treatment which Congress has plainly guarded against in crafting a balanced, federally-directed immigration enforcement scheme.

Mandatory state alien inspection schemes and attendant federal verification requirements will impermissibly impair and burden the federal resources and activities of DHS. S.B. 1070's mandate for verification of alien status will necessarily result in a dramatic increase in the number of verification requests being issued to DHS, and will thereby place a tremendous burden on DHS resources, necessitating a reallocation of DHS resources away from its policy priorities. As such, the federal government will be required to divert resources from its own, carefully considered enforcement priorities—dangerous aliens who pose a threat to national security and public safety—to address the work that Arizona will now create for it. Such interference with federal priorities, driven by state-imposed burdens on federal resources, constitutes a violation of the Supremacy Clause. Section 2 conflicts with and otherwise stands as an obstacle to the full purposes and objectives of Congress, and its enforcement would further conflict with the enforcement prerogatives and priorities of the federal government. Moreover, Section 2 does not promote any legitimate state interest.

Section 3 of S.B. 1070

Section 3 of S.B. 1070 makes it a new state criminal offense for an alien in Arizona to violate [the federal law that] requires every alien to "at all times carry with him and have in his personal possession any certificate of alien registration or alien registration receipt card issued to him," [and] which penalizes the willful failure to apply for registration when required. Section 3 of S.B. 1070 provides a state penalty of up to $100 and up to twenty days imprisonment for a first offense and thirty days imprisonment for any subsequent violation.

Section 3 of S.B. 1070 is preempted by the comprehensive federal alien registration scheme, which provides a standard for alien registration in a single integrated and all-embracing system. Section 3 of S.B. 1070 conflicts with and otherwise stands as an obstacle to the full purposes and objectives of Congress in creating a uniform and singular federal alien registration scheme.

Section 3 [further] demands the arrest and prosecution of all aliens who do not have certain enumerated registration documents. But several classes of aliens who are eligible for humanitarian relief are simply not provided with registration documents while their status is being adjudicated by the federal government. S.B. 1070 thus seeks to criminalize aliens whose presence is known and accepted by the federal government (at least during the pendency of their status review) and thereby conflicts with and otherwise stands as an obstacle to the full purposes and objectives of Congress in providing certain forms of humanitarian relief. Additionally, Section 3 of S.B. 1070 is a key part of Arizona's new immigration policy as it is tantamount to a regulation of immigration, in that it seeks to control the conditions of an alien's entry and presence in the United States without serving any traditional state police interest. Accordingly, Section 3 of S.B. 1070 is preempted by the federal government's recognized exclusive authority over the regulation of immigration.

Section 4 of S.B. 1070

Section 4 of S.B. 1070 makes it a felony for "a person to intentionally engage in the smuggling of human beings for profit or commercial purpose." The statute defines "smuggling of human beings" as the "transportation, procurement of transportation or use of property...by a person or an entity that knows or has reason to know that the person or persons transported...are not U.S. citizens, permanent resident aliens or persons otherwise lawfully in this state or have attempted to enter, entered or remained in the United States in violation of law."

Arizona's alien smuggling prohibition is preempted by federal law. There are several key differences between the federal and Arizona alien smuggling provisions that demonstrate that Arizona's alien smuggling prohibition actually regulates conditions of unlawful presence and not smuggling at all. First, Arizona's alien smuggling law, unlike the federal criminal provisions, is not limited to transportation that is provided "in furtherance" of unlawful immigration, but instead prohibits the knowing provision of any commercial transportation services to an alien unlawfully present in the United States. Second, unlike federal law, Arizona's alien smuggling law not only criminalizes the conduct of the transportation provider but has been used, in conjunction with Arizona's conspiracy statute, to prosecute the unlawfully present alien. Third, Arizona's smuggling provision is not targeted at smuggling across the United States' international borders. As a result of these differences, taken both separately and in tandem, Arizona's smuggling prohibition regulates the conditions of an alien's entry and continued presence in the United States, by essentially banning an unlawfully present alien from using commercial transportation. Although a state is free, in certain instances, to regulate conduct that is not regulated by the federal government, the differences between Section 4 and federal anti-smuggling law convert Arizona's alien smuggling prohibitions into a preempted regulation of immigration. Additionally, Arizona's smuggling prohibition will result in special, impermissible burdens for lawfully present aliens, who will predictably be impeded from using commercial transportation services due to the strictures of Section 4. Arizona's smuggling prohibition thus conflicts with and otherwise stands as an obstacle to the full purposes and objectives of Congress in creating a comprehensive system of penalties for aliens who are unlawfully present in the United States.

Section 5 of S.B. 1070

Section 5 of S.B. 1070 makes it a new state crime for any person who is "unauthorized" and "unlawfully present" in the United States to solicit, apply for, or perform work. Arizona's new prohibition on unauthorized aliens seeking or performing work is pre-empted by the comprehensive federal scheme of sanctions related to the employment of unauthorized aliens. The text, structure, history, and purpose of this scheme reflect an affirmative decision by Congress to regulate the employment of unlawful aliens by imposing sanctions on the employer without imposing sanctions on the unlawful alien employee. Arizona's criminal sanction on unauthorized aliens stands as an obstacle to the full purposes and objectives of Congress's considered approach to regulating employment practices concerning unauthorized aliens, and it conflicts with Congress's decision not to criminalize such conduct for humanitarian and other reasons. Enforcement of this new state crime additionally interferes with the comprehensive system of civil consequences for aliens unlawfully present in the United States by attaching criminal sanctions on the conditions of unlawful presence, despite an affirmative choice by Congress not to criminalize unlawful presence.

Section 5 of S.B. 1070 also makes it a new state crime for a person committing any criminal offense to (1) "transport…an alien…, in furtherance of the illegal presence of the alien in the United States,…if the person knows or recklessly disregards" that the alien is here illegally; (2) "conceal, harbor or shield…an alien from detection…if the person knows or recklessly disregards the fact that the alien" is unlawfully present; or (3) "encourage or induce an alien to come to or reside in this state if the person knows or recklessly disregards the fact that such…entering or residing in this state is or will be in violation of law." This provision exempts child protective service workers, first responders, and emergency medical technicians. This provision contains no further exceptions, including for organizations exempted by federal law from criminal liability, such as religious organizations which "encourage, invite, call, allow, or enable" an alien to volunteer as a minister or missionary.

Arizona's new state law prohibition of certain transporting, concealing, and encouraging of unlawfully present aliens is preempted by federal law. This new provision is an attempt to regulate unlawful entry into the United States (through the Arizona border). The regulation of unlawful entry is an area from which states are definitively barred by the U.S. Constitution. Additionally, because the purpose of this law is to deter and prevent the movement of certain aliens into Arizona, the law restricts interstate commerce. Enforcement and operation of this state law provision would therefore conflict and interfere with the federal government's management of interstate commerce, and would thereby violate Article I, Section 8 of the U.S. Constitution.

Section 6 of S.B. 1070

Section 6 of S.B. 1070 amends a preexisting Arizona criminal statute governing the circumstances under which law enforcement officers can make a warrantless arrest. Section 6 allows the arrest of anyone whom the officer has probable cause to believe "has committed any public offense that makes the person removable from the United States," and does not require coordination with DHS to confirm removability. The warrantless arrest authority provided by Section 6 applies to persons who have committed an offense in another state when an Arizona law enforcement official believes that offense makes the person removable. Arizona law previously allowed for the warrantless arrest of anyone who was suspected of having committed a misdemeanor or felony in Arizona. Although Section 6 authorizes warrantless arrests based on crimes committed out of state, it does so only if the officer believes the crime makes the individual removable. Thus, Section 6 is not intended to serve any new law enforcement interest. Rather, the purpose of Section 6, especially when read in light of S.B. 1070's overall purpose, is plain: Section 6 provides additional means to arrest aliens in the state on the basis of immigration status.

Section 6 makes no exception for aliens whose removability has already been resolved by federal authorities, despite the fact that only the federal government can actually issue removal decisions. Section 6 will therefore necessarily result in the arrest of aliens based on out-of-state crimes, even if the criminal and immigration consequences of the out-of- state crime have already been definitively resolved. For that reason, as with Section 2, Section 6 of S.B. 1070 interferes with the federal government's enforcement prerogatives and will necessarily impose burdens on lawful aliens in a manner that conflicts with the purposes and practices of the federal immigration laws. Additionally, Section 6 will result in the arrest of aliens whose out-of-state crimes would not give rise to removal proceedings at all.

Wherefore, the United States respectfully requests the following relief [be granted by the district court]:

1. A declaratory judgment stating that Sections 1-6 of S.B. 1070 are invalid, null, and void; [and]

2. A preliminary and a permanent injunction against the State of Arizona, and its officers, agents, and employees, prohibiting the enforcement of Sections 1-6 of S.B. 1070;...

Arizona's Law Encouraging Citizen Identity Checks by Police: Permissible State Action

ATTORNEYS REPRESENTING ARIZONA AND ITS GOVERNOR, JANICE K. BREWER

Janice K. Brewer and the State of Arizona oppose plaintiff's [U.S. government's] motion [that] seeks to enjoin enforcement of S.B. 1070 or the "Act." S.B. 1070 is Arizona's legitimate and constitutionally permissible response to the crushing personal, environmental, criminal, and financial burdens thrust upon the State as a consequence of illegal immigration and the lack of comprehensive enforcement activity by the federal government and certain Arizona "sanctuary" cities. The Arizona Legislature enacted S.B. 1070 primarily to require that Arizona's law enforcement officers cooperate in the enforcement of federal immigration laws and, pursuant to the State's broad police powers, to establish state crimes that mirror existing federal laws.

Plaintiff seeks to enjoin S.B. 1070 as facially [obviously] unconstitutional. Plaintiff's claims find no support in the Constitution or federal law and, in many instances, contravene express congressional intent. Plaintiff bears a heavy burden of establishing that Sections 2 through 6 of S.B. 1070 are unconstitutional in *all* of their applications, that plaintiff will be *irreparably* harmed if the law is not enjoined, and that plaintiff's interests in enjoining Sections 2 through 6 outweigh Arizona's interests in having S.B. 1070 implemented. Plaintiff attempts to meet this burden by relying on faulty premises and inapposite case law. Plaintiff will not suffer *any* harm, much less irreparable harm, if S.B. 1070 is implemented because the Act requires only that Arizona's law enforcement officers act in accordance with their constitutional authority and congressionally established federal policy. Plaintiff is not entitled to an injunction.

THE SUPREMACY CLAUSE

The Supremacy Clause governs state action in two ways. First, it requires states to uphold federal law. Second, the Supremacy Clause prohibits states from regulating in areas reserved to the federal government and from enacting laws that "interfere with, or are contrary to" federal law. Plaintiff frames the issues in this lawsuit in terms of federal preemption, arguing that Arizona's legitimate policy choices contravene federal immigration policy and priorities. S.B. 1070 does nothing of the sort. Arizona merely seeks to assist with the enforcement of existing federal immigration laws in a constitutional manner. It is plaintiff that is attempting to impose immigration policies and priorities that contravene and conflict with federal law and unambiguous congressional intent.

CONGRESS' REGULATION OF IMMIGRATION

The Immigration and Nationality Act (INA), which Congress originally enacted in 1952, generally regulates the conditions upon which aliens may enter and remain in the country and, with limited exceptions, charges the Secretary of the Department of Homeland Security (DHS) with the administration and enforcement of the nation's immigration and naturalization laws. The DHS agencies charged with securing the nation's borders are: (1) ICE; (2) U.S. Customs and Border Protection; (3) the Transportation Security Administration; and (4) the U.S. Coast Guard. ICE is responsible for interior enforcement of the federal immigration laws. Its mandate includes, among other things, "detaining illegal immigrants and ensuring their departure (or removal) from the United States."

The federal government has faced two significant obstacles in the interior enforcement of its immigration laws. First, Congress and DHS have devoted over five times more resources in terms of staff and budget on border enforcement than on interior enforcement. Second, certain state and local governments have implemented policies that either discourage or severely restrict law enforcement officers from assisting in the enforcement of federal immigration laws. [An example is] the Executive Order the Mayor of New York City issued in 1989 prohibiting, with limited exceptions, "any City officer or employee from transmitting information regarding the immigration status of any individual to federal immigration authorities." Interior enforcement problems have had serious consequences. For example, the Center for Immigration Studies found that eight of the 48 *al Qaeda* foreign born terrorists operating in the United States since 1993 worked in the United States illegally.

Both the Executive and Congress each have expressed the desire to improve interior enforcement through increased cooperation between federal, state, and local authorities. In 1995, the President issued a Memorandum stating that: "It is a fundamental right and duty for a nation to protect the integrity of its borders and its laws." To further this objective, the President directed the Department of Justice (DOJ) to, among other things, ensure that "all necessary steps [be] taken to increase coordination and cooperative efforts with State, and local law enforcement officers in identification of criminal aliens."

In 1996, Congress established a federal policy of encouraging cooperation between federal, state, and local authorities in enforcing the federal immigration laws through two amendments to the INA. [One amendment's] stated purpose was "to give State and local officials the authority to communicate with [ICE] regarding the presence, whereabouts, or activities of illegal aliens." Several provisions of [the Second Amendment] also were designed to encourage cooperation between federal, state, and local law enforcement officers regarding violations of federal immigration laws. In accordance with these federal policies and statutes, numerous federal, state, and local governments have successfully cooperated in the enforcement of federal immigration laws.

ARIZONA'S ENACTMENT OF S.B. 1070

Despite these strong federal policies of cooperative enforcement of the federal immigration laws, interior enforcement remains weak. In 2006, the House Committee on Homeland Security concluded that "[t]he existing resources of the U.S. Border Patrol and local law enforcement *must continue to be enhanced* to counter the cartels and the criminal networks [illegal aliens] leverage to circumvent law enforcement." Yet, federal law enforcement estimates that *only* "10 percent to 30 percent of illegal aliens are actually apprehended and 10 percent to 20 percent of drugs are seized." As President Obama aptly stated: "the system is broken" and "everybody knows it."

These enforcement problems have been particularly acute in Arizona for two reasons. First, the federal government has failed to secure Arizona's border. Second, several Arizona cities implemented "sanctuary" policies limiting or restricting law enforcement officers' ability to cooperate with the federal government in the enforcement of the federal immigration laws. This cooperative *non*-enforcement of the federal immigration laws has resulted in a significant presence of illegal aliens in Arizona and numerous incidents of serious violence against Arizonans, including the homicide of eight Phoenix police officers since 1999. Almost 50% of illegal aliens enter the United States through Arizona. The Arizona Department of Corrections has estimated that criminal aliens make up more than 17% of Arizona's prison population and 21.8% of felony defendants in Maricopa County [the Phoenix area] Superior Court.

Faced with the ever-escalating social, economic, and environmental costs caused by illegal immigration, the Arizona Legislature determined that it had to take action. After considering these issues and receiving input from numerous and diverse organizations, the Arizona Legislature enacted S.B. 1070 to eliminate sanctuary city policies, to encourage—and, in some instances, mandate—assistance with the enforcement of federal immigration law, and, pursuant to the State's broad police powers, to adopt state crimes that mirror existing federal laws.

The Pertinent Provisions of S.B. 1070

Section 2 has twelve subsections. Plaintiff purports to challenge all of Section 2, but addresses only subsections B and H in its motion. Subsection B states, in pertinent part:

> For any lawful stop, detention *or arrest* made by a law enforcement official or a law enforcement agency of this state…where *reasonable suspicion* exists that the person is an alien *and* is unlawfully present in the United States, a reasonable attempt shall be made, when practicable, to determine the immigration status of the person, except if the determination may hinder or obstruct an investigation. Any person who is arrested shall have the person's immigration status determined before the person is released. The person's immigration status shall be verified with the federal government. A law enforcement official or agency may not consider race, color or national origin in implementing the requirements of this subsection except to the extent permitted by the United States or Arizona Constitution.

Plaintiff argues that S.B. 1070 will require Arizona's law enforcement officers "to verify the immigration status of every person who is arrested in the state," even if no reasonable suspicion of unlawful presence exists. However, this interpretation is inconsistent with the State's interpretation. Moreover, the plaintiff's interpretation ignores recognized principles of statutory construction and defies common sense. The State interprets S.B. 1070 to read that *only* where a reasonable suspicion exists that a person arrested is an alien and is unlawfully present in the United States *must* the person's immigration status be determined before the person is released. [It makes common sense that] the Arizona Legislature could not have intended to compel Arizona's law enforcement officers to determine and verify the immigration status of *every single person* arrested—even for U.S. citizens and when there is absolutely no reason to believe that the person is unlawfully present in the country.

Plaintiff's interpretation suggests the word "person" in the second sentence should be understood to mean both U.S. citizens and aliens. However, a U.S. citizen does not have an immigration status and nowhere in the INA does federal law ascribe an immigration status to any category of U.S. citizen. Accordingly, the only interpretation of the second sentence that is plausible is that "person" means "such person"—namely, aliens referred to in the first sentence where reasonable suspicion exists that the alien is unlawfully present in the United States.

S.B. 1070 does not authorize indefinite detention. S.B. 1070 does not expressly limit the time during which a law enforcement officer may detain an arrested person pending an investigation into his or her immigration status. [However, the law must] be construed in a manner that preserves its constitutionality and is consistent with the Arizona Legislature's intent. The statutory history [of S.B. 1070] confirms that the Arizona Legislature did *not* intend to authorize indefinite detention. Thus, S.B. 1070 must be construed to limit the detention of any person pending an investigation into the person's immigration status to a reasonable time.

Section 3 reinforces and mirrors federal law by imposing the *same* misdemeanor penalties as federal law imposes for violations the INA. The only difference between this provision and the federal statutes is that S.B. 1070 "does not apply to a person who maintains authorization from the federal government to remain in the United States."

Section 4 modifies [existing Arizona law only insofar as it clarifies] law enforcement officers' existing authority to "stop any person who is operating a motor vehicle if the officer has reasonable suspicion to believe the person is in violation of any civil traffic law."

Section 5 will add two provisions to the Arizona Criminal Code. First, [it will be] a Class 1 misdemeanor [1] for an occupant of a motor vehicle…to attempt to hire or pick up passengers for work…if the motor vehicle…impedes the normal movement of traffic; [2] to enter a motor vehicle [in these circumstances]; and [3] or for a person who is who is an unauthorized alien to knowingly [seek or perform] work in a public place. Second, [section 5] will make it unlawful for a person *who is in violation of a criminal offense* to transport, move, conceal, harbor, or shield unlawful aliens, or to encourage an alien to come to this state if the person knows or recklessly disregards that the person would be violating immigration laws to do so. S.B. 1070 is designed to deter persons from inducing persons to enter or remain in the state unlawfully for the purpose of assisting with their criminal enterprise.

Section 6 adds to the authority Arizona peace officers have under [existing law] to arrest a person without a warrant by authorizing such arrests when "the officer has probable cause to believe…[t]he person to be arrested has committed any public offense that makes the person removable from the United States." This provision is based upon a memorandum the DOJ's Office of Legal Counsel prepared in which it concluded that federal law does not "preclude state police from arresting aliens on the basis of civil deportability." Neither Section 6 nor any other federal, state, or local law authorizes Arizona's law enforcement officers to determine whether a person is removable. If, however, a law enforcement officer receives confirmation from the federal government or its authorized agent that a person is removable, this provision permits the officer to handle the initial arrest and processing. S.B. 1070 further reduces the federal government's burden by permitting the officer to transport the person to a federal facility.

S.B. 10 AND THE U.S. CONSTITUTION

None of the Challenged Sections of S.B. 1070 Are Preempted

To establish its claim that federal law preempts S.B. 1070 [under the Supremacy clause], plaintiff must demonstrate that: (1) S.B. 1070 purports to regulate immigration, an exclusively federal power; that (2) federal law occupies the field [that is, Congress intends federal law to be exclusive in that area]; or (3) S.B. 1070 conflicts with federal law. Plaintiff must also overcome the presumption, which the Supreme Court has held applies "[i]n all pre-emption cases,…that the historic police powers of the States were not to be superseded by the Federal Act unless that was the clear and manifest purpose of Congress." Plaintiff has not met that burden with respect to any of its challenges to Sections 2 through 6 of S.B. 1070.

S.B. 1070's sections do not conflict with federal law and priorities. [The sections] will not result in the harassment of lawfully present persons. Plaintiff argues that [the S.B. 1070 sections 2 through 6] conflict with "federal law and priorities" because their enforcement will result in the harassment of lawfully present aliens and, therefore, are "at odds with congressional objectives."

Section 3 of S.B. 1070 neither conflicts with federal law nor regulates in a federally occupied field. Plaintiff first argues that Section 3, which incorporates the federal penalties for violations of the INA, "is preempted because it legislates in an area fully occupied by Congress." Nothing in the history of the INA supports such a conclusion. Congress enacted these statutes in 1952 and has since amended the INA five times, but has never expressly preempted concurrent state regulation. Further, the applicable federal regulations do not indicate any intent to preempt state law and the Supreme Court has repeatedly held that it expects "an administrative regulation to declare any intention to pre-empt state law with some specificity." Plaintiff also argues that S.B. 1070 "conflicts with federal law and enforcement priorities in that field." But all S.B. 1070 does is require that persons comply with federal law.

Section 4 of S.B. 1070 does not conflict with federal law. Plaintiff's argument that Arizona's smuggling statute conflicts with federal law confuses several principles of preemption. First, plaintiff erroneously contends that a mere *difference* between [Arizona law] and the federal smuggling statute is a conflict. To establish conflict preemption, plaintiff must demonstrate that compliance with both State and federal law is impossible, [or that] the state law stands as an obstacle to the accomplishment and execution of the full purposes and objectives of Congress. The only alleged conflict that plaintiff identifies is that the Arizona statute is broader than the federal statute. This fact, however, neither impedes the federal government's ability to prosecute persons for smuggling under *its* smuggling statute nor makes it impossible for a person to comply with both laws.

Second, plaintiff ignores the requisite mental state for a conviction under [Arizona law]. Under the plain language of the statute, a person can be convicted of smuggling *only* if the State proves beyond a reasonable doubt that the person charged: (1) "with the intent to promote or aid human smuggling"; (2) "intentionally transport[s] or procure[s] the transport of a person who is [unlawfully present]…in Arizona"; (3) for a commercial purpose; and (4) "while knowing or having reason to know that the person being transported is [unlawfully present]…in Arizona."

Section 5 of S.B. 1070 does not regulate immigration. Plaintiff's argument that [it does], takes an overly broad and unsupported view of what it means to "regulate immigration." A statute is a "regulation of immigration" if it defines who should or should not be admitted into the country, and the conditions under which *a legal entrant* may remain. The Supreme Court "has never held that every state enactment which in any way deals with aliens is a regulation of immigration and thus per se pre-empted by this constitutional power. In fact, the Court has expressly held that "the States do have some authority to act with respect to illegal aliens, at least where such action mirrors federal objectives and furthers a legitimate state goal."

S.B. 1070 does not purport to regulate who should or should not be admitted to the United States or the conditions upon which *a legal entrant* may remain. Rather, S.B. 1070 will make it unlawful for a person ***who is in violation of a criminal offense*** to transport, move, conceal, harbor, or shield unlawful aliens, or to encourage an alien to come to this state if the person knows or recklessly disregards that the person would be violating immigration laws to do so. The fact that this statute applies *only* to persons who engage in such conduct while committing some other criminal offense demonstrates that it is designed to deter *criminals* from using illegal aliens to assist in their criminal conduct or enterprise.

[**Section 6** of S.B. 1070 does not conflict with federal authority.] Plaintiff argues that S.B. 1070, which authorizes warrantless arrests of aliens who are removable, "does not depend upon coordination with DHS to verify removability." This is simply incorrect. Nothing in either S.B. 1070 or any other provision of state or federal law authorizes Arizona's law enforcement officers to make determinations regarding a person's removability. Under S.B. 1070, Arizona's law enforcement officers will regularly communicate with DHS regarding the immigration status of aliens. There is a substantial likelihood that, in doing so, DHS will confirm that a particular alien is removable. If DHS does so, S.B. 1070 merely provides Arizona's law enforcement officers with the ability to arrest and transport the person directly to DHS for processing, thereby *reducing* the burden on DHS.

S.B. 1070 will not burden federal resources. Plaintiff's second argument—that S.B. 1070 will "burden federal resources and impede federal enforcement and policy priorities"—is equally flawed. The sole mission of DHS is to carry out the will of Congress. Here, Congress has not only codified a federal policy of *encouraging* cooperation among federal, state, and local authorities in the enforcement of federal immigration laws, but it has *mandated* that DHS respond to the inquiries Arizona's law enforcement officers will make under S.B. 1070. DHS simply has no choice but to allocate its resources in a manner that enables it to comply with this congressional mandate.

In any event, plaintiff's speculation that S.B. 1070 will "burden federal resources and impede federal enforcement and policy priorities" is based entirely upon plaintiff's misconception that Arizona's law enforcement officers will contact LESC for "*every* person stopped who is reasonably suspected to be unlawfully present **and** *every* person arrested in the state. Not only is this argument inconsistent with the manner in which Arizona expects the Act to be appropriately implemented, but it ignores the fact that many law enforcement agencies across the country already are doing precisely what S.B. 1070 requires.

S.B. 1070 Correctly Adopts Federal Law as the Policy of Arizona

Plaintiff also seeks to invalidate S.B. 1070 on the ground that it allegedly attempts to set immigration policy at the state level. However, Arizona's policy of cooperative enforcement of the federal immigration laws and "attrition through enforcement" incorporate, among other things, the cooperative enforcement policies that Congress clearly established in statutes such as the INA. Even plaintiff acknowledges that: "It is certainly a primary objective of federal law to prevent aliens from unlawfully entering and residing in the United States...." And, plaintiff cannot cite to any *congressional* policy that S.B. 1070 supposedly contravenes.

Plaintiff's argument also neglects to demonstrate how the policies underlying S.B. 1070 will (on their face) interfere with any DHS or DOJ enforcement priorities. Arizona cannot require the federal government to take any action with respect to any illegal alien within Arizona's borders—nor does S.B. 1070 attempt to do so. S.B. 1070 merely requires, in limited circumstances, that Arizona's law enforcement officers exercise their existing authority to communicate with the federal government regarding possible immigration violations. This requirement cannot, as plaintiff argues, "force a diversion of federal resources away from federal priorities" because *Congress* determines federal priorities and Congress has not only invited such inquiries but has *required* ICE to respond to them. Further, because S.B. 1070 does not (and could not) provide Arizona's law enforcement officers any authority to determine who should or should not remain in the country, S.B. 1070 does not interfere with the federal government's interest in providing humanitarian relief. In fact, S.B. 1070 expressly requires that the section "be implemented in a manner consistent with federal laws regulating immigration."

S.B. 1070 Does Not Violate the Commerce Clause

The only provision of S.B. 1070 that plaintiff claims violates the Commerce Clause is Section 5. Statutes that do not discriminate and impose no burdens on interstate commerce do not violate the Commerce Clause. Further, even statutes that impose incidental burdens on interstate commerce do not violate the Commerce Clause if they regulate even-handedly to effectuate a legitimate local public interest, and the burden imposed is outweighed by the benefits to the state. Plaintiff generally alleges that S.B. 1070 "restricts the interstate movement of aliens in a manner that is prohibited by [the Commerce Clause]." Plaintiff's argument is misguided as S.B. 1070 does not restrict the interstate movement of aliens nor discriminate against or burden interstate commerce.

In fact, S.B. 1070 does not even address whether aliens can or cannot come to the State, nor does it regulate entry in any way. S.B. 1070 simply provides that individuals, *who are in violation of a criminal offense,* cannot also transport, move, conceal, harbor or shield *illegal* aliens within the state *in furtherance of their unlawful presence,* nor can they encourage an *illegal* alien to *illegally* enter or reside in the state. Plaintiff's misunderstanding about the application of S.B. 1070 and its speculation about the Act's alleged potential impact on interstate commerce is not sufficient to establish a violation of the Commerce Clause. S.B. 1070 does not discriminate against out-of-state interests, burden commerce, or create a preference for in-state commerce.

Plaintiff's Argument That S.B. 1070 Interferes with Foreign Policy [Ignores] the *De Canas* Test

Plaintiff's argument that S.B. 1070 "is independently preempted because it impermissibly conflicts with U.S. foreign policy" is unsupported by the controlling Supreme Court precedent. The premise of plaintiff's argument is that, because S.B. 1070 applies to illegal aliens, it is *per se* preempted under the federal government's foreign affairs power. But plaintiff fails to recognize that the Supreme Court [in *De Canas v. BICA*, 1976] has already rejected the position plaintiff advances and explicitly held that "the fact that aliens are the subject of a state statute" does not mandate a finding of preemption.

De Canas addressed the same type of regulation that is at issue here—regulation designed to address harm specific to Arizona and that touches upon aliens that the federal government has determined are *not lawfully present* in the country. None of the cases plaintiff cites involve the preemption of state regulation touching upon illegal aliens. *De Canas* controls the preemption inquiry and, for the reasons set forth above, plaintiff has not demonstrated preemption under the *De Canas* test.

Plaintiff also seeks to establish that it will suffer irreparable harm if S.B. 1070 is enacted by arguing that S.B. 1070 will interfere with plaintiff's "ability to manage foreign policy." This argument fails to establish irreparable harm because the criticism Arizona has received following S.B. 1070's passage has had little (if anything) to do with any provision in the Act. Arizona and Mexico continue to work together on areas of mutual concern. And, federal officials have, at the very least, been a substantial factor in coloring foreign officials' negative perceptions.

For example, before Governor Brewer even signed S.B. 1070, President Obama criticized the Act by stating that it was "misguided" and instructed the DOJ to evaluate whether the law would violate civil rights. President Obama further stated that a federal solution was necessary to avoid "open[ing] the door to irresponsibility by others," and referred to "the recent efforts in Arizona" as "threaten[ing] to undermine basic notions of fairness that we cherish as Americans." Secretary Janet Napolitano also appeared on television to assert that S.B. 1070 was "bad law enforcement law," after which she admitted that she had not read the Act. [U.S. Attorney General] Eric Holder expressed a concern about the bill as it relates to racial profiling even though he later acknowledged having only "glanced at the bill." And Secretary of State Hillary Clinton announced [that she] expected "a significant negative response from the international community."

Instead of educating the international community about existing U.S. immigration laws, President Obama, Secretary Napolitano, Attorney General Holder, and Secretary Clinton have allowed S.B. 1070 to be distorted in Latin America and around the world. Based on all these statements and misrepresentations, it is impossible to determine to what extent, if any, the foreign policy impact of S.B. 1070 arises out any actual provision of the Act.

THE BALANCE OF EQUITIES TIPS SHARPLY IN ARIZONA'S FAVOR

Plaintiff will not suffer any harm (let alone irreparable harm) if S.B. 1070 goes into effect. Arizona, by contrast, is suffering serious consequences under the status quo. There can be no dispute that Arizona has a serious illegal immigration problem. In 2009, there were approximately 500,000 people in Arizona who were not lawfully present in this country. Arizona has repeatedly asked for federal assistance in dealing with the influx of illegal aliens in Arizona. On June 23, 2010, Governor Brewer wrote to President Obama and explained that "the need for action to secure Arizona's border could not be clearer" and proposed a four-point strategy for addressing Arizona's border-control issues. And, as recently as July 2010, Arizona Attorney General Terry Goddard wrote to President Obama to address the "rampant trafficking of drugs, humans, guns and money across our border" caused by the Mexican drug cartels, which Goddard believes to be "responsible for the murders of more than 22,700 people south of our border since 2007."

Arizona's interest in having S.B. 1070 enforced substantially exceeds plaintiff's supposed interest in having S.B. 1070 enjoined. Enjoining the enforcement of S.B. 1070 would inflict significant and tangible, irreparable harm upon the State and its citizens. Among the documented harms demonstrated by the State herein are: (i) Citizens, including police officers and their families, are exposed to injury and death; (ii) Individuals are subjected to the presence of drug cartels and criminal activity; and (iii) Citizens are denied the use of public lands deemed unsafe and dangerous. These are not speculative, hypothetical harms. These are real-life experiences which have substantially affected the quality of life in Arizona and will continue to do so at an increasing rate if S.B. 1070 is enjoined.

For the foregoing reasons, Governor Brewer and the State of Arizona respectfully request that the Court deny plaintiff's requested injunction.

THE CONTINUING DEBATE
Arizona's Law Encouraging Citizen Identity Checks by Police

What Is New

Passage of S.B. 1070 set off widespread protest. President Barack Obama repeatedly condemned the act. So did numerous other prominent figures including Roman Catholic Cardinal Roger M. Mahony of Los Angeles, who compared the ability of Arizona authorities to demand documents with "Nazism," and Mexico's President Felipe Calderón, who decried S.B. 1070 for "using racial profiling as a basis for law enforcement." Most Americans disagreed, however. Typifying survey results, a *Washington Post* poll in June 2010 found 58% of Americans supporting the law. With regard to legal case that the readings in this debate are part of, U.S. district court judge Susan Bolton soon ruled that Arizona could not put most of S.B. 1070 into effect. Arizona appealed to the Ninth Circuit of the U.S. Court of Appeals, which in 2011 upheld the district court. Arizona then appealed to the Supreme Court, which will almost certainly finally decide the fate of S.B. 1070 in a ruling on that case or one of the others filed against the law. However, other states are considering their own approaches to unauthorized immigrants. In August 2010, for example, Florida's attorney general proposed legislation that would include not only having police check immigration papers, but longer detention of suspects during the investigation process and separate state penalties for being an unauthorized alien, and each such initiative will likely face legal challenges.

Where to Find More

Background material on federalism as a constitutional issue is available in Louis Fisher and Katy Harriger, *American Constitutional Law: Vol. 1, Constitutional Structures: Separated Powers and Federalism* (Carolina Academic Press, 2009). On federalism and immigration, see Daniel Booth, "Federalism on ICE: State and Local Enforcement of Federal Immigration Law," *Harvard Journal of Law & Public Policy* (June 2006). One place to keep up on developments regarding the *United States v. Arizona* is on the Web site of LawBrain at http://lawbrain.com/wiki/ Arizona_Senate_Bill_1070. To get background on a suit against S.B. 1070 on civil right grounds, *Friendly House v. Whiting,* read the briefs supporting and opposing the law on the Web site of American Immigration Council at www.legalactioncenter.org/ FriendlyHouse-v-Whiting-AmicusBriefs.

What More to Do

As you consider this debate, focus on the federalism issue and try to not let you views on other related issues such as civil rights influence your views here. It is possible, for example, to find the civil rights impact of S.B. 1070 abhorrent, yet to also believe that Arizona was within its authority as a state to pass the law as far as the issues of the supremacy clause, the commerce clause, and foreign policy. The authority of the state on this dimension does not mean the courts in another case could not strike down the law as a civil rights violation. Federalism is an important aspect of the constitutional structure, and an ongoing issue how the powers of the federal government and those of the states interact.

3   CIVIL LIBERTIES

THE PHRASE "UNDER GOD" IN THE PLEDGE OF ALLEGIANCE:
Violation of the First Amendment *or* Acceptable Traditional Expression?

VIOLATION OF THE FIRST AMENDMENT

ADVOCATE: Douglas Laycock, Professor, School of Law, University of Texas; and Counsel of Record for 32 Christian and Jewish clergy filing an amicus curiae brief with the Supreme Court in *Elk Grove School District v. Newdow*

SOURCE: A discussion of the topic "Under God? Pledge of Allegiance Constitutionality," sponsored by the Pew Forum on Religion and Public Life and held before the National Press Club, Washington, D.C., March 19, 2004

ACCEPTABLE TRADITIONAL EXPRESSION

ADVOCATE: Jay Alan Sekulow, Chief Counsel, American Center for Law and Justice; and Counsel of Record for 76 members of Congress and the Committee to Protect the Pledge filing an amicus curiae brief with the Supreme Court in *Elk Grove School District v. Newdow*

SOURCE: A discussion of the topic "Under God? Pledge of Allegiance Constitutionality," sponsored by the Pew Forum on Religion and Public Life and held before the National Press Club, Washington, D.C., March 19, 2004

This debate focuses on the establishment clause of the Constitution's First Amendment, which requires that "Congress shall make no law respecting an establishment of religion." It is clear that the authors of the First Amendment were reacting against the British practice of establishing and supporting an "official" church, in that case the Church of England. Also certain is that Congress meant the amendment to prohibit any attempt to bar any religion or religious belief. There the certainties end. For example, freedom of religion does not mean that the government cannot proscribe certain religious practices. Polygamy, animal sacrifice, and taking illegal drugs are just a few of the practices exercised in the name religion that have been legally prohibited with subsequent court approval.

Nevertheless, religion has always had a presence in government in the United States. The Great Seal of the United States, adopted in 1782 (and found on the back left of one dollar bills) contains an "all seeing eye of Providence," which probably means God, especially given that it is framed in a triangle, thought to represent the Christian trinity. The Great Seal also contains the Latin phrase "annuit coeptis," which translates as "It/He (Providence/God) has favored our undertakings." Also, first adopted in 1964 and currently on all U.S. paper currency is the motto "In God We Trust." That phrase is also found in the fourth stanza of the Star Spangled Banner (written 1813; officially adopted 1931), which concludes, "And this be our motto: 'In God is our trust.'" Finally, in 1957 Congress added "under God" after "one nation" to the Pledge of Allegiance. This last reference to God is the specific issue in this debate.

Government also has and continues to support religion and to choose among religions in other ways. For example, the military employs chaplains for all the major religious faiths, but does not employ atheist counselors. There is also a level of choosing among religions in having chaplains for the major religions, but not for the lesser-known ones. Each year the president lights an immense Christmas tree, although these days in a bow to restrictions on religious displays on public property the giant fir is called the "national tree" and is lighted as part of the "Pageant of Peace," which, of course, corresponds with the Christmas season. Historically, it has been common to find the Ten Commandments carved in the walls of public buildings or otherwise displayed in them.

Traditionally, displays of the Ten Commandments or similar religious symbols on public property, prayers in public schools, references to God on the country's currency, or affirmations of patriotism were not high-profile issues. This began to change because of the increasing stress on civil rights and liberties and because in *Everson v. Board of Education* (1947) the Supreme Court ruled that the due process cause of the Fourteenth Amendment made the establishment clause of the First Amendment applicable to the states, as well as federal government. During the ensuing years, a significant number of cases involving practices at the state and local levels were brought before the Supreme Court. With regard to the establishment clause, the Court struck down prayers and religious invocations in public schools, most religious displays on public property, and other explicit and implicit supports of religion by public officials. However, the Supreme Court has also allowed religious groups to meet in public buildings as long as there is no discrimination, and has supported prayers opening legislative sessions and having student groups fees go to student religious groups.

In this setting, Michael Newdow filed suit arguing that a California rule requiring students to recite the Pledge of Allegiance with its affirmative reference to God violated the establishment clause of the First Amendment. A U.S. District Court ruled for the school district, but the Ninth Circuit of the U.S. Court of Appeals found for Newdow, and the Elk Grove school district appealed to the U.S. Supreme Court. Shortly before the High Court heard oral arguments, two opposing attorneys who had filed amicus curiae ("friend of the court") briefs with the Court debated the issue and responded to questions from the audience in the readings that follow.

POINTS TO PONDER

➤ Expressing an absolutist position when writing the majority opinion in the *Everson* case, Justice Hugo Black argued that the wall between church and state "must be kept high and impregnable. We [should] not approve any breach." What would be the implications of adopting that no-compromise standard?

➤ Compare the argument of Douglas Laycock that the Pledge, as government-sanctioned religious expression, is "coercive" and Jay Sekulow's contention that the phrase "under God" is merely a "historical statement" reflecting the belief in God by most Americans throughout history.

➤ Does it make any difference that students are not required to say the Pledge, only that schools must lead its recitation?

The Phrase "Under God" in the Pledge of Allegiance: Violation of the First Amendment

DOUGLAS LAYCOCK

Jay [Sekulow, the author of the second article in this debate] and I were on the same side in a case [*Locke v. Davey*, 2004] that the [Supreme] Court decided earlier this year, involving the student from Washington [State] who wanted to take his state scholarship to go to seminary with it. With this case, we're on opposite sides. How does that happen? What's up with me? Explaining that is relevant to what I think about the Pledge of Allegiance.

I come to these cases with a fairly simple theory, which is that people of every religion, including the majority and the minority, and people of no religion at all, are entitled to believe their own beliefs, speak their own beliefs, and act on their own beliefs as long as they're not hurting anybody else, and to be left alone by government and have government not take sides. And a corollary of that is that none of these groups can use the government to try to force the other side to join in or participate in their own religious observances. So when government tries to stop a student prayer club from meeting on its own after school, I think government is wrong. And when that student prayer club—or the supporters of that student prayer club—moves into the classroom and tries to induce everyone else who didn't want to come to participate anyway, I think they're wrong. And I think the Pledge of Allegiance falls on that side of the line.

The country has been fighting about this issue in various forms since the 1820s, when Catholics objected to Protestant religious observances in public schools. We've gotten better about it. In the 1840s and '50s, we had mobs in the street; we had people dead. We don't do that to each other any more, and that's progress. And "one nation under God" may seem like a pretty minimal violation of whatever principle is at stake here. The Supreme Court for 40 years has said consistently, without an exception, that government may not sponsor religious observances in the public schools, and they've said it with respect to things that were pretty short. The first school prayer case, *Engel v. Vitale* in 1962, was a pretty generic, monotheistic prayer composed not by clergymen but by the New York Board of Regents, and it was 22 words long, and the Court said you can't ask children to recite that prayer.

Now we're down to only two words, and it's not a prayer, and it's mixed up in the Pledge of Allegiance, and the question is, Does that change the answer? And the Supreme Court has repeatedly suggested, never in a holding, but over and over in what lawyers call dictums—side comments explaining what this opinion doesn't decide—there is some kind of threshold. It's got to be big enough to matter before it's an Establishment Clause violation [of the First Amendment to the Constitution]. There are little, ceremonial, rote, repetition things that the Court is not going to get involved in striking down. "In God We Trust" on the coins is a classic example; various state mottos around the country; certainly religious references in historical documents and in politicians' speeches, the Supreme Court is not going to strike down. And they have said—without a holding—two or three times that the Pledge of Allegiance is like "In God We Trust" on the coins. It's very short, and it's repeated by rote, and nobody really thinks about it much. Well, most people don't really think about it much.

The Court may say the Pledge of Allegiance—the religious part of the Pledge of Allegiance—is just too short to worry about. It's what lawyers call *de minimis*. That may happen.

I think the Pledge of Allegiance is different from all these other examples of things that might be de minimis. It's different from "In God We Trust" on the coins. It's different from politicians making speeches and so forth. The reason it's different is really unique in the culture. Government doesn't do this to adults; it doesn't do this to children in any other context. In the Pledge of Allegiance, we ask every child in the public schools in America every morning for a personal profession of faith. You don't have to take out your coin and read and meditate on "In God We Trust." You don't have to pay any attention when the politician is talking, and lots of us don't.

But this asks for a personal affirmation: I pledge allegiance to one nation under God. Now if God does not exist, or if I believe that God does not exist, then that isn't one nation under God. We can't have a nation under God unless there is a God. It doesn't say one nation under our god, or some gods, or one of the gods. It pretty clearly implies there is only one God, and if there is only one God, then the God of the Pledge is the one true God, and other alleged gods around the world are false gods.

It says one other thing about this God—it doesn't say much, can't say much in two words—but the nation is "under God." God is of such a nature that God exercises some sort of broad superintending authority so that it is possible for a whole nation to be under Him. Now that doesn't exclude many folks, but it excludes some, right? This is not God as First Cause who set the universe in motion and doesn't intervene any more; this is not God as a metaphor for all the goodness imminent in the universe or imminent in the population. This is God exercising some kind of authority over at least this nation; maybe over all nations.

It's a pretty generic concept of God, and it's comfortable for a lot of people. But we may overestimate how many people. The largest private opinion polls have about 15 percent of the population not subscribing to any monotheistic conception of God. Who is in that 15 percent? Buddhist and other non-theists, Hindus and other polytheists, those with no religion, atheist, agnostic, humanist, ethical culturalists. That's 15 percent of the population, with 7.2 million children in public schools who are being asked to personally affirm every morning a religious belief that is different from the religious belief that is taught or held in their home and by their parents. And it is the personal affirmation request in the Pledge, it seems to me, that makes the Pledge unique. It is different from all the other kinds of ceremonial deism that go on in the country.

In the attempt to defend the Pledge, government and the various friends of the Court supporting the Pledge have said a remarkable variety of things, but probably the most common thing they've said is variations on what appears in the brief of the United States. It is not religious. We don't mean for them to take it literally. We ask the children to say the nation is under God, but we don't expect them to really believe that the nation is under God. Here is a quote from the government's brief: "What it really means is, I pledge allegiance to one nation, founded by individuals whose belief in God gave rise to the governmental institutions and political order they adopted, indivisible, with liberty and justice for all."

Now if that were what it means, if anybody thought that was what it meant, we would not have had the great political outcry in response to the Ninth Circuit's decision. If people want to get mad about this because it had some recital about what the founders believed, or because of the other point the government makes—that it's in reference to historical and demographic facts that most Americans over time have believed in God—that would be one thing. But people don't get angry at a recital of historical and demographic facts. People get angry because they know what it means; it's plain English. They believe what it means, they want people to say what it means, they want their kids to say what it means. And I'll tell you a dirty little secret: They want to coerce other kids to say what it means and what they believe to be true. They know that "under God" means under God.

And if it doesn't mean under God, if we were to take the government seriously for asking children every morning to say the nation is under God but not to mean the nation is under God, well, Christians and Jews have a teaching about that, too. "Thou shalt not take the name of the Lord Thy God in vain." If we don't mean it, if it's a vain form of words that doesn't mean what it says, then it is indeed a taking of the name of the Lord in vain. That is why the [amicus curiae] brief that I filed [with the Supreme Court in the case of *Elk Grove School District v. Newdow*] is on behalf of 32 Christian and Jewish clergy who do care, not only about not coercing other people to practice their religion, but also care that if we are going to practice religion, we mean it seriously. We don't want a watered down religion that we don't really believe.

Jay Sekulow's version [in an opposing amicus curiae brief] is a little different. He says there's a category—and there's some of this in the government's brief as well—of patriotic observances with religious references. You can't do religion in the school, but you can do patriotism with a religious reference. The consequence of that would be, I suppose, that we could undo all the school prayer cases as long as we wrapped them in a coat of patriotism.

Mingling the patriotic and the religious seems to me to make it worse, not better. Think about what the Pledge does to a child who cannot in good faith affirm that the nation is under God and who actually thinks about it. And let me tell you, kids think about it. You don't think about it if you're comfortable with it, if it doesn't challenge anything you believe, you blur right over it. You can say it pretty fast, and most of us don't stop to reflect on the Pledge anymore. But for kids who don't believe it, and maybe most especially for kids who once went to a church and now don't believe it, whether or not to say "under God" becomes a big issue. I don't claim it becomes a big issue for all 7.2 million whose parents show up in opinion polls, but for a substantial minority of kids, to say "under God" or not becomes an issue.

Some kids drop it out. One of the saving graces here is that it's only two words, so you can get away with dropping it out, and your friends may not notice. But there are people who refuse to say those two words because they don't believe them, and there are a few who refuse to say those two words because it's religious in a governmental context, and it shouldn't be there. It belongs somewhere else.

And for the child who cannot say it, here's what we do by putting the religious reference in the middle of the Pledge of Allegiance to the nation: If you are doubtful about the existence of God, you are of doubtful loyalty to the nation. What kind of a citizen can you be? You can't even say the Pledge of Allegiance in the prescribed form that Congress has written. You can't pledge your loyalty to the nation without pledging your belief in the existence of God.

Now over and over and over the Supreme Court has said the reason it will not allow the government itself to take a position on a religious question, will not allow the government to endorse a religious viewpoint or an anti-religious viewpoint is because government should not make any citizen's political standing in the community depend upon his religious beliefs, not even implicitly, not even by implication. The Court says repeatedly that if the government says this is a Christian nation or this is a religious nation, then non-Christians and non-religious folks will think the government really views them as a second-class citizens. That's pretty indirect and implicit. This is very direct and explicit. Now, children, it is time to pledge your allegiance to the United States of America, and to do that, you have to pledge that the nation is under God. We have linked religion and politics, religion and patriotism, religious faith and patriotic standing inseparably right in the middle of one sentence. And the only way to avoid the religious part is literally to drop out mid-sentence and then come back in.

What would follow from a Supreme Court either striking down or upholding the Pledge? I think because of the fact that the Pledge is unique in asking for a personal affirmation, not much follows about other cases from a decision striking it down. Political volcano is going to follow, but not much is going to follow legally. "In God We Trust" doesn't come off the coins, the other religious references in the school curriculum don't come out. Of course the government can teach historical documents that have religious references in them because that is part of the history curriculum. I think they can teach music with religious references in it because that's music. It's important in the culture. I think schools should be more sensitive than they are about the problems faced by nonbelieving children when they're asked to sing that music. I think we can deal with those problems, but I don't think the Constitution requires that all—indeed, I think it forbids— certainly, it's sound educational policy—forbids stripping all religious references out of history. Religion is part of history.

None of those things ask the child to personally affirm his belief that the nation is under God, so in this sense, the Pledge case is unique. A decision taking "under God" out of the Pledge would not really portend much change on anything else.

A decision upholding the Pledge, well, you've got to see how they write it. If the Court wants to say the Pledge is special, we're going to let this go by, but it doesn't mean we're unraveling all the school prayer cases, it doesn't mean anything else much changes. They can write this very narrowly. There is a whole list of objective factors that are special about the Pledge that cut the other way. They could say it is only two words; it is recited by rote; it is not a prayer; it has been around in exactly the same form for 50 years before we got a hold of it; kids don't have to say it—we settled that in 1943 [in West Virginia v. Barnette]; they don't have to say it. For those reasons, in combination with all those reasons, we're going to uphold this. Nothing else will satisfy all those reasons. Nothing else is only two words, for starters, and that would be an opinion that doesn't change much.

If they write an opinion that's like the government's brief—we're going to declare that this really isn't religious—the problem with that is that it's completely standardless and therefore it's completely boundless. It's a fiat. The plain language is religious, but five of us on the Supreme Court—hey, with five votes, you can do anything—we're going to tell the country this is not religious. The Fifth Circuit recently held the Ten Commandments are not religious. A big monument across the top, giant letters, "I am the Lord, thy God. Thou shalt have no other gods before me." Not religious, the Fifth Circuit [of the U.S. Court of Appeals] says.

If the Supreme Court adopts that kind of approach—we'll just decree things not to be religious—then everything's up for grabs. If you're going to arbitrarily decree religious things to be secular, you can do it in any case, and district judges will be asked to do it in any case. So that would be a much scarier opinion, a much more potentially wide-ranging opinion, and then other possibilities sort of range in between. Any religion is okay if you're wrap it in patriotism. I think that's pretty wide open, too, because political officers can be pretty clever about wrapping things in patriotism.

So we may get an opinion either way—we may get a very narrow opinion either way or a very broad opinion, particularly if they uphold it. Watch not only for the result; watch for how they write it.

Question: Please comment on the "notion…of ceremonial deism," the idea that "references to God become meaningless if recited often enough in public places."

Mr. Laycock: I think you're right. I think the principal religious division in the country used to be Protestant-Catholic. It's not that anymore. It is a continuum from intense anti-religion to intensely religious. Intensely devout Protestants, Catholics, Muslims, Jews find themselves on the same side of a lot of issues, given that divide, and ceremonial deism is very comfortable for the vast range in the middle. The religious center in America is low-intensity theist.

I think these ceremonial references are very problematic for the anti-religious and for the seriously religious, and many of the seriously religious, in good faith, defend that kind of watered-down ceremonial deism in court on the theory that it's better than nothing; that's all they'll let us have, that's all we can get in a government-sponsored forum, and it's not for me to tell them they're making a mistake. But it seems to me it is a mistake, and a lot of folks who are intensely religious aren't comfortable with it, and to some extent, it is a position only for the Court. So the Justice Department, representing the United States, says, This is not religious at all. But the form letter from the White House that goes out to people who write in about this issue says it is profoundly religious. They're telling the Court one thing and the public something completely different. The ceremonial deism is a placeholder.

Question: Just to follow up,…comment on whether there is a path that we go down that essentially declares that the public realm—whatever is supported by government—must necessarily be godless, or is there an alternative to this? Does this case take you there or does it not necessarily take you there?

Mr. Laycock: There's no path that leads to the public sphere being godless. There is a path that leads to any activity sponsored by government being godless. The simple absolutist rule is that if the government's sponsoring it, there's no mention of God. In the public schools, the Court has never found a case where a government could mention God, but they've never said this is an absolutist rule with no exceptions either.

This case does not take us there. It does not present the question whether there can ever be any exceptions because this case has the unique feature of requesting a personal affirmation. So a decision in this case wouldn't say anything about whether the rule about what the teacher can do is absolute or the rule about what the president or the governor or the mayor at a public ceremony can do. That's never going to be absolute.

Question: I was wondering what implications this case would have for currency in the message "In God We Trust" on the U.S. dollar notes and coins?

Mr. Laycock: I'm sure there are people who fear it portends that any governmental reference to God goes, and so the currency all has to be changed. I don't think that follows at all because no one has to agree with the currency or pledge allegiance to the currency or even pay any attention to what it says on the currency, beyond the number.

Question: [You argue] "that the Pledge requires an affirmation of personal faith and consequently has got to go." Mr. Sekulow argues, "no, it doesn't—it's not an affirmation of personal faith, so it's okay. One point of view that's not represented here…is that yes, it requires an affirmation of personal faith and that's fine. And the Court should say that's fine. Is that a possible outcome? Can you play around with that a little bit?

Mr. Laycock: I think that's quite unlikely. It's not impossible, but let me just give you 30 seconds of the background. What the Court has said over the years on political issues the government can try to lead public opinion—which it does all the time, it tries to rally public support for its own agenda—but it cannot coerce people to agree with the government or to say that they agree with the government. And that's why in 1943, when the Pledge was entirely secular, it didn't have "under God" in it, and the Pledge case got to the Supreme Court, they said, You can't make students say it. Any student can opt out, but the teacher can lead it. On religious questions in the school prayer cases, they've said opt out isn't enough, because it's really outside the government's jurisdiction, the government isn't responsible for leading public opinion on religion, so the government can't do it at all. It can't ask the kids, even with an opt-out right, to say anything religious, and that's why I agree with Jay [Selulow].

It would be quite unlikely for them to say this really is religious, it really is an affirmation of faith and the government can ask you to say it as long as it gives you the right to opt out. That would be a striking departure from the structure of doctrine they've set up over the past 60 years.

Question: Much has been made of the fact that there are only two words here, but one of those words is a preposition, which, to at least some ears, implies a particular type of God, one that we are under, one that is transcendent. And I wonder if consideration of that aspect would move this particular phrase beyond ceremonial deism? I guess my concern is that if you reject the historical document argument, it does seem to imply that we're asking people to affirm a particular type of God, which in 2004, many, many people do not affirm.

Mr. Laycock: I think that if you want to talk about history, let's talk about history. "One nation under God" does not talk about history. It talks about theology and the relation of this nation today to God today and it does say we're under, that is a particular kind of God. I don't think that's going to trouble the Court much because it doesn't eliminate many conceptions of God, but it does eliminate some, as I said. But it's hard to talk about God without talking about some conception of God. It's impossible to be truly neutral in God-talk because humans have evolved too many radically diverse understandings of God.

Question: If our nation was not under Christianity at the birth of our Constitution, which I think scholars generally acknowledge Thomas Jefferson, whether he was a deist or a heretical Christian or a Unitarian, whatever he was, he was a religious man, obviously. But whether he was a Christian or not isn't relevant as far as the Constitution goes. But why did our Constitution refer to a Christian Sabbath, not a Jewish or a Muslim or an atheist Sabbath? And why was the document dated in the year of our Lord? Would anyone dare to say that Lord is anyone other than Jesus Christ?

Mr. Laycock: I agree with most of what Jay just said. Let me elaborate a little bit further and add a piece that I think is very important here. The founding generation fought hard about religious liberty, but they fought about the issues that were controversial in their time. And the religious liberty issue that was controversial in their time was how do you fund the church? And it was controversial because Protestants disagreed about it, because Episcopalians and Congregationalists had had tax support and nobody else did, and fixing that, not surprisingly, produced a huge fight.

They did not fight about these sort of religious references in public documents and public events because there was broad diversity of opinion, but the country was overwhelmingly Protestant and there wasn't any disagreement there big enough to get a fight going. The disagreement became big enough to get a fight going in the 1820s, when they started creating public schools and conservative Protestants said you Unitarians—Horace Mann was a Unitarian, and he was the founder of the public school movement—you Unitarians are putting watered down Christianity. It's not much more than Unitarianism in the public schools. We want real religion in the public schools. And then the huge Catholic immigration began and you got much bigger fights between Protestants and Catholics about what to do with the schools. And really, today's battles over prayer in the public schools and funding for private religious schools both of those battles date to those early 19th century disputes and the Protestant-Catholic conflicts that comes all the way down.

Now if the Religion Clauses of First Amendment are a guarantee of principle that government will leave each of us alone, give us as much religious liberty as we can, that principle encountered a whole new set of applications when religious diversity became greater and when the public schools got going. And so to say that in the Declaration of Independence, which is our founding political theory but it's also a political document to rally opinion, that they invoked both the secular rationale, natural law, and the religious rationale, nature's God and our Creator, they did both, that's true. And that was shrewd, but I don't think that tells us anything about how the government should handle religion when it has other people's children in its custody.

The Phrase "Under God" in the Pledge of Allegiance: Acceptable Traditional Expression

JAY ALAN SEKULOW

First, let me say that I probably agree with Doug [Laycock] on more cases than I disagree. In fact, the very first case I argued at the Supreme Court of the United States [*Airport Commissioners v. Jews for Jesus*]—which seems like a long time ago, because it was—Justice [Sandra Day] O'Connor wrote for the Court, and she relied primarily on an article that was written by Professor Laycock. So I've always appreciated that unanimous opinions are rare and getting rarer every day, especially in the Religion Clause cases.

Let me give you five reasons why the Pledge of Allegiance is constitutional and should be affirmed by the Court as not violating the Establishment Clause [of the First Amendment].

1. The Pledge of Allegiance is not in a form of prayer.
2. The Pledge of Allegiance does not refer to Christianity or any other particular religion.
3. The religious portion of the Pledge of Allegiance is only two words.
4. The Pledge of Allegiance was recited unchanged for 50 years before the Court considered the question.
5. And no one can be required to recite the Pledge of Allegiance.

That's the closing portion of the [amicus curiae] brief Professor Laycock filed [in *Elk Grove School District v. Newdow*], where he argued that if the Court was going to rule in favor the Pledge of Allegiance, here's five ways to do it. And it may well be what the Supreme Court does, because it does give a very specific approach, and I think a fairly persuasive one.

Doug [Laycock] talked about the 40 or 50 years of history when the Supreme Court has dealt with the school prayer issue and not allowing for school prayer in that context. There's another history that's over 200 years now, and it goes something like this: "God save the United States and this Honorable Court"—that's how this Supreme Court oral argument's going to start when Dr. [Michael] Newdow presents his arguments before the Supreme Court [in *Elk Grove School District v. Newdow*] next Wednesday.

So the fact of the matter is that the Supreme Court itself has had this cry as part of its opening ceremony described as an invocation. Students attend oral arguments frequently, including kids in high school and even elementary school. And when those justices stand up or walk in, the students stand up. And while they don't have to repeat it, students also don't have to repeat the Pledge of Allegiance, and correctly so, since the Supreme Court's decision in [*West Virginia State Board of Education v. Barnette* (1943)], which is now dating back almost 60 years, said you can't be compelled to violate your conscience [by being required to recite the Pledge of Allegiance], and in that way, if you are objecting to the form of the Pledge of Allegiance.

I think that the words "God save the United States and this Honorable Court," like the words of the Pledge of Allegiance, echo what our founding fathers thought, and that was that our freedoms, rights and liberties are derived not from government but rather from God granting them to mankind. And in a sense, it's a very Lockean [English political philosopher John Locke, 1632–1704] concept. Thomas Jefferson talks about it. And even, of course, in the Declaration of Independence itself, how often have we learned or were required to learn and recite in school the words, the famous portion of the Declaration of Independence where it's written, "We hold these truths to be self-evident, that all men are created equal, endowed by their Creator with certain unalienable rights. Amongst them are life, liberty and the pursuit of happiness."

If the Pledge of Allegiance were to say something like that, I would suspect that there would be the same objection. Why? Because of its reliance on a Creator, and it is a concept where the Creator endows us with our rights. But in the context of the history of our country, that makes a lot of sense. Our country was founded on the concepts that the rights of man don't derive from a king and they can't be taken away from us by a king. The rights of mankind, the basic rights of mankind—liberty, freedom, the things that we cherish in this country—derive from a Creator. That's what our founding fathers mean.

It's often talked about, Thomas Jefferson's famous letter [in 1801] to the Danbury Baptist Connecticut Association, where he talked about what he called the "high and mighty duty in this wall of separation between church and state." There's something else that Jefferson wrote several years before he wrote that famous letter to the Danbury Baptists, and that was during the debates on the First Amendment and also in discussions with friends about the concept of liberty. He wrote, "Can the liberties of a nation be thought secure when we have removed their only firm basis, a conviction in the minds of the people that the liberties are a gift of God and that they are not violated but with His wrath?"

Now, Thomas Jefferson, in the classic understanding of his religious belief, would not fall within what most people would consider an orthodox Christian position. In my view of history anyway, I would not consider him to be—and I'm not speaking as a theologian—he had various views on religion and faith. I don't think faith was insignificant in his life, I don't mean to suggest that at all, but it wouldn't be what we would typically talk about today as a Protestant form of Christianity or Catholic form of Christianity. He kind of had his view of faith, Christianity, and the deity of Jesus, and that's a whole different topic.

But he recognized something very fundamental in that our rights don't come from a king; they are endowed to us. So if the requirement of the school district in *Elk Grove* was that we begin each school day by reminding ourselves, as students, that we should remember the history of this great nation, that we are endowed by our Creator with these rights, they're inalienable, and that the Creator bestowed them upon us—life, liberty and the pursuit of happiness—I submit that many people, Dr. Newdow included, would object, saying again it's this compelled reliance.

Now, nobody can be compelled, nor should they be, as I said, to recite the Pledge. Let's talk about the more recent history, and that is, what happened in 1954? Now, of course, the issue upon which certiorari is granted—and I am frequently reminded of that both when I'm watching arguments and when I argue them myself—is not the congressional action here, which is interesting. The United States asked for review of the 1954 congressional act amending the Pledge of Allegiance. The Supreme Court denied review there. They granted the school district's policy for review, which is a policy that said the school day will start with a patriotic expression. The Pledge of Allegiance would meet that patriotic expression.

In 1954, though, when the Pledge was modified to include the phrase "under God," what was motivating Congress? There were a lot of things motivating Congress. We were in the midst of the Cold War. There was this desire to treat and to establish the difference between how we viewed our rights and liberties, and how communism viewed these things, which is any rights that you have, whatever they might be, are derived from the state; the state is supreme. Congress, reflecting, again, on what the founding fathers thought, said, No, it doesn't work that way. We believe the foundation of our country is different, and this shows the difference. We believe that our rights come from God to mankind.

And I don't know if this is a true fact or not, but it's in one of the briefs, that Dr. Newdow is actually an ordained minister with the Universal Life Church, and I'm not sure if that's correct. What the Universal Life Church has as one of their—and I know they have a pretty broad view of what constitutes God—mission statements, it says that—and they use the phrase "gods" in terms of recognizing that individuals, us, are given what he calls "God-given rights"—freedoms, liberties. Again, this is part of the American experience.

Now, no one's required to believe that, and I don't think that that's the intent of saying the Pledge. Students who don't want to participate don't have to participate, and I think acknowledging the historical significance of how our rights are derived in the foundation of America is correct. The idea that you would be able to tell a student, You cannot be compelled to memorize the Declaration of Independence—which many of us remember having to do—and recite it because of its reference to a Creator, I would think would be wrong. Now, could you argue that there should be a religious exemption? Probably you could argue that under the Free Exercise Clause. These days, though, I don't know if any of us would be too persuasive on how that would go. But I will tell you this much: that is the historical fact. Our founding fathers did recognize—This was part of the Lockean concept of the rights of mankind, and you don't have to be a historian to check this out....

But I don't think it's correct contextually, with due respect, and that is "one nation"—the Pledge of Allegiance, "I pledge allegiance..." one nation under God," and of course ellipses in between. But that's not what the Pledge of Allegiance says. It doesn't say "one nation under God," and context matters in Establishment Clause cases. And I think the context of the Pledge and the history of how this country came into existence is going to point to what I would expect to be a Supreme Court decision affirming the constitutionality of the Pledge.

Let me close with this, and then I know there's going to be some questions. I think it would be revisionist history if we're going to start saying that students cannot say the Pledge of Allegiance, and revisionist in this context: the history, granted, of the Pledge itself is only 50 years old—it's not that old. But I'll tell you something: the religious heritage of the country goes back to its founding, and whether you take the very strict view of church-state separation or a more accommodationist view, or somewhere in between, denying the history is denying the fact. And I think that mandating a change in the Pledge or finding that those statements, those two words, as Professor Laycock pointed out so well in his brief, those two words create a constitutional crisis, I would hope the Court does not go there.

Question: [Please comment on the] notion...of ceremonial deism...the idea that "references to God become meaningless if recited often enough in public places."

Mr. Sekulow: I'll go quickly, because I addressed the issue and covered it, but I'll give you two quick thoughts.

I don't for those who are anti-religious—and I know there are people who are anti-religious—I mean, the fact of the matter is you could be anti-something or pro-something;

it's a free country, and neither the anti-religious nor the majority religion have a veto right over everybody else. And I think that's one thing.

Number two, a lot of people on my side of these issues normally, Doug [Laycock], get nervous about the phrase ceremonial deism. I've never had a problem with it. I think what Justice O'Connor said is right. It's one of these phrases that does tend to solemnize an occasion. It expresses hope for the future and reflects our past, but again, you're not compelling anybody to say this. You're not compelling anybody to believe this, but I suspect there'll be a lot of questions—I mean, I'm guessing again—on the issue of ceremonial deism. I've had that happen on a couple of the cases that I argued on those issues where prayer came up, and even in some of the earlier cases, in the early '90s. That's an issue that's going to come up. The ceremonial deism question is going to, I think, play in this probably significantly.

Question: Just to follow up,…comment on whether there is a path that we go down that essentially declares that the public realm—whatever is supported by government—must necessarily be godless, or is there an alternative to this? Does this case take you there or does it not necessarily take you there?

Mr. Sekulow: I think this case says you don't have to be godless. You can accurately reflect the historical precedent of the country's founding. That's how I would pitch this case. If I were arguing this case to the Court, I would be talking about the historic fact of patriotic expression. Sure, it's got religious overtones, but so does the "Star Spangled Banner" and a host of other religious music and songs and documents of our country. It's part of who we are.

So, yes, I think it can reflect—If you don't want to be in a situation where the next thing—and maybe some do—that we're fighting over is whether you really can have those students memorize the Declaration of Independence and be required to recite it as my teacher required me to recite it flawlessly, and if you didn't do it flawlessly you did it again, and it could go on, for many of us, for weeks.

Question: "I was wondering what implications this case would have for currency in the message "In God We Trust" on the U.S. dollar notes and coins?

Mr. Sekulow: I do think the lawsuit will follow, though. If the Pledge of Allegiance is declared unconstitutional—There have already been a series of cases on the national motto. Most recently, I handled one in Kansas. The district court ruled in our favor, and there was no appeal taken in that case. But I would expect that whether it applies or not, you will see those kind of lawsuits being filed if they declare the Pledge unconstitutional.

Whether they'll succeed or not, that's going to depend on how this opinion's written and what the Court says. But to say that it's not going to have far reaching consequences if the Pledge is struck down as unconstitutional—even if it is a four-four decision, which, as Professor Laycock said, is just an affirmance of the judgment—I will tell you that there will be school districts all over the United States that are going to say, Well, look, we're going to not read the tea leaves here. We don't want to get sued and lose again, so we're just going to stop saying the Pledge. I think that will be a ripple effect of this, too.

Question: Mr. Laycock argues "that the Pledge requires an affirmation of personal faith and consequently has got to go." Mr. Sekulow argues, "no, it doesn't—it's not an affirmation of personal faith, so it's okay." One point of view that's not represented here…is that yes, it requires an affirmation of personal faith and that's fine. And the Court should say that's fine. Is that a possible outcome? Can you play around with that a little bit?

Mr. Sekulow: I can't imagine the Court saying that—if they hold the Pledge constitutional, I think—actually, if they hold the Pledge constitutional, I think, it's going to be for the five reasons that Professor Laycock laid out in his brief. I think that is a pretty straightforward way for the Court to go if they decide it's constitutional. I can't imagine them saying the Pledge is constitutional, and you must believe it when you say it.

Question: Much has been made of the fact that there are only two words here, but one of those words is a preposition, which, to at least some ears, implies a particular type of God, one that we are under, one that is transcendent. And I wonder if consideration of that aspect would move this particular phrase beyond ceremonial deism? I guess my concern is that if you reject the historical document argument, it does seem to imply that we're asking people to affirm a particular type of God, which in 2004, many, many people do not affirm.

Mr. Sekulow: But it's an historical fact that the phrase under God—Most people think it originated in the Gettysburg Address, when President Lincoln said "This nation under God shall have a new birth of freedom." But actually it predates that by almost a hundred years, because General Washington—I think he was Colonel Washington then actually—in his order to the Continental Army said, "Millions of lives are in jeopardy, both born and unborn"—talking about posterity—"and this army under God"—now, does that mean that this army's under God? That's how they viewed the interplay of Divine Providence. That's what they meant by that.

And, again, the Pledge is an historic statement. You can't change the history; you can debate what the history means, but the words they used are—Fortunately for all of us, we have them, and that's what they meant and that's what they said....

Let's say you don't agree with the historical document, say the Declaration of Independence. Again, Mrs. Sopher requiring us to memorize it when I was in junior high. There's no dispute that that's what the document says. It says we're endowed by our Creator with these rights. It was a Lockean concept that rights derived not from the King of England, because then the king could take them away, but derived from God to mankind. That's what they thought, whether they were deists or whatever their views were theologically, that is what their overall and overarching propositions were, and that's their thought process. So you could say you don't agree with the historical documents or you don't assume they're historic, you could argue anything, but I think they're pretty clear.

Question: If our nation was not under Christianity at the birth of our Constitution, which I think scholars generally acknowledge Thomas Jefferson, whether he was a deist or a heretical Christian or a Unitarian, whatever he was, he was a religious man, obviously. But whether he was a Christian or not isn't relevant as far as the Constitution goes. But why did our Constitution refer to a Christian Sabbath, not a Jewish or a Muslim or an atheist Sabbath? And why was the document dated in the year of our Lord? Would anyone dare to say that that Lord is anyone other than Jesus Christ?

Mr. Sekulow: I've just completed a dissertation on a lot of the historical backgrounds, mostly focusing on the Supreme Court justices, not on the founding fathers. But what becomes very clear is that a lot of terminology was used by the founding fathers and by Supreme Court justices that we take in one context and, culturally, at the time, meant something very different. It's not to say that they were not people of faith, but there is no doubt about it, I mean, if you study history in America, it was a pretty broad—even within the founding fathers, a pretty broad swath of faith.

And statements like "In the year of our Lord" were the customary ways in which these documents were signed. It does not mean that they were anti-religious. Obviously they included them in there. The Declaration of Independence, I think, as a foundational document established how Americans viewed the relationship between rights, liberty, mankind and God, and I think they did it in one document and actually in one portion of that document.

A lot of the justices, for instance, had said this is a Christian nation, in 1892, 1864. We're Unitarians. Now, I'm not saying that they weren't Unitarians, weren't Christians, it's just that it wasn't what you would typically think of as Protestantism as we know it. So you've got to look at the cultural context to understand.

Now, having said all of that, to remove that history, I think, would be very dangerous. The fact that there was this general belief in the way rights derived to mankind, to remove that, I think, would be wrong....

THE CONTINUING DEBATE:
The Phrase "Under God" in the Pledge of Allegiance

What Is New

The Supreme Court in essence ducked when it ruled in *Elk Grove Unified School District v. Newdow*. Instead of deciding the question, the Court dismissed the case on the grounds that since Michael Newdow's ex-wife had custody of their daughter, he did not have "standing" (enough legal interest) to sue on the girl's behalf. That probably only put off the day when the Supreme Court will have to rule. New lawsuits have been filed, and U.S. district court judges in California and Florida have ruled the Pledge unconstitutional. However, in the latest legal ruling, the California-based Ninth Circuit of the U.S. Court of Appeals upheld the Pledge by a vote of 2 to 1, including describing its religious references as "ceremonial and patriotic [in] nature." The decision is available at Rutgers University's *Jurist* dated March 11, 2010, online using the drop-down menu at www.jurist.law.pitt.edu/gazette.

Where to Find More

One site of a group that believes in a wall between church and state is the "nontheist" Freedom From Religion Foundation at www.ffrf.org/. Taking the opposite view is the Rutheford Institute at www.rutherford.org/issues/religiousfreedom.asp/. A comprehensive view of the Supreme Court's role in the church-state issue is Kent Greenawalt's two-volume set, *Religion and the Constitution*; Volume 1: *Free Exercise and Fairness* and Volume 2: *Establishment and Fairness* (Princeton University Press, 2006, 2008). The history of and controversies about the Pledge itself can be found in Richard J. Ellis, *To the Flag: The Unlikely History of the Pledge of Allegiance* (University of Kansas Press, 2005).

What to More to Do

The Supreme Court has sometimes drawn a line between what religious expressions are not permissible and which merely reflect tradition and are permissible. To ponder this distinction, draw up a list of a few expressions of religion ranging from "In God We Trust" on U.S. currency to forced prayers in school and indicate which (if any) are permissible and which are not. Explain the distinction, and also discuss the "OK" and "Not OK" lists of others in your class. Once your views are clear, try jotting down some notes for a hypothetical essay, "How High Should the Wall Between Church and State Be?"

4   CIVIL RIGHTS

CALIFORNIA'S PROPOSITION 8 BARRING GAY MARRIAGES:
Equal Rights Violation of the U.S. Constitution *or* Valid State Law?

EQUAL RIGHTS VIOLATION OF THE U.S. CONSTITUTION

ADVOCATE: Attorneys representing plaintiffs Kristen M. Perry, et al. and the City of San Francisco seeking to have California's constitutional clause barring gay marriage declared a violation of the U.S. Constitution

SOURCE: *Kristin M. Perry, et al., Plaintiffs, and the City and County of San Francisco, Plaintiff-Intervenor, v. Arnold Schwarzenegger, et al., Defendants, and Proposition 8 Official Proponents Dennis Hollingsworth, et al., Defendant-Intervenors*; Case 3:09-cv-02292-VRW; U.S. District Court for the Northern District of California; Responses to Court's Questions for Closing Arguments, June 15, 2010

VALID STATE LAW

ADVOCATE: Attorneys representing Proposition 8 official proponents Dennis Hollingsworth, et al., seeking to have California's constitutional clause barring gay marriage upheld

SOURCE: *Kristin M. Perry, et al., Plaintiffs, and the City and County of San Francisco, Plaintiff-Intervenor, v. Arnold Schwarzenegger, et al., Defendants, and Proposition 8 Official Proponents Dennis Hollingsworth, et al., Defendant-Intervenors*; Case 3:09-cv-02292-VRW; U.S. District Court for the Northern District of California; Responses to Court's Questions for Closing Arguments, June 15, 2010

The origins of the gay rights issue in the United States began in 1610 when colonial Virginia made sexual contact between same-sex individuals a criminal offense. Thereafter, federal and state policy mostly worked against gays throughout most of U.S. history. This began to change in the 1960s as part of the general civil right movement. Led by Illinois, which decriminalized sexual acts between same-sex adults, laws relating to intimate homosexual relations began to change slowly. Ultimately, the Supreme Court in *Lawrence v. Texas* (2003) declared all such laws unconstitutional. Other laws and policy related to behavior traditionally associated with opposite-sex individuals also changed. In an early instance, a male student in Providence, Rhode Island, successfully sued his school in 1980 to force it to allow him to bring a male date to the senior prom. Social attitudes against homosexuals also moderated, and in 1967, Massachusetts elected the first country's openly gay state legislator. There are now several openly gay members of Congress.

Inevitably, the issue of whether to legalize gay marriages came to the fore. The first major event occurred in 1996 when a judge in Hawaii ruled that barriers to same-sex marriages violated the state constitution. Even though Hawaii soon amended its constitution to reinstitute the ban, an alarmed Congress passed, and President Bill Clinton signed, the Defense of Marriage Act (DOMA, 1996) barring U.S. recognition of same-sex marriages and allowing states not to recognize same-sex marriages licensed by other states. Then in 1999, Vermont's Supreme Court ruled that the state constitution entitled same-sex couples to the same benefits and protections as married heterosexual couples. The following year, Vermont's legislature enacted a civil union bill granting legal status to gay couples. In response, many state legislatures and, in numerous other instances, their citizens through referendums passed laws and even state constitutional amendments barring gay marriages. But some courts and legislatures moved in the opposite direction by allowing civil union and even gay marriages.

The genesis of the events immediately leading to the readings in this debate began in May 2008 when the California Supreme Court ruled the state's ban on same-sex marriage violated the state's constitution. Six months later, California's voters negated that decision by passing a referendum, Proposition 8, with a 52% majority that amended California's constitution to bar same-sex marriage. Gay-rights supporters filed suit challenging the validity of Proposition 8 court on technical grounds, but in May 2009 the state's supreme rejected the appeal.

That set the stage for a female couple and a male couple to file *Perry, et al. v. Schwarzenegger* to be filed in the U.S. District Court in San Francisco. The suit argues that Proposition 8 violates the equal protection clause of the Fourteenth Amendment and other parts of the U.S. Constitution. To avoid one bit of possible confusion, note that Arnold Schwarzenegger is technically the defendant as the state's governor, but he opposed Proposition 8 and refused to defend it in court. As a result, anti–gay marriage groups intervened and defending the law in lieu of the governor.

The trial phase of the case began in January 2009 and included not just legal arguments about the Constitution but also testimony about such issues as whether sexual orientation is innate or a matter of choice and the impact of such matters as gay child rearing and other family-related activities. At the end of the trial, Judge Vaughn R. Walker posed a series of questions to the plaintiffs, those seeking to overturn Proposition 8, and to the defendants, proponents of upholding it. The two readings that follow are respectively the replies of the plaintiffs and the defendants [defendant-intervenors] to those questions.

POINTS TO PONDER

➤ The only time clergy can perform a legal act is by marrying people. This arguably conflicts with the First Amendment. Some people advocate having marriages a purely a religious or personal pledge with no legal consequences and having all couples who want a legal connection to do so through a civil union.

➤ Part of the argument is whether the courts should give sexual-orientation, as a classification of people, the same special protections against discrimination given to groups based on race, religion, age, and some other demographic traits. What in principle should determine whether any group is afforded such special protections?

➤ In a democracy, should the courts care that Proposition 8 was passed by California's voters rather than by its legislature?

California's Proposition 8 Barring Gay Marriages: Equal Rights Violation of the U.S. Constitution

ATTORNEYS REPRESENTING PLAINTIFFS KRISTEN M. PERRY, ET AL.

RESPONSES TO QUESTIONS DIRECTED TO PLAINTIFFS

QUESTION: Assume the evidence shows Proposition 8 is not in fact rationally related to a legitimate state interest. Assume further the evidence shows voters genuinely but without evidence believed Proposition 8 was rationally related to a legitimate interest. Do the voters' honest beliefs in the absence of supporting evidence have any bearing on the constitutionality of Proposition 8?

ANSWER: To survive rational basis review, a classification must "bear a rational relationship to an independent and legitimate legislative end." A "law will be sustained" under the rational basis standard *only* "if it can be said to *advance* a legitimate government interest" (emphasis added). [Quotations herein are, unless otherwise attributed, taken from court decisions, usually those of the Supreme Court. Because of space limitations, the citations could not be included, but are available in the original document.] Accordingly, if this Court finds that "the evidence shows Proposition 8 is not in fact rationally related to a legitimate state interest"—as Plaintiffs proved at trial—then Prop. 8 could not survive even rational basis review (let alone, the more stringent requirements of intermediate and strict scrutiny). The voters' allegedly "genuine"—but erroneous—views to the contrary would be insufficient to sustain Prop. 8 because the genuinely held beliefs of voters who enact an arbitrary, irrational, and discriminatory law cannot shield the measure from constitutional scrutiny. Voters' unfounded and discriminatory stereotypes are not a substitute for *proof* that a law actually furthers a legitimate state interest. Indeed, those who disfavor a particular group often genuinely believe and accept negative stereotypes about the disfavored group, even where such stereotypes are wholly unsubstantiated. The constitutionally relevant question for rational basis purposes is whether Prop. 8 in fact "advance[s] a legitimate government interest"—not whether the voters *believed* that it did. In that case, the court found that there was an "absence of" proof that New York's prohibition on marriage by individuals of the same sex failed to further a legitimate state interest. Here, in contrast, Plaintiffs conclusively proved at trial that Prop. 8 does not advance any legitimate state interest, and that it is therefore irrational and unconstitutional under any standard of scrutiny.

QUESTION: What evidence supports a finding that maintaining marriage as an opposite-sex relationship does not afford a rational basis for Proposition 8?

ANSWER: Merely "maintaining marriage as an opposite-sex relationship" is not by itself a rational basis for Prop. 8. As an initial matter, neither tradition nor moral disapproval is a sufficient basis for a State to impair a person's constitutionally protected right to marry. Moreover, the evidence demonstrates that maintaining marriage as an opposite-sex relationship to the exclusion of loving and committed gay and lesbian couples does not promote any legitimate government interest. To the contrary, doing so causes irreparable harm to gay men and lesbians and their families, and is fundamentally stigmatizing and discriminatory.

QUESTION: Until very recently, same-sex relationships did not enjoy legal protection anywhere in the United States. How does this fact square with plaintiffs' claim that marriage between persons of the same sex enjoys the status of a fundamental right entitled to constitutional protection?

ANSWER: The Supreme Court "has long recognized that freedom of personal choice in matters of marriage and family life is one of the liberties protected by the Due Process Clause of the Fourteenth Amendment." Plaintiffs are seeking invalidation of the discriminatory restrictions that Prop. 8 imposes on the existing constitutional right to marry—which is "fundamental[ly] importan[t] for all individuals." Those existing "constitutional protection[s]" for "personal decisions relating to marriage" extend to individuals in a loving, committed relationship with a person of the opposite sex or the same sex because, no matter the sex of the individuals involved in the relationship, marriage is an "expression of emotional support and public commitment" essential to personal fulfillment. Thus, just as the plaintiffs in *Loving v. Virginia*, (1967), were not asking the Supreme Court to recognize a new right to interracial marriage, Plaintiffs here are not asking this Court to recognize a new fundamental right to same-sex marriage. They are instead seeking access to an existing constitutional right that has long been denied to gay men and lesbians. The mere longevity of those discriminatory and irrational restrictions on the right to marry is a constitutionally inadequate ground for continuing to exclude gay men and lesbians from this "vital personal right." [In *Loving v. Virginia*, the Supreme Court struck down a Virginia law that barred marriages between people of different races.]

QUESTION: What is the import of evidence showing that marriage has historically been limited to a man and a woman? What evidence shows that that limitation no longer enjoys constitutional recognition?

ANSWER: Evidence that marriage historically has been limited to a man and a woman does not insulate Prop. 8 from constitutional attack. The historical exclusion of gay men and lesbians from marriage is consistent with the uncontroverted [unchallenged] evidence in this case that gay men and lesbians have suffered a history of discrimination and unequal treatment in virtually all aspects of their lives. Moreover, although there have historically been discriminatory restrictions imposed on marriage, eliminating those restrictions has not deprived marriage of its vitality and importance, but has, in fact, strengthened marriage as a social institution. For example, slaves historically were not allowed to marry but gained that right after emancipation. Similarly, although bans on interracial marriage had their origins in the colonial period, were eventually enacted by 41 States, and remained on the books in more than a dozen States as late as 1967, such restrictions are unthinkable—and flatly unconstitutional—today. Although longstanding, none of these discriminatory restrictions on marriage ever "enjoy[ed] constitutional recognition"—and nor do discriminatory measures that restrict marriage to individuals of the opposite sex.

QUESTION: What empirical data, if any, supports a finding that legal recognition of same-sex marriage reduces discrimination against gays and lesbians?

ANSWER: Uncontroverted evidence demonstrates that invalidating Prop. 8 would immediately and significantly reduce discrimination against gay men and lesbians by removing discriminatory restrictions that prohibit individuals of the same sex from marrying in California.

Affording gay men and lesbians the right to marry would also reduce discrimination by providing them with access to certain tangible benefits, such as health insurance, that flow directly from marriage. Moreover, empirical studies from jurisdictions where marriage between individuals of the same sex is permitted demonstrate the salutary benefits that flow from permitting gay men and lesbians to marry. Empirical evidence also demonstrates that marriage correlates with a variety of measurable health benefits that extend to the married individuals and their children. Indeed, empirical studies have established that gay men and lesbians living in States that do not provide them with antidiscrimination protections are at a significantly higher risk of suffering from psychiatric disorders.

Finally, substantial evidence demonstrates that gay and lesbian couples are stigmatized because they cannot marry. Prop. 8 necessarily relegates the relationships of gay and lesbian individuals to second-class status by communicating the official view that their committed relationships are less worthy of recognition than comparable heterosexual relationships. The resulting harm from that stigmatization is profound and far-reaching.

QUESTION: Even if enforcement of Proposition 8 were enjoined, plaintiffs' marriages would not be recognized under federal law. Can the court find Proposition 8 to be unconstitutional without also considering the constitutionality of the federal Defense of Marriage Act?

ANSWER: Yes. Plaintiffs have challenged only Prop. 8 in this litigation. The Court need not—and in the absence of a federal defendant, should not—address the federal Defense of Marriage Act in this litigation. It may be that the Court's ruling will have implications for the Defense of Marriage Act and other similar laws that discriminate against gay men and lesbians. But such implications, if any, will depend on the parameters of this Court's decision

QUESTION: What evidence supports a finding that the choice of a person of the same sex as a marriage partner partakes of traditionally revered liberties of intimate association and individual autonomy?

ANSWER: Testimony of multiple experts and of Plaintiffs themselves confirms that these liberties are precisely what is at stake in the choice of a same-sex marriage partner. Describing why she is a plaintiff in this case, Sandy Stier explained that "I would like to get married, and I would like to marry the person that I choose and that is Kris Perry." Ms. Stier went on to explain that she feels it is important for the next generation "to at least feel like the option to be true to yourself is an option that they can have, too." Similarly, an American Psychoanalytic Association Position Statement on marriage by same-sex couples has explained that "the milestone of marriage moves a couple and its children into full citizenship in American society."

Of course, the importance that attaches to the "choice" of a person of the same sex as a marriage partner does not mean that gay men and lesbians choose their sexual orientation or could choose to marry a person of the opposite sex. Gay men and lesbians, like all other citizens, have the right to choose the individual with whom they wish to spend their life in marriage. The evidence in this case clearly demonstrates, however, that the vast majority of individuals experience little or no choice in their sexual orientation, and that marrying someone of the opposite sex is not a realistic, viable option for gay men and lesbians.

RESPONSES TO QUESTIONS DIRECTED TO PROPONENTS

QUESTION: Assuming a higher level of scrutiny applies to either plaintiffs' due process or equal protection claim, what evidence in the record shows that Proposition 8 is substantially related to an important government interest? Narrowly tailored to a compelling government interest?

ANSWER: There is no evidence in the record to suggest that Prop. 8 is even rationally related to a legitimate government interest—let alone, substantially related to an important government interest or narrowly tailored to further a compelling government interest. To the contrary, Prop. 8 causes irreparable harm to gay men and lesbians and their families, and is fundamentally discriminatory. Indeed, Proponents cannot conceivably satisfy the requirements of either intermediate or strict scrutiny because they rely exclusively on hoc rationalizations and do not defend any of the arguments advanced in support of Prop. 8 during the campaign itself—such as the purported risk that, in the absence of Prop. 8, children would be taught in school about marriage between individuals of the same sex. The Supreme Court has made clear, however, that, to survive heightened scrutiny, the "justification[s]" offered to defend a discriminatory measure "must be genuine, not hypothesized or invented post hoc in response to litigation."

QUESTION: What evidence in the record supports a finding that same-sex marriage has or could have negative social consequences?

ANSWER: There [is no] evidence in the record that could support a finding that marriage by individuals of the same sex would in fact have negative implications. While Proponents subjected each of the credible and well-qualified experts called by Plaintiffs to lengthy cross-examination, none offered any testimony that would lend support to the premise that allowing gay men and lesbians to marry has or could have negative consequences.

QUESTION: If the motion is granted, is there any evidence to support a finding that Proposition 8 advances a legitimate governmental interest?

ANSWER: There is no evidence in the record to support a finding that Prop. 8 advances legitimate government interests. As Plaintiffs have explained in detail, the record in this case clearly demonstrates that Prop. 8 in fact serves no legitimate government interest.

QUESTION: Why should the court assume that the deinstitutionalization of marriage is a negative consequence?

ANSWER: To the extent that "deinstitutionalization" includes the removal of unfounded and discriminatory restrictions on one or both of the participants in a marriage, this Court should not assume that outcome to be a negative one, and the evidence proves otherwise. For example, as explained by Dr. Nancy Cott, the removal of historically accepted restrictions on the freedom and individuality of women in a marriage, and the lifting of restrictions that have existed over time concerning marriage across different races, are positive developments that have fulfilled the meaning of marriage and helped it to remain a vibrant and important social institution. But even to the extent one assumes that the "deinstitutionalization" of marriage is a harmful or negative thing, the record is devoid of credible, reliable evidence sufficient to show that affording gay men and lesbians the right to marry would lead to such deinstitutionalization. To the contrary, the evidence shows that removing a remaining, unfounded and discriminatory restriction from the meaning of marriage would strengthen, rather than weaken, the institution.

QUESTION: What evidence in the record shows that same-sex marriage is a drastic or far-reaching change to the institution of marriage?

ANSWER: Simply put, there is no evidence that permitting same-sex couples to marry would effect a drastic or far-reaching change to the institution of marriage. First, as Professor Cott testified, civil marriage has never been a static institution. Historically, it has changed, sometimes dramatically, to reflect the evolving needs, values, and understanding of society. Indeed, the institution of marriage has changed repeatedly over its history, from the elimination of the doctrine of coverture [the possession of all of a wife's rights by her husband], to permitting interracial couples to marry, to permitting "no fault" divorces. The institution has easily weathered those changes, and is still seen as a significant institution resonating with social meaning. And allowing same-sex couples to marry is no more drastic than any of those changes.

QUESTION: What evidence in the record shows that same-sex couples are differently situated from opposite-sex couples where at least one partner is infertile?

ANSWER: No evidence in the record shows that same-sex couples are differently situated from opposite-sex couples where at least one partner is infertile. In fact, Plaintiffs presented testimony from Dr. Anne Peplau establishing, based on years of research, that same-sex couples and opposite-sex couples are fundamentally the same in terms of their relationships, what they are looking for in a relationship, and what makes the relationship successful or unsuccessful.

QUESTION: Assume the evidence shows that children do best when raised by their married, biological mother and father. Assume further the court concludes it is in the state's interest to encourage children to be raised by their married biological mother and father where possible. What evidence if any shows that Proposition 8 furthers this state interest?

ANSWER: There is no evidence that Prop. 8 furthers any state interest that may exist in encouraging children to be raised by their married, biological mother and father. Prop. 8 does not change California's laws and policies that permit gay and lesbian individuals to have, adopt, or raise children. Nor does prohibiting marriage by individuals of the same sex have any effect on whether biological parents will choose to raise their biological children or whether biological parents will choose to marry or remain married to raise those children. To the contrary, to the extent the State has an interest in what is "best" for children, the evidence shows that Prop. 8 affirmatively harms the interests of children and does not promote the achievement of good child-adjustment outcomes. By denying same-sex couples with children the right to marry, Prop. 8 deprives the children of those couples the legitimacy that marriage confers on children and the sense of security, stability, and increased well-being that accompany that legitimacy. Indeed, the evidence shows that Prop. 8 stigmatizes the children of same-sex couples by relegating their parents to the separate and unequal institution of domestic partnership. Moreover, because certain tangible and intangible benefits flow to a married couple's children by virtue of the State's (and society's) recognition of that bond, Prop. 8 denies children of same-sex couples access to those benefits.

QUESTION: Why is legislating based on moral disapproval of homosexuality not tantamount to discrimination? What evidence in the record shows that a belief based in morality cannot also be discriminatory? If that moral point of view is not held and is disputed by a small but significant minority of the community, should not an effort to enact that moral point of view into a state constitution be deemed a violation of equal protection?

ANSWER: Legislative action based on moral disapproval of gay men and lesbians as a group is discrimination, and mere moral disapproval is not a legitimate government interest. Accordingly, whether that "moral point of view" is held unanimously—or whether it is disputed by a significant minority of the population—it is not a sufficient basis for sustaining legislation.

QUESTION: What harm do proponents face if an injunction against the enforcement of Proposition 8 is issued?

ANSWER: Excluding individuals of the same sex from the institution of marriage harms Plaintiffs, their children, and hundreds of thousands of other gay men and lesbians (and their families) throughout California. Allowing gay men and lesbians to marry harms no one. Indeed, Proponents' counsel admitted that Proponents "don't know" what effect, if any, marriage by individuals of the same sex would have on opposite-sex marriage. Tellingly, Proponents presented no evidence whatsoever that the 18,000 same-sex marriages that took place between the California Supreme Court's decision in the Marriage Cases and the passage of Prop. 8 have harmed Proponents or anyone else.

RESPONSES TO QUESTIONS DIRECTED TO PLAINTIFFS AND PROPONENTS

QUESTION: What does the evidence show the difference to be between gays and lesbians, on the one hand, and heterosexuals on the other? Is that difference one which the government "may legitimately take into account" when making legislative classifications?

ANSWER: The evidence demonstrates that gay and lesbian individuals and heterosexuals are similarly situated with respect to marriage. The only difference is that gay and lesbian individuals desire to marry a person of the same sex and heterosexual individuals desire to marry a person of the opposite sex. But this difference is not one that the government "may legitimately take into account" when making legislative classifications because it "bears no relation to ability to perform or contribute to society."

Moreover, any difference with respect to procreation is not a basis for barring gay men and lesbians from marrying because marriage has never been limited to procreative unions. And, to the extent that Proponents claim that gay and lesbian couples are less stable and monogamous in their relationships than heterosexual couples, there is no empirical support for this negative stereotype.

QUESTION: What does the evidence show the definition (or definitions) of marriage to be?

ANSWER: Marriage is fundamentally an intimate commitment between two people who choose to build a life and home together—with or without children. This definition of marriage recognizes that, for many, marriage may include childrearing or the legitimization of children, but at its core, procreation is not required for a relationship to constitute a "marriage" as understood through the history of our Nation.

QUESTION: What does it mean to have a "choice" in one's sexual orientation?

ANSWER: Having a "choice" necessarily entails being able to voluntarily decide between two (or more) viable options. Having "choice" in one's sexual orientation would amount to choosing the sex of the person to whom one is attracted. Not surprisingly, no party argued or put on any evidence that heterosexuals feel as though they have a "choice" regarding the sex to which they are attracted. And the overwhelming evidence demonstrates that the same is true for gay men and lesbians.

Notably, despite Proponents' repeated attempts to conflate the two concepts, "choice" is not the same thing as "change." Some percentage of individuals may experience a change in their sexual orientation at some point during their lifetime, but that does not mean that the individual could at any point voluntarily choose to change his or her sexual orientation. There are many reasons why a change may occur—for example, a man may be married to a woman before he realizes that he is gay. But, by definition, "choice" requires a voluntary decision, and there is no testimony or evidence to support the notion that one consciously decides on his or her sexual orientation. As the "Report of the American Psychological Association Task Force on Appropriate Therapeutic Responses to Sexual Orientation" explained:

> [E]nduring change to an individual's sexual orientation is uncommon…[T]he results of scientifically valid research indicate that it is unlikely that individuals will be able to [voluntarily] reduce same-sex attractions or increase other-sex sexual attractions.

QUESTION: If spouses are obligated to one another for mutual support and support of dependents, and if legal spousal obligations have no basis in the gender of the spouse, what purpose does a law requiring that a marital partnership consist of one man and one woman serve?

ANSWER: Plaintiffs agree that spouses are obligated to one another for mutual support and the support of dependants. Plaintiffs further agree that the sex of the spouse is irrelevant to legal spousal obligations. Indeed, changes in society have led spousal roles to become more gender-neutral over time, and changes in the law have ended gender-determined roles for spouses. Accordingly, there is no purpose in limiting marriage to opposite-sex couples. Individuals in marriages of two men or two women are equally capable—and equally obligated—to provide mutual support and support for their dependents as individuals in opposite-sex marriages.

QUESTION: The California Family Code requires that registered domestic partners be treated as spouses. Businesses that extend benefits to married spouses in California must extend equal benefits to registered domestic partners. If, under California law, registered domestic partners are to be treated just like married spouses, what purpose is served by differentiating—in name only—between same-sex and opposite-sex unions?

ANSWER: The fact that California grants gay and lesbian individuals virtually all the tangible rights associated with marriage but denies them the label of "marriage" serves no purpose but to stigmatize and discriminate against gay and lesbian individuals.

The word "marriage" has a unique meaning, and there is a significant symbolic disparity between domestic partnership and marriage. The unique cultural value and social meaning of "marriage" cannot compare to the legal benefits of domestic partnerships. Domestic partnerships—even if they confer virtually all the material benefits of marriage—stigmatize gay and lesbian individuals and relegate them to the status of second-class citizens.

Prop. 8 reflects and propagates the stigma that gay and lesbian individuals do not have intimate relations similar to those of heterosexual couples and conveys the State's judgment that same-sex couples are inherently less deserving of society's full recognition through the status of civil marriage than heterosexual couples. This distinction is stigmatizing—and thus unconstitutional.

QUESTION: What evidence, if any, shows whether infertility has ever been a legal basis for annulment or divorce?

ANSWER: The ability or willingness of married couples to produce children has never been a prerequisite to the validity of a marriage under American law. There is no evidence in the record that an opposite-sex couple not capable of procreating together has ever been barred from marrying simply because their union would not be naturally procreative. Accordingly, Proponents' assertion that "the institution of marriage is, and always has been, uniquely concerned with promoting and regulating naturally procreative relationships between men and women" is factually incorrect and has no support in the trial record.

QUESTION: What are the constitutional consequences if the evidence shows that sexual orientation is immutable for men but not for women? Must gay men and lesbians be treated identically under the Equal Protection Clause?

ANSWER: As a threshold matter, the evidence conclusively demonstrates that sexual orientation is not a choice—it is not consciously changeable for the vast majority of men or women, whether they are heterosexual, gay, or lesbian. Moreover, even if sexual orientation were changeable, gay men, lesbians, and heterosexuals should all be treated equally under the Equal Protection Clause. Because sexual orientation is properly considered a suspect or quasi-suspect classification, discrimination based on sexual orientation is inherently suspect whether it targets a gay man, a lesbian, or a heterosexual.

QUESTION: If the court finds Proposition 8 to be unconstitutional, what remedy would "yield to the constitutional expression of the people of California's will [as expressed in the Prop. 8 referendum]"?

ANSWER: No remedy short of an order permanently enjoining Prop. 8's enforcement in its entirety would be sufficient. If a state constitutional provision is inconsistent with the Fourteenth Amendment of the U.S. Constitution, it can no longer be given effect—regardless of its level of public support.

California's Proposition 8 Barring Gay Marriages: Valid State Law

ATTORNEYS REPRESENTING PROPOSITION 8 OFFICIAL PROPONENTS DENNIS HOLLINGSWORTH, ET AL.

RESPONSES TO QUESTIONS DIRECTED TO PROPONENTS

QUESTION: Assuming a higher level of scrutiny applies to either plaintiffs' due process or equal protection claim, what evidence in the record shows that Proposition 8 is substantially related to an important government interest? Narrowly tailored to a compelling government interest?

ANSWER: Because Proposition 8 neither infringes a fundamental right nor discriminates on the basis of sex, and because gays and lesbians are not entitled to heightened protection under the Equal Protection Clause, Proposition 8 is subject only to rational basis review. Even if heightened scrutiny applied, however, Proposition 8 would readily satisfy such scrutiny.

California's interest in increasing the likelihood that children will be born to and raised by their biological mothers and fathers in stable and enduring family units is a government interest of the highest order. Not only is this core procreative purpose of marriage "fundamental to our very existence and survival," indeed, "It is hard to conceive an interest more legitimate and more paramount for the state than promoting an optimal social structure for educating, socializing, and preparing its future citizens to become productive participants in civil society." [Quotations herein are, unless otherwise attributed, taken from court decisions, usually those of the Supreme Court. Because of space limitations, the citations could not be included, but are available in the original document.] For all of these reasons, the Supreme Court has recognized that marriage is "the foundation of the family and of society, without which there would be neither civilization nor progress."

Thus, "it seems beyond dispute that the state has a compelling interest in encouraging and fostering procreation of the race and providing status and stability to the environment in which children are raised. This has always been one of society's paramount goals." For the same reasons, California has a compelling interest in proceeding with caution when considering changes to the vital institution of marriage that could well weaken that institution and the critically important interests it has traditionally served.

As explained more fully in our responses to [other] questions, Proposition 8 furthers these interests by preserving the traditional definition and form of marriage and by providing special encouragement and recognition to those relationships that uniquely further California's interests in increasing the likelihood that children will be born to and raised by their natural parents in stable and enduring family units.

Proposition 8 is substantially related to at least the two important interests identified above. It does not matter that California could have done more to further these interests, for example by refusing to accommodate either the vested interests of a limited number of same-sex couples who acted in reliance on the California Supreme Court's decision prior to the enactment of Proposition 8 or the interests of gay and lesbian families that are served by domestic partnerships that offer essentially the same rights and obligations of marriage. To the contrary, it is well settled that the Constitution "does not require that a regulatory regime single-mindedly pursue one objective to the exclusion of all others to survive…intermediate scrutiny." Simply put, the fact that California has "struck its own idiosyncratic balance between various important but competing state interests" does not render "its asserted interest" in responsible procreation and parenting "any less substantial than in the states" that have taken a different approach.

Nor does the fact that California permits opposite-sex couples who cannot, or do not intend to, have children to marry render Proposition 8 unconstitutionally over-inclusive. For one thing, allowing such couples to marry does further the State's interest in increasing the likelihood that children will be born to and raised by their natural parents in enduring family units because it reinforces social norms that seek to channel intimate heterosexual relationships into marriage.

The fact that California permits gays and lesbians—as well as single individuals and cohabiting heterosexual couples—to adopt does not in anyway undermine the States' interest in increasing the likelihood that children will be born and raised by their natural parents in stable, enduring family units. Rather, it simply reflects an attempt to provide for the practical reality that this ideal is not always possible. It is simply implausible that by recognizing and making provisions for the reality that an ideal will not be achieved in all cases, the State somehow abandons its interests in promoting and increasing the likelihood of that ideal. Likewise, the fact that California has opted to encourage, rather than require, that opposite-sex couples procreate only within marriage and stay together to raise their children, does not render Proposition 8 unconstitutional.

Allowing [heterosexual] couples to marry furthers the State's interest in other ways as well. Most obviously, couples who do not plan to have children may experience accidents or change their plans, and some couples who do not believe they can have children may discover otherwise. And even in cases of obvious infertility, it is usually the case that only one spouse is infertile. In such cases marriage furthers the State's interest in responsible procreation by decreasing the likelihood that the fertile spouse will engage in sexual activity with a third party, for the State's interest is served not only by increasing the likelihood that procreation occurs within stable family units, but also by decreasing the likelihood that it occurs outside of such units.

Moreover, attempting to determine on a case-by-case basis whether each heterosexual couple seeking to marry will have children would be intolerably burdensome, intrusive, and impractical. As another district court has recognized, because such an approach is simply not a "real alternative" for achieving the state's "compelling interest in encouraging and fostering procreation…and providing status and stability to the environment in which children are raised," allowing "legal marriage as between all couples of opposite sex" is "the least intrusive alternative available to protect the procreative relationship."

Thus, even if intermediate scrutiny applied, no principle of constitutional law bars California from foregoing an implausible and Orwellian attempt to police fertility and childbearing intentions and relying instead on the common-sense presumption that opposite-sex couples are, in general, capable of procreation. Indeed, applying intermediate scrutiny in a closely analogous context, the Supreme Court rejected as "ludicrous" an argument that a law criminalizing statutory rape for the purpose of preventing teenage pregnancies was "impermissibly overbroad because it makes unlawful sexual intercourse with prepubescent females, who are, by definition, incapable of becoming pregnant."

Finally, because there is a clear biological difference between opposite-sex couples who, at least as a general matter, are capable of natural procreation (both intentionally and unintentionally) and same-sex couples who are categorically incapable of natural procreation, California's separate treatment of these two types of couples is neither surprising nor troublesome from a constitutional perspective. Given that same-sex couples and opposite-sex couples are not similarly situated with respect to the state's interest in channeling potentially procreative relationships into stable and enduring family units, intermediate scrutiny does not require the State to prove that limiting marriage to opposite-sex couples is "necessary" to further this interest. In all events, there are very good reasons to believe that redefining marriage to include same-sex couples could weaken that institution and the interests it has always served. In light of these risks, the traditional opposite-sex definition of marriage as reflected in Proposition 8 is substantially related to the State's important interests in increasing the likelihood that children will be born to and raised by their biological mothers and fathers in stable and enduring family units and proceeding with caution when considering changes to the vital institution of marriage that could well weaken that institution and the critically important interests it has traditionally served. For essentially the same reasons, the traditional definition of marriage reflected in Proposition 8 is narrowly tailored to at least the compelling interests identified above.

QUESTION: What evidence in the record supports a finding that same-sex marriage has or could have negative social consequences? What does the evidence show the magnitude of these consequences to be?

ANSWER: There is substantial common ground among the parties relating to the fact that there will be significant consequences flowing from the adoption of same-sex marriage. Professor [Nancy] Cott has acknowledged that the adoption of same-sex marriage will change the public meaning of marriage, that a change in the social meaning of marriage will unquestionably have real world consequences, and that whatever these consequences are, they will be momentous. As Professor Cott told National Public Radio when Massachusetts legalized same-sex marriage: "One could point to earlier watersheds, but perhaps none quite so explicit as this particular turning point," and she added at trial that same-sex marriage is "arguably a highly distinctive turning point." There is ample evidence supporting Professor Cott's view that same-sex marriage would represent a watershed turning point in the history of this venerable institution. For example:

• According to Joseph Raz, professor at both Oxford University and Columbia Law School, "there can be no doubt that the recognition of gay marriages will affect as great a transformation in the nature of marriage as that from polygamous to monogamous or from arranged to unarranged marriage."

• Yale Law School professor and prominent gay rights advocate William Eskridge believes that "enlarging the concept [of marriage] to embrace same-sex couples would necessarily transform it into something new."

Professor Cott also admits that it is not possible to predict with precision the consequences that will flow from same-sex marriage. But there is a wealth of evidence in the record as to the likely negative consequences. Taken together, the evidence supporting these findings strongly suggests that redefining marriage to include same-sex unions will change the public meaning of marriage in ways that will weaken the social norms that seek to discourage procreative sexual relationships and childrearing outside of marital bonds. Redefining marriage in this way would also change its focus from the needs of children to the desires of the adult partners, suggesting that the latter are paramount, as well as weaken the social understanding that, all else being equal, what is best for a child is to be raised by its married, biological parents and to have a mother and father. All of these changes are likely to reduce the willingness of biological parents, especially fathers, to make the commitments and sacrifices necessary to marry, stay married, and play an active role in raising their children. The evidence suggests that as a result, there will be lower marriage rates, higher rates of divorce and cohabitation, more out of wedlock children, and fewer children raised by both of their biological parents.

First, extending marriage to same-sex couples would eliminate the state's ability to specially promote those relationships that uniquely further the vital societal purpose of channeling potentially and naturally procreative conduct into stable and enduring family units. This would have particularly negative consequences for the involvement of fathers in raising their children. The link marriage provides between sex and procreation helps to increase the likelihood that fathers will care for their children.

Second, and relatedly, extending marriage to same-sex couples would likely accelerate and perhaps even complete the "deinstitutionalization of marriage." We discuss deinstitutionalization in more detail in response to the fourth question posed to us, which specifically addresses the concept. In short, a range of social science scholars agree that there is a connection between same-sex marriage and the deinstitutionalization of marriage.

Third, leaving aside the obvious fact that it is far too soon to draw any firm empirical conclusions based on the scant experience with same-sex marriage in those few jurisdictions that have adopted it, the evidence shows that concerns about the potential harms from same-sex marriage have not been negated by experience in those few places where it has been adopted. For example, since becoming the first nation in the world to institute same-sex marriage in 2001, there have been a number of worrisome trends in the Netherlands, including:

- Fewer marriages. There was an average yearly decrease of .07 in the marriage rate from 2001 through 2008, following an average yearly increase of .02 from 1994 through 2000.

- More single-parent families. Single-parent families (as a percentage of all families) increased by an average of .08% annually from 2001 to 2008, after increasing by an average of only .032% annually from 1994 to 2000.

- More unmarried parents raising children. From 2001 to 2008, non-married cohabiting couples with children (as a percentage of all cohabiting couples) increased at a 30% greater average annual rate than it had from 1994 to 2000.

- More opposite-sex couples choosing an alternative status over marriage. In 2001, 2.05% of all opposite-sex couples entering marriage or a new registered partnership chose a partnership. By 2008, that figure climbed to 9.14%.

The evidence also shows that even some same-sex marriage advocates recognize the common-sense wisdom in taking a cautious approach to making such a significant change to the institution of marriage. Indeed, in 2008 leading same-sex marriage advocate Jonathan Rauch recommended that "the way to do this is let different states do different things. Let's find out how gay marriage works in a few states. Let's find out how civil unions work. In the meantime, let the other states hold back."

Refining marriage to include same-sex unions would have other consequences as well. For one thing, it would indisputably eliminate the State's ability to provide special encouragement and recognition to those relationships most likely to further core interests that marriage has traditionally served, namely increasing the likelihood that children will be born to and raised by their natural parents in stable and enduring family units. In addition, such a redefinition will likely infringe, or at least threaten, the First Amendment and other fundamental liberty interests of institutions, parents, and other individuals who support the traditional opposite-sex definition of marriage on religious or moral grounds.

QUESTION: If the motion is granted, is there any other evidence to support a finding that Proposition 8 advances a legitimate governmental interest?

ANSWER: There is a large volume of evidence demonstrating that Proposition 8 advances legitimate government interests. First, by restoring the traditional definition of marriage, Proposition 8 advances the government interests in marriage, especially increasing the likelihood that children will be born to and raised by both their natural parents in stable and enduring family units. Authorities from a wide range of disciplines recognize these as primary interests advanced by marriage.

Second, restoring the traditional definition of marriage also enables California to proceed with caution when considering changes to the fundamental and critical social institution of marriage. In particular, it allows California to observe the results of same-sex marriage in other jurisdictions that have adopted it. As leading same-sex marriage advocate Jonathan Rauch has said: "Let's find out how gay marriage works in a few states. Let's find out how civil unions work. In the meantime, let the other states hold back."

Third, the evidence also demonstrates that Proposition 8 advances a series of other legitimate interests including ensuring democratic control over important social policy, treating different things differently, both in language and in law, and accommodating the First Amendment and other fundamental liberty interests of institutions, parents, and other individuals who support the traditional opposite-sex definition of marriage on religious or moral grounds. In addition, Proposition 8 forestalls the harms that would flow from same-sex marriage.

QUESTION: Why should the court assume that the deinstitutionalization of marriage is a negative consequence?

ANSWER: The court need not assume that the deinstitutionalization of marriage is a negative consequence. The evidence shows that deinstitutionalization weakens marriage, and hence weakens its ability to fulfill its vital societal purposes. Andrew Cherlin, a sociologist at Johns Hopkins University, defines deinstitutionalization as "the weakening of the social norms that define people's behavior in a social institution such as marriage." This weakening of social norms with respect to marriage entails shifting the focus of marriage from serving vital societal needs to facilitating the personal fulfillment of individuals. In other words, people become less likely "to focus on the rewards to be found in fulfilling socially valued roles such as the good parent or the loyal and supportive spouse"; instead "personal choice and self-development loom large in people's construction of their marital careers."

A principal societal purpose of marriage is channeling naturally procreative relationships into stable, long-lasting unions. Deinstitutionalization weakens marriage's ability to perform this function, and thus would likely result in high levels of nonmarital childbearing, cohabitation, and divorce. These consequences directly and negatively impact children. As a leading survey of social science research explains: "Children in single-parent families, children born to unmarried mothers, and children in stepfamilies or cohabiting relationships face higher risks of poor outcomes than do children in intact families headed by two biological parents. Parental divorce is also linked to a range of poorer academic and behavioral outcomes among children. There is thus value for children in promoting stable, strong marriages between biological parents.

QUESTION: What evidence in the record shows that same-sex marriage is a drastic or far-reaching change to the institution of marriage?

ANSWER: The limitation of marriage to opposite-sex unions has been a fundamental, definitional feature of that institution throughout history at common law, in this Country and, almost without exception, in every civilized society that has ever existed. And, with only a handful of exceptions, the same is true today. Redefining marriage to include same-sex unions would constitute a drastic and far-reaching change to that institution.

QUESTION: What evidence in the record shows that same-sex couples are differently situated from opposite-sex couples where at least one partner is infertile?

ANSWER: Same-sex couples are differently situated from opposite-sex couples where at least one partner is infertile in at least three ways. First, determining infertility in opposite-sex couples is extremely burdensome and intrusive, and is not always 100 percent reliable. Second, the fertile partner in an opposite-sex couple is capable of procreative sexual activity with a third party, and allowing all opposite-sex couples to marry discourages the fertile partner of a sterile spouse from engaging in such potentially procreative activity with other individuals. Third, the marriage of opposite-sex couples reinforces social norms that discourage heterosexual intercourse—which generally is potentially procreative—outside the framework of marriage.

QUESTION: Assume the evidence shows that children do best when raised by their married, biological mother and father. Assume further the court concludes it is in the state's interest to encourage children to be raised by their married biological mother and father where possible. What evidence if any shows that Proposition 8 furthers this state interest?

ANSWER: The traditional institutional of marriage has always been understood to further society's interest in increasing the likelihood that children will be raised by their biological mother and father in a stable and enduring family unit. Because Proposition 8 simply restores the opposite-sex definition and form of marriage that has prevailed all but universally throughout history and that continues to prevail in all but a handful of jurisdictions today, the evidence that Proposition furthers society's interest in increasing the likelihood that children will be raised by their biological mother and father in a stable and enduring family unit is the same evidence that establishes that marriage furthers this interest.

The traditional opposite-sex definition of marriage reflected in Proposition 8 is closely aligned with this central concern of that institution. Because sexual relationships between members of the opposite sex can in most cases produce children, either intentionally or not, such relationships have the potential to further—or harm—this vital interest in a way, and to an extent, that other types of relationships do not. By providing special recognition and encouragement to committed opposite-sex relationships, Proposition 8 seeks to channel potentially procreative conduct into relationships where that conduct is likely to further, rather than harm, these interests. Further, by maintaining the traditional definition of marriage, Proposition 8 avoids those harms to the institution of marriage and the purposes it has traditionally served that would very likely flow from the "watershed" redefinition of that institution urged by Plaintiffs.

QUESTION: Why is legislating based on moral disapproval of homosexuality not tantamount to discrimination? What evidence in the record shows that a belief based in morality cannot also be discriminatory? If that moral point of view is not held and is disputed by a small but significant minority of the community, should not an effort to enact that moral point of view into a state constitution be deemed a violation of equal protection?

ANSWER: As an initial matter, Proposition 8 does not legislate based on moral disapproval of homosexuality. Proposition 8 furthers important government interests that have nothing to do with such disapproval. Indeed, it does not matter that voters may have supported Proposition 8 for a variety of reasons, including arguably illegitimate ones. This court must uphold Proposition 8 so long as furthering a legitimate interest is at least one of the purposes of the statute, and may not reject the asserted reasons for the enactment of Proposition 8 unless it determines they could not have been a goal of the legislation. As the Supreme Court has repeatedly explained, even when heightened scrutiny applies, "it is a familiar practice of constitutional law that this court will not strike down an otherwise constitutional statute on the basis of an alleged illicit legislative motive."

Further, religious support for the traditional definition of marriage has a doctrinal and historical basis in the sacred nature of matrimony, which is wholly distinct from religious teachings regarding homosexuality and cannot reasonably be equated with moral disapproval of homosexuality. Religious teachings regarding the sacred nature of marriage developed without regard to issues of sexual orientation, predating by millennia the movement for same-sex marriage. Indeed, it is only that very recent movement that has introduced discussion of sexual orientation into religious discourse regarding marriage.

Furthermore, even if Proposition 8 were based on moral disapproval of homosexual conduct, it would not be unconstitutional. While Proponents have not argued that a belief based in morality can never be discriminatory, it is plain that moral disapproval of homosexual conduct is not tantamount to animus, bigotry, or discrimination. On the contrary, religions that condemn homosexual conduct also teach love of gays and lesbians. To be sure, moral disapproval of homosexual conduct cannot be enforced "through operation of the criminal law," and thus cannot support a law seeking to criminalize "the most private human conduct, sexual behavior, and in the most private of places, the home." But it does not follow that moral considerations cannot influence the formation of public policy. On the contrary, it is well settled that a State need not promote or facilitate what it cannot prohibit. Thus, for example, although with few exceptions a State cannot prohibit abortions, the Supreme Court has "unequivocally" held "that a state has no constitutional obligation to fund or promote abortion" and "is not required to show a compelling interest for its policy choice to favor normal childbirth."

As the Supreme Court has explained, there is a basic difference between direct state interference with a protected activity and state encouragement of an alternative activity consonant with legislative policy. Constitutional concerns are greatest when the State attempts to impose its will by force of law; the State's power to encourage actions deemed to be in the public interest is necessarily far broader." Under these precedents, the fact that a State may not criminalize intimate same-sex relationships in no way suggests that it cannot draw a distinction between such relationships and traditional opposite-sex marriages by preserving the traditional understanding of marriage.

Finally, marriage is inextricably intertwined with religious and moral concerns. As with other issues that are inextricably intertwined with moral values, such as the death penalty, gambling, obscenity, prostitution, and assisted suicide, legislation regarding marriage must inevitably choose between, or attempt to balance, competing moral views. It is not only inevitable, but entirely proper, that voters' decisions be informed by their most deeply held values and beliefs as such debates are resolved, as they should be, through the democratic process.

QUESTION: What harm do proponents face if an injunction against the enforcement of Proposition 8 is issued?

ANSWER: This Court has already held that Proponents have a "significant protectable interest in defending Proposition 8" that is not adequately represented by any other party. That interest would obviously be harmed by an injunction against enforcement of Proposition 8. Additionally, Proponents would be harmed by the issuance of an injunction against the enforcement of Proposition 8 in their capacities as agents for the People and Government of the State of California, recognized as such under state law to defend, in lieu of the defendant public officials, the constitutionality of Proposition 8.

QUESTIONS TO PLAINTIFFS AND PROPONENTS

QUESTION: What does the evidence show the difference to be between gays and lesbians, on the one hand, and heterosexuals on the other? Is that difference one which the government "may legitimately take into account" when making legislative classifications?

ANSWER: First, it is undeniable that only the sexual union of a man and a woman is capable of producing offspring. This unique property of opposite-sex relationships is why marriage is "fundamental to our very existence and survival." The government may legitimately take into account this indisputable biological difference between opposite-sex and same-sex couples.

Second, it is undeniable that only the union of a man and a woman can provide a child with both of its biological parents. The government may legitimately take this into account when making legislative classifications. Social science research indicates that, on average, the ideal family structure for a child is a family headed by two biological parents in a low-conflict marriage. Furthermore, for most children the alternative to being raised by their married, biological parents is being raised by a single parent or in a step-family. As the eminent sociologist Kingsley Davis explained, "the creation, nurture, and socialization of the next generation" are "vital and extremely demanding tasks" for which "society normally holds the biological parents responsible."

Third, it is undeniable that only the union of a man and a woman can provide a child with both a father and a mother. This is another unique property of opposite-sex unions that may form a legitimate basis for legislative classifications. Indeed, "the accumulated wisdom of several millennia of human experience" has not discovered a child-rearing model superior to that centered on the child's married mother and father.

Finally, the evidence demonstrates—and Plaintiffs' experts acknowledge—that there are other meaningful differences between gay and lesbian relationships and heterosexual relationships.

QUESTION: What does the evidence show the definition (or definitions) of marriage to be?

ANSWER: The evidence shows that marriage is, as Justice [John Paul] Stevens has put it, "a license to cohabit and produce legitimate offspring." Marriage confers societal approval to engage in procreative sexual intercourse and the birth of children. This definition of marriage is supported by the historical and anthropological record.

QUESTION: What does it mean to have a "choice" in one's sexual orientation?

ANSWER: Professor [Gregory] Herek's study, referenced by the court, found that 13 percent of self-identified gay men, 30 percent of self-identified lesbians, 41 percent of self-identified bisexual men, and 55 percent of self-identified bisexual women reported that they experienced some, a fair amount, or a lot of choice with respect to their sexual orientation, with the balance reporting that they experienced little choice, or no choice. These statistics, at face value, are wholly inconsistent with any finding that gays and lesbians are a class defined by an immutable characteristic. Indeed, statistics such as these would be unthinkable with respect to other classes, such as race or sex, which the Supreme Court has held to be entitled to heightened protection under the Equal Protection Clause.

Nor does the fact that any given individual reported that he or she experiences little or no choice with respect to his or her sexual orientation mean that his or her sexual orientation has not changed in the past, or that it might not change in the future. This sort of fluidity would be unthinkable with respect to other classes, such as race or sex, which the Supreme Court has held to be entitled to heightened protection under the Equal Protection Clause.

Finally, the fact that substantial numbers of gays, lesbians, and bisexuals reported that they experienced at least some choice with respect to their sexual orientation establishes that that orientation is not determined solely by accident of birth. Not only have plaintiffs presented no evidence that sexual orientation is determined in this manner, but a substantial body of evidence indicates that sexual orientation is not so determined. The American Psychiatric Association [has said], "There are no replicated scientific studies supporting any specific biological etiology for homosexuality."

QUESTION: If spouses are obligated to one another for mutual support and support of dependents, and if legal spousal obligations have no basis in the gender of the spouse, what purpose does a law requiring that a marital partnership consist of one man and one woman serve?

ANSWER: The equal treatment under law of each spouse without respect to gender is an analytically separate issue from the State's interest in preserving the traditional definition of marriage. As explained above, the traditional definition of marriage serves a myriad of governmental interests.

QUESTION: The California Family Code requires that registered domestic partners be treated as spouses. Businesses that extend benefits to married spouses in California must extend equal benefits to registered domestic partners. If, under California law, registered domestic partners are to be treated just like married spouses, what purpose is served by differentiating—in name only—between same-sex and opposite-sex unions?

ANSWER: The California Court of Appeals answered this question when it upheld the California Legislature's decision to differentiate, in name only, between registered domestic partners and married spouses. By retaining the traditional opposite-sex definition of marriage, California preserves the abiding link between that institution and the vital social interests that are implicated by the uniquely procreative capacity of male-female unions and provides special recognition and encouragement to those unions that uniquely serve its interest in increasing the likelihood that children will be born to and raised by both of their natural parents in stable and enduring family units. At the same time, the parallel institution of domestic partnerships recognizes and honors the committed loving relationships of gays and lesbians. These parallel institutions seek to respect and accommodate differing types of relationships that have differing natural capacities and thus serve differing societal interests. It is not irrational that they be called by different names.

Relatedly, redefining marriage to include same-sex couples would work a profound transformation in the meaning and nature of the institution. We cannot escape the reality that the shared societal meaning of marriage—passed down through the common law into our statutory law—has always been the union of a man and a woman. To alter that meaning would render a profound change in the public consciousness of a social institution of ancient origin. It is not unreasonable for the State to proceed incrementally and with caution in balancing the competing interests in this novel and controversial area.

In sum, by retaining the traditional definition of marriage while extending the rights and benefits of marriage to same-sex couples through domestic partnerships, California seeks both to preserve the institution of marriage and its traditional purposes and to recognize and honor gay and lesbian relationships. Nothing in the Constitution requires the state categorically to favor one of these values over the other.

QUESTION: What evidence, if any, shows whether infertility has ever been a legal basis for annulment or divorce?

ANSWER: California courts have allowed annulment on the basis of fraud only "if the fraud relates to a matter which the state deems vital to the marriage relationship." As recently as 2005, the California Court of Appeals has held that procreation is such a vital matter. In fact, "annulments on the basis of fraud are generally granted only in cases where the fraud related in some way to the sexual or procreative aspects of marriage." Thus, the California Court of Appeals has held that an annulment should be granted where one spouse fraudulently concealed known sterility from the other. The justification for the rule is the central place of procreation in marriage.

The historic basis for these legal rules is the centrality of procreation to the institution of marriage. As one commentator explained, "since marriage is a sexual relation, having in view the propagation of the species, a man or woman so imperfect in the sexual organism as to be perpetually and incurably incapable of the connection which precedes parentage cannot enter into indissoluble matrimony with another having no notice of the incapacity."

QUESTION: What are the constitutional consequences if the evidence shows that sexual orientation is immutable for men but not for women? Must gay men and lesbians be treated identically under the Equal Protection Clause?

ANSWER: As an initial matter, the evidence makes clear that sexual orientation is not immutable, either for gay men or for lesbians. Proponents acknowledge, however, that the evidence indicates that there are differences between how gay men and lesbians experience sexual orientation and that for many women, in particular, sexual orientation is a very fluid construct. If this Court were to find, however, that sexual orientation is immutable for gay men but not for lesbians, Proponents are aware of no constitutional precedent for treating gay men and lesbians differently for purposes of a sexual orientation classification under the Equal Protection Clause.

Even if it were appropriate to distinguish between gays and lesbians for purposes of the Equal Protection Clause, a finding that sexual orientation is immutable for gay men would satisfy only one of the requirements for heightened protection; they would still need to satisfy the other requirements for heightened scrutiny, including a lack of political power.

QUESTION: If the court finds Proposition 8 to be unconstitutional, what remedy would "yield to the constitutional expression of the people of California's will [as expressed in the passage of the Prop. 8 referendum]"?

ANSWER: If, as Plaintiffs maintain, Proposition 8 cannot be reconciled with its own non-retrospective application, as interpreted by the California Supreme Court, or with any other feature of California law, the remedy that would "yield to the constitutional expression of the people of California's will" is sustaining Proposition 8 by giving it retrospective effect or invalidating the conflicting feature of California law. Several factors support this conclusion. Proposition 8 is a provision of the California Constitution, and thus "constitutes the ultimate expression of the people's will." The people of California have consistently expressed their commitment to maintaining the institution of marriage in its traditional form as the union of a man and a woman. A contrary result would entail the conclusion that the California judiciary and legislature—the very bodies the people's initiative process is designed to control—have the power to secure the invalidation of a state constitutional provision under the federal constitution by issuing judicial decisions or passing laws that rationally cannot be squared with the expressed will of the people.

[N.B. Unlike the plaintiffs that answered questions to the other side (the proponents/defendants), the proponents did not choose to answer the questions to the plaintiffs. That commentary, had it existed, would have been included here.]

THE CONTINUING DEBATE:
California's Proposition 8 Barring Gay Marriages

What Is New

In August 2010 Judge Vaughn Walker of the U.S. District Court in San Francisco handed down his decision in *Perry v. Schwarzenegger*. He found Proposition 8 to be unconstitutional. After briefly suspending his order not to enforce Proposition 8, he made it permanent. However, before any gay marriages could take place, the Ninth Circuit of the U.S. Court of Appeals ordered that the ban on gay marriages in California remain in place while the opponents of Judge Walker's ruling appealed it. As of September 2011, the Ninth Circuit had not yet ruled, and the ban remained in place. But whatever the decision at that level, the issue will almost certainly be appealed to the Supreme Court. As for the court of public opinion, a May 2011 Gallup poll found that for the first time, a majority of Americans (53%) were in support of same-sex marriages.

Where to Find More

For the gay and lesbian perspective, access the Web sites of the Human Rights Campaign at www.hrc.org/ and the National Gay and Lesbian Taskforce at www.thetaskforce.org/. Among those organizations opposing gay marriages are the American Family Association at www.afa.net/ and the Alliance Defense Fund at www.alliancedefensefund.org/. The legality of gay marriages and other forms of union in the 50 states is available at usmarriagelaws.com/. For the international impacts of gay marriages, read M. V. Lee Badgett, *When Gay People Get Married: What Happens When Societies Legalize Same-Sex Marriage* (New York University Press, 2009).

What More to Do

The original documents that served as a base for the two readings were both much longer than the edited versions here, with each side offering an extended legal and substantive justification of their position. One approach to organizing a discussion in class would be to divide the class into groups, assign each one or more of the issues identified in the judge's questions, then have the groups do an in-depth analysis and bring their findings to class.

AMERICAN PEOPLE/
POLITICAL CULTURE

THE CULTURAL ASSIMILATION OF IMMIGRANTS:
The Melting Pot Is Broken *or* Blending Satisfactorily?

THE MELTING POT IS BROKEN

ADVOCATE: John Fonte, Director, Center for American Common Culture, Hudson Institute

SOURCE: Testimony during hearings on "Comprehensive Immigration Reform: Becoming Americans—U.S. Immigrant Integration" before the U.S. House of Representatives, Committee on the Judiciary, Subcommittee on Immigration Citizenship, Refugees, Border Security, and International Law, May 16, 2007

BLENDING SATISFACTORILY

ADVOCATE: Gary Gerstle, James Stahlman Professor, Department of History, Vanderbilt University

SOURCE: Testimony during hearings on "Comprehensive Immigration Reform: Becoming Americans—U.S. Immigrant Integration" before the U.S. House of Representatives, Committee on the Judiciary, Subcommittee on Immigration Citizenship, Refugees, Border Security, and International Law, May 16, 2007

The face of America is changing. A nation that was once overwhelmingly composed of European heritage whites is becoming more diverse ethnically and racially. In 1960 the U.S. population was approximately 82% white, 11% black, and 6% Hispanic, 0.5% Asian American, and 0.5% Native American. By 2010 the U.S. population had become 66% white, 13% African American, 15% Latino, 5% Asian American, 1% Native American, and 2% multiracial. This diversification is expected to continue, with the U.S. Census Bureau estimating that in 2050, the U.S. population will be 52% white, 24% Latino, 15% African American, 9% Asian American, and 1% Native American. One reason for the change is varying fertility rates, which is the average number of children a woman in her child-bearing years will have. In 2000 the fertility rate was 2.0 for whites, 2.1 for African Americans, 2.3 for Asian Americans, 2.5 for Native Americans, and 2.9 for Hispanics.

Immigration changes are a second factor accounting for growing diversity. As late as the 1950s, more than 70% of immigrants were coming from Europe or from Canada and other European-heritage countries. Then Congress amended the immigration laws in 1965 to eliminate the quota system that favored immigration from Europe. Now, only about 16% of newcomers are from Europe, compared to 48% from Latin America and the Caribbean, 32% from Asia, and 4% from Africa. Adding to this influx are those who come to the United States without going through established immigration procedures. There are an estimated 10 million such immigrants in the United States, and between 400,000 and 500,00 new ones were arriving each year. About 80% of these illegal immigrants are from Central America, espccially Mexico.

Not only the racial and ethnic composition of those coming to the United States changed dramatically since the 1960s. There has also been a dramatic increase in the number of immigrants. Legal immigration has nearly tripled from an annual average of 330,000 in the 1960s to annual averages of 978,000 in the 1990s and 1,016,000 between 2000 and 2006. These numbers seems huge, but relative to the U.S. population they are not as high as earlier periods in history. For example, the immigrants who arrived during the decade 1900–1909 equaled 10.4% of the population. Those arriving legally in the ten years between 1997 and 2006 came to 2.9% of the population, with the net inflow of about 4 million illegal immigrants during those years increasing that figure to about 4.3%.

The classic image Americans have of what has occurred with immigrants is in the melting pot analogy, with new immigrants being "Americanized," that is learning English and adopting existing American values and customs. In reality, of course, new immigrants also changed the nature of the American "stew" in the pot by introducing new words, ideas, foods, and other things that existing Americans adopted. Be that as it may, the increased rate of immigration and its increasingly non-European complexion have raised concerns in some quarters that the melting pot is not working adequately and even that some immigrants have no wish to blend in. This view came into particular focus with the book, *Who We Are: The Challenges to America's National Identity* (Simon & Schuster, 2004) written by Harvard University political scientist Samuel P. Huntington. As the *Washington Post* noted, Huntington posed "some of the most critical questions facing our nation" including, "How can a people already preoccupied with ethnic identity absorb and acculturate the millions of immigrants being driven to our shores by global economics?" and "How in the long run will America cohere if everyone feels they belong to a minority?" Huntington was concerned about the melting pot, and his view is furthered in the first reading by John Fonte of the conservative think tank, the Hudson Institute. That is followed by a much more optimistic view of the assimilation process given by historian Gary Gerstle of Vanderbilt University.

POINTS TO PONDER

➤ The traditional goal has been a cultural melting pot in which immigrants merged into existing American culture. Some people now advocate multiculturalism, the coexistence of more than one culture. What are the benefits and drawbacks of the melting pot and multicultural images?

➤ There are people who argue that at least some of those who raise concerns about assimilation are closet racists who are concerned about the "de-Europanization" of the United States, both in culture and the color of its citizen's skins. What is your view?

➤ Think about what changes to immigration policy and naturalization (becoming a U.S. citizen) policy you might make.

The Cultural Assimilation of Immigrants: The Melting Pot Is Broken

JOHN FONTE

WHAT DO WE MEAN BY INTEGRATION?

Let us start by using the more serious and vigorous term "assimilation." There are different types of assimilation: linguistic, economic, cultural, civic, and patriotic. Linguistic assimilation means the immigrant learns English. Economic assimilation means the immigrant does well materially and, perhaps, joins the middle class. Cultural assimilation means that the immigrant acculturates to the nation's popular cultural norms (for both good and ill). Civic assimilation or civic integration means that the immigrant is integrated into our political system, votes, pays taxes, obeys the law, and participates in public life in some fashion.

These forms of assimilation are necessary, but not sufficient. We were reminded again last week, in the Fort Dix conspiracy that there are naturalized citizens, legal permanent residents, and illegal immigrants living in our country who speak English, are gainfully employed (even entrepreneurs) who would like to kill as many Americans as possible [Fort Dix conspiracy: Six foreign-born Muslim men were arrested in May 2007 and charged with plotting to detonate a terrorist bomb at the U.S. Army installation. Three of the men were illegal immigrants, one was a naturalized citizen, one was a legal immigrant, and the status of the six man was unknown]. The type of assimilation that ultimately matters most of all is patriotic assimilation: political loyalty and emotional attachment to the United States. What do we mean by patriotic assimilation? First of all, patriotic assimilation does not mean giving up all ethnic traditions, customs, cuisine, and birth languages. It has nothing to do with the food one eats, the religion one practices, the affection that one feels for the land of one's birth, and the second languages that one speaks. Multiethnicity and ethnic subcultures have enriched America and have always been part of our past since colonial days.

Historically, the immigration saga has involved some "give and take" between immigrants and the native-born. That is to say, immigrants have helped shape America even as this nation has Americanized them. On the other hand, this "two way street" is 2 not a fifty-fifty arrangement. Thus, on the issue of "who accommodates to whom"; obviously, most of the accommodating should come from the newcomers, not from the hosts.

So what is patriotic assimilation? (or as well shall soon discuss "Americanization"). Well, one could say that patriotic assimilation occurs when a newcomer essentially adopts American civic values, the American heritage, and the story of America (what academics call the "narrative") as his or her own. It occurs, for example, when newcomers and their children begin to think of American history as "our" history not "their" history. To give a hypothetical example, imagine an eighth-grade Korean-American female student studying the Constitutional Convention of 1787.

Does she think of those events in terms of "they" or "we"? Does she envision the creation of the Constitution in Philadelphia as something that "they" (white males of European descent) were involved in 200 years before her ancestors came to America, or does she imagine the Constitutional Convention as something that "we" Americans did as part of "our" history? Does she think in terms of "we" or "they"? "We" implies patriotic assimilation. If she thinks in terms of "we" she has done what millions of immigrants and immigrant children have done in the past. She has adopted America's story as her story, and she has adopted America's Founders—[James] Madison, [Alexander] Hamilton, [Benjamin] Franklin, [George] Washington—as her ancestors. (This does not mean that she, like other Americans, will not continue to argue about our history and our heritage, nor ignore the times that America has acted ignobly).

OUR HISTORIC SUCCESS WITH AMERICANIZATION

Historically America has done assimilation well. As *Washington Post* columnist Charles Krauthammer put it, "America's genius has always been assimilation, taking immigrants and turning them into Americans."

This was done in the days of Ellis Island because America's leaders including Democrat [President] Woodrow Wilson and Republican [President] Theodore Roosevelt believed that immigrants should be "Americanized."

They were self-confident leaders. They were not embarrassed by the need to assimilate immigrants into our way of life and by explicitly telling newcomers that "this is what we expect you to do to become Americanized." Indeed, they didn't use weasel words like "integration," that suggests a lack of self-confidence. They believed in "Americanization." For example, on July 4, 1915 President Woodrow Wilson declared National Americanization Day. The President and his cabinet addressed naturalization ceremonies around the nation on the subject of Americanization. The most powerful speech was delivered by future Supreme Court Justice, Louis Brandeis at Faneuil Hall in Boston in which Brandeis declared that Americanization meant that the newcomer will "possess the national consciousness of an American."

In a sense the views of Theodore Roosevelt, Woodrow Wilson and Louis Brandeis on the need to foster assimilation go back to the Founders of our nation. Indeed, President George Washington explicitly stated the need to assimilate immigrants in a letter to Vice President John Adams. [Washington wrote:]

> The policy or advantage of [immigration] taking place in a body (I mean the settling of them in a body) may be much questioned; for, by so doing, they retain the language, habits, and principles (good or bad) which they bring with them. Whereas by an intermixture with our people, they, or 4 their descendants, get assimilated to our customs, measures, laws: in a word soon become one people.

The Present Day: Americanization and Anti-Americanization

During the 1990s, one of the great members of the House of Representatives, the late Congresswoman Barbara Jordan (D-TX) called for a revival of the concept of Americanization and for a New Americanization movement. Jordan wrote an article in the *New York Times* on September 11, 1995 entitled the "The Americanization Ideal," in which she explicitly called for the Americanization of immigrants. We should heed her words today. Unfortunately, for decades we have implemented what could truly be called anti-Americanization, anti-assimilation, and anti-integration policies—Multilingual ballots, bi-lingual education, [presidential] executive order 13166 that insists on official multilingualism, immigrant dual allegiance including voting and running for office in foreign countries, and the promotion of multiculturalism over American unity in our public schools. [Executive Order 13166, Improving Access to Services for

Persons With Limited English Proficiency, issued August 11, 2000.] The anti-assimilation policies listed above did not place in a vacuum. They are all connected and related to the larger picture. All of these policies and attitudes have hurt assimilation.

Let us examine how assimilation has become more problematic in recent years. Traditionally the greatest indicator of assimilation is intermarriage among ethnic groups and between immigrants and native-born. Unfortunately a new major study published in the *American Sociological Review* by Ohio State Professor Zhenchao Qian found a big decline in inter-ethnic marriage. Professor Qian declared, "These declines…are significant a departure from past trends" and "reflect the growth in the immigrant population" with Latinos marrying Latinos and Asians marrying Asians.

The survey found that even as recently as the 1970s and 1980s there was an increase in intermarriage between immigrants and native born citizens. In the 1990s however, this situation was reversed with intermarriage between immigrants and native-born declining. Mass low-skilled immigration was an implicit factor cited in the *Ohio State University Research Bulletin*. The researchers pointed out the immigrants with higher education levels were more likely to marry outside their immediate ethnic group and the reverse was true for immigrants with less education. In recent years our immigration policy favors the less education and lower skilled.

My fellow witness, Professor Rumbaut has done some excellent work examining assimilation among the children of immigrants. With Professor Alejandro Portes he produced the "The Children of Immigrants Longitudinal Study," of over 5,000 students from 49 schools in the Miami, Florida and San Diego, California areas. Portes carried out the research in Miami. Their joint findings were published by the University of California Press in 2001 as *Legacies: The Story of the Immigrant Second Generation*. The parents of the students came from 77 different countries, although in the Miami area they were 5 primarily from Cuba, Haiti, Nicaragua, and Columbia. In San Diego there were large numbers from Mexico, the Philippines, and Viet Nam.

Portes and Rumbaut pointed out that it is significant that although the youths' knowledge of English increased during their three or four years of school between the longitudinal interviews, their American identity decreased:

> Moreover, the direction of the shift is noteworthy. If the rapid shift to English…was to have been accompanied by a similar acculturative shift in ethnic identity, then we should have seen an increase over time in the proportion of youths identifying themselves as American, with or without a hyphen, and a decrease in the proportion retaining an attachment to a foreign national identity. But…results of the 1995 survey point in exactly the opposite direction.

In other words, linguistic assimilation has increased, but patriotic assimilation has decreased. After four years of American high school the children of immigrants are less likely to consider themselves Americans. Moreover, the heightened salience (or importance) of the foreign identity was very strong. Portes and Rumbaut declare that:

Once again, foreign national identities command the strongest level of allegiance and attachment: over 71% of the youths so identifying considered that identity to be very important to them, followed by 57.2% hyphenates [as in, for example, Irish-American], 52.8% of the pan-ethnics [such as Latino, a regional, rather than specific country reference], and only 42% of those identifying as plain American. The later [plain American] emerges as the "thinnest" identity. Significantly, in the 1995 survey, almost all immigrants groups posted losses in plain American identities....Even private-school Cubans, over a third of whom had identified as American in 1992, abandoned that identity almost entirely by 1995–1996.

In 2002 the Pew Hispanic Survey revealed that around seven months after 9/11 only 34% of American citizens of Hispanic origin consider their primary identification American. On the other hand, 42% identified first with their parent's country of origin (Mexico, El Salvador, etc.) and 24% put ethnic (Latino, Hispanic) identity first.

An empirical survey of Muslims in Los Angeles was conducted in the 1990s by religious scholar Kambiz Ghanea Bassiri (a professor at Reed College). The study found that only one of ten Muslim immigrants surveyed felt more allegiance to the United States than to a foreign Muslim nation. Specifically, 45% of the Muslims surveyed had more loyalty to an Islamic nation-state than the United States; 32% said their loyalties "were about the same" between the U.S. and a Muslim nation-state; 13% were "not sure" which loyalty was stronger; and 10% were more loyal to the United States than any Muslim nation. All of this data suggests problems with assimilation.

In a Chicago *Tribune* article on April 7, the head of the Office of New Americans in Illinois, the person in charge of assimilation in the state, made the following statement. "The nation-state concept is changing. You don't have to say, 'I am Mexican,' or, 'I am American.' You can be a good Mexican citizen and a good American citizen and not have that be a conflict of interest. Sovereignty is flexible."

He is a dual citizen who is actively involved in Mexican politics. He votes in both the U.S. and Mexico and is active in political campaigns in both nations. His political allegiance is clearly divided. He will not choose one nation over the other. One hundred years ago the President of the United States in 1907, Theodore Roosevelt, expressed a different point of view:

> If the immigrant who comes here in good faith becomes an American and assimilates himself to us, he shall be treated on an exact equality with everyone else, for it is an outrage to discriminate against any such man because of creed, or birth-place, or origin. But this is predicated upon the man's becoming in very fact an American, and nothing but an American...There can be no divided allegiance here. we have room for but one sole loyalty and that is a loyalty to the American people.

Those are two very different views of the meaning of the oath of allegiance in which the new citizens promises to "absolutely and entirely" renounce all allegiance to any foreign state.

What is to be done?

What do we do then, in a practical sense? For one thing, it makes no sense to enact so-called comprehensive immigration reform, which means both a slow motion amnesty and a massive increase in low skilled immigration further exacerbating our assimilation problems. What we do need is comprehensive assimilation reform for those immigrants who are here legally

First, we have to dismantle the anti-assimilation regime of foreign language ballots, dual allegiance voting by American citizens in foreign countries, bi-lingual education, and executive order 13166.

Second, we should follow Barbara Jordan's lead and explicitly call for the Americanization of immigrants, not integration.

Third, we should enforce the oath of allegiance. The Oath should mean what it says:

> I hereby declare, on oath, that I absolutely and entirely renounce and abjure all allegiance and fidelity to any foreign prince, potentate, state, or sovereignty, of whom or which I have heretofore been a subject or a citizen; that I will support and defend the Constitution and laws of the United States of America against all enemies foreign and domestic; that I will bear true faith and allegiance to the same; that I will bear arms on behalf of the United States when required by law; that I will perform noncombatant service in the Armed Forces of the United States when required by law; that I will perform work of national importance under civilian direction when required by law; and that I take this obligation freely, without any mental reservation or purpose of evasion; so help me God.

Clearly, if we are a serous people, naturalized citizens should not be voting and running for office in their birth nations.

Fourth, Senator Lamar Alexander of Tennessee has introduced bi-partisan legislation "to promote the patriotic integration of prospective citizens into the American way of life by providing civics, history and English as a second language courses." There is a "specific emphasis" on "attachment to the principles of the Constitution" and to the "heroes of American history (including military heroes)." This initiative will be administered by the Office of Citizenship in the United States Citizenship and Immigration Services (USCIS). Also, this legislation incorporates "a knowledge and understanding of the Oath of Allegiance into the history and government test given to applicants for citizenship." This amendment passed the Senate last year by 91–1. Its enactment should be implemented with or without any "comprehensive" measure.

Fifth the mandate of the Office of Citizenship should be to assist our new fellow citizens in understanding the serious moral commitment that they are making in taking the Oath, and "bearing true faith and allegiance" to American liberal democracy.

Because we are a multiethnic, multiracial, multireligious country, our nationhood is not based on ethnicity, race, or religion, but, instead, on a shared loyalty to our constitutional republic and its liberal democratic principles. If immigration to America is going to continue to be the great success story that it has been in the past, it is essential that newcomers have an understanding of and attachment to our democratic republic, our heritage, and our civic principles.

To this end, the Office of Citizenship should strengthen the current educational materials used by applicants for American citizenship. Since the Oath of Allegiance is the culmination of the naturalization process, an examination of the Oath and what it means, "to bear true faith and allegiance" to the United States Constitution should be part of those educational materials, and should be included on any citizenship test. Further, the Office could (1) examine ways to make citizenship training and the swearing-in ceremony more meaningful; (2) cooperate with other government agencies that work with immigrants such as the U.S. Department of Education's English Literacy-Civics 8 program; and (3) continue to reexamine the citizenship test to see how it can be improved (as it is currently doing, so kudos to the Office of Citizenship on this point). Sixth English Literacy Civics (formerly English as a Second Language-Civics or ESLCivics) is a federal program that provides grants to teach English with a civics education emphasis to non-native speakers. The program is administered by the U.S. Department of Education through the states. The money goes to adult education schools, community colleges, and non-governmental organizations to integrate civic instruction into English language learning.

Logically, EL-Civics is a program that should promote the Americanization of immigrants. As noted, in becoming American citizens, immigrants pledge, "True faith and allegiance" to American liberal democracy. This requires some knowledge of our history and our values. If the money expended annually on EL-Civics assisted our future fellow citizens in understanding America's heritage and civic values, the money would be well spent. This appears to have been the intent of Congress in creating the program in the first place.

Unfortunately, there are problems with EL-Civics programs. In many federally funded EL-Civics classes "civics" is defined narrowly as pertaining almost exclusively to mundane day to day tasks such as how to take public transportation or make a doctor's appointment. Obviously, these "life-coping skills" (as they are called in the jargon) could be part of EL-Civics classes, but the classes should focus primarily on American values, or what veteran civic educator Robert Pickus calls "Idea Civics."

The problem is that many state guidelines for EL-Civics are rigid and inflexible. These state guidelines have been influenced heavily by language professionals; who define "civics" in a very narrow way, and resist the idea of teaching American values through English language training.

It is time to put American civic principles at the head of the taxpayer supported English Literacy Civics program. Federal guidelines to the states should be revised, insisting on the use of solid content materials that emphasize our American heritage, and our civic and patriotic values. In our post-9-11 world, "Idea Civics," that will assist newcomers in understanding the meaning of "bearing true faith and allegiance" to our democratic republic must be emphasized.

In sum, it is time to promote the patriotic assimilation of immigrants into the mainstream of American life. Today as in the past, patriotic assimilation is a necessary component of any successful immigration policy. This does not mean that we should blindly replicate all the past Americanization policies of Theodore Roosevelt and Woodrow Wilson. But it does mean that we have much to learn from our great historical success. In the final analysis it means that we should draw on a usable past, exercise common sense, and develop an Americanization policy that will be consist with our principles and effective in today's world.

What about "Comprehensive Immigration Reform"?

The irony is that so-called "comprehensive" immigration reform is not "comprehensive." There are no serious assimilation components to the legislation. Moreover the eventual promised amnesty and the massive increase in low-skilled immigration promoted formula would weaken assimilation. Assimilation policy cannot be separated from immigration policy. We need comprehensive assimilation reform (for legal immigrants), before we need comprehensive immigration.

Unfortunately, comprehensive immigration reform is primarily about the special needs of particular businesses, not the interests of the American people as a whole, ignores assimilation and puts the market over the nation, but Americans must always remember that we are a nation of citizens before we are a market of consumers.

The Cultural Assimilation of Immigrants: Blending Satisfactorily

GARY GERSTLE

Since its founding, the United States has arguably integrated more immigrants, both in absolute and relative terms, than any other nation. In the years between the 1820s and 1920s, an estimated 35 million immigrants came to the United States. Approximately 40 to 50 million more came between the 1920s and 2010s, with most of those coming after 1965. The successful integration of immigrants and their descendants has been one of the defining features of American society, and, in my view, one of this country's greatest accomplishments. Can we find descendants of the immigrants who came in such large numbers one hundred years ago who today do not regard themselves as Americans? We can probably identify a few, but not many. Even those groups once known for their resistance to Americanization—Italians, for example—today count themselves and are considered by others as being among the America's most ardent patriots. Throughout the nation's history, moreover, newer Americans and their descendants have contributed a dynamic quality to our society through their Americanization. As President Woodrow Wilson proudly told a group of immigrants in 1915, America was "the only country in the world that experiences a constant and repeated rebirth," and the credit went entirely to the "great bodies of strong men and forward-looking women out of other lands" who decided to cast their lot with America.

In my testimony today, I have four aims: first, to acquaint you with the so-called "new immigrants" who came by the millions to the United States one hundred years ago and who were widely regarded as lacking the desire and ability to integrate themselves into American society; second, to discuss with you how these immigrants and their children confounded their critics by becoming deeply and proudly American; third, to lay out for you what I think a successful process of immigrant integration requires; and fourth, to suggest to you ways this earlier experience of successful integration can guide an exploration of the prospects of integrating immigrants who are living in America today.

My most important point is twofold. First, that the United States has been enormously successful in making Americans out of immigrants, even among immigrant populations who were thought to have cultures and values radically different from America's own. Second, immigrant integration does not happen overnight. Typically it takes two generations and requires both engagement on the part of immigrants with American democracy and an opportunity for them to achieve economic security for themselves and their families. If we approach questions of immigration today with a realistic and robust sense for what a successful process of immigrant incorporation requires, we have reason to be optimistic that America will once again demonstrate its remarkable ability to absorb and integrate foreign-born millions.

THE "NEW IMMIGRANTS" OF ONE HUNDRED YEARS AGO

An estimated 24 million immigrants came to the United States between the 1880s and the 1920s. They entered a society that numbered only 76 million people in 1900. A large majority of these new immigrants came from Europe, and they came mostly from impoverished and rural areas of eastern and southern Europe: from Italy, Russia, Poland, Lithuania, Hungary, Slovakia, Serbia, Greece, and other proximate nations or parts of the Austro-Hungarian Empire. Few of these immigrants were Protestant, then the dominant religion of the United States; most were Catholic, Christian Orthodox, or Jewish. The integration process of these turn-of-the century immigrants, however, was not quick and it was not easy. Indeed, the label applied to these immigrants—"the new immigrants"—was meant to compare them unfavorably to the "old immigrants" who had come prior to 1880 from the British Isles, Germany, and Scandinavia and who were then thought to have been the model immigrants: industrious, freedom-loving, English-speaking, and ardently patriotic. If I could parachute you, the members of this Subcommittee into American society in a year when the "new immigration" was at its height—in 1910, for example, or 1920—you would encounter a pessimism about the possibilities of integrating these immigrants more intense than what exists in American society today. That the outcome was so positive and so at variance with the pessimistic expectations of 1910 or 1920 should caution us against giving ourselves over to pessimism today.

In the early years of the twentieth century, a majority of Americans were Protestants who cared deeply about the Protestant character of their society. Protestantism, in their eyes, had given America its mission, its democracy, its high regard for individual rights, and its moral character. These Americans worried that the largely Catholic, Orthodox, and Jewish immigrants who dominated the ranks of the "new immigrants" would subvert cherished American ideals, and that the great American republic would decline or even come to an end.

America, at the time, was also a deeply racist society. Black-white segregation was at its height. Chinese immigrants had been largely barred from coming to the United States in 1882 and Japanese immigrants were largely barred in 1907. A naturalization law stipulated that only those immigrants who were free and white were eligible for citizenship, a law that effectively prohibited almost all East and South Asians immigrants from becoming citizens between 1870 and 1952. For a twenty year period in the early twentieth century, the U.S. government attempted to rule that several peoples from the Middle East and West Asia, including Arabs and Armenians, were nonwhite and thus also ineligible for U.S. citizenship. In 1924, Congress stopped most eastern and southern Europeans from coming to the United States because these peoples were also now thought to be racially inferior and thus incapable of assimilating American civilization and democracy. This is how a member of Congress (Fred S. Purnell of Indiana, R) described eastern and southern European immigrants in 1924, [saying,] "There is little or no similarity between the clear-thinking, self-governing stocks that sired the American people and this stream of irresponsible and broken wreckage that is pouring into the lifeblood of America the social and political diseases of the Old World."

Purnell quoted approvingly the words of a Dr. Ward, who claimed that Americans had deceived themselves into believing that "we could change inferior beings into superior ones." Americans could not escape the laws of heredity, Ward argued. "We cannot make a heavy horse into a trotter by keeping him in racing stable. We can not make a well bred dog out of mongrel by teaching him tricks." The acts that Ward dismissed as "tricks" including the learning by immigrants of the Gettysburg Address and the Declaration of Independence.

Given these attitudes, it is not surprising that many immigrants felt unwelcome in the United States. Nevertheless, America was then what it is today: a society for the enterprising, for those who wanted to raise themselves up in the world. Many immigrants perceived America as a land in which they could improve their economic circumstances. They worked endless hours to make that happen. But would America become for them more than a place to work? Would it become their home, a place where they would feel comfortable, where they would raise their families, where they could come to consider themselves—and be considered by others as—Americans? Many immigrants doubted that this would ever be the case. Many intended to make some money in the United States and return home. In the early years of the 20th century, it is estimated that the repatriation rates (those who chose to return home) among Italian immigrants ran as high as 40 to 50 percent. Among immigrants from the Balkans in the years prior to the First World War, it is estimated that as many 80 percent returned home. Those who did not or could not return to their original lands often sent remittances to their families in Europe. For many of these immigrants, becoming U.S. citizens and learning English were goals that were secondary to the primary challenge of earning a living and raising the standard of one's family, either in the United States or one's home country. Yet these immigrants and their children did become integrated into America and deeply committed to America. How and when did this integration happen?

INTEGRATING THE "NEW IMMIGRANTS"

Three factors are particularly important for understanding the integration of the "new immigrants": learning to practice American democracy; the transition in immigrant communities from the first to second generation; and the achievement of economic security.

Practicing American Democracy: As anti-immigrant sentiment grew in America across the early decades of the 20th century, immigrants who had been reluctant to enter American politics now believed that they had no alternative but to become so involved, if only to protect their most basic interests. In the 1920s, they began to naturalize and then to vote in large numbers. Immigrants wanted to elect representatives who supported their freedom to enter the United States, to pursue a trade or occupation of their choice, to school their children and raise their families in ways that corresponded to their cultural traditions and religious beliefs. They also wanted the government to end discrimination against immigrants in employment, housing, and education. Immigrants lost some major elections, as in 1928, when Herbert Hoover (R) defeated the pro-immigrant candidate, Al Smith (D) [for the presidency], but they also scored some major victories, as when Franklin D. Roosevelt (D) won a landslide re-election in 1936 with the help of millions of new voters, many of them immigrant, casting their ballots for the first time. These immigrant voters believed that FDR was opening up American politics to immigrant participation in ways that few previous presidents had done. In response to this opening, these new immigrants and their children became an important part of the Democratic Party voting majority that would keep Democrats in the White House and in control of Congress for a majority of years between the mid-1930s and late 1960s.

Political parties were important in brokering the entrance of immigrants into American politics. The Democratic Party in particular played a pivotal role not just in registering immigrants to vote but in teaching them the practical arts of American politics—running for office, building constituencies, raising money for campaigns, getting out the vote, writing legislation and building coalitions. The "political boss" and "political machines" were central institutions in many American cities of the time, and both played important roles in bringing immigrants into politics. Although the national Republican Party was not as important as the Democratic Party in assisting immigrants, particular state and local Republican parties often were important players in this brokerage process.

The ability of immigrants to participate in politics and to feel as though their votes made a difference was crucial to their engagement with and integration into America. In the 1920s and 1930s, immigrants began to assert their Americanness and their right to participate in debates about America's best interests. In the short term, this generated more political conflict than political consensus, as immigrant Americans often disagreed sharply with the native-born about what course to chart for America's future, and whether (and how) to open up American workplaces, occupations, universities, and neighborhoods to the full participation of immigrants. But there can be no doubt that immigrant engagement in American politics, with all the conflict it entailed, worked to bind the native-born and foreign born together, and make both groups feel part of one American nation. And that engagement worked, too, to change America in ways that allowed Catholics and Jews to assert their claims on America and to assert that they had as much right to live in America, to speak on its behalf, and to access its opportunities as did long-settled populations of American Protestants.

Generational Transition: Equally important to the integration of the new immigrants was a shift in the balance of power within immigrant families from the first to second generation. This shift occurred sometime between the 1920s and the 1940s, as the immigrant generation aged and the second generation came into maturity. The children of immigrants (or those who had come to America as very small children) were comfortable with their Americanness in ways that their parents frequently had not been. Some of this second-generation Americanization occurred invisibly, through the daily experiences of these children with American society—walking down the streets of their cities, scouring the ads in newspapers and magazines for alluring consumer goods, listening to the radio, going to the movies, playing sports, and discovering the latest innovation in American popular music. Popular culture in America has always been a great assimilator. Some of the second generation's Americanization occurred more formally, through institutions, most notably high schools (which significantly expanded their enrollments in the 1930s and 1940s) and the World War II military, which took more than sixteen million young Americans out of their homes and neighborhoods between 1941 and 1945, mixed them up with other young Americans from every region of the country, and then asked every one of them to give their life for their country.

Even prior to their entry into these powerful institutions, mother-tongue monolingualism had fallen dramatically among these young men and women. For the second generation, bilingualism or English monolingualism became the norm; the third generation, meanwhile, was almost entirely English monolingual. Most members of the third generation could not speak and not even understand the language of their grandparents. By this time, too, many private institutions in "new immigrant" ethnic communities— churches, synagogues, fraternal and charitable organizations, ethnic newspapers— had begun to see themselves as agents of Americanization, in part to keep the younger generation engaged with issues of concern to the ethnic community.

Economic Security: We should not underestimate the importance of economic security in persuading immigrants to cast their lot with America. The welfare of one's family was almost always a key consideration for the "new immigrants" of the early 20th century. While some immigrants found opportunities in America and prospered, many were stuck in low paying, unskilled jobs in American manufacturing and construction, with little promise of advancement and no security that they would be able to keep even these jobs. Many had to make do with wages that were chronically insufficient. Many lived with the fear that they would fail as breadwinners, that the American dream would never be theirs, and that their employers would toss them aside for yet younger and cheaper workers. When the Great Depression plunged the U.S. economy into crisis for twelve long years, this fear spread to the second generation who were trying to find their first jobs at a time when neither the private nor public sector was able to bring the nation's unemployment rate below 15 percent. In these dire circumstances, many immigrants and their children began to turn to collective institutions of economic self help, the most important of which was the labor movement. Labor unions were Americanizing institutions during these years, convincing ethnic workers both that they had rights as American workers and that their ability to improve their circumstances would contribute to the overall well-being of American society. Labor movement advocates argued that wages must be raised to a decent level, that hours of work should not exceed human endurance, that the government must make some provision for those who lost their jobs through no fault of their own, and that those who had spent a life time at work should be rewarded by the government with an old age pension. The labor movement provided critical support for two of the most important government policies of the 1930s and 1940s, the Social Security Act and the GI Bill of Rights, both of which meant a great deal to the new immigrants and their children. One can make the case that the labor movement played a major role in helping to lift immigrant workers and their children out of poverty and thereby in giving them a stake in the American dream.

To identify the labor movement as an important institution of immigrant incorporation is to venture onto controversial political terrain. But whatever one thinks of the proper role of labor unions, it remains the case that questions of economic security and opportunity must be part of our discussion of immigrant integration. An immigrant population that finds itself unable to move out of poverty or to gain the confidence that it can provide a decent life for their children is far more likely to descend into alienation than to embrace America.

By 1950s, the integration of the "new immigrants" and their children had been successfully accomplished. Most of the children and grandchildren of these immigrants were enthusiastic Americans. But the success of the process had taken forty to fifty years and had required immersion in the practice of American democracy, a transition in generational power from the first o the second generation, and the achievement of economic security.

TODAY'S IMMIGRANTS: QUESTIONS AND ANSWERS

Today's immigrants are sometimes depicted by their critics as are far more different from "us" than were past waves of immigrants and as far less interested in integrating themselves into American society. The charge is also leveled that there are simply too many of immigrants residing in America today for this country to absorb and integrate.

Below I examine each of these beliefs in light of the background I have provided on the "new immigrants" who came between the 1880s and 1920s.

1. *Are today's immigrants too different from "us?"* Immigrants today are different from earlier waves of immigrants in the diversity of their origins, in the diversity of their economic backgrounds, and in the fact that a majority are nonwhite. At earlier periods of U.S. history, most immigrants came from Europe. Today they come from every continent, with South America (and Latin America more generally), Asia, and Africa being the largest sources. Today's immigrants are also more diverse in economic backgrounds than any previous wave of immigrants. In earlier waves, the immigrants were overwhelmingly poor and generally lacking in education. Such individuals are amply represented in the ranks of immigrants today, but so too are those who are highly trained professionals, managers, and small retailers who have decided that their skills will be more fully used and rewarded in the United States than at home, and that the opportunities for their children will be greater here as well. Thus the proportions of professionals and managers in the immigrant streams coming from the Philippines, India, Taiwan, and Korea regularly reach or exceed fifty percent. These immigrants are generally thought not to be "problem immigrants" and so they don't form a significant part of our discussion about immigration today. But these kinds of immigrants are well represented in today's immigrant population, especially among those groups who have come from East and South Asia. They are generally thought to be important contributors to America, and so they should be included in any overall assessment of current immigration.

Discussion of today's immigrants generally focuses on those who are at the poor end of the immigrant spectrum. Poverty alone, of course, is hardly a distinguishing feature of today's immigrants, since past groups of immigrants were overwhelmingly poor. What does distinguish today's immigrant poor is that they are nonEuropean. Coming from nonEuropean cultures, they are sometimes thought by their critics to lack the cultural attributes—what we commonly refer to as the values of "western civilization"— that allowed earlier waves of poor immigrants to climb out of their poverty, to embrace America's creed of freedom and individualism as their own, and to become active contributors to American enterprise and American democracy.

The irony of this critique is that the "Europeans" held up as model immigrants of yesteryear were, at the time of their immigration, depicted much as poor nonwhite immigrants are today: as so racially and culturally different from Americans, as so different from the earlier waves of immigrants who had come from western and northern Europe, that they could never close the gap between who they were and what "we," America, wanted them to be. Because they were allegedly unassimilable, the United States made a fateful decision in the 1920s to all but close its immigrant gates to eastern and southern Europeans. America was successful in barring them from entry, but it was wrong to believe that they lacked the ability to integrate themselves into American society. As I have argued in earlier sections of this testimony, the millions of eastern and southern Europeans already here did Americanize, and today we celebrate them as exemplary Americans. Why repeat that earlier mistake today and designate large sections of the world's population as inappropriate material for inclusion in America? To do so is not only to discriminate on the grounds of race but also to confess our own lack of faith in the promise and transformative power of American freedom.

2. *Are today's immigrants too little interested in integrating themselves into American society?* It is true that many immigrants today retain strong ties to their homeland and

that many return home or aspire to do so. Technological innovations have made travel back and forth relatively easy, and the communications revolution has made it possible to stay in constant and instantaneous touch with one's family and friends back home. Many immigrants are not eager to relinquish the cultures they brought with them. Among adult immigrants who work in unskilled occupations where literacy is not important (construction, agriculture, landscaping, and personal services), some are slow to learn English. But these patterns are hardly novel. To the contrary, they are similar to patterns evident among the European immigrants who came at the beginning of the twentieth century. They are patterns that tend to be characteristic of immigrant groups in which recent arrivals form a large part of the immigrant population.

If we want to develop an accurate picture of the progress of integration (or lack thereof), we should not be content to take snapshots of a group at a particular point in time. We should want to supplement those snapshots with an examination of immigrants across time and across generations. Studies done by social scientists are beginning to supply us with this kind of data, and they are revealing patterns of integration that are similar to those associated with European immigrants a hundred years ago. For example, among the children of Latino immigrants, the rates of Spanish monolingualism (those who speak only Spanish) are very low and the rates of English-Spanish bilingualism are very high. Moreover, English monolingualism has made surprising inroads among the children of Latino immigrants, so much that some Latino parents worry that their children are losing touch with their cultural roots. These patterns become even more pronounced among third generation immigrants. The patterns of language loss and acquisition among today's immigrant generations, in other words, seem to be similar to those that shaped the lives of the European immigrants who came one hundred years ago.

Successful integration depends not simply on language and generational transition but on immigrant engagement with American democracy and on the experience of economic opportunity, advancement, and security. Some social scientists have argued that institutions that were once so important in involving past generations of immigrants in American politics (political parties) and for helping them to achieve economic security (the labor movement) have either so changed in nature or have become so weak that they can no longer perform a similar function with today's immigrants. There is some truth to this argument, although the events of the past two years have demonstrated both that political parties still retain the capacity to mobilize immigrants and that labor unions, in cities such as Los Angeles where they remain strong, can still play an important role in promoting immigrant economic interests. Nevertheless, it seems clear that the successful integration of today's immigrants requires either that these older institutions find ways to broaden their involvement with immigrants or that other institutions step forward to engage immigrants in the practice of American democracy and to assist the poor among them with the pursuit of economic opportunity and security. Among Latino immigrants, the Catholic Church has demonstrated that it can become an important mechanism for immigrant integration. Ideally, institutions that assist immigrants in the pursuit of economic opportunity will bring them into alliance rather than conflict with the native-born poor.

3. *Has the number of immigrants coming to America reached such a numerical level that integration has become impossible?* In absolute terms, the number of immigrants is at all time high: approximately 35 million. A few years ago, the number arriving in a single

year passed one million and topped the previous one year record that had been record-ed in the early years of the twentieth century. In proportional terms, however, we have not yet reached the immigrant density that prevailed in America in the early twentieth century. The million who were arriving annually in those years were entering a society that possessed between one-fourth and one-third the population of America today. To reach that earlier level of immigrant density, America would have to admit three to four million immigrants a year and sustain that rate for a decade or more.

It is possible, of course, for a society to reach levels of saturation whereby the num-bers coming overwhelm mechanisms of integration. Saturation can be a national phe-nomenon or one that affects a particular region or city. Current immigrant density in the United States, however, is not at an all time high. Moreover, it is wrong to assume that demography is destiny, and that, for the sake of integration, we must close the immigrant gates once a pre-selected immigration density index is reached. If we can put in place mechanisms or institutions that broaden immigrant immersion in the practice of American democracy and broaden the access of poor immigrants to economic oppor-tunity and security, then we can have every reason to believe that the integration of this wave of immigrants will be as successful as the last one was. The process will take time and we should expect it to be complex and contentious. But it can yield success, prov-ing yet again the remarkable ability of America to take in people from very different parts of the world, to make them into Americans, and to allow them an important role in defining what it means to be an American.

THE CONTINUING DEBATE:
The Cultural Assimilation of Immigrants

What Is New

Perhaps because of the stumbling economy, American attitudes toward undocumented immigrants have become less open than a few years earlier. When asked in 2010 whether immigration reform should focus on allowing (1) "illegal immigrants who have jobs to become legal U.S. residents," or (2) "developing a plan for stopping the flow of illegal immigrants into the U.S. and for deporting those already here" only 42% favored emphasizing legalization, while 57% wanted to stress interdiction and deportation. Yet this opinion about undocumented immigrants has not led to a strong move to cut legal immigration. According to another 2010 poll, a plurality of Americans (47%) wanted current immigration levels to remain the same, 35% wanted them decreased, and 17% wanted them increased. This is actually more open than attitudes in 1995, when a majority (51%) wanted a decrease, only 42% favored the status quo, and a scant 3% supported an increase. As for the melting pot idea, 2010 found 60% favoring that approach over 34% who thought immigrants should strive to maintain their culture.

Where to Find More

A review of immigration policy is Jeb Bush and Thomas F. McLarty, chairs, Report of the Independent Task Force on U.S. Immigration Policy (Council on Foreign Relations, 2009). Current immigration statistics are available from the Department of Homeland Security at www.dhs.gov/files/statistics/. Also see the Congressional Budget Office's *Immigration Policy of the United States* (February 2006) at the agency's Web site, www.cbo.gov/. A group favoring tough immigration laws is NumbersUSA at www.numbersusa.com/. An opposing viewpoint is held by the National Immigration Forum at www.immigrationforum.org/.

What More to Do

One thing to do is to be careful of the history of immigration. It is common to think that things once went smoothly and now have somehow gone off the tracks. Is that true? Talk to people who are, say, third and fourth generation Americans and see what they can recall about how fast their parents, grandparents, and great grandparents "melted in the pot." Then talk to first or second generation Americans, especially from the newer immigrant groups, such as Latinos. Also explore the data on the acculturation of immigrants from these groups and the generations that follow them at the Pew and Kaiser sites noted above and others that are available. Has acculturation really slowed?

PARTICIPATION

REQUIRING PHOTO IDENTIFICATION TO VOTE:
Protecting the Integrity of Elections *or* Suppressing Voter Turnout?

PROTECTING THE INTEGRITY OF ELECTIONS

ADVOCATE: Hans von Spakovsky, Senior Legal Fellow, Center for Legal & Judicial Studies, Heritage Foundation

SOURCE: "Voter Photo Identification: Protecting the Security of Elections," Legal Memorandum #70, Heritage Foundation, July 13, 2011

SUPPRESSING VOTER TURNOUT

ADVOCATE: Shirley Jackson Lee, Democrat, U.S. House of Representatives, Texas

SOURCE: "Voter Suppression and Voter ID," remarks to the U.S. House of Representatives, *Congressional Record*, July 19, 2011

This debate partly involves the collision to two dynamics in American politics. One of those is the effort to increase voter turnout in elections by making it easier to vote. The second movement involves greater scrutiny of people by increased requirements to show identification and by making it more difficult to create fake driver's licenses and other forms of identification.

Increasing voter turnout is certainly a laudable goal. Turnout among the voting-age population of Americans is, at an average of 54% in recent presidential elections, lower than the 63% average for other democracies with presidential elections. There are some mitigating factors, principally the fact that immigrants who are not yet citizens and therefore ineligible to vote make up 8.6% of the U.S. adult population, but these factors do not entirely explain Americans' low turnout.

Numerous steps have been taken in recent decades to increase turnout. Among the changes have been allowing voter registration through motor vehicle departments when getting a license, mail-in voter registration, and shortening the time between registration deadlines and elections to allow, in some cases, even election-day registration. Additionally, most states now permit people to vote up to six weeks before election day, and 29% of all Americans who voted took advantage of that option in 2008.

Colliding with the movement to increase turnout by easing barriers to voting has been the effort to increase identification requirements. Those who favor this cite one or more of three concerns. One is terrorism. Those who raise this point note that the government's official post-9/11 report advised that, "At many entry points to vulnerable facilities, including gates for boarding aircraft, sources of identification are the last opportunity to ensure that people are who they say they are." Illegal aliens are a second concern for many. Those who raise this issue urge more fraud-proof IDs and a greater need to uncover undocumented residents and prevent them for getting jobs, government services, and other benefits. The closely connected third concern is that the electoral process is being compromised by ineligible individuals such as illegal aliens, other noncitizens, and convicted felons using fake IDs to vote. Proposals to implement a national ID card have not succeeded in Congress, but several states have tightened requirements for voter identification. Moreover, Congress did pass the REAL ID Act of 2005 mandating that beginning in 2008 states institute federal technological standards and verification procedures to issue driver's licenses and other state identification cards. Some states have moved to comply, while others have refused to implement the act or dragged their feet. Furthermore, with Janet Napolitano, who opposed the act while governor of Arizona, serving as the Secretary of Homeland Security (which administers the act), there has been no pressure from the Obama administration on states to comply.

In our first reading, Hans von Spakovsky, an analysts at the conservative think tank, the Heritage Foundation, argues that requiring voters to authenticate their identity is a reasonable and easily met requirement and will not negatively impact turnout. Disagreeing, Democratic Texas Congresswoman Shirley Jackson Lee—who according to the *National Journal,* is among the 20% most liberal members of the House of Representatives—terms voter ID as oppressive, compares it to the now-banned poll taxes of yesteryear, and calls for returning to the once standard and acceptable ID requirements such as a birth certificates, a current utility bill, or government check so that seniors and others will not be stopped from voting.

POINTS TO PONDER

➤ When considering this issue, take care not to conflate the issue of voter ID with concerns about terrorism or the non-voter related status and activities of illegal aliens. The issues are largely separate.

➤ Pay careful attention to, and perhaps do some of your own, research into the level of voter fraud through the use of poor or faked IDs. Is the cost of the "fix" (IDs, perhaps enhanced ones) justified by the problem?

➤ Should there be, as some advocate, some level of effort required to vote so that voters are those who have enough interest, have acquired some information about the candidates and issues, and are not simply casting random, uninformed votes?

Requiring Photo Identification to Vote: Protecting the Integrity of Election

Hans Von Spakovsky

Many state legislatures are considering whether to improve election integrity by requiring voters to produce a photograph identification card (voter ID) when they vote at their polling places on Election Day. Georgia, Indiana, Texas, Rhode Island, South Carolina, and Kansas have answered that question with a resounding "yes" by implementing such voter-ID laws. Those states understand that the United States has an unfortunate history of voter fraud and that requiring individuals to authenticate their identity at the polls is a fundamental and necessary component of ensuring the integrity of the election process.

Every individual who is eligible to vote should have the opportunity to do so. It is equally important, however, that the votes of eligible voters are not stolen or diluted by a fraudulent or bogus vote cast by an ineligible or imaginary voter. The evidence from academic studies and actual turnout in elections is also overwhelming that—contrary to the shrill claims of opponents—voter ID does *not* depress the turnout of voters, including minority, poor, and elderly voters.

THE NEED FOR VOTER ID

Requiring voters to authenticate their identity at the polling place is necessary to protect the integrity of elections and access to the voting process. Every illegal vote steals or dilutes the vote of a legitimate voter. Opponents of voter ID claim that it can only prevent impersonation fraud at the polls, which rarely happens. That assertion is incorrect. Voter ID can prevent and deter:

• Impersonation fraud at the polls;

• Voting under fictitious voter registrations;

• Double voting by individuals registered in more than one state or locality; and

• Voting by illegal aliens, or even legal aliens who are still not entitled to vote since state and federal elections are restricted to U.S. citizens.

As the Commission on Federal Election Reform, headed by former President Jimmy Carter and former Secretary of State James Baker, said in 2005:

> The electoral system cannot inspire public confidence if no safeguards exist to deter or detect fraud or to confirm the identity of voters. Photo IDs currently are needed to board a plane, enter federal buildings, and cash a check. Voting is equally important.

Voter fraud does exist, and criminal penalties imposed after the fact are an insufficient deterrent to protect against it. For example, in *Crawford v. Marion County Election Board*, the 2008 case in which the U.S. Supreme Court upheld Indiana's voter ID law, the Court said that despite such criminal penalties:

> It remains true, however, that flagrant examples of such fraud in other parts of the country have been documented throughout this Nation's history by respected historians and journalists, that occasional examples have surfaced in recent

years…that…demonstrate that not only is the risk of voter fraud real but that it could affect the outcome of a close election.

For those trying to defend America's electoral integrity, the stakes are high. The relative rarity of voter fraud prosecutions for impersonation fraud, as the Seventh Circuit Court of Appeals pointed out in the Indiana case, can be "explained by the endemic underenforcement" of voter fraud cases and "the extreme difficulty of apprehending a voter impersonator" without the tools—a voter ID—needed to detect such fraud. This nation should not tolerate even one election being stolen, but without the tools to detect these illegal schemes, it is hard to know just how many close elections are being affected.

In 1984, a dramatic example of such fraud was revealed by a New York State grand jury. The grand jury detailed a widespread conspiracy that operated without detection for 14 years in Brooklyn. This conspiracy involved not only impersonation of legitimate voters at the polls, but also voting under fictitious names. As a result, thousands of fraudulent votes were cast in state and congressional elections.

One of the witnesses before the grand jury described how he led a crew of eight individuals from polling place to polling place to vote. Each member of his crew voted in excess of 20 times, and there were approximately 20 other such crews operating during that election. This extensive impersonation fraud and voting under bogus voter registrations could have been stopped and detected if New York had required voters to authenticate their identity at the polls.

According to the grand jury in the Brooklyn case, the advent of mail-in registration—a form of registration that was implemented nationally with the passage of the National Voter Registration Act of 1993—was also a key factor in perpetrating the fraud. In recent elections, officials have detected numerous fraudulent voter registration forms, many of which were submitted by ACORN—the ethically challenged organization that has been found to have engaged in the submission of tens of thousands of invalid voter registration forms in multiple jurisdictions. Given that most election jurisdictions engage in minimal to nonexistent screening efforts, however, there is no way to know how many invalid registrations slipped through. In states without identification requirements, election officials have no way to prevent the casting of fraudulent votes by unscrupulous individuals based on fictitious voter registrations.

The problem of possible double voting by someone who is registered in two states is illustrated by one of the Indiana voters highlighted by the League of Women Voters in their *Crawford v. Marion County Election Board* amicus brief. This voter was used by the league as an example of someone who had difficulty voting because of the voter ID requirement. However, after an Indiana newspaper interviewed this voter, it turned out that the problems she encountered stemmed from her trying to use a Florida driver's license to vote in Indiana. Not only did she have a Florida driver's license, but she was also registered to vote in Florida where she owned a second home. In fact, she had claimed residency in Florida by filing for a homestead exemption on her property taxes, which is normally only available to individuals who claim residency in a state. So the Indiana law worked as intended: It prevented someone from illegally voting twice.

Since the vast majority of states (and the federal government) will not issue an official identification to an illegal alien, requiring state or federally issued photo IDs can also prevent noncitizens, particularly illegal aliens, from voting in elections. Given the increase in reports of noncitizens voting, such measures are needed. For example:

- The Colorado secretary of state recently testified before Congress that a check of the voter registration rolls indicated over 11,000 individuals who were non-citizens at the time they registered to vote, at least 5,000 of whom likely voted.
- New Mexico Secretary of State Dianna Duran, reported that a preliminary check of voter registration rolls had already found 37 noncitizens that had voted in New Mexico elections.

States that issue driver's licenses to noncitizens who are in the United States legally (and those few remaining states like New Mexico that issue driver's licenses to illegal aliens) should ensure that such licenses note on their face that the holder is *not* a U.S. citizen.

Even though a small amount of fraud can sometimes tip a close election, there is no evidence that there is "massive" voter fraud in the United States—either in general or in any specific state. In fact, election officials around the country do a good job overall of administering elections, especially given their lack of resources. But there are recurring problems with America's voter registration system because many states do not do an adequate job of checking the accuracy and validity of new voter registrations.

The potential for abuse and the casting of fraudulent ballots by ineligible voters (like illegal aliens or persons registered in more than one state) or in the names of fake voters, dead voters, or voters who have moved but whose names remain on the registration list exists, and such fraud has occurred in many reported cases. As the Supreme Court recognized, there is a "real risk that voter fraud could affect a close election's outcome." There are enough incidents and reported cases of actual voter fraud to make it very clear that America must take the steps necessary to make such fraud harder to commit. Requiring voter ID is just one such common-sense step that can stop or deter many of these problems.

VOTER ID DOES NOT REDUCE TURNOUT

States must protect the security of the election process, but they must also ensure that every eligible individual is able to vote. Not only does voter ID help to prevent fraudulent voting, but where it has been implemented, it has not reduced turnout. Despite many false claims to the contrary, there is no evidence that voter ID decreases the turnout of voters or has a disparate impact on minority, poor, or elderly voters; the overwhelming majority of Americans have a photo ID or can easily obtain one. Democratic Senator Harold Metts, who sponsored Rhode Island's voter ID law, said that "as a minority citizen and a senior citizen, I would not support anything that I thought would present obstacles or limit protections."

Numerous studies have borne out the fact that requiring an ID to vote does not depress turnout. For example:

- A study by the University of Missouri on turnout in Indiana showed that turnout actually *increased* by about 2 percentage points overall in Indiana in 2006 in the first election after the voter ID law went into effect. There was no evidence that counties with higher percentages of minority, poor, elderly, or less-educated populations suffered any reduction in voter turnout. In fact, "the only consistent and statistically significant impact of photo ID in Indiana is to increase voter turnout in counties with a greater percentage of Democrats relative to other counties."

- In September 2007, The Heritage Foundation released a study analyzing the 2004 election turnout data for all states. This study found that voter ID laws do not reduce the turnout of voters, including African-Americans and Hispanics. Such voters were just as likely to vote in states with ID as in states where just their names were asked at the polling place.

- A study by the University of Delaware and the University of Nebraska–Lincoln examined data from the 2000, 2002, 2004, and 2006 elections. At both the aggregate and individual levels, the study found that voter ID laws do not affect turnout, including across racial/ethnic/socioeconomic lines. The study concludes that "concerns about voter identification laws affecting turnout are much ado about nothing."

- A survey by American University of registered voters in Maryland, Indiana, and Mississippi to see whether registered voters had photo IDs concluded that "showing a photo ID as a requirement of voting does not appear to be a serious problem in any of the states" because "[a]lmost all registered voters have an acceptable form of photo ID." Less than 0.5 percent of respondents had neither a photo ID nor citizenship documentation. A 2008 election survey of 12,000 registered voters in all 50 states found that fewer than nine people were unable to vote because of voter ID requirements.

- In 2010, a Rasmussen poll of likely voters in the United States showed overwhelming support (82 percent) for requiring photo ID in order to vote in elections. This support runs across ethnic and racial lines; Rasmussen reports that "[t]his is a sentiment that spans demographics, as majorities in every demographic agree."

- A similar study by John Lott in 2006 also found no effect on voter turnout and, in fact, found an indication that reducing voter fraud (through means such as voter ID) may have a positive impact on voter turnout.

That is certainly true in a classic case of voter fraud committed in Greene County, Alabama. In that county, which is 80 percent African-American, voter turnout increased after several successful voter fraud prosecutions instilled new confidence in local voters regarding the integrity of the election process.

Actual election results in Georgia and Indiana also confirm that suppositions about voter ID hurting minority turnout are incorrect. Turnout in both states increased more dramatically in 2008 in both the presidential preference primary *and* the general election in the first presidential elections held after their photo ID laws went into effect than they did in some states *without* photo ID.

There was record turnout in Georgia in the 2008 presidential primary election—over 2 million voters, more than twice as much as in 2004 when the voter photo ID law was not in effect (the law was first applied to local elections in 2007). The number of African-Americans voting in the 2008 primary also doubled from 2004. In fact, there were 100,000 more votes in the Democratic primary than in the Republican primary, and the number of individuals who had to vote with a provisional ballot because they had not obtained the free photo ID available from the state was less that 0.01 percent.

In the 2008 general election when President Barack Obama was elected, Georgia, with one of the strictest voter ID laws in the nation, had the largest turnout in its history—more than 4 million voters. Democratic turnout was up an astonishing 6.1 percentage points from the 2004 election when there was no photo ID requirement, the fifth largest increase of any state.

Overall turnout in Georgia went up 6.7 percentage points, the second highest increase in the country and a striking jump even in an election year when there was a general increase in turnout over the prior presidential election. The black share of the statewide vote increased from 25 percent in 2004 to 30 percent in 2008 according to the Joint Center for Political and Economic Studies. And according to Census Bureau surveys, 65 percent of the black voting-age population voted in the 2008 election compared to only 54.4 percent in 2004, an increase of over 10 percentage points.

By contrast, the Democratic turnout in the nearby state of Mississippi, also a state with a high percentage of black voters but without a voter ID requirement, increased by only 2.35 percentage points. Turnout in the 2010 congressional election in Georgia was over 2.6 million voters—an increase of almost 500,000 voters over the 2006 election. While only 42.9 percent of registered black Georgians voted in 2006, 50.4 percent voted in 2010 with the voter ID law in effect, an increase of over 7 percentage points. As Georgia's secretary of state recently pointed out, when compared to the 2006 election, voter turnout in 2010 "among African Americans outpaced the growth of that population's pool of registered voters by more than 20 percentage points."

The Georgia voter ID requirement went into effect because it was upheld in final orders issued by every state and federal court in Georgia that reviewed the law, including the Eleventh Circuit Court of Appeals and, most recently, the Georgia Supreme Court. As these courts held, such an ID requirement is not discriminatory and does not violate the Constitution or any federal voting rights laws, including the Voting Rights Act of 1965.

In Georgia, as has happened in every state that has considered voter ID legislation, organizations like the ACLU and the NAACP made specious claims that there were hundreds of thousands of voters without photo ID. Yet when dismissing all of their claims, the federal court pointed out that after two years of litigation, none of the plaintiff organizations like the NAACP had been able to produce a single individual or member who did not have a photo ID or could not easily obtain one. The district court judge concluded that:

> [This] failure to identify those individuals "is particularly acute" in light of the Plaintiffs' contention that a large number of Georgia voters lack acceptable Photo ID…. [T]he fact that Plaintiffs, in spite of their efforts, have failed to uncover anyone "who can attest to the fact that he/she will be prevented from voting" provides significant support for a conclusion that the photo ID requirement does not unduly burden the right to vote.

Clearly, such erroneous claims are an attempt only to frustrate proponents of voter ID.

In Indiana, which the U.S. Supreme Court said has the strictest voter ID law in the country, turnout in the Democratic presidential preference primary in 2008 quadrupled from the 2004 election when the photo ID law was not in effect—in fact, there were 862,000 more votes cast in the Democratic primary than in the Republican primary. In the general election in November, the turnout of Democratic voters increased by 8.32 percentage points from 2004, the largest increase in Democratic turnout of any state in the nation. According to Census Bureau surveys, 59.2 percent of the black voting-age population voted in the 2008 election compared to only 53.8 percent in 2004, an increase of over 5 percentage points.

The neighboring state of Illinois, with no photo ID requirement and President Obama's home state, had an increase in Democratic turnout of only 4.4 percentage points—only half of Indiana's increase. Turnout in the 2010 congressional election in Indiana was almost 1.75 million voters, an increase of more than 77,000 voters over the 2006 election. Indiana was one of the states with a "large and impressive" increase in black turnout in the 2010 election: "the black share of the state vote was higher in 2010 than it was in 2008, a banner year for black turnout." In fact, the black share of the total vote went from only 7 percent in 2008 to 12 percent in 2010 (this in the state with the strictest voter ID law in the country).

One misleading story constantly relied on by opponents of Indiana's ID law is the claim that elderly nuns in Indiana "were turned away from the polls for lack of picture IDs." In fact, the nuns had pointedly refused to obtain photo IDs to vote prior to the election and were turned away from the polls by another nun who ran the convent precinct, violating federal and state law that required her to provide the nuns with provisional ballots. Those ballots would have been counted if the nuns had gone to the county clerk's office within 10 days after the election to show an ID or sign an affidavit testifying to their identity. An office where they could have easily obtained an ID was only two miles from the convent. These nuns were also all over 65, automatically entitling them to vote by absentee ballot without an ID.

The nuns could have voted without difficulty were it not for their refusal (not inability) to comply with Indiana law and the refusal of the precinct election official, their fellow sister, to comply with federal and state law. This incident raises the question of whether the entire incident was trumped up to generate misleading news from gullible reporters and sympathetic activists.

Just as in the federal case in Georgia, the federal court in Indiana noted the complete inability of the plaintiffs in that case to produce anyone who would not be able to vote because of the photo ID law:

> Despite apocalyptic assertions of wholesale voter disenfranchisement, Plaintiffs have produced not a single piece of evidence of any identifiable registered voter who would be prevented from voting pursuant to [the photo ID law] because of his or her inability to obtain the necessary photo identification. Similarly, Plaintiffs have failed to produce any evidence of any individual, registered or unregistered, who would have to obtain photo identification in order to vote, let alone anyone who would undergo any appreciable hardship to obtain photo identification in order to be qualified to vote.

Despite the efforts of opponents of voter ID, such specious claims have failed to gain traction in any courtroom across the country.

Finally, opponents of voter ID laws have charged that requiring an ID, even when it is free, is a "poll tax" because of the incidental costs, such as possible travel to a registrar's office or obtaining a birth certificate, that may be involved. Such a "poll tax" claim, for instance, was recently raised in Georgia. The federal court, however, dismissed this claim, agreeing with the Indiana federal court that:

[Such an argument] represents a dramatic overstatement of what fairly constitutes a "poll tax." Thus, the imposition of tangential burdens does not transform a regulation into a poll tax. Moreover, the cost of time and transportation cannot plausibly qualify as a prohibited poll tax because those same "costs" also result from voter registration and in-person voting requirements, which one would not reasonably construe as a poll tax.

Clearly, these absurd cries of "poll tax," are simply another tactic in the increasingly desperate campaign against voter ID legislation.

CONCLUSION

Despite all of the evidence to the contrary, opponents of voter ID refuse to admit that voter turnout is unaffected by such a requirement. Their claim that the implementation of voter ID laws "smacks of vote suppression" is preposterous and an outrageous libel on the American people and their elected representatives. The vitriolic rhetoric engaged in by opponents of voter ID is a sign of desperation; their claims of "suppression" and "intimidation" have been shown to be completely untrue.

America is one of the only democracies in the world that does not uniformly require voters to present photo ID when they vote. Across the globe, democracies administer such a requirement without any problems and without any reports that their citizens are in any way burdened when voting.

In fact, America's southern neighbor Mexico, which has a much larger rate of poverty than the United States, requires both a photo ID and a thumbprint to vote—and turnout has increased in Mexican elections since this requirement went into effect in the 1990s. Mexico's voter ID laws are also credited with reducing the fraud that had prevailed in many Mexican elections and "allowing the 2000 election of Vicente Fox, the first opposition party candidate to be elected president of Mexico in seventy years."

Requiring voters to authenticate their identity is a perfectly reasonable and easily met requirement. Such measures are supported by the vast majority of voters of all races and ethnic backgrounds. As the U.S. Supreme Court has noted, voter ID protects the integrity and reliability of the electoral process. All states have a valid and legitimate state interest not only in deterring and detecting voter fraud, but also in maintaining the confidence of their citizens in the security of U.S. elections.

Requiring Photo Identification to Vote: Suppressing Voter Turnout

Shirley Jackson Lee

I rise to oppose the epidemic across America of voter suppression and requiring voter ID.

Do you realize that in almost every election in my own State of Texas there has been discrimination, intimidation to voters? Where we used to be able to use a birth certificate, a utility bill, government check, paycheck, and other documents, now we cannot because someone suggests that someone will steal someone's birth certificate to impersonate a voter. I don't think that's right.

What we need now is to eliminate the poll tax of the 21st century. Barbara Jordan [once an African American member of Congress and Democrat from Texas] recognized that voting is a right, not a privilege, and she stood in the gap to ensure that Texas was covered by the Voting Rights Act. Barbara Jordan would not be here today if we had the voter intimidation that we're seeing growing across America.

Eliminate voter intimidation by elimination of the oppressive voter ID requirement by returning to the standard and acceptable requirements such as birth certificates, current utility bill, government check which provide the protection to protect the vote so that seniors and others will not be stopped from voting.

INTRODUCTION

Today, we address an issue that disturbs the very foundation of our Nation; the right of each and every citizen to participate in electing their representatives in government. Enshrined in our Constitution by our Nation's founders, this fundamental right is the linchpin of our democracy.

Unfortunately, the right to vote was not recognized for all people in this country at its inception. Indeed, for the several decades after the signing of the Constitution, the right to vote belonged to white men who owned property alone.

Through a long-fought effort by dedicated activists, courageous legislators and judges, and with the gradual evolution of public sentiment, the voting franchise was extended by law to all white men, non-white men, women, native Americans, and then finally, to all citizens over the age of 18.

However, even though the right to vote was legally recognized for all citizens of age, there have always been sinister efforts to suppress the vote of certain citizens who were guaranteed the right to vote by the Constitution.

Through poll taxes, grandfather clauses, literacy tests, intimidation and outright violence, voter suppression remained an agenda by those who do not believe in the principle of one person, one vote, and who seek to keep certain groups from participating in our democracy.

VOTER ID

Voter photo identification legislation a recent phenomenon and the latest tactic of the voter suppression agenda. Only a decade ago, in any of our 50 states, a voter could set out on election Tuesday and be permitted to vote in his or her respective state without being required to present a photo ID to election officials.

Alarmingly, since that time, 15 states have adopted photo ID requirements for voting. In fact, at least 34 states have introduced legislation requiring voters to produce photo IDs at the voting booth in this year alone. Seven states, including my home state of Texas, have adopted the strictest form of voter photo ID legislation with the fewest exceptions.

This raises the question: what caused these states to, after more than two centuries of holding elections without photo ID requirements, impose such a burden on voters? Proponents of these laws argue that voter identification fraud is an epidemic in America, while there has been little documented evidence. Voter impersonation fraud occurs when one person votes using the identity of another.

In order to obtain a state-issued photo ID valid under these statues, states often charge fees. Moreover the documents used for proof of identity in order to obtain photo IDs, such as birth certificates and social security cards, also cost money. When added together, along with transportation costs, the amount of money required to obtain an acceptable form of identification can be substantial for a citizen who lacks the financial means to do so.

Harper v. Virginia Board of Elections, a Supreme Court case decided in 1966, outlawed the Jim Crow requirement that a citizen pay a poll tax in order to be allowed to vote in an election. In its decision, the Court said—quote—"We conclude that a State violates the Equal Protection Clause of the Fourteenth Amendment whenever it makes the affluence of the voter or payment of any fee an electoral standard."

However, with voter photo ID requirements, those who would suppress the rights of citizens to vote would have vote a way to implement a backdoor poll tax. Voters without valid, non-expired state or federal government issued identification documents will be burdened with the expenses of obtaining one of those prescribed forms of ID.

Because of the state's so-called "rational basis" for requiring photo identification in order to vote, Indiana's state photo ID law was upheld by the Supreme Court in *Crawford* in 2008.

The effects of such a ruling are unduly discriminatory and target specific groups of voters: low income voters, racial and ethnic minorities, senior citizens, disabled voters, and college students. I will leave you to guess which party has been behind the concerted and overzealous efforts by state legislatures and governors to push these discriminatory bills.

Eleven percent of the population, or roughly 21 million people, do not have a government-issued photo identification document.

Nationwide, depending on the state, African-Americans are 2 or 3 times as likely as their white counterparts to lack government-issued photo identification. Nearly a fifth of our seniors do not have government-issued photo IDs.

We must remember that voting is a right under our Constitution, not a privilege. We must prevent this effort to turn back the hands of time in order to prevent eligible voters from exercising their Constitutional rights.

TEXAS

Now, I am sad to report that my home state of Texas has been the latest victim of the systematic effort to suppress votes all around America. In late May [2011], [Republican] Governor Rick Perry signed into law the Texas iteration of voter photo identification legislation, which was based upon the extremely restrictive Indiana photo ID law.

The history and current state of discriminatory voter suppression in Texas is so pervasive that any substantive change to its election law must be submitted by preclearance to the Department of Justice under Section 5 of the Voting Rights Act. This makes Texas one of the 9 states in our country that must submit election law alterations, such as photo ID requirements, to the Department of Justice before the changes are permitted to take effect. The law is set to take effect in January next year.

Currently, Texas election law allows voters to use their birth certificate, a current utility bill, a government check, a paycheck, official mail addressed to them, and other documents in lieu of a driver's license issued by the state or a U.S. passport. These documents have long been sufficient in the state of Texas to prove one's identity for the purposes of voting.

However, once the new law takes effect, those alternative forms of identification will be unavailable to citizens of Texas. In fact, Texan voters will be unable to use their birth certificate, which is issued by the State of Texas, in order to vote.

Now, this fact is particularly revealing, especially in light of the purported reason for passing voter photo identification legislation, which is to combat a "supposed" widespread problem of voter impersonation fraud.

If we are to accept their argument that the voter photo ID laws are for the purpose of preventing voter impersonation fraud, then why not continue to allow people to use birth certificates? By banning citizens from using their state-issued birth certificates, we are required to believe the ridiculous and unfounded notion of people stealing other people's birth certificates in order to show up at an election to vote! Where is the sense in that? I don't know about you, but I have never heard a single case in which a person stole someone else's birth certificate and then showed up at the polls and voted as that person.

No, the fact that birth certificates were removed from Texas election law as a permissible form of identification reveals that voter impersonation fraud is merely a pretextual argument; a guise under which the real purpose of suppressing the votes of certain people can be achieved. That is something for which we cannot stand.

However, while a birth certificate is no longer good enough to prove your identity for the purpose of voting in the State of Texas, "coincidentally," the new law does allow voters to use concealed handgun licenses in order to be permitted to cast their ballots.

There is no doubt that the Texas Voter ID law was specifically crafted with the intent to impose new obligations on the rights of certain Texans to vote, while attempting to preserve the rights of other citizens they believe to be predisposed to voting a certain way.

This is wrong in the State of Texas, and it is wrong in America.

CONCLUSION

In the *Harper* Supreme Court case, Justice Douglas closed his majority opinion with these words: "Wealth or fee paying has, in our view, no relation to voting qualifications; the right to vote is too precious, too fundamental to be so burdened or conditioned."

THE CONTINUING DEBATE
Requiring Photo Identification to Vote

What Is New

With the Democrats and Republicans in a virtual standoff in Congress, efforts to increase identification requirements in federal elections and countervailing proposals to bar states from imposing tighter requirements are stalemated. That leaves the action on this issue in the states. As of August 2011, twenty states had no ID requirements to vote. Of the thirty states with a requirement, seven accept only a photo ID. Another seven ask for a photo ID but allow people without one to vote if they swear to their identity or meet some other criterion. And sixteen states accept either photo or non-photo IDs such as a utility bill. The trend is toward tightening ID requirements. Five of the seven states that accept only photo IDs added that requirement during 2011. Efforts to challenge enhanced requirements as unconstitutional have largely failed, with the Supreme Court rejecting challenges to changes by Arizona (2006) and Indiana (2007).

Where to Find More

Voter identification requirements in the states are available from the National Conference of State Legislatures at www.ncsl.org/. Look for "Elections and Campaigns" under the drop-down menu "Legislatures and Election." For a review of the factors that lead states to adopt or reject enhanced voter ID requirements, read Kathleen Hale and Ramona McNeal, "Election Administration Reform and State Choice: Voter Identification Requirements and HAVA," *Policy Studies Journal* (2010). What Americans think about this debate is examined in Michael Alvarez, Thad E. Hall, Ines Levin, and Charles Stewart III, "Voter Opinions about Election Reform: Do They Support Making Voting More Convenient?" *Election Law Journal* (2011).

What More to Do

Consider the voter photo ID issue at two levels. At one, presenting a driver's license or some other photo ID is neither a huge barrier to a legitimate voter nor to someone who is ineligible to vote but is willing to go to the effort and expense of getting a fake ID. At the second level, this debate is being driven by the REAL ID Act of 2005 and its strict requirements for getting a state-issued photo ID. Under that act, state-issued licenses and other ID cards will only be acceptable for federal purposes (such as boarding aircraft) if the card has specific tamper-proof qualities, has a barcode or other machine-readable feature, and is issued only after an individuals presents verifiable documents giving their social security number, legal status, address, birth date, and other personal information. Opponents fear that this approaches a national ID card and that the machine-readable aspect will allow the government to track people as not only the government, but banks, stores, and others ask for the ID to conduct business.

7

MEDIA

THE FUTURE OF QUALITY JOURNALISM:
Imperiled *or* Secure?

IMPERILED

ADVOCATE: David Simon, creator and executive producer of the HBO television series *The Wire*

SOURCE: Testimony during hearings on Senate Subcommittee on "The Future of Journalism" before the U.S. Senate, Committee on Commerce, Science, and Transportation; Subcommittee on Communications, Technology, and the Internet, May 6, 2009

SECURE

ADVOCATE: Arianna Huffington, founder of the *Huffington Post*

SOURCE: Testimony during hearings on Senate Subcommittee on "The Future of Journalism" before the U.S. Senate, Committee on Commerce, Science, and Transportation; Subcommittee on Communications, Technology, and the Internet, May 6, 2009

Journalism is undergoing profound change. Until about 40 years ago, the daily sources of news easily available to most Americans were limited to one newspaper, perhaps two in the larger cities, and to the three major broadcast television networks, ABC, CBS, and NBC. Then, like now, radio was ubiquitous, but its role in news delivery was marginal.

Then technology began to rapidly and dramatically reconfigure the news media. In 1980 CNN began broadcasting on the technological upstart, cable television. Then Fox network with its news programming was launched, in the 1990s Microsoft and NBC joined to begin MSNBC, cable companies added foreign sources of news like the BBC, and specialty new channels like the Weather channel and CNBC (business) emerged, as did Univision and other foreign language networks with newscasts. The advent of the Internet further accelerated change. Now almost all U.S. daily newspapers and scores of foreign dailies, often in English, are available online. All the broadcast and cable news networks and many of their foreign counterparts are also available online. Beyond these, there is a wide range of relatively new ways to transmit news widely and quickly. Some are organized operations such as the liberal *Huffington Post*, edited by the author of the second article in this debate, the conservative *Drudge Report*, and the less ideological *Politico.com*. At the other end of the organizational range are the billions of email and text messages that people use daily to exchange their views individually. For collective interchanges, there are at least 112 million blog sites. Almost all of this wide array of Internet sites are free, and many include streaming video and other innovative techniques to enhance their product.

Because such ways of transmitting news are so new and because getting good data is exceptionally difficult, it is unclear what their overall impact is or will be. For now, though, consider the following indications of the rise of non-traditional sources of news:

• 37% of Americans go online daily to get news, and another 8% do so 3 to 5 days a week.

- 29% reported recently getting online news from a source other than a newspaper Web site.
- 27% report getting a news story from a friend by email within the last week.
- 14% report sending a news story to a friend by email within the last week.
- 36% have news feeds on their homepage.
- 15% regularly and 21% sometimes read blogs about politics or current events.
- 3% regularly and 9% sometimes read online magazines such as *Salon* or *Slate*.
- 10% regularly and 20% sometimes get news through social networking pages such as MySpace and Facebook.
- 6% regularly and 18% sometimes share information about local, national, or international news through a social networking page.

Among the traditional sources of news, newspapers have suffered most from this competition. Most Americans (61%) still cite television as their primary news source, but in 2007 the Internet (17%) replaced newspapers (16%) as the second-most used primary source. Concomitantly, daily newspaper circulation between 1985 and 2008 sagged 62 to 48 million copies. Drops in circulation led to declines in ad revenues. These forced major cutbacks, with newspapers losing 17% of their staff between 2001 and 2008. The increases that print newspapers have gained in online readership and ad revenue have fallen far short of losses from their print side. As a result, some papers like the *Baltimore Examiner*, *Tucson Citizen*, and *Cincinnati Post* have closed. The *Seattle Post-Intelligencer*, *Detroit Free Press*, *Christian Science Monitor*, and others have either gone entirely online or only publish printed editions a few times a week.

The debate here is about the "so what" of this shift in the sources of news. David Simon sees dire results from the decline of newspapers. He partly blames the newspaper industry, but whatever the cause, he believes that in-depth professional journalism is in danger, thereby endangering the ability of the people to keep track of their government. He views news sources like the *Huffington Post*, as "parasites" that contribute little more than "repetition" and "froth." Anne Huffington disagrees, and sees the new era of journalism as a "golden age" of increased opportunities for people to get news through a range of quality sources.

While the debate here focuses on newspapers, television news is also struggling. The number of people watching the evening news on one of the major broadcast or cable networks fell 35% to 26.3 million between 1993 and 2008. Adding to the worries that many have about the traditional press is the criticism that it has tried to boost its audience and revenues by "dumbing down" its coverage to the point where it is ever harder to distinguish, for example, between the *CBS Evening News* and *Entertainment Tonight*, which follows on many CBS stations.

POINTS TO PONDER

➤ Simon implicitly equates professional journalists with high-quality news. Do you agree that newspaper offer high-quality journalism?

➤ Think about what sources you go to for news, and ask yourself why you use these sources.

➤ Consider Huffington's praise of "citizen journalism," and ask yourself whether you agree.

The Future of Quality Journalism: Imperiled

DAVID SIMON

Thank you all for the invitation and opportunity to speak on this issue today, but I start by confessing reluctance.

My name is David Simon, and I used to be a newspaperman in Baltimore. Head and heart, I was a newspaperman from the day I signed up at my high school paper until the day, eighteen years later, when I took a buyout from the *Baltimore Sun* and left for the fleshpots of Hollywood [Simon became involved in popular entertainment, most notably creating the HBO police series set in Baltimore, *The Wire*].

To those colleagues who remain at newspapers, I am therefore an apostate, and my direct connection to "newspapering"—having ended in 1995—means that as a witness today, my experiences are attenuated.

Ideally, rather than listening to me, you should be hearing from any number of voices of those still laboring in American journalism. I am concerned that the collective voice of the newsroom itself—the wisdom of veteran desk editors, rewrite men and veteran reporters is poorly represented in this process. But of course newspapers are obliged to cover Congress and its works, and therefore the participation of most working journalists in today's hearing would compromise some careful ethics. I know your staff tried to invite working journalists but were rebuffed on these grounds. And so, tellingly, today's witness list is heavy with newspaper executives on the one hand, and representatives of the new, internet-based media on the other.

And so, I've accepted the invitation, though to be honest, I'm tired of hearing myself on this subject; I've had my say in essays that accompany this testimony, and in the episodes of a recent television drama, and I would be more inclined to hear from former colleagues if they were in a position to speak bluntly....

What I say will likely conflict with what representatives of the newspaper industry will claim for themselves. And I can imagine little agreement with those who speak for new media. From the captains of the newspaper industry, you will hear a certain "martyrology"—a claim that they were heroically serving democracy to their utmost only to be undone by a cataclysmic shift in technology and the arrival of all things web-based. From those speaking on behalf of new media, weblogs and that which goes twitter, you will be treated to assurances that American journalism has a perfectly fine future online, and that a great democratization in newsgathering is taking place.

In my city, there is a technical term we often administer when claims are plainly contradicted by facts on the ground. We note that the claimant is, for lack of a better term, full of it. Though in Baltimore, of course, we are explicit with our nouns.

High-end journalism is dying in America and unless a new economic model is achieved, it will not be reborn on the web or anywhere else. The internet is a marvelous tool and clearly it is the informational delivery system of our future, but thus far it does not deliver much first-generation reporting. Instead, it leeches that reporting from mainstream news publications, whereupon aggregating web sites and bloggers contribute little more than repetition, commentary and froth. Meanwhile, readers acquire news from the aggregators and abandon its point of origin—namely the newspapers themselves.

—In short, the parasite is slowly killing the host.

It is nice to get stuff for free, of course. And it is nice that more people can have their say in new media. And while some of our internet commentary is—as with any unchallenged and unedited intellectual effort—rampantly ideological, ridiculously inaccurate and occasionally juvenile, some of it is also quite good, even original.

Understand here that I am not making a Luddite argument against the internet and all that it offers. But democratized and independent though they may be, you do not—in my city—run into bloggers or so-called citizen journalists at City Hall, or in the courthouse hallways or at the bars and union halls where police officers gather. You do not see them consistently nurturing and then pressing sources. You do not see them holding institutions accountable on a daily basis.

Why? Because high-end journalism—that which acquires essential information about our government and society in the first place—is a profession; it requires daily, full-time commitment by trained men and women who return to the same beats day in and day out until the best of them know everything with which a given institution is contending. For a relatively brief period in American history—no more than the last fifty years or so—a lot of smart and talented people were paid a living wage and benefits to challenge the unrestrained authority of our institutions and to hold those institutions to task. Modern newspaper reporting was the hardest and in some ways the most gratifying job I ever had. I am offended to think that anyone, anywhere believes American institutions as insulated, self-preserving and self-justifying as police departments, school systems, legislatures and chief executives can be held to gathered facts by amateurs pursuing the task without compensation, training, or for that matter, sufficient standing to make public officials even care to whom it is they are lying or from whom they are withholding information.

The idea of this is absurd, yet to read the claims that some new media voices are already making, you would think they need only bulldoze the carcasses of moribund newspapers aside and begin typing. They don't know what they don't know—which is a dangerous state for any class of folk—and to those of us who do understand how subtle and complex good reporting can be, their ignorance is as embarrassing as it is seemingly sincere. Indeed, the very phrase citizen journalist strikes my ear as nearly Orwellian. A neighbor who is a good listener and cares about people is a good neighbor; he is not in any sense a citizen social worker. Just as a neighbor with a garden hose and good intentions is not a citizen firefighter. To say so is a heedless insult to trained social workers and firefighters.

—So much for new media. But what about old media?

When you hear a newspaper executive claiming that his industry is an essential bulwark of society and that it stands threatened by a new technology that is, as of yet, unready to shoulder the same responsibility, you may be inclined to empathize. And indeed, that much is true enough as it goes.

But when that same newspaper executive then goes on to claim that this predicament has occurred through no fault on the industry's part, that they have merely been undone by new technologies, feel free to kick out his teeth. At that point, he's as fraudulent as the most self-aggrandized blogger.

Anyone listening carefully may have noted that I was bought out of my reporting position in 1995. That's fourteen years ago. That's well before the internet ever began to seriously threaten any aspect of the industry. That's well before Craigslist and department-store consolidation gutted the ad base. Well before any of the current economic conditions applied.

In fact, when newspaper chains began cutting personnel and content, their industry was one of the most profitable yet discovered by Wall Street money. We know now—because bankruptcy has opened the books—that the *Baltimore Sun* was eliminating its afternoon edition and trimming nearly 100 editors and reporters in an era when the paper was achieving 37 percent profits. In the years before the internet deluge, the men and women who might have made *The Sun* a more essential vehicle for news and commentary—something so strong that it might have charged for its product online—they were being ushered out the door so that Wall Street could command short-term profits in the extreme.

Such short-sighted arrogance rivals that of Detroit in the 1970s, when automakers—confident that American consumers were mere captives—offered up Chevy Vegas, and Pacers and Gremlins without the slightest worry that mediocrity would be challenged by better-made cars from Germany or Japan.

In short, my industry butchered itself and we did so at the behest of Wall Street and the same unfettered, free-market logic that has proved so disastrous for so many American industries. And the original sin of American newspapering lies, indeed, in going to Wall Street in the first place.

When locally-based, family-owned newspapers like *The Sun* were consolidated into publicly-owned newspaper chains, an essential dynamic, an essential trust between journalism and the communities served by that journalism was betrayed.

Economically, the disconnect is now obvious. What do newspaper executives in Los Angeles or Chicago care whether or not readers in Baltimore have a better newspaper, especially when you can make more putting out a mediocre paper than a worthy one? The profit margin was all. And so, where family ownership might have been content with 10 or 15 percent profit, the chains demanded double that and more, and the cutting began—long before the threat of new technology was ever sensed.

But editorially? The newspaper chains brought an ugly disconnect to the newsroom, and by extension, to the community as well. A few years after the A.S. Abell Family sold *The Sun* to the Times-Mirror newspaper chain, fresh editors arrived from out of town to take over the reins of the paper.

They looked upon Baltimore not as essential terrain to be covered with consistency, to be explained in all its complexity year in and year out for readers who had and would live their lives in Baltimore. Why would they? They had arrived from somewhere else, and if they could win a prize or two, they would be moving on to bigger and better opportunities within the chain.

So, well before the arrival of the internet, as veteran reporters and homegrown editors took buyouts, newsbeats were dropped and less and less of Baltimore and central Maryland were covered with rigor or complexity.

In a city in which half the adult black males are without consistent work, the poverty and social services beat was abandoned. In a town where the unions were imploding and the working class eviscerated, where the bankruptcy of a huge steel manufacturer meant thousands were losing medical benefits and pensions, there was no longer a labor reporter. And though it is one of the most violent cities in America, the Baltimore courthouse went uncovered for more than a year and the declining quality of criminal casework in the state's attorney's office went largely ignored.

Meanwhile, the editors used their manpower to pursue a handful of special projects, Pulitzer-sniffing as one does. The self-gratification of my profession does not come, you see, from covering a city and covering it well, from explaining an increasingly complex and interconnected world to citizens, from holding basic institutions accountable on a daily basis. It comes from someone handing you a plaque and taking your picture.

The prizes meant little, of course, to actual readers. What might have mattered to them, what might have made the *Baltimore Sun* substantial enough to charge online for content would have been to comprehensively cover its region and the issues of that region, to do so with real insight and sophistication and consistency.

But the reporters required to achieve such were cleanly dispatched, buyout after buyout, from the first staff reduction in 1992 to the latest round last week, in which nearly a third of the remaining newsroom was fired. Where 500 men and women once covered central Maryland, there are now 140. And the money required to make a great newspaper—including, say, the R&D funding that might have anticipated and planned for the internet revolution—all of that went back to Wall Street, to CEO salaries and to big-money investors. The executives and board chairman held up their profit margins and got promoted; they're all on some golf course in Florida right now, comfortably retired and thinking about things other than journalism. The editors took their prizes and got promoted; they're probably on what passes for a journalism lecture circuit these days, offering heroic tales of past glory and jeremiads about the world they, in fact, helped to bring about.

—But the newspapers themselves?

When I was in journalism school in the 1970s, the threat was television and its immediacy. My professors claimed that in order to survive, newspapers were going to have to cede the ambulance chasing and reactive coverage to TV and instead become more like great magazines. Specialization and detailed beat reporting were the future. We were going to have to explain an increasingly complex world in ways that made us essential to an increasingly educated readership. The scope of coverage would have to go deeper, address more of the world not less. Those were our ambitions. Those were my ambitions.

In Baltimore at least, and I imagine in every other American city served by newspaper-chain journalism, those ambitions were not betrayed by the internet. We had trashed them on our own, years before. Incredibly, we did it for naked, short-term profits and a handful of trinkets to hang on the office wall. And now, having made ourselves less essential, less comprehensive and less able to offer a product that people might purchase online, we pretend to an undeserved martyrdom at the hands of new technology.

I don't know if it isn't too late already for American newspapering. So much talent has been torn from newsrooms over the last two decades and the ambitions of the craft are now so crude, small-time and stunted that it's hard to imagine a turnaround. But if there is to be a renewal of the industry a few things are certain and obvious:

First, cutting down trees and printing a daily accounting of the world on paper and delivering it to individual doorsteps is anachronistic. And if that is so, then the industry is going to have to find a way to charge for online content. Yes, I have heard the post-modern rallying cry that information wants to be free. But information isn't. It costs money to send reporters to London, Fallujah and Capitol Hill, and to send photographers with them, and to keep them there day after day. It costs money to hire the best investigators and writers and then to back them up with the best editors. It costs money to do the finest kind of journalism. And how anyone can believe that the industry can fund that kind of expense by giving its product away online to aggregators and bloggers is a source of endless fascination to me. A freshman marketing major at any community college can tell you that if you don't have a product for which you can charge people, you don't actually have a product.

Second, Wall Street and free-market logic, having been a destructive force in journalism over the last few decades, are not now suddenly the answer. Raw, unencumbered capitalism is never the answer when a public trust or public mission is at issue. If the last quarter century has taught us anything—and admittedly, with too many of us, I doubt it has—it's that free-market capitalism, absent social imperatives and responsible regulatory oversight, can produce durable goods and services, glorious profits, and little of lasting social value. Airlines, manufacturing, banking, real estate—is there a sector of the American economy where laissez-faire theories have not burned the poor, the middle class and the consumer, while bloating the rich and mortgaging the very future of the industry, if not the country itself? I'm pressed to think of one.

Similarly, there can be no serious consideration of public funding for newspapers. High-end journalism can and should bite any hand that tries to feed it, and it should bite a government hand most viciously. Moreover, it is the right of every American to despise his local newspaper—for being too liberal or too conservative, for covering X and not covering Y, for spelling your name wrong when you do something notable and spelling it correctly when you are seen as dishonorable. And it is the birthright of every healthy newspaper to hold itself indifferent to such constant disdain and be nonetheless read by all. Because in the end, despite all flaws, there is no better model for a comprehensive and independent review of society than a modern newspaper. As love-hate relationships go, this is a pretty intricate one. An exchange of public money would pull both sides from their comfort zone and prove unacceptable to all.

But a non-profit model intrigues, especially if that model allows for locally-based ownership and control of news organizations. Anything that government can do in the way of creating non-profit status for newspapers should be seriously pursued. And further, anything that can be done to create financial or tax-based incentives for bankrupt and near-bankrupt newspaper chains to transfer or even donate unprofitable publications to locally-based non-profits should also be considered.

Lastly, I would urge Congress to consider relaxing certain anti-trust prohibitions with regard to the newspaper industry, so that the *Washington Post*, the *New York Times* and various other newspapers can sit down and openly discuss protecting their copyright from aggregators and plan an industrywide transition to a paid, online subscriber base. Whatever money comes will prove essential to the task of hiring back some of the talent, commitment, and institutional memory that has been squandered.

Absent this basic and belated acknowledgment that content has value—if indeed it still does after so many destructive buyouts and layoffs—and that content is what ultimately matters, I don't think anything else can save high-end, professional journalism.

The Future of Quality Journalism: Secure

Arianna Huffington

Thank you for inviting me to be a part of today's discussion on the future of journalism. Like any good news story, let me start with the headline: Journalism Will Not Only Survive, It Will Thrive.

Despite all the current hand wringing about the dire state of the newspaper industry—well-warranted hand wringing, I might add—we are actually in the midst of a Golden Age for news consumers. Can anyone seriously argue that this isn't a magnificent time for readers who can surf the net, use search engines, and go to news aggregators to access the best stories from countless sources around the world—stories that are up-to-the-minute, not rolled out once a day? Online news also allows users to immediately comment on stories, as well as interact and form communities with other commenters.

Since good journalism plays an indispensable role in our democracy, we all have a vested interest in making sure that our journalistic institutions continue producing quality reporting and analysis. But it's important to remember that the future of quality journalism is not dependent on the future of newspapers.

Consumer habits have changed dramatically. People have gotten used to getting the news they want, when they want it, how they want it, and where they want it. And this change is here to stay.

As my compatriot Heraclitus put it nearly 2,500 years ago: "You cannot step into the same river twice." [Huffington's maiden name is Stassinopoulos]

The great upheaval the news industry is going through is the result of a perfect storm of transformative technology, the advent of Craigslist, generational shifts in the way people find and consume news, and the dire impact the economic crisis has had on advertising. And there is no question that, as the industry moves forward and we figure out the new rules of the road, there will be—and needs to be—a great deal of experimentation with new revenue models. But what won't work—what can't work—is to act like the last 15 years never happened, that we are still operating in the old content economy as opposed to the new link economy, and that the survival of the industry will be found by "protecting" content behind walled gardens. We've seen that movie (and its many sequels, including TimesSelect). News consumers didn't like them, and they closed in a hurry.

And the answer can't be content creators attacking Google and other news aggregators. No, the future is to be found elsewhere. It is a linked economy. It is search engines. It is online advertising. It is citizen journalism and foundation-supported investigative funds. That's where the future is. And if you can't find your way to that, then you can't find your way.

Online video offers a useful example of the importance of being able to adapt. Not that long ago, content providers were committed to the idea of requiring viewers to come to their site to view their content—and railed against anyone who dared show even a short clip.

But content hoarding—the walled garden—didn't work. And instead of sticking their finger in the dike, trying to hold back the flow of innovation, smart companies began providing embeddable players that allowed their best stuff to be posted all over the web, accompanied by links and ads that helped generate additional traffic and revenue.

When I hear the heads of media companies talking about "restricting" content or describing news aggregators as "parasites," I can't help feeling the same way I did in 2001, when I was one of the cofounders of The Detroit Project, and watched as the heads of the auto industry decided that instead of embracing the future they would rather spend considerable energy and money lobbying the government for tax loopholes for gas-guzzling behemoths, fighting back fuel efficiency standards, and trying to convince consumers through billions in advertising that SUVs were the cars that would lead America into the 21st century.

Instead of trying to hold back the future, I suggest that media executives read *The Innovator's Dilemma* by Clayton Christensen, and see what he has to say about "disruptive innovation" and how, instead of resisting it, you can seize the opportunities it provides.

And that's why it's imperative that Congress and the FCC [Federal Communications Commission] make sure they have in place smart policies that bridge the digital divide, ensure competition among Internet service providers, and protect innovators and consumers from attempts to undermine net neutrality or impose unjustified charges—like metering—on Internet users.

Digital news is a classic case of "disruptive innovation"—a development that newspapers ignored for far too long.

Even so, I think all the obituaries for newspapers we're hearing are premature. Many papers are belatedly but successfully adapting to the new news environment. Plus, it's my feeling that until those of us who came of age before the Internet all die off, there will be a market for print versions of newspapers. There is something in our collective DNA that makes us want to sip our coffee, turn a page, look up from a story, say, "Can you believe this?" and pass the paper to the person across the table. Sure, you could hand them your Blackberry or laptop…but the instinct is different (and, really, who wants to get butter or marmalade on your new MacBook Pro?).

I firmly believe in a hybrid future where old media players embrace the ways of new media (including transparency, interactivity, and immediacy) and new media companies adopt the best practices of old media (including fairness, accuracy, and high-impact investigative journalism).

This hybrid future will include nonprofit/for profit hybrids, like the Investigative Fund the *Huffington Post* recently launched.

As the newspaper industry continues to contract, one of the most commonly voiced fears is that serious investigative journalism will be among the victims of the scaleback. And, indeed, many newspapers are drastically reducing their investigative teams. Yet, given the multiple crises we are living through, investigative journalism is all the more important. For too long, whether it's coverage of the war in Iraq or the economic meltdown, we've had too many autopsies and not enough biopsies.

The Investigative Fund is our attempt to change this—backed by nonprofit foundations interested in giving freelance reporters, many of whom have lost their jobs, the ability to pursue important stories. Others, like ProPublica, The Center for Public Integrity, Spot.US, and The Center for Investigative Reporting are pursuing different not-for-profit investigative models. More will follow.

We will also see more citizen journalism—not as a replacement for traditional journalists, but as a way of augmenting their coverage.

"Citizen Journalism" is shorthand for a collection of methods for producing content by harnessing the power of a site's community of readers, and making it a key element of the site's editorial output. These engaged readers can, among other things, recommend stories, produce raw data for original reported stories, write original stories themselves, record exclusive in-the-field video, search through large amounts of data or documents for hidden gems and trends, and much more. By tapping this resource, online news sites can extend their reach and help redefine newsgathering in the digital age.

In the process, they will also expand their online community—which, in turn, will attract more users and help build a more viable business model.

For too long, traditional media have been afflicted with Attention Deficit Disorder—they are far too quick to drop a story—even a good one, in their eagerness to move on to the Next Big Thing. Online journalists, meanwhile, tend to have Obsessive Compulsive Disorder...they chomp down on a story and stay with it, refusing to move off it until they've gotten down to the marrow.

In the future, these two traits will come together and create a much healthier kind of journalism. The discussion needs to move from "How do we save newspapers?" to "How do we strengthen journalism—via whatever platform it is delivered?"

We must never forget that our current media culture led to the widespread failure (with a few honorable exceptions) to serve the public interest by accurately covering two of the biggest stories of our time: the run-up to the war in Iraq and the financial meltdown.

That's why, as journalism transitions to a new and different place, the emphasis should not be on subsidizing what exists now but on how to rededicate ourselves to the highest calling of journalists—which is to ferret out the truth, wherever it leads. Even if it means losing our all-access-pass to the halls of power.

Unfortunately, this is a concept that has fallen out of favor with too many journalists who, like Pontius Pilot, wash their hands of finding the truth and instead are obsessed with a false view of "balance" and the misguided notion that every story has two sides. And that the truth can be found somewhere in the middle. But not every story has two sides and the truth is often found lurking in the shadows. The earth is not flat. Evolution is a fact. Global warming is real.

The most exciting thing for both journalists and news consumers, is the fact that technology will continue to give readers more and more control over what kind of information they get, and how that information will be presented. The days of publishing pooh-bahs dictating what is important and what is not are over. And thank goodness. As the legendary journalist I.F. Stone once said of a leading newspaper of his time: it's a particularly exciting paper to read because "you never know on what page you will find a page-one story."

We stand on the threshold of a very challenging but very exciting future. Indeed, I am convinced that journalism's best days lie ahead—just so long as we embrace and support innovation and don't try to pretend that we can somehow hop into a journalistic Way Back Machine and return to a past that no longer exists and can't be resurrected.

THE CONTINUING DEBATE:
The Future of Quality Journalism

What Is New

The decline in circulation of newspapers continues and has even accelerated, dropping by about 20% during the period March 2009–September 2010 alone. Reflecting this ongoing trend, 166 newspapers closed or ceased publishing printed edition between 2008 and late 2010. Because of the financial pressures, the surviving papers reduced their staffs by about 35,000 during the period, thus cutting down on news coverage. Americans are divided about what it portends. A 2009 poll found that 61% believe that they would "still be able to get the information they need as citizens," if the newspaper in their community shut down. Also worrisome for newspapers, in 2011 only 28% of Americans expressed significant confidence in newspapers, while 40% had only "some" confidence, and 31% had little or no confidence in them, with 1% unsure.

Where to Find More

A first-rate source for more information on newspapers and all the other news media is the annual port, *State of the News Media*, by the Pew Research Center's Project for Excellence in Journalism at www.stateofthemedia.org. More on newspapers specifically can be found on the Web site of the American Society of Newspaper Editors at www.asne.org/. To follow the media more generally, go to National Public Radio's *On The Media* program found at www.onthemedia.org/. The hearings in Congress at which Simon and Huffington testified sparked considerable interest in the media. One commentary is John Nichols, "David Simon, Arianna Huffington and the Future of Journalism," *The Nation*, May 11, 2009, at www.thenation.com. From a political science perspective, the future of journalism is heavily connected to the issue about the role the press plays in democracy and governance. A good look at that is Doris Graber, "The Media and Democracy: Beyond Myths and Stereotypes," *Annual Review of Political Science* (2003).

What More to Do

First, discuss how important newspapers are to society, particularly democracy. Thomas Jefferson once said that, if it was "left to me to decide whether we should have government without newspapers, or newspapers without a government, I should not hesitate a moment to prefer the latter." Do you agree? If you are worried about the decline of newspapers, and also what many see as the "infotainmentization" of television news, what would you do to fix that? Expanding public funding of public television news, giving commercial stations tax breaks for news operations, designating newspapers as tax exempt organizations, or making newspaper subscriptions tax deductible are a few ideas. Brainstorm to find others and debate them.

8   INTEREST GROUPS

PERMITTING CORPORATIONS TO PARTICIPATE IN ELECTION CAMPAIGNS:
A Blow to Democracy *or* Constitutionally Appropriate?

A BLOW TO DEMOCRACY

ADVOCATE: Monica Youn, Counsel at the Brennan Center for Justice at the New York University School of Law

SOURCE: Testimony during hearings on the "First Amendment and Campaign Finance Reform After *Citizens United*," before the Committee on the Judiciary, U.S. House of Representatives, February 3, 2010

CONSTITUTIONALLY APPROPRIATE

ADVOCATE: M. Todd Henderson, Assistant Professor of Law, University of Chicago Law School

SOURCE: "*Citizens United*: A Defense," Faculty Blog, University of Chicago Law School, March 12, 2010

Elections are big business. During the 2008 election cycle (2007–2008) alone, candidates, parties, interest groups, and individuals spent approximately $5.5 billion on the campaigns for the nominations and election for federal, state, and local offices. Of this total, almost two-thirds went to federal elections, including $2 billion to the presidential campaign and another $1.5 billion or so to the campaigns for Congress.

Although some wealthy candidates spend millions of their own dollars trying to get elected, more than 95% of the overall money that goes to influencing who gets nominated for and elected to Congress comes from sources other than the candidates themselves. In an ideal democracy, most of this money would come from small donations by a sizeable proportion of the electorate supporting one or another candidate. Reality is different. The vast majority of money comes from "big money" sources. Only about 15% of the money donated to congressional candidates for the 2008 campaigns came from small donors (those giving less than $1,000), while about 45% came from large donors. Political action committees (PACs) representing interest groups accounted for about another 25% of congressional campaign funds. Tax-exempt advocacy groups (TAGs) are also major players in the campaign finance picture. Also called 501(c) groups and 527 groups in reference to the sections of the Internal Revenue Code designating them as tax exempt, TAGs are not supposed to support or oppose the election of candidates for federal office. Nevertheless, a significant percentage of the more than $400 million that TAGs spent promoting their causes during the 2008 election cycle went to de facto partisan electoral activity.

Concern about the impact of big money on elections led Congress to enact the Federal Election Campaign Act (FECA) in 1971 to limit individual and PAC "hard money" contributions to political parties and candidates. The FECA did not cover "soft money" that various groups use to oppose or support federal candidates without donating to any candidate directly. In part to address soft money, Congress in 2002 enacted the Bipartisan Campaign Reform Act (BCRA). Among other things, the act prohibits federal candidates from raising or spending soft money and also limits its flow into federal elections via state and local party funds. The act also expanded the definition of campaign advertisements (versus issue ads) by specifying that messages depicting a candidate prior to an election and targeting that candidate's constituency are campaign communications subject to federal regulations. These two laws have helped restrain the flow of big money into politics, but their impact has been limited by Supreme Court decisions voiding some of their provisions as violations of the First Amendment. Most importantly for this debate, the Court ruled in *Citizens United v. FEC* (2010) that the BCRA's provision prohibiting corporations from sponsoring independent "electioneering communications" close to elections was an unconstitutional restraint on free speech. Corporations, it should be noted, are considered legal "persons" with at least some constitutional rights under Supreme Court decisions dating as far as *Dartmouth College v. Woodward* (1819) and *Santa Clara County v. Southern Pacific Railroad* (1886). Also worth noting is that the Court's decision in *Citizens United* probably means that the BCRA's limits on labor union electioneering are also unconstitutional.

What *Citizens United* did not do, despite much erroneous reporting, was to strike down long-standing laws that bar corporations (since 1907) and unions (since 1947) from giving money directly to federal candidates and political parties. The justices did, however, invalidate state laws barring corporate independent election activity, thereby reversing the Court's decision in *Austin v. Michigan Chamber of Commerce* (1990) upholding a Michigan law barring corporations from using their funds to support or oppose a candidate independently.

Fueled at least in part by the worry that *Citizens United* will result in increased spending by corporations to help Republicans, the decision drew an angry condemnation by President Obama and congressional Democrats. In the first reading, Marcia Youn of the Brennan Center at NYU's School of Law, tells a congressional hearing that the Court's *Citizens United* decision was misguided and will harm the democratic process by increasing the influence of big money in politics. University of Chicago Law School Professor M. Todd Henderson disagrees in the second reading. He contends that the Supreme Court made the appropriate decision in *Citizens United* and that the decision enhances democracy by increasing the number of views expressed.

POINTS TO PONDER

➢ If corporations, which are organizations, can have their "free speech" limited, can unions, advocacy groups, and other organizations also be restricted from using their money to independently support candidates?

➢ Youn and Henderson have very different views of what the *Citizens United* decision will mean in terms of corporate political spending. Whose view seems more likely to be right?

➢ If restraining corporate political spending both restrains free speech and serves to keep the political playing field more even between wealthy interests and others, which is more important?

Permitting Corporations to Participate in Election Campaigns: A Blow to Democracy

MARCIA YOUN

Since its creation in 1995, the Brennan Center has focused on fundamental issues of democracy and justice, including research and advocacy to enhance the rights of voters and to reduce the role of money in our elections. That work takes on even more urgency after the United States Supreme Court's decision in *Citizens United v. Federal Election Commission* on January 21, 2010. *Citizens United* rivals *Bush v. Gore* [2000] for the most aggressive intervention into politics by the Supreme Court in the modern era. Indeed, *Bush v. Gore* affected only one election; *Citizens United* will affect every election for years to come. [In *Bush v. Gore*, the Supreme Court rejected a challenge to Florida's awarding of its electoral votes to George W. Bush, thereby, in effect, giving him a majority of the Electoral College votes and the presidency.]

[There is a] five-vote majority on the Supreme Court [that] has imposed a radical concept of the First Amendment, and used it to upend vital protections for a workable democracy. We must push back against this distorted version of the Constitution. We must insist on a true understanding of the First Amendment as a charter for a vital and participatory democracy. And there are other values in the Constitution, too, that justify strong campaign laws—values such as the central purpose of assuring effective self-governance.

The Court blithely asserts that unlimited corporate spending poses no threat of corruption. That is simply not the case. We urge, above all, that this committee build a record to expose the actual workings of the campaign finance system. Such a record is vital for the public's understanding, and even more to make clear to Justices in future litigation that a strong record undergirds strong laws.

THE POLITICAL STAKES OF *CITIZENS UNITED*

Last week, the Supreme Court's decision in *Citizens United v. FEC* undermined 100 years of law that restrained the role of special interests in elections. By holding—for the first time—that corporations have the same First Amendment rights to engage in political spending as people, the Supreme Court re-ordered the priorities in our democracy—placing special interest dollars at the center of our democracy, and displacing the voices of the voters. There is reason to believe that future elections will see a flood of corporate spending, with the real potential to drown out the voices of every-day Americans. As Justice [John Paul] Stevens warned in his sweeping dissent, American citizens "may lose faith in their capacity, as citizens, to influence public policy" as a result.

After news of the *Citizens United* ruling sent shock waves through political, legal, and news media circles throughout the nation, some commentators took a jaundiced view, arguing, in essence, that since the political system is already awash in special-interest dollars, this particular decision will have little impact. It is undoubtedly true that heretofore, corporations have engaged in large-scale spending in federal politics—primarily through political action committees ("PACs") and through more indirect means such as lobbying and nonprofit advocacy groups. However, the sums spent by corporations in previous elections are miniscule in comparison to the trillions of dollars in corporate profits that the Supreme Court has now authorized corporations to spend to influence the outcome of federal elections. The difference, in short, changes the rules of federal politics.

Prior to *Citizens United*, a corporation that wished to support or oppose a federal candidate had to do so using PAC funds—funds amassed through voluntary contributions from individual employees and shareholders who wished to support the corporation's political agenda. Such funds were subject to federal contribution limits and other regulations. Now however, the *Citizens United* decision will allow corporations that wish to directly influence the outcome of federal elections to draw from their general treasury funds, rather than PAC funds, to support or oppose a particular candidate. This difference is significant enough to amount to a difference in kind rather merely a difference in degree, as demonstrated by the following:

- In the 2008 election cycle, the nation's largest corporation, Exxon-Mobil, formed a PAC that collected approximately $700,000 in individual contributions. Thus, Exxon-Mobil was limited to spending this amount on advertisements directly supporting or opposing a federal candidate. During the same 2008 election, Exxon-Mobil's corporate profits totaled more than $80 billion. Thus, *Citizens United* frees this one corporation to increase its direct spending in support or opposition to federal candidates by more than 100,000 fold.

- During the 2008 election cycle, all winning congressional candidates spent a total of $861 million on their campaigns—less than one percent of Exxon-Mobil's corporate profits over the same period.

Furthermore, corporations have demonstrated that they are willing to spend vast sums of money to influence federal politics. Since corporations have been banned from contributing to candidates and restricted in their campaign spending, their political spending has generally taken the form of lobbying.

- In the same year that it was able to raise only $700,000 for its federal PAC, Exxon Mobil spent $29 million on lobbying.

- In 2008, the average expenditures in a winning Senate race totaled $7.5 million and $1.4 million for the House.

- The health care industry in 2009 spent approximately $1 million per day to lobby Congress on health care reform.

- During the 2008 election, all congressional candidates spent a total of $1.4 billion on their campaigns. This is only 26 percent of the $5.2 billion corporations spent on lobbying during the same two-year period.

Thus, merely by diverting a fraction of their political spending budgets from lobbying to direct campaign advocacy, corporations could easily outspend the candidates themselves by a factor of many multiples. The same is true even if one factors in party spending:

- The single largest lobbying organization—the U.S. Chamber of Commerce—spent more than $144 million in lobbying, grassroots efforts, and advertising in 2009, compared to $97.9 million spent by the RNC and $71.6 million spent by the DNC. Thus, this single corporate-backed trade association is able to outspend the national committees of both political parties *combined.*

- According to *The Atlantic*'s Marc Ambinder, the Chamber's 2009 spending included electioneering in the Virginia and Massachusetts off-year elections, as well as "sizeable spending on advertising campaigns in key states and districts aimed at defeating health care, climate change, and financial reform legislation."

Even corporations that are reluctant to throw their hat into the ring of political spending may find themselves drawn into the fray just to stay competitive in the influence-bidding arms race this decision creates.

Indeed, despite the campaign finance regulations that—until *Citizens United*—attempted to protect our democracy against overt influence-peddling, there are numerous examples to demonstrate that absent such safeguards, special interests will attempt to use all means at their disposal to insure favorable legislative treatment.

• In 2006, the FEC levied a $3.8 million fine—the agency's largest in history—against mortgage giant Freddie Mac for illegally using corporate treasury funds to raise over $3 million for members of the House subcommittee that had regulatory authority over that corporation. Approximately 90% of those funds directly benefited the chair of the subcommittee.

Moreover, corporate campaign ads may be a much more effective route than lobbying for corporations to pressure elected officials to comply with their agendas. Even the most aggressive lobbying effort cannot exert the same direct political pressure on an elected official that a campaign expenditure can. Such corporate campaigning impacts the political survival of elected officials in a way that mere lobbying cannot. An elected official might hesitate to oppose a corporation on a particular piece of legislation if she knows that the corporation could unleash a multimillion attack ad blitz in her next reelection campaign.

Such an example came before the Court just last year in *Caperton v. Massey Coal Co.* In that case, the Supreme Court recognized that large independent expenditures can create actual and apparent bias in the context of judicial elections. In *Caperton,* the CEO of a coal company with $50 million at stake in a case before the West Virginia Supreme Court spent almost $3 million dollars in independent expenditures in support of that candidate's campaign. Writing for the majority, Justice Kennedy, wrote that such large expenditures—expenditures which exceeded the combined expenditures of both candidate committees by $1 million—had "a significant and disproportionate influence on the electoral outcome" and created a "serious, objective risk of actual bias."

In *Citizens United,* the Supreme Court has handed corporate special interests a loaded weapon—whether they ever fire the weapon is, arguably, beside the point. There is every reason to believe that the threat of corporate funded campaign attack ads is likely to distort policy priorities and to allow special interests to dominate federal politics. Perhaps even more profoundly, the Court in *Citizens United* has given the stamp of constitutional approval to corporate electioneering. The Court has invited corporations into elections, telling them that they have a First Amendment right to spend their vast resources to try to influence the outcome of an election. If even a few major corporations with stakes in current policy battles take the Court up on its invitation, the resulting wave of special interest money could undermine the foundations of our democracy.

THE ROBERTS COURT'S "DEREGULATORY TURN"

The limits on corporate campaign spending at issue in *Citizens United* represent the fourth time challenges to campaign finance laws have been argued before the Roberts Court, and the fourth time the Roberts Court majority has struck down such provisions as unconstitutional. As Professor Richard Hasen has explained, this "deregulatory turn" represents an about-face—by contrast, the Rehnquist Court had generally taken a deferential approach to campaign finance reform regulations enacted by federal and state lawmakers. However, now that Chief Justice [John] Roberts and Justice [Samuel] Alito have replaced Chief Justice [William] Rehnquist and Justice [Sandra Day] O'Connor on the Supreme Court, the newly constituted majority has moved with stunning haste to dismantle decades-old safeguards intended to limit the effect of special interest money in politics. Indeed, as Justice Stevens wryly noted, "The only relevant thing that has changed since *Austin* and *McConnell* is the composition of this Court."

With *Citizens United,* the current Supreme Court's majority's hostility to campaign finance law has become apparent to even the most casual observer. At oral argument in *Citizens United,* Justice Antonin Scalia exemplified the majority's unwarranted suspicion of long-standing campaign finance reform safeguards, assuming in his questions that such safeguards represented nothing more than incumbent self-dealing:

> Congress has a self-interest. I mean, we—we are suspicious of congressional action in the First Amendment area precisely because we—at least I am—I doubt that one can expect a body of incumbents to draw election restrictions that do not favor incumbents. Now is that excessively cynical of me? I don't think so.

Justice [Anthony] Kennedy also speculated during oral argument that "the Government [could] silence a corporate objector" who wished to protest a particular policy during an election cycle. Similarly, in the *Citizens United* opinion, Justice Kennedy simply assumed, without any factual basis, that Congress' motives were invidious, stating of the law at issue, "[i]ts purpose and effect are to silence entities whose voices the Government deems to be suspect." And Chief Justice Roberts famously expressed his impatience with campaign finance safeguards, striking down regulations on corporate electioneering in the *Federal Election Commission v. Wisconsin Right to Life* decision, saying "Enough is enough." The Court has used its skepticism of congressional motives—based not on facts or a record below but on the instincts of a majority of justices—to justify its utter lack of deference to legislative determinations in this arena. Such a cavalier dismissal of Congress' carefully considered legislation ignores the years of hearings, record, debate and deliberation involved in creating these reforms.

Unfortunately, *Citizens United* will not be the Roberts Court's last word on the issue. Seeking to take advantage of the majority's deregulatory agenda, the same coalition of corporate-backed groups that filed the *Citizens United* lawsuit have launched an armada of constitutional challenges to state and federal reforms, now advancing rapidly toward the Supreme Court.

These challenges include attacks on public financing systems, campaign finance disclosure requirements, "pay-to-play" restrictions on government contractors and lobbyists, and "soft money" restrictions on political parties and political action committees. Challengers seek to use the First Amendment as a constitutional "trump card" to strike down any reform that attempts to mitigate special interest domination of politics. Several of these challenges will be ripe for decision by the Supreme Court within the year.

This committee has an important role to play in helping to create a factual record that would correct unfounded assumptions about money and politics embedded in the Court's decisions, and could be useful in defending both new and existing reforms against judicial overreaching. In addition, we urge the committee to endorse several reforms to counter the impact of *Citizens United*—supporting public financing of congressional and presidential elections; enacting federal voter registration modernization legislation; and enacting federal legislation that requires shareholder approval for corporate political spending, as well as effective disclosure of such spending.

CONCLUSION—ADVANCING A VOTER-CENTRIC VIEW OF THE FIRST AMENDMENT

Perhaps the most troubling aspect of *Citizens United*—worse than its political implications, worse than its aggressive deregulatory stance—is that the Court embraces a First Amendment where voters are conspicuously on the sidelines. At the start of the *Citizens United* opinion, Justice Kennedy correctly noted that "The right of citizens to inquire, to hear, to speak, and to use information to reach consensus is a precondition to enlightened self-government and a necessary means to protect it." As the opinion proceeded, however, it became evident that the majority was in fact taking a myopic view of campaign finance jurisprudence, one that focuses exclusively on campaigns—candidates, parties and corporate interests—at the expense of the voting citizenry. The Court's ultimate judgment held, in effect, that whatever interest is willing to spend the most money has a constitutional right to monopolize political discourse, no matter what the catastrophic result to democracy.

This aspect of *Citizens United*—like many others—constitutes a break with prior constitutional law. The Court has long recognized that "constitutionally protected interests lie on both sides of the legal equation." Accordingly, our constitutional system has traditionally sought to maintain a balance between the rights of candidates, parties, and special interests to advance their own views, and the rights of the electorate to participate in public discourse and to receive information from a variety of sources. It is crucial that this committee and Congress recognize the Roberts Court's one-sided view of the First Amendment as a distortion—one which threatens to erode First Amendment values under the guise of protecting them. In truth, our constitutional jurisprudence incorporates a strong First Amendment tradition of deliberative democracy—an understanding that the overriding purpose of the First Amendment is to promote an informed, empowered, and participatory electorate. This is why our electoral process must be structured in a way that "build(s) public confidence in that process," thereby "encouraging the public participation and open discussion that the First Amendment itself presupposes." In this post-*Citizens United* era, a robust legislative response will be critical. It is similarly imperative, however, that we reframe our constitutional understanding of the First Amendment value of deliberative democracy. In the longer term, reclaiming the First Amendment for the voters will be the best weapon against those who seek to use the "First Amendment" for the good of the few, rather than for the many.

Permitting Corporations to Participate in Election Campaigns: Constitutionally Appropriate

M. TODD HENDERSON

Let me say at the outset, some of my prior beliefs. First, I believe in the marketplace of ideas and think that more speech is generally better than less speech. I believe the Founders shared this belief and enshrined it in the "no law" component of the First Amendment. I believe this is especially true for speech about politics. Why else would we allow the Nazis to march in Skokie? [This is a reference to a 1978 decision by an Illinois court that under the First Amendment a neo-Nazi group could march and proclaim its views in Skokie, Illinois, a suburb of Chicago with a large Jewish population.] Other countries don't let Nazi's march because they (rightfully) view their ideas as repugnant. But we let them march. We do so because we are more confident in our citizens' ability to know right from wrong, to look beyond rhetoric for substance, and to be able to weigh competing claims of truth. If we didn't trust the people to make decisions based on all available information, if we didn't trust the people to be able to filter speech according to its source and content, if we didn't trust the people to know what is good for them, we wouldn't let the Nazi's march. But we let them march.

Second, I believe that we should view extensions of government activity under a presumption of error, especially where there is no evidence of a market failure or where the case for government regulation is suspect, say because of the potential for an incumbency bias or the possibility of abuse by the forces of totalitarianism. The control we have over our government, which, after all, has a monopoly on legal physical violence, is tenuous and something that requires constant vigilance. Giving incumbent politicians the ability to write rules that will make it more likely they will be reelected is something that should be done only, if at all, in the face of overwhelming evidence of the inability of citizens to make sensible political decisions in the absence of these rules.

Third, I believe that people generally want to restrict "corporations" in the abstract from influencing politics, a belief that is born out by recent polling data showing about 70% of people disagree with the result in *Citizens United*. In other words, if we voted on *Citizens United*, I think we would have voted the other way. As I describe below, I do not think this should matter. Based on the first two priors, I think the Court got the case right, and that its countermajoritarian instincts here are a sign of strength in the decision, not weakness.

Here are some thoughts about the case and its aftermath.

First, I think it is amusing how the case is perceived on both sides of the political aisle. Political commentators on the Left have said the case has "more dire implications than Dred Scott" and that "within 10 years every politician in this country will be a prostitute." [In *Dred Scott v. Sandford* (1857) the Supreme Court ruled that escaped slave Dred Scott could not sue for his freedom in federal court because he was property, not a citizen.] Or take this zinger from Justice [John Paul] Stevens's opinion: "The Court's ruling threatens to undermine the integrity of elected institutions across the Nation" and "do damage to this institution" as well.

The law that was struck down was passed in 2002: The Bipartisan Campaign Reform Act. It was upheld against a facial challenge in a 2003 case called McConnell, which was based on a precedent from 1990, called *Austin* [*v. Michigan Chamber of*

Commerce]. So pick your time period, pre 2002, pre 1990, whichever. Were all politicians prostitutes of corporate interests, whatever that is, in 1989?

Or, looking at the issue another way, does the fact that the conduct permitted by *Citizens United* was legal in 26 states prior to *Citizens United,* suggest that politicians are hopelessly corrupt in over half our states? What about the fact that prior to the case, companies, unions, and advocacy groups and other agglomerations of individual interests that chose the corporate form could do exactly what *Citizens United* allows them to do if the speech was funneled through "separate segregated funds," commonly known as Political Action Committees? The belief in disaster must be based on a claim that when corporations or unions can fund political speech directly, from so-called treasury funds, instead of indirectly, the flood gates will open and companies will spend much, much more on politics. This is a claim about how corporations act that is highly suspect, a point I will return to in a moment.

Moreover, what about all the money the so-called special interests spend on lobbying members of our legislatures? The campaign finance laws say nothing about this, and which is more likely to influence public policy creation, a drug company running an ad in New Jersey 30 days before the election telling citizens that Senator Henderson is a Marxist who wants to nationalize drug development or that same company spending millions on lobbyists to jawbone existing legislators about the virtues of our current system?

A final point about the hysteria: Do critics of more political speech have such little faith in the people to make decisions that the inevitable consequence of more information about politics will be to bias it in a socially negative direction? Was it really the case that 2 U.S.C. section 441(b), the law at issue in the case, is all that was preserving our democracy? I for one have more faith in the strength of our Union and the wisdom of the people than to think that the byzantine structure of federal election law is all that distinguishes American politics from that of the Ukraine or Nigeria. Even if you believe, as many do, that the average corporation is analogous to the National Socialist party, this does not mean we must necessarily regulate their speech. Remember, we let the Nazis speak.

On the Right the fans are just as simple minded. An op-ed in the *Wall Street Journal* after the decision argued (lamely) that *Citizens United* is a key victory for business in the battle to reduce the influence of trial lawyers. The unstated suggestion is that companies will give more money and this is a good thing. This is highly suspect, and I suspect that businesses are not in favor of the decision. Every penny spent to influence law is a penny not spent to pay managers, hire workers, innovate, or make shareholders wealthy.

Campaign finance laws can be thought of as a solution to a simple collective action problem: every firm would prefer not to pay politicians not to treat them badly, but none individually have an incentive to refrain from doing so absent collective agreement of the same. An obvious solution to the collective action problem is an agreement among firms to refrain from spending on politics. But this agreement would be illegal under our antitrust laws. Campaign finance laws may be a rough substitute. (Note the irony that laws restricting speech are necessary because of other laws prohibiting firms from acting rationally in their self-interest.)

The zero-sum game aspect of corporate giving can be seen by looking at the donations by businesses in the 2008–2009 election cycle. Business corporations gave $1.96 billion to political campaigns, 50.6% to Republicans, 49.4% to Democrats. They play both sides, making claims of *Citizens United* meaning more corporate influence or better for Republicans somewhat fanciful.

While we are on the subject of partisanship, it is interesting to compare business giving with that by the other major corporate contributors—labor unions, specifically public-employee unions. Unions donated $674 million in 2008–2009 (about one third of what businesses gave), but they gave overwhelmingly to Democrats (92% to 8%). The net contributions from "corporations" were $1.6 billion for Democrats and $1.0 billion for Republicans. The conservative majority of the Court hardly gave Republicans a gift, assuming these ratios continue when the rules are liberalized across the board, and we have no reason to believe they won't be. (For reference, one candidate, our president, raised nearly $1 billion in donations from individuals in that year.)

So it is not at all clear that this case will make things worse or that it favors one political party or the other. It is not even clear that it favors things corporate or business over things uncorporate. After all, there are corporations on the side of almost all issues, especially when we remember that the ACLU, NRA, Sierra Club, AARP, Citizens United, and others are corporations too. Are those anti-corporate readers out there afraid of all of them or just some of them? If you like the ACLU and the Sierra Club, but not the NRA and the AARP, and as a consequence want to ban the speech of the former and not the latter, this is the road to totalitarianism. The Supreme Court is adamant that restrictions on speech cannot be based on content. Tolerating the speech of those we disagree with is one of our most sacred core values.

This case is about just this kind of toleration and the threat of unchecked political power. To see this, consider this passage from the Court in *Citizens United*:

> The law before us is an outright ban, backed by criminal sanctions. Section 441b makes it a felony for all corporations—including nonprofit advocacy corporations—either to expressly advocate the election or defeat of candidates or to broadcast electioneering communications within 30 days of a primary election and 60 days of a general election. Thus, the following acts would all be felonies under §441b: The Sierra Club runs an ad, within the crucial phase of 60 days before the general election, that exhorts the public to disapprove of a Congressman who favors logging in national forests; the National Rifle Association publishes a book urging the public to vote for the challenger because the incumbent U.S. senator supports a handgun ban; and the American Civil Liberties Union creates a Web site telling the public to vote for a presidential candidate in light of that candidate's defense of free speech. These prohibitions are classic examples of censorship.

Let me reframe the Court's holding: the government may not ban political documentaries in the 60 days before an election. This is the end of democracy? The government tried to ban speech about government! Imagine a [Sarah] Palin Administration banning the Michael Moore movie "Dumb as the Average Moose," before the 2016 presidential election? How would those on the Left react to that decision?

The [U.S.] Solicitor General [Elena Kagan] admitted during oral argument that the logical extreme of the law would allow the government to ban book publishers, who happen to have chosen to organize their economic affairs as corporations, from publishing political books before elections. Yes, you read that right. Book banning. This goes to the heart of the First Amendment. Imagine James Madison and Thomas Jefferson traveled to our era and asked about the Bill of Rights. If *Citizens United* came out the other way, we would have to tell them that virtual child pornography and pole dancing are protected by the First Amendment, but books or documentaries about politicians are not. I'm not suggesting that we limit our constitutional interpretation to a what-would-the-Founders-think analysis or even to the plain text (which, by the way, says Congress shall pass no law restricting the freedom of speech), but if the First Amendment means anything, it means protecting speech about politics.

Of course, one could argue that books or documentaries about politicians are OK, so long as the speaker was you or me or all of us acting together, so long as we didn't organize as a corporation. But why should the value of political speech be determined by whether the entity doing the speaking or enabling the speaking is a corporation or person, partnership, or sole proprietorship? Or whether the corporation speaking was a "media corporation," a class of corporations that were exempted from the regulation. So our First Amendment, as previously interpreted, said that the *New York Times* or Fox News could say whatever they want about politics whenever they wanted, but that the ACLU and Apple could not. I see no basis for this in the text of the Amendment or in common sense. What is the difference between a non-media company and a media company? What if Apple started a newspaper? Could it then speak? How about a blog? Is that media? Why should Rupert Murdoch [head of a huge multimedia empire including Fox Network] get to spend and say what he wants on politics, but not News Corp. [the corporation Murdoch controls]? And what is the reason for encouraging businesses that want to speak to choose to organize as partnerships or individuals instead or corporations? Imagine a corporation with one owner—should the corporation not be allowed to speak the same as its sole owner?

One possibility is a concern that when News Corp. spends money on politics, it is spending shareholders' money, or, depending on your point of view, employees' money or other stakeholders' money. This is as true as it is irrelevant. For one, investing is voluntary, and there is no demand for any individual firm's stock. If you own shares in Exxon Mobil, and it decides to spend $1 million to fund ads supporting Sarah Palin for president, you can convert your shares to cash and buy shares of Apple Computer, which is running ads supporting President Obama's reelection. The only time this voting with your feet argument doesn't work is if the conduct causing you to sell also is the cause of a loss of firm value, thus making your shares worth less than they would have been. Given the trivial amounts firms spend or could possibly spend on politics, this is in the world of law-school hypotheticals. (ExxonMobil had political expenditures of about $500,000 in 2008, on profits of nearly $50 billion, or less than 0.001%. We will, of course, have to wait and see how much they spend next year, but, for the reasons I describe below, I'd be shocked if it was orders of magnitude more. Even if they spent 1,000 times more, the expenditures would be only 1 percent of profits, something unlikely to move the stock price needle significantly.)

Business corporations exist to make money, and donations to candidates will be aimed in that direction. Insofar as they are, shareholders should be happy, and if they aren't, they can exert influence by selling their shares. If instead, the claim is just corporate influence, as opposed to this agency costs story, then we are back to puzzles about individual contributions, donations by PACs, lobbyists, and so on. Corporations spend handsomely to lobby politicians, and shareholders don't complain. Why? Because presumably the lobbying is about increasing firm value—that is, making money for shareholders. Why do we think other forms of political spending would be different?

Moreover, firms are very jealous and protective of their reputations. Do you think Nike is going to risk its brand by spending billions to elect politicians that may offend 49% of the population? And if they do, don't we have faith in other constraints on such attempts at manipulation? Consumer boycotts, news reports, publicity by non-profits, and so on are likely to cause firms to be quite cautious in their attempts to buy politicians outright.

Finally there is the claim that business are creatures of the state and therefore the state should be able to tell them what to do. This certainly used to be the case, when state legislatures gave businesses permission to do only certain things in return for, well, political contributions and favors. But thankfully we've moved past this so-called concession theory. The concession theory is plainly inconsistent with the contractarian model of the firm, which treats corporate law as nothing more than a set of standard form contract terms provided by the state to facilitate private ordering. Limited liability can be created by contract as easily as it can by state diktat, and no matter what, if we have this view of government power, it has no end. Everything exists in some way because of government action or inaction, but that is not the basis of our government. We believe our rights exist not because of the government, but rather the other way around—the government exists to protect our preexisting rights.

Let me close with three final observations.

First, I think the case is interesting in how it reveals the schism on the Court (and in all of politics) between those with faith in experts and those with faith in markets. The campaign finance laws, and the dissenters' views of elections law, are premised on a belief that we can design rules, no matter how layered and complex, that can be implemented by well-meaning bureaucrats with the result that we can take the money/corporate influence/corruption out of politics and finally create Democracy. These people are uncomfortable with uncertainty and unknown outcomes, and believe we should plan our way to some sort of utopia. The *Citizens United* majority, on the other hand, seems to have a distrust in experts and regulating natural things out of existence, preferring instead to rely on markets to work toward the optimal state of affairs. Of course, there is a tradeoff between a belief in centralized versus diffuse knowledge, and the question is how much of each. In short, I think the *Citizens United* majority looked at the elaborate regulatory regime, the relative ineptness of the Federal Election Commission bureaucrats charged with implementing it, and decided to err on the side of the marketplace of ideas.

Second, we should not forget the history of our regulation of corporate speech, which, by the way, survives *Citizens United*. The first law banning corporate contributions in federal political elections was based in part about the content of corporate speech. The Tillman Act, passed in 1907 is named for Senator Benjamin Ryan "Pitchfork Ben" Tillman from South Carolina, one of the most reprehensible public servants in our history. Tillman argued that, "The negro must remain subordinated or be exterminated," and openly called for the murder of blacks in order to, "keep the white race at the top of the heap." Tillman wanted to restrict corporate speech to reduce the influence of Northern corporations, which were opposed to segregation. We should not condemn restrictions of corporate speech for this reason, but we should remember that the motives behind allegedly idealistic legislation are not always what they seem. Sometimes corporations have good things to say; sometimes they have bad things to say. Telling them they cannot speak prevents us from hearing both during a crucial period before our elections.

Finally, some critics deride the case as "activist" and inconsistent with claims about the proper judicial role made by some of the justices in the majority. Of course the claim of activism is as silly as the claim of courts as simply calling balls and strikes, as the Chief Justice [John Roberts] has argued. Some of the Court's job is calling balls and strikes, but most is about policy. And, some of the best court decisions are countermajoritarian. Consider *Meyer v. Nebraska* (1923), which dealt with a state law banning foreign language instruction for young children, passed during the anti-German hysteria of World War I. The Nebraska Supreme Court had upheld the ban, writing, "The legislature had seen the baneful effects of permitting foreigners, who had taken residence in this country, to rear and educate their children in the language of their native land."[Justice] Oliver Wendell Holmes followed his views about judicial restraint and dissented. But the Court got it right. Activism was essential to preserve our liberty.

In *Citizens United,* the Court decided that we cannot trust the government to tell us what we should be hearing about our political system. In the view of this corporate law professor, this is a victory for our democracy.

THE CONTINUING DEBATE:
Permitting Corporations to Participate in Election Campaigns

What Is New

Congress did nothing in the aftermath of the *Citizens United* decision to try to mitigate the impact of the decision. At least one reason is that incumbents in Congress are much more likely to get large donations from interests groups and other corporations than are challengers. Therefore it is to the disadvantage of the incumbents, whether Republican or Democrat, to limit the flow of money. The 2010 congressional elections were the most expensive in U.S. history, but it is not clear how much the *Citizens United* decision played a part in the sharply increased flow of money into the electoral process. As Campaign Finance Institute executive director Michael Malbin put it, "While the decision enables more direct business participation, it does not mean more business corporations will feel an incentive to act in this way....The evidence so far is mixed; any conclusion is highly premature." The upcoming 2012 presidential and congressional elections will provide a much clearer view of the impact of the Supreme Court's decision on campaign finance.

Where to Find More

Details of campaign fund raising and spending, including by your members of Congress, are on the site of The Center for Responsive Politics at www.opensecrets.org/. Also good is the Hoover Institution's site on campaign finance at www.campaignfinancesite.org/. More officially, you can find information from the Federal Elections Commission at www.fec.gov/. Good information on reform legislation and regulations should also be on the site of the Campaign Legal Center at www.campaignlegalcenter.org/.

What More to Do

This is one of those cases where the details are very important. Even if you support reform, it is important to see that at some point limiting what individuals and groups can spend to influence elections begins to unduly restrict their free speech and their right to try to influence policy—abilities that are at the core of democracy. It is also worth considering how appropriate it is to distinguish between organizations based on their professed purpose: business, union, civic organizations, ideological groups, and so on. Also, should wealth be a barrier to fully airing one's views, even if they are corporate? Yet democracy also entails some degree of equality among people's ability to have influence, and the money factor clearly skews that. What would you advise Congress to do, if anything?

POLITICAL PARTIES

TEA PARTY MEMBERS:
Irresponsible Zealots *or* Responsibly Dissenting Citizens?

IRRESPONSIBLE ZEALOTS

ADVOCATE: Frank Lautenberg, Member, U.S. Senate, Democrat, New Jersey

SOURCE: "Toxic Tea," remarks to the U.S. Senate, *Congressional Record*, March 10, 2011

RESPONSIBLY DISSENTING CITIZENS

ADVOCATE: Mitch McConnell, Minority Leader, U.S. Senate, Republican, Kentucky

SOURCE: "Tea Party," remarks to the U.S. Senate, *Congressional Record*, March 31, 2011

The United States in one of a small minority of countries that have a two-party system, one in which only two parties hold almost all elective offices. Moreover, the United States is arguably the world's purist two-party system. Every U.S. president since 1853 has been a Democrat or a Republican, and the two parties combined have held at least 96 percent of the seats in Congress since 1863.

Still minor parties have been and remain common in the United States, and they have sometimes risen to so-called "third party" status and played an important part in American politics. Third parties have been most likely to emerge during times of high political stress, with many third party followers being drawn from among alienated members of one or both of the two major parties. The Republican Party emerged in the 1850s when the issue of allowing slavery in new territories divided both the Democrats and the Whig Party, with anti-slavery elements of each joining in the new party. The first Republican president, Abraham Lincoln, had served in the Illinois legislature and the U.S. House of Representatives as a Whig, and Lincoln's first vice president, Hannibal Hamlin was a former Democratic member of Congress.

The current era of American history is also one of great stress. Social issues such as abortion divide the country and compromise is difficult. Changes in the demographic composition of the country, with the minority populations growing rapidly, are causing cultural angst among many. And most recently the faltering economy and soaring budget deficits have increased the feeling among most Americans that the country is in trouble. In this atmosphere, a dissident movement has emerged. Named after the raiders of the Boston Tea Party in 1773, the Tea Party movement began to form in 2008 and 2009 through a campaign to send tea bags as symbols of protest to members of Congress. Numerous Tea Party organizations sprang up, and in 2010 the political weight of the movement was evident in its ability to help determine the outcome of numerous elections, mostly by either playing a strong role in determining who Republican candidates were and/or who won the final election. However, no central Tea Party structure has emerged. For example, one Web site lists more than 90

Tea Party groups in Michigan alone, ranging from the Ann Arbor Tea Party to the Wolverines for Liberty in Lake City. As such, the Tea Party remains a loosely connected mélange of state and local groups, and it is debatable whether the Tea Party is a movement, a splinter group of the Republican Party, or an emerging third party.

Who are the Tea Party's supporters? They are overwhelmingly white, over age 45, and identify as Republicans and conservatives. A majority of Tea Party supporters are men, earn at least $50,000 a year, and are Protestants. At least 85 percent of all Tea Partiers believe the national debt, the size and power of the federal government, and terrorism each seriously endangers the country and that it is headed in the wrong direction. Most Tea Partiers reject the idea that the problems that minorities face stem mostly from discrimination and strongly support halting illegal immigration and deporting most undocumented immigrants. Such ideas attract many Americans, with a poll in 2010 showing about 30 percent of them saying they supported the Tea Party.

The following debate focuses on the nature of the Tea Party. New Jersey's Democratic U.S. Senator Frank Lautenberg claims that driven by its Tea Party element, the Republic Party is brewing up a "toxic tea" for Americans. Kentucky Republican and Senate Minority Leader Mitch McConnell portrays Tea Party members as everyday Americans from across the country who are distressed by both parties that they have decided to stand up and make their voices heard.

POINTS TO PONDER

➤ Where, if any place, is the line between someone who is an unreasoning fanatic and someone who is resolutely committed to his/her principles?

➤ A core Tea Party principal is opposition to "big government"—big taxes, big programs, big power. Where do you stand on this idea?

➤ Is it better to have political parties that are closer to the center, and thus better able to compromise, or farther apart ideologically, and thus better able to offer a clear choice to voters?

Tea Party Members:
Unreasoning Zealots

Frank Lautenberg

Everyone is aware of how deeply concerned the American people are about staying in their homes, about having adequate health care, and about providing education and a better path for the lives of their children. But everyone also knows there is a group calling themselves the tea party, and they are busy trying to eliminate those opportunities.

In Wisconsin, a tea party Governor is trying to take away workers' collective bargaining rights to be represented. It is like going into a courtroom without a lawyer.

In Florida, another tea party Governor has killed the critical high-speed rail project by rejecting Federal grants of $2.4 billion to move it along. He threw it away, threw it back—$2.4 billion. Here in Congress, tea party activists have seized control of the Republican side of the aisle. But it is far from a tea party for lots of jobless people and those qualified to study in college but unable to pay the freight. Now that they are in power, we see them brewing a toxic tea—a dangerous concoction that will create pain for our children and ultimately bring shame to our country.

We know cutting critical programs now brings sky-high prices later—in more illnesses and a less educated society. So we look at the future, we say we have to invest in our children, our environment, and medical research. But every time they hear something we need, they say no. They insist on saying no to 200,000 little kids who now go to Head Start Programs that help them in the earliest stages of life, when learning is fun and curiosity abounds. Look here. We see a young child's face through the window. They are holding back 218,000 Head Start kids from learning to learn. They ought to visit these schoolrooms and be upfront with these children and their parents and say, Sorry, America can't help you.

That is not all. Look at what they want to do to higher education. We say we must invest in Pell grants which make the dream of college a reality for millions of disadvantaged Americans. They say, Sorry, your country can't help you. They say no to future employers. Too bad we don't have enough qualified workers, so maybe the employers then can appropriately say, Oh, well, ship the jobs overseas. That is the alternative. Is that what we want America to do? They say no, even though the unemployment rate is twice as large for those who lack a bachelor's degree as for college graduates.

They are unable to look at a simple chart such as this one: There we can see the way the arrow is pointed, with the year 2000 over here and the year 2009 over here, and we see rising tuitions. That is what is happening. Therefore, it tells us how difficult it is for those who don't have the money, the family support financially, and won't able to take advantage of the Pell grants, because they want to slash them. They want to get them off the record as much as they can.

The chart shows between a $10,000 and $15,000 tuition rate in 2001. In 2008 and 2009, we are somewhere close to $20,000 a year. Do we want to force middle-class citizens to take on more debt in order to attend college or slam shut the campus doors on them altogether?

I know the value of government investment in college education firsthand. I came from a poor working-class family. I was a teenager when I enlisted in the Army. My father was on his deathbed. He died and left a 37-year-old widow, myself, and my 12-

year-old sister. Thanks to the GI bill, I attended college at Columbia and later cofounded a company with two other fellows—a company that was started with nothing. We had zero in funding. We put together a few hundred bucks. Now that company employs 45,000 employees in 23 countries, based in New Jersey. Jobs in this country. We built the "greatest generation" out of those educational opportunities we had in the military, and we were moving America to the top of the economic ladder.

Government investment in my education made all the difference in my life, and now the 45,000 people who work for ADP. Now Republicans want to take away opportunities such as that from young people. These are people who go into a business, have an education, learn something about how to operate a business, but also learn how we ought to be creating job opportunities and economic development for all in our country.

That is not all the House Republicans have in store for our country. We have to protect women's health, but they won't listen. They want to wipe out funding for title X. Title X offers women access to critical health services, including cervical cancer tests, breast cancer screenings, encouragement to think about family planning and how they are going to get by. But these people on the other side don't want to hear it. They don't care. They don't care that title X offers women access to take care of their health at all times.

Millions of poor women benefit from title X. So killing it will take care away from those who need it most. Title X funding for women's health: House GOP, tea partiers, lots of them, eliminate $1 billion for women's care. They cancel funding for 2 million breast cancer screenings. How cruel is that in this country of ours? If you have money, you can take care of yourself. If you don't, too bad. Well, that is not the way we want to do it. That is not the way we want to do it on this side of the aisle. They are cutting off resources for 2.2 million cervical cancer screenings. What a horror that is. What did these women do to deserve higher health risks during their lifetimes?

But it gets worse. The Republicans are also going after medical research. We say we must invest in finding cures and treatment for millions of children suffering from asthma, diabetes, autism, and pediatric cancer, to name a few of those health-damaging afflictions. To these children they say, You know what. If you don't feel good, maybe you should go to an emergency room with your parents. Stand in line. Too bad. We would like to help, but we can't do that.

The National Institutes of Health [NIH] is making strides in fighting childhood diseases, but the Republicans want to reduce NIH's ability to do their research by taking $1 billion out of the their budget. If you want to see bravery, look into the eyes of a child struggling with leukemia, and look in the parents' eyes, and you will see tears, often no hope.

Look at what the Republicans want to do to our environment. We say we must invest in the Clean Air Act, a law that spares millions of children from suffering from asthma, and the Republicans say, No can do. They say you can't restrict polluters with regulations. It is too cumbersome. And if you don't like regulations, for instance, take a look at this bothersome thing we have in America called red lights. They are cumbersome. They stop traffic. These people don't want regulations, so we ought to get rid of the red lights and let the traffic move, but watch yourself when you get to the intersection.

Maybe they want to get rid of the air traffic control system. Pilots have to wait for some government bureaucrat to tell them where and when they can fly? What a nerve that is to interfere with these regulations and rules.

The Republicans also want to let mercury back into our air. Mercury is brain poisoning for children. They also want to stop us from restricting soot pollution. Look at the picture. Soot is ugly when it is pouring from a smokestack, but it is even uglier inside a child's lungs. This is a picture we see in many places in our country.

Several years ago I wrote a law called the Right to Know. It says to people who live in areas where there are chemicals present—either manufacturing, chemicals being stored or transported—so people could know if they hear a particular alarm, they have to respond to it and report it to the fire department. We had an incident in Elizabeth, NJ, some years ago when a group of firemen responded to a chemical fire and, in some instances, their protective uniforms melted. That is the kind of situation we want to avoid. We want people to know what is being stored, what is being released into the air in case of a fire.

Finally, when we say we have to clean the water our children drink, the Republican answer is, Oh, we can't handle that. It costs too much. So they cut the funding that helps States protect our drinking water from *E. coli*, arsenic, and other dangerous substances. The water is not safe for dishwashing, much less consumption.

The House GOP keeps on brewing their toxic tea for America. Ask any parent if they want their kids to drink from that teapot. They don't, and we shouldn't make them do it. We need to gather together for things such as birthday parties and school graduations and lots of smiles instead of their toxic tea parties.

Let's reject the House Republican tea party approach to funding our government. When they say, hey, join us for a cup of toxic tea, we must say, no, we have had this long enough, and we are not going to stand for it anymore.

[Colleagues,] you know very well that what we are looking at is very constricted budgets. One doesn't have to be an economist or a business executive to know that when there is a financial statement, it comes in two parts. One part is the expenses you need with which to operate. The other is the revenues that permit the companies and the organizations to function. What we are looking at is revenues. I know the [that many of you] share that position with me. We have discussed it.

Why should people who have the means, who have the good fortune to make lots and lots of money—we saw something this afternoon on a chart that had janitors in New York City at some locations paying a higher tax rate on their earnings than those who earn a million dollars or more. That is not fair. So if we want to do the right thing, we have to introduce revenues into the budget. We have to restore the cuts they want to make on the other side. We want to restore children's health. We want to make sure the NIH is producing as much as it can, and we want to turn America back to a lot more smiles than we have seen.

Tea Party Members:
Responsibly Dissenting Citizens

MITCH MCCONNELL

Anyone who follows national politics knows that when it comes to a lot of the issues Americans care about most, Democratic leaders in Washington are pretty far outside the mainstream. That is why we have one Democratic leader coaching his colleagues to describe any Republican idea as extreme, and that is why other Democrats are attempting to marginalize an entire group of people in this country whose concerns about the growth of the Nation's debt, the overreach of the Federal Government, and last year's health care bill are about as mainstream as it gets.

I am referring, of course, to the tea party—a loosely knit movement of everyday Americans from across the country who got so fed up in the direction they saw lawmakers from both parties taking our country a couple years ago that they decided to stand up and make their voices heard. Despite the Democratic leadership's talking points, these folks are not radicals. They are our next-door neighbors and our friends. By and large, they are housewives, professionals, students, parents, and grandparents. After last fall's election, a number of them are now Members of Congress.

Later on today, we will hear from many of them outside the Capitol. These are everyday men and women who love their country and who do not want to see it collapse as a result of irresponsible attitudes and policies that somehow persist around here despite the warning signs we see all around us about the consequences of fiscal recklessness. They are being vilified because, in an effort to preserve what is good about our country, they are politely asking lawmakers in Washington to change the way things are done around here. So this morning I thought we could step back and take a look at some of the things they are proposing and then let people decide for themselves who they think is extreme.

At a time when the national debt has reached crisis levels, members of the tea party are asking that we stop spending more than we take in. In other words, they are asking that Washington do what any household in America already does. They want us to balance our budget, and they do this because they know their history and that the road to decline is paved with debt. Is that extreme?

They want us to be able to explain how any law we pass is consistent with the Constitution. This means that as we write new laws, they want us to be guided by the document that every single Senator in this Chamber has sworn to uphold. Is that extreme?

They want us to cut down on the amount of money the government spends. This year, the Federal Government in Washington is projected to spend about $1.6 trillion more than it has.

That means we will have to borrow it from somewhere else, driving the national debt even higher than it already is. What is more, the Obama administration plans to continue spending like this for years, so that within 5 years, the debt will exceed $20 trillion. Given these facts, you tell me: Is it extreme to propose that we cut spending?

What else? Well, a lot of people in the tea party think the health care bill the Democrats passed last year should be repealed and replaced with real reforms that actually lower costs. Is that extreme?

Here is a bill that is expected to lead to about 80,000 fewer jobs, which will cause Federal health care spending to go up, compel millions to change the health care plans they have and like, and which is already driving individual and family insurance premiums up dramatically. Businesses are being hammered by its regulations and its mandates. A majority of States are working to overturn it. Two Federal judges have ruled one of its central provisions violates the U.S. Constitution.

None of this sounds extreme to me. In fact, if you ask me, the goals of the tea party sound pretty reasonable. These folks recognize the gravity of the problems we face as a nation and they are doing something about it for the sake of our future. They are engaged in the debate about spending and debt, which is a lot more than we can say about the President and many Democrats here in Congress. They are making their voices heard and they have succeeded in changing the conversation here in Washington from how to grow government to how to shrink it.

In my view, the tea party has had an overwhelmingly positive impact on the most important issues of the day. It has helped focus the debate. It has provided a forum for Americans who felt left out of the process to have a voice and make a difference. It is already leading to good results.

It may take some time, but thanks to everyday Americans like these getting involved, speaking their minds, and advocating for commonsense reforms, I am increasingly confident we will get our fiscal house in order. Republicans are determined to do our part to advance the goals I have mentioned. That is why we have been fighting to cut spending in the near term, and that is why we will soon be proposing a balanced budget amendment. American families have to balance their budgets; so should their elected representatives in Washington. It is not too much to expect that lawmakers spend no more than they take in, unless you think it is extreme to balance the books.

That brings us to the heart of the matter. The last time the Senate voted on a balanced budget amendment, in 1997, the Federal deficit was a little over $100 billion. Today, it is about $1.6 trillion. Back then, the national debt was about $5.5 trillion. Today, it is closer to $14 trillion. Back then, the amendment failed by just one vote—just one. Today, Democrats are already lining up against it.

What is extreme is the thought that government can continue on this reckless path without consequence. What is extreme is thinking we can blithely watch the Nation's debt get bigger and bigger and pretend it doesn't matter. What is extreme is spending more than $1.5 trillion than we have in a single year. This is the Democrats' approach. That is what is extreme.

The sad truth is, as our fiscal problems have become deeper, Democrats in Washington and many others in statehouses across the country have become increasingly less concerned about the consequences. Look no farther than the ongoing spending debate in which Democrats have fought tooth and nail over a proposal to cut a few billion dollars at a time when we are borrowing about $4 billion a day and our national debt stands at $14 trillion; the President has set the debate out entirely; and Democrats have the nerve to call anyone who expresses concern an extremist. If you are wondering where the tea party came from, look no further than that.

THE CONTINUING DEBATE:
Tea Party Members

What Is New

As of mid 2011, 60 of 242 House Republicans (24 percent) and 4 of 47 Senate Republicans (9 percent) were members of the Tea Party Caucus in Congress. The Tea Party was particularly in the news during the struggle in 2011 over the conditions that should prevail to allow raising the national debt limit. During the negotiations that were largely conducted between Republican House Speaker John Boehner and Democratic President Barack Obama, members of the House Tea Party Caucus were widely reported to have been a key factor in forcing Obama to give way on his wish to raise taxes and spare social welfare programs from cuts. Critics of the Tea Party castigated its legislators for intransigence and playing politics with the national economy, and 66 Republicans, including most Tea Party Caucus members, voted against the compromise package that Speaker Boehner and President Obama hammered out. Yet so did 95 House Democrats, most of them from the most liberal wing of their party. Thus the ideologues from both parties, not just the Tea Partyers, voted no.

Where to Find More

A look at Tea Party adherents and their impact on politics is available in Scott Rasmussen and Doug Schoen, *Mad As Hell: How the Tea Party Movement Is Fundamentally Remaking Our Two-Party System* (Broadside Books, 2011). Yet more information can be found at Pollingreport.com at www.pollingreport.com/ by searching the term "Tea Party." A positive view of the Tea Party is relayed by former House Republican leader Dick Armey and Matt Kibbe in *Give Us Liberty: A Tea Party Manifesto* (William Morrow, 2010). A strongly critical analysis has been written by Jill Lepore in *The Whites of Their Eyes: The Tea Party's Revolution and the Battle over American History* (Princeton University Press, 2010).

What More to Do

Form your own opinion of the Tea Party. Search the net to find some of the many, many sites of Tea Party adherents to get a flavor of what the movement's supporters want. Even better, contact one or more adherents. The Web site of the Tea Party Patriots at www.teapartypatriots.org/ has a function that lets you seek out Tea Party groups by ZIP code. So find one near you, interact with group members, and see if you find them patriots or nut cases.

10 VOTING/CAMPAIGNS/ELECTIONS

ELECTING THE PRESIDENT
Adopt the National Popular Vote Plan *or* Preserve the Electoral College?

ADOPT THE NATIONAL POPULAR VOTE PLAN

ADVOCATE: National Popular Vote, an advocacy organization

SOURCE: "Agreement Among the States to Elect the President by National Popular Vote," from the Web site of National Popular Vote, April 29, 2009

PRESERVE THE ELECTORAL COLLEGE

ADVOCATE: John Samples, Director, Center for Representative Government, Cato Institute

SOURCE: "A Critique of the National Popular Vote Plan for Electing the President," *Policy Analysis*, October 13, 2008

Most Americans do not understand clearly how they elect their presidents. When one poll asked "What is meant by the Electoral College?" only 20% of those surveyed correctly responded that it elected the president. Another 35% gave various incorrect answers, and 46% admitted they did not know. Another survey asked how the election would be resolved if there was a tie in the Electoral College. "By the House of Representatives," the correct answer, was chosen by 25% of the respondents, while 24% incorrectly chose the Senate. Another 32% thought that whomever had won the popular vote would become president, 2% guessed that a coin toss would decide the election, and 17% said they did not know.

It is worrisome that most people did not know what the Electoral College is, but they can hardly be blamed for not knowing the intricacies of the complex procedure. Basically, the Electoral College is an indirect process for selecting the U.S. president. Each state selects a number of electors equal to its combined representation in the U.S. House and Senate, and the District of Columbia gets three electors, for a total of 538 electors. The exact process for choosing electors varies by state, but as a general rule each party or candidate selects a slate of electors. It is for one of these slates that the people vote in November. In all states except Maine and Nebraska, there is a "winner-take-all" system in which the slate that receives the most votes wins. Then the individual electors cast their separate ballots for president and vice president in December. The ballots are sent to Congress, where they are counted in early January. It takes a majority of all electoral votes (270) to win. If no individual receives a majority, then the House selects a president from among the candidates with the three highest electoral votes. Each state casts one vote in the House, and it requires a majority of the states (26) to win. The Senate, with each member voting individually, chooses a vice president from among the top two electoral vote recipients. This type of election by Congress as happened twice (1800 and 1824).

You will see in the following readings that there are many objections to, and countering defenses of, the Electoral College. The most important is that it is possible for one candidate to win the popular vote and another to win the Electoral College and become president. This has occurred three times (1876, 1888, and 2000). In 2000, Al Gore received 51,003,238 popular votes to only 50,459,624 votes for George W. Bush in the 2000 presidential election. Yet Bush became president when he received 271 electoral votes to Gore's 266. More generally, the winning candidate's share of the popular vote and share of the electoral vote are never the same. In 2008, for example, Barack Obama received 67.8% of the electoral votes, while getting only 52.9% of the popular vote.

Whether such outcomes are acceptable is for you to decide, but they are a product of the way the electoral college was consciously designed. Congress is constructed to balance the equality of the states in a federal system (with each state getting two votes in the Senate) and the idea of majority rule (with each state's population largely determining its number of seats in the House). Thus, there was never any assumption that the president should or would be elected by a majority popular vote when the delegates at the Constitutional Convention in Philadelphia created the Electoral College. Indeed, a second motive for the Electoral College was to insulate the selection of president from the people. As Alexander Hamilton explained in *Federalist* #68 (1788), he and others worried that the "general mass" would not "possess the information and discernment requisite to such complicated investigations," raising the possibility of "tumult and disorder." This is part of the reason why the Constitution left it up to each state to determine how its electors are chosen. At first most states had their legislature choose the electors. During the first presidential election in 1789, the electors were chosen by popular vote in only four states. It was the presidential election in 1804 before a majority of states used the popular vote to pick electors, and the last state legislature did not give up its ability to choose electors until South Carolina did so in 1860.

Over time members of Congress have introduced over 700 proposals to reform or eliminate the Electoral College, and polls dating back to 1944 show a majority of Americans up until the 1960s favoring its dissolution. Yet it survives in part because amending the Constitution is so difficult. Some years ago, those who favor electing the president by popular vote thought of a possible way to get around the need for a constitutional amendment and launched an effort to institute the National Popular Vote (NPV) plan. It is well described in the first reading, which also advocates its adoption and decries the Electoral College. The second reading defends the Electoral College in general and criticizes the NPV plan as an alternative.

POINTS TO PONDER

➤ Remember that it is possible to both (a) favor eliminating or revising the Electoral College and (b) oppose the NPV plan.

➤ Which is more important, the aspect of federalism that is part of the Electoral College vote calculation or the "majority rules" aspect of the NPV plan?

➤ What do you make of the arguments that the NPV plan is/is not constitutional?

Electing the President:
Adopt the National Popular Vote Plan

NATIONAL POPULAR VOTE

The National Popular Vote bill would guarantee the Presidency to the candidate who receives the most popular votes in all 50 states (and the District of Columbia).

The National Popular Vote bill has been enacted by states possessing 61 electoral votes—23% of the 270 necessary to activate the law (Hawaii, Washington, Illinois, New Jersey, and Maryland).

The bill has passed 27 legislative chambers in 17 states, including Arkansas, California, Colorado, Hawaii, Illinois, Maine, Maryland, Massachusetts, Michigan, Nevada, New Jersey, New Mexico, North Carolina, Oregon, Rhode Island, Vermont, and Washington.

The bill is currently endorsed by 1,659 state legislators—763 sponsors (in 48 states) and an additional 896 legislators who have cast recorded votes in favor of the bill.

In numerous Gallup polls conducted since 1944, about 70% of Americans have supported a national popular vote for President (with only about 20% opposed and about 10% undecided). The *Washington Post*, Kaiser Family Foundation, and Harvard University poll show 72% support for direct nationwide election of the President.

State-level polls (most taken after the November 2008 election) show strong support for a national popular vote for president in battleground states, small states, Southern states, border states, and numerous other states. Support is strong among Republican voters, Democratic voters, and independent voters, as well as every demographic group surveyed. State polls have been conducted in Arkansas (80%), California (70%), Colorado (68%), Connecticut (73%), Delaware (75%), Kentucky (80%), Maine (77%), Massachusetts (73%), Michigan (73%), Mississippi (77%), Missouri (70%), New Hampshire (69%), Nebraska (74%), Nevada (72%), New Mexico (76%), New York (79%), North Carolina (74%), Ohio (70%), Pennsylvania (78%), Rhode Island (74%), Vermont (75%), Virginia (74%), Washington (77%), and Wisconsin (71%). Details, including cross-tabs, are available at www.NationalPopularVote.com/.

The *New York Times* endorsed National Popular Vote's plan (March 14, 2006) by calling it an "innovative new proposal" and "an ingenious solution" urging that "Legislatures across the country should get behind it." The *Chicago Sun-Times* called National Popular Vote's plan "thinking outside the box" and said "It's time to make the change with this innovative plan" (March 1, 2006). The *Minneapolis Star-Tribune* said "It's a lot to ask the Legislature to do the right thing and endorse the new compact. But it really should. So should other states—both red and blue—join, for the sake of a better democracy" (March 27, 2006). The *Los Angeles Times* endorsed the plan on June 5, 2006. The *Sacramento Bee* endorsed the bill saying "The governor and senators can get this process rolling in other states by acting this session" (June 3, 2006). Common Cause and Fair Vote have also endorsed the plan.

The National Advisory Board of National Popular Vote includes former congressmen John Anderson (R-Illinois and later independent presidential candidate), John Buchanan (R-Alabama—the first Republican elected to represent Birmingham), Tom Campbell (R-California), and Tom Downey (D-New York), and former Senators Birch Bayh (D-Indiana), David Durenberger (R-Minnesota), and Jake Garn (R-Utah).

The National Popular Vote bill is described in the 620-page book, *Every Vote Equal: A State-Based Plan for Electing the President by National Popular Vote*. The book was first released at National Popular Vote's press conference on February 23, 2006 in Washington, DC.

SHORTCOMINGS OF THE CURRENT SYSTEM

The current system of electing the president has several shortcomings—all stemming from the winner-take-all rule (i.e., awarding all of a state's electoral votes to the presidential candidate who receives the most popular votes in each state).

Because of the state-by-state winner-take-all rule, a candidate can win the presidency without winning the most popular votes nationwide. There have been four "wrong winner" elections out of the nation's 56 presidential elections. This is a failure rate of 1 in 14. But because half of American presidential elections are landslides (i.e., a margin of greater than 10% between the first- and second-place candidates), the failure rate is actually 1 in 7 among the non-landslide elections. Given that we are currently in an era of non-landslide presidential elections (1988, 1992, 1996, 2000, 2004, and 2008), it is not surprising that we have already had one election in this recent string of six elections won by the second-place candidate. Moreover, a shift of a handful of votes in one or two states would have elected the second-place candidate in five of the last 12 presidential elections. A shift of 60,000 votes in Ohio in 2004 would have elected Kerry, even though President Bush was ahead by 3,500,000 votes nationwide. A switch of fewer than 22,000 votes in 2004 in New Mexico, Nevada, and Iowa would have wiped out President Bush's majority in the Electoral College. The second-place candidate was elected in 2000, 1888, 1876, and 1824.

Another shortcoming of the current system is that voters in two thirds of the states are effectively disenfranchised in presidential elections because they do not live in closely divided "battleground" states. Under the winner-take-all rule, presidential candidates have no reason to poll, visit, advertise, organize, or campaign in states that they cannot possibly win or lose. In 2008, candidates concentrated over two-thirds of their campaign visits and ad money in just six states and 98% in just 15 states. This means that voters in two thirds of the states are ignored in presidential elections.

Both shortcomings have a single cause—the states' use of the winner-take-all rule. The winner-take-all rule is not mentioned in the U.S. Constitution. It is not a federal law. It was not the choice of the Founding Fathers. It was used by only three states in the nation's first presidential election. The winner-take-all rule exists only in state law. States have the power to change these state laws at any time.

HOW THE NATIONAL POPULAR VOTE BILL WOULD WORK

At the present time, the Electoral College reflects the voters' *state-by-state* choices for president in 48 states. In Maine and Nebraska, the Electoral College reflects the voters' *district-by-district* choices. The United States can have nationwide popular election of the president if the states change the manner of choosing their presidential electors so that the Electoral College reflects the voters' *nationwide* choice. This means changing the state laws that establish the state-level winner-take-all rule (or, in Maine and Nebraska, the district level winner-take-all rule).

Under the state legislation proposed by National Popular Vote, the popular vote counts from all 50 states and the District of Columbia would be added together to obtain a national grand total for each presidential candidate. Then, state election officials in all states participating in the plan would award their electoral votes to the presidential candidate who receives the largest number of popular votes in all 50 states and the District of Columbia.

Under the proposal, no state would act alone in offering to award its electoral votes to the nationwide winner. Instead, the National Popular Vote plan would take effect only when the plan has been enacted by states collectively possessing a majority of the electoral votes—that is 270 of the 538 electoral votes. This threshold guarantees that the presidential candidate receiving the most popular votes nationwide would win enough electoral votes in the Electoral College to become president. The 270-vote threshold corresponds essentially to states representing a majority of the people of the United States. The result would be that every vote in all 50 states and the District of Columbia is equally important in presidential elections.

The National Popular Vote plan is an interstate compact—a type of state law authorized by the U.S. Constitution that enables states to enter into a legally enforceable contractual obligation to undertake agreed joint actions. There are hundreds of interstate compacts, and each state in the United States belongs to dozens of compacts. Examples of interstate compacts include the Colorado River Compact (allocating water among seven western states), the Port Authority (a two-state compact involving New York and New Jersey), and the Multi-State Tax Compact. Some compacts involve all 50 states and the District of Columbia. Interstate compacts are generally subject to congressional consent.

As an additional benefit, National Popular Vote's plan would eliminate the (unlikely) possibility of faithless presidential electors. The presidential candidate receiving the most popular votes in all 50 states and the District of Columbia would receive a guaranteed majority of at least 270 electoral votes coming from the states enacting the compact, and the nationwide winner candidate would receive additional electoral votes from whatever non-compacting states happened to be carried by the nationwide winner. Thus, in practice, the presidential candidate receiving the most popular votes nationwide would end up with about three-quarters of the electoral votes—more than enough to eliminate the remote possibility that an unfaithful elector could affect the outcome.

Because the presidential candidate receiving the most popular votes nationwide would be guaranteed enough electoral votes in the Electoral College to become president, another benefit of the National Popular Vote plan is that it would eliminate the possibility of a presidential election being decided by the House of Representatives (where each state would have one vote) and the vice-presidential election being decided by the U.S. Senate.

Nationwide election of the president would reduce the possibility of close elections and recounts. The current system regularly manufactures artificial crises even when the nationwide popular vote is not particularly close. Even though President Bush was 3.5 million votes ahead of Kerry in 2004 on election night, the nation had to wait until Wednesday to see if Kerry would dispute Ohio's all-important 20 electoral votes. A shift of 60,000 votes in Ohio in 2004 would have given Kerry a majority of the electoral votes, despite President Bush's 3,500,000-vote lead in the nationwide popular vote. Similarly, the disputed 2000 presidential election was an artificial crisis created by one candidate's 537-vote lead in Florida in an election in which the other candidate had a 537,179-vote lead nationwide (1,000 times greater). In the nation's most controversial presidential election, Tilden's 3.1%-lead in the popular vote in 1876 was greater than Bush's substantial 2.8%-lead in 2004; however, a constitutional crisis was created by very small popular-vote margins in four states (889, 922, 1,050, and 1,075). With a single massive pool of 122,000,000 votes, there is less opportunity for a close outcome or recount (and less incentive for fraud) than with 51 separate smaller pools, where a few hundred popular votes can decide the presidency.

To prevent partisan mischief between the November voting by the people and the mid-December meeting of the Electoral College, the compact contains a six-month blackout period if any state ever wishes to withdraw from the compact. The blackout period starts on July 20 of each presidential election year and runs through the January 20 inauguration. Interstate compacts are contracts. It is settled compact law and settled constitutional law that withdrawal restrictions—very common in interstate compacts—are enforceable because the U.S. Constitution prohibits a state from impairing any obligation of contract.

Under existing law in 48 of the 50 states, the state's electoral votes are cast by a group of presidential electors who were nominated by the political party whose presidential candidate carried their particular state. People nominated for this position are almost invariably long-time party officials or activists. Under the proposed compact, the 270 or more electoral votes possessed by the states belonging to the compact would be cast by a group of presidential electors nominated by the political party whose candidate won the nationwide vote in all 50 states and the District of Columbia. This group of electors—sufficient to guarantee the election of a president—would reflect the will of the voters nationwide. None of these presidential electors would be voting contrary to his or her political inclinations or conscience. Instead, the 270 (or more) presidential electors associated with the candidate who won the nationwide vote would simply vote for their own party's presidential nominee (i.e., the nationwide choice of the voters from all 50 states and the District of Columbia). This approach implements the desire of an overwhelming majority of Americans (over 70% in recent polls), namely that the candidate who gets the most votes nationwide should become president.

Some may argue that voters would be uncomfortable with the electoral votes of their state being cast for a candidate that won the national popular vote—but not necessarily their state's vote. However, the public is not attached to the current system. Indeed, less than 20% of the public supports it. A nationwide popular vote for president inherently means that the winner would no longer be determined on the basis of which candidate carries individual states but, instead, on the basis of which candidate receives the most citizen votes in all 50 states and the District of Columbia. All of the 270 (or more) presidential electors from the states enacting the compact will be from the political party associated with the nationwide winner. When these electors cast their votes for the candidate who received the most votes nationwide, they will be implementing the method of electing the president that has long been supported by an overwhelming majority of Americans; the method that the people's elected representatives have enacted into law; and the method under which the campaign will have been conducted.

THE EXCLUSIVE POWER OF THE STATES TO AWARD
THEIR ELECTORAL VOTES

The U.S. Constitution gives the states exclusive and plenary control over the manner of awarding their electoral votes. The manner of conducting presidential elections is covered in Article II, Section 1, Clause 2 of the U.S. Constitution. "Each State shall appoint, in such Manner **as the Legislature thereof may direct**, a Number of Electors...." (emphasis added).

The constitutional wording "as the Legislature thereof may direct" contains no restrictions. It does not encourage, discourage, require, or prohibit the use of any particular method for awarding a state's electoral votes. In particular, the U.S. Constitution does not mention two of the most prominent present-day features of American presidential elections—the winner-take-all rule (awarding all of a state's electoral votes to the candidate winning the state) and citizen voting for president. These features were not part of the original Constitution, nor were they installed by any subsequent federal constitutional amendment. Instead, these features were established by state laws that were enacted, over a period of decades, on a state-by-state basis.

The winner-take-all rule was used by only three states when the Founding Fathers went back to their states to organize the nation's first presidential election in 1789. Today, it is used by 48 of the 50 states. A federal constitutional amendment was not required, nor used, to enact the winner-take-all rule in these 48 states. The 48 states simply used the power that the Founding Fathers gave them to enact this particular method for awarding their electoral votes on a state-by-state basis. The states may change their decisions concerning the winner-take-all rule, at any time, by enacting a different state law.

Only half the states participating in the nation's first presidential election gave voters a voice in presidential elections, whereas no state legislature has chosen the state's presidential electors since 1876. A federal constitutional amendment was not required, nor used, to confer the presidential vote on the people. States simply enacted state laws implementing this concept.

The fact that Maine enacted a congressional-district system in 1969 (and Nebraska did the same in 1992) is a reminder that the manner of awarding electoral votes is entirely a matter of state law. Maine and Nebraska did not need a federal constitutional amendment to modify the winner-take-all rule because the winner-take-all rule was never part of the U.S. Constitution in the first place. The legislatures of Maine and Nebraska simply used the power that the Founding Fathers gave the states to decide how to award their electoral votes.

The U.S. Supreme Court has repeatedly characterized the authority of the states over the manner of awarding their electoral votes as "plenary" and "exclusive."

In short, there is nothing in the U.S. Constitution that needs to be changed in order to implement nationwide popular vote of the president. This change can be accomplished in the same manner as the current system was originally adopted—namely the states using their exclusive and plenary power to decide the manner of awarding their electoral votes.

NATIONWIDE POPULAR ELECTION WILL GIVE A VOICE TO SMALL STATES

It is sometimes asserted that the current system helps the nation's least populous states. It is also sometimes asserted that the small states confer a partisan advantage on one political party. In fact, neither statement is true.

Twelve of the 13 smallest states are almost totally ignored in presidential elections because they are politically non-competitive. Idaho, Montana, Wyoming, North Dakota, South Dakota, and Alaska regularly vote Republican, and Rhode Island, Delaware, Hawaii, Vermont, Maine, and DC regularly vote Democratic. These 12 states together contain 11 million people. Because of the two electoral-vote bonus that each state receives, the 12 non-competitive small states have 40 electoral votes.

However, the two-vote bonus is an entirely illusory advantage to the small states. Ohio has 11 million people and has "only" 20 electoral votes. As we all know, the 11 million people in Ohio are the center of attention in presidential campaigns, while the 11 million people in the 12 non-competitive small states are utterly irrelevant. Nationwide election of the president would make each of the voters in the 12 smallest states as important as an Ohio voter.

The fact that the bonus of two electoral votes is an illusory benefit to the small states has been widely recognized by the small states for some time. In 1966, Delaware led a group of 12 predominantly low-population states (North Dakota, South Dakota, Wyoming, Utah, Arkansas, Kansas, Oklahoma, Iowa, Kentucky, Florida, Pennsylvania) in suing New York in the U.S. Supreme Court. Delaware and the other states argued that New York's use of the winner-take-all rule effectively disenfranchised voters in their states. The Court declined to hear the case (presumably because of the well-established constitutional provision that the manner of awarding electoral votes is exclusively a state decision). Ironically, defendant New York is no longer a closely divided "battleground" state (as it was in the 1950's and 1960's) and today suffers the very same disenfranchisement as the 12 non-competitive small states. A vote in New York is, today, equal to a vote in Wyoming—both are equally worthless and irrelevant in presidential elections.

NATIONWIDE POPULAR ELECTION WILL MEAN A 50-STATE CAMPAIGN

Although no one can accurately predict exactly how a presidential campaign would be run if every vote were equal throughout the United States, it is clear that presidential candidates would have to run 50-state campaigns. It would be politically impossible, under a nationwide vote, for presidential candidates to ignore two-thirds of the states, as they now do.

In round numbers, both major party candidates have time for about 450 campaign visits during a three-month presidential campaign (coincidentally, a number that is roughly equal to the number of congressional districts in the country, namely 435). Presidential candidates now concentrate their 450 visits heavily in battleground states, such as Ohio and Wisconsin, while virtually ignoring the equally-populous near-by states of Illinois and Indiana. In a nationwide vote for president, every vote would be equally important throughout the country. The Republican Party would suddenly care about whether its share of the vote in Indiana was 58% or 62% (as opposed to its 60% share in 2004), and it would therefore campaign in Indiana. Similarly, the Democratic Party would campaign in Indiana because it would care whether its (losing) share was 38%, 40%, or 42%. Therefore, in a nationwide vote for president, both presidential candidates would have to start paying specific attention to issues of concern to Indiana. Failure to campaign in every state, or failure to campaign in the current spectator states, would be punished as surely and severely as a gubernatorial or senatorial candidate is punished if he or she ever seems to be ignoring areas inside a state, presidential candidates could not continue to concentrate over two-thirds of their campaign visits in just six states, and over 80% in just nine states. Thus, in a nationwide vote, each presidential campaign would have to reallocate its limited campaigning resources over all the states. On average, candidates would allocate one visit to each congressional district.

A small state such as Idaho with two congressional districts could reasonably expect two visits from both the Democratic candidate and the Republican candidate.

Currently, of course, Idaho receives no attention from either party because the Republican candidate has nothing to gain in Idaho, and the Democratic candidate has nothing to lose. Although Idaho would undoubtedly continue to deliver a popular-vote majority to the Republican presidential candidate, every vote in Idaho would suddenly matter to both the Democrat and the Republican candidates. It would be folly for John Kerry to write off Idaho because he would care if he lost Idaho by 227,000 versus a somewhat smaller or larger number. Similarly, it would be folly for George Bush to take Idaho for granted because he would care if he won by 227,000 versus some larger or smaller number. As the *Idaho State Journal* editorialized in 2004, "As we enter the home stretch of the quadrennial horse race known as the presidential election, it's time to remember that this is an election for the president of the United States of America—all 50 states, not an election for the president of the Swing States of America."

The expenditure of money for advertising, organizing, and campaigning is allocated in a manner that parallels campaign visits. In round numbers, both major-party candidates (and their closely allied groups) had about a half billion dollars at their disposal in 2004 (that is, an average of roughly $1 million for each of the nation's 435 congressional districts). Under a nationwide vote, each presidential campaign would have to reallocate its campaigning resources over all the nation's 435 congressional districts. Thus, on average, candidates could be expected to allocate one visit to each congressional district and $1,000,000.

Although it is sometimes conjectured that a national popular election would focus only on big cities, it is clear that this would not be the case. Evidence as to how a nationwide presidential campaign would be run can be found by examining the way presidential candidates *currently* campaign *inside* battleground states. Inside Ohio or Florida, the big cities do not receive all the attention. And, the cities of Ohio and Florida certainly do not control the outcome in those states. Because every vote is equal inside Ohio or Florida, presidential candidates avidly seek out voters in small, medium, and large towns. The itineraries of presidential candidates in battleground states (and their allocation of other campaign resources in battleground states) reflect the political reality that every gubernatorial or senatorial candidate in Ohio and Florida already knows—namely that when every vote is equal, the campaign must be run in every part of the state.

Further evidence of the way a nationwide presidential campaign would be run comes from national advertisers who seek out customers in small, medium, and large towns of every small, medium, and large state. A national advertiser does not write off Indiana or Illinois merely because a competitor makes more sales in those particular states. Moreover, a national advertiser enjoying an edge over its competitors in Indiana or Illinois does not stop trying to make additional sales in those states. National advertisers go after every single possible customer, regardless of where the customer is located.

Electing the President: Preserve the Electoral College

John Samples

The U.S. Constitution provides for the election of the president of the United States in Article II, section 1 and in the Twelfth Amendment. Article II states: "Each State shall appoint, in such Manner as the Legislature thereof may direct, a Number of Electors, equal to the whole Number of Senators and Representatives to which the State may be entitled in the Congress." The Twelfth Amendment provides for the casting of electoral ballots, a majority of which suffices for election. For well over a century, almost all states have elected to cast their votes by the unit rule in which the winner in a state receives all of that state's electoral votes. The National Popular Vote (hereinafter NPV) plan proposes an interstate compact to bring about direct election of the president of the United States. States that join the compact would agree to cast their electoral votes for the winner of the national popular vote for president. The compact would become valid once states with a majority of presidential electors sign on. Congress must approve of the compact before states can agree to it. By July 1, 2008, four states—Hawaii, Illinois, New Jersey and Maryland—had passed NPV; the four together control 50 electoral votes. Supporters also say the proposal has been introduced in 42 states. They hope NPV will govern the 2012 presidential election. I begin this analysis by examining the differences between NPV's plan for electing the president and the Constitution's method for doing so. I then turn to NPV's effects on the relative influence of the states in presidential elections. Although the NPV seeks to equalize the power of voters, it is Congress and state legislators that will decide the fate of this proposal. The latter will wish to know if the NPV enhances or depreciates the influences of their constituents on a presidential election. Finally, I will evaluate the costs and benefits of NPV.

NPV AND THE STATUS QUO

NPV sets as its goal implementing a nationwide popular election of the president and vice president, a significant change from the constitutional status quo. Under NPV, presidential electors "would reflect the nationwide will of the voters—not the voters' separate statewide wills." The states that are parties to the compact would award all their electoral votes to "the presidential slate receiving the most popular votes in all 50 States and the District of Columbia." Taken together, those votes would number at least 270 electoral votes, i.e. the necessary majority for election.

NPV does not necessarily impose election by a majority. If a plurality suffices for election, a majority of voters may have chosen someone other than the winner. Under NPV, the nation is the electoral district. In the current way of electing the president, the states are important. States qua states are represented in a presidential election because electors are allocated on the basis of both population and states. State legislatures also decide how to allocate their electors. Each state constitutes an electoral district for purposes of allocating a state's electors. NPV thus proposes to change the way Americans elect a president by eliminating the states as election districts in favor of the nation.

The current system allows states more choices in how to allocate electors. As noted, NPV proposes a winner-take-all system that follows the national popular vote; each state in the compact allocates all its electors to the candidates with the most popular votes nationwide. The Constitution empowers state legislatures to decide how to allocate electors. In practice, almost all states have selected a winner-take-all rule for allocating their electoral votes. A few states have chosen other methods of allocation, now and in the past. All votes would be equally weighted under NPV. As we shall later learn, there are several ways of measuring the influence of individual votes under the Electoral College. Clearly the framers did not intend to create a means to elect presidents that depended on equal weighting of individual votes. The representation given states qua states precluded such equality from the start. This move toward equal weighting of votes also suggests how different NPV would be from the constitutional status quo.

We may summarize the differences between the two ways of electing a president. The Constitution assigns importance to the states in electing the president. NPV recognizes only a national electoral district in which individuals cast equally-weighted votes. The states matter only as contractors to the NPV compact; the agreement itself makes the allocation of state electors a function of a plurality of voters in the national district. The constitutional plan does not restrict how states may allocate their electors although almost all have chosen a winner-take-all system. NPV requires the states to have a winner-take-all system that follows the votes of a national plurality or majority. The actual majority or plurality vote for president in a state has no influence on the election of the president. In general, NPV proposes two changes to the current means of electing the U.S. president. It eliminates states as electoral districts in presidential elections. It creates through a state compact a national electoral district for the presidential election. In that way, the NPV advances a national political identity for the United States.

THE INTERESTS OF THE STATES

The U.S. Constitution allocates electors to the states on the basis of their population (each gets one per House seat) and their equality (because each gets two electors regardless of size) (Article II, section 1). The most populous states would be less influential in electing the president than they would be under a direct election proposal. This difference is not large. The constitutional plan (known as the electoral college) reflects population by allocating electors according to House membership, which is four times greater than the Senate membership. Moreover, a state's influence in an actual presidential election may depend on more than its relative population. A state whose electoral votes are crucial to determining the winner of an election enjoys more influence than a state whose votes do not affect the outcome of the election. State legislatures will likely decide the fate of the NPV. Although many factors will affect these decisions, each legislature is likely to consider whether NPV increases or decreases the influence of their state over the presidential election. There are two ways to look at the question of which states would win and which would lose by moving to direct elections. First, I will examine the question on the basis of state's share of the total electors and its eligible voters (*the relative measure*). Next, I will turn to some estimates of the relative influence of each state in determining the winner of the presidency (*the power measure*).

The Relative Measure

Under the current system, a particular state's influence over a presidential election may be measured by dividing a state's electoral votes by the total electoral votes for the nation. The influence of a state under direct election is measured by dividing the number of eligible voters in a state in 2000 by the total number of eligible voters in the nation in 2000. The absolute gain or loss of a state from moving to direct election equals the difference between this measure of its influence under the electoral college and the same number under direct election. This absolute measure of state influence is difficult to interpret. I have thus constructed a relative measure of how much each state wins or loses from direct election. The relative gain or loss of a state equals its absolute gain or loss divided by the measure of its influence under the electoral college.

NPV would move us from the presidential status quo to direct election. Twenty states may expect to gain from moving to direct election. Most of these gains are quite small. Six states may expect to gain more than 10 percent in influence according to this measure. In contrast, 29 states and the District of Columbia lose influence from the move to direct election. Of those, 20 states and the District of Columbia may be expected to lose more than 10 percent of their influence over the presidential election by the change. A large part of this group would lose about half their current influence over the presidential election.

Power Measures

In practice, the influence of a state in selecting a president depends on how likely it is that the state will cast the pivotal vote that constitutes a majority in the electoral college for a candidate. States that are more likely to cast the deciding vote have more influence over the selection. If the deciding vote were distributed randomly, larger states would tend to be more powerful in presidential elections simply because they have more electoral votes, the Senate bonus not withstanding. Of course, the deciding vote in the electoral college has not been distributed randomly. States that are more competitive are more likely to cast the deciding vote. In other words, battleground states will have the most actual influence over the presidential outcome.

State officials who wish to determine whether their state benefits from the electoral college face the daunting task of determining whether their state is likely to be competitive (i.e. likely to cast a deciding vote for president). We might reasonably assume that the NPV would enact direct election of the president for the foreseeable future. A state legislator thus would like to know whether their state will be competitive in the future. No study has offered that knowledge. A study by George Rabinowitz and Stuart Elaine Macdonald ["The Power of the States in U.S. Presidential Elections," *American Political Science Review* (1986)] has estimated which states have the most influence under the current electoral college plan, taking into account their likely competitiveness. We can also examine in a less systematic way which states have been competitive in recent elections.

Rabinowitz and Macdonald collected data about the partisan and ideological leanings of the states in presidential elections from 1944 to 1980. They then simulated a large number of elections to determine how often a state occupies the pivotal position in a presidential election. The results of that simulation are interesting. Once again, the most powerful state comes first in the list, the least influential at the bottom. The power of a state in the electoral college is highly correlated to its size. California is by far the most influential state followed by Texas, New York, Illinois, and Ohio. States with small populations also tend to have less influence by the Rabinowitz-Macdonald measure. That is not surprising. Large states are less likely to be politically or otherwise homogeneous, which may be related to more competition in presidential elections.

In contrast to the earlier ranking of states, the Rabinowitz-Macdonald measures suggests that large states have the most influence in the selecting of a president. Where the voting measure suggests that large states would benefit by moving to direct election, the Rabinowitz-Macdonald study suggests they dominate the current system.

Another study found that voters in large states have more influence over presidential elections than voters from small states. Lawrence Longley and James Dana ["The Biases of the Electoral College in the 1990s," *Polity* (1992)] examined the relative influence of voters within states in the 1990s.

They did not attempt to estimate how likely it was a state would be competitive as part of their investigation. Instead, they calculated both the likelihood that a state would cast the pivotal vote in the electoral college and that a voter could change the way his state's electoral votes were cast by changing his vote. Longley and Dana found that citizens in all but six of the states have lower than average voting power in presidential elections. Voters in the six most populous states have greater than average influence. The study concluded, "the electoral college in the 1990s contains partially countervailing biases which result in a net advantage to large states as much as 2.663 to one, and a net *disadvantage* to states with from 3 to 21 electoral votes." [emphasis in original]

Two recent studies offer new insights about the power of voters and states under the electoral college and under the direct vote. Jonathan Katz, Andrew Gelman, and Gary King ["Empirically Evaluating the Electoral College," in *Rethinking the Vote: The Politics and Prospects of American Election Reform,* ed. Ann N. Crigler, Marion R. Just, and Edward J. McCaffery (New York: Oxford University Press, 2004)] examined the relative power of a vote under the electoral college and a direct vote system. Looking at presidential elections since 1960, they found minimal difference between the two systems in the estimated average probability of a voter being decisive. The method of voting did not affect the actual power of voters in these presidential elections.

The most recently published study of the electoral college uses a different measure of power: candidate attention to a state as measured by the number of visits. This measure of power fits well with the concerns of the NPV proposers who criticize the current system because only a few states receive attention from candidates under the electoral college. David Strömberg ["How the Electoral College Influences Campaigns and Policy: The Probability of Being Florida," *American Economic Review* (2008)] examines the actual number of visits to all states in the presidential elections from 1948 to 2000. He then constructs a model to predict the number of visits each state would receive under direct election of the president. He calculates which states will gain and lose visits under each voting system. Strömberg also concludes that small states do not benefit from the electoral college on balance.

By Strömberg's calculations, [the] twenty states that control 221 electoral votes would receive more visits under a direct vote for president; [the] twenty states that control 210 electoral votes receive more visits under the electoral college. Ten states and the District of Columbia (107 electoral votes) neither gain nor lose visits by moving to a direct vote. Looked at this way, the states that would benefit from a direct vote are 49 electoral votes short of the majority needed to pass NPV. The states that would gain comprised 41 percent of eligible voters in the 2006 elections; the states that would lose under direct election comprised 38 percent which implies that 21 percent of the nation's eligible voters lives in states that would neither gain nor lose by moving to direct election. In sum, the same number of states would lose from a direct vote as would gain, and the losers control almost as many electoral votes as the gainers. Finally, if we add the states that have reason to be indifferent since they neither gain nor lose from a direct vote to the states that would lose visits, we discover a coalition of states who have no reason to move to a direct vote and control a majority of 317 electoral votes. The number of eligible voters tells a similar story. Fifty-nine percent of eligible voters in 2006 lived in states that would either lose influence under direct election or would be indifferent about moving away from the electoral college.

Implications

It is often said that the electoral college benefits small states that block efforts to amend the Constitution to institute direct election of the president. This assumption implies most states would benefit from moving to direct election but are stymied by the supermajority requirements of amending the basic law and the determination of small states to hold on to their privileges. In fact, these matters are much more complicated than most people assume.

In practice, actual influence under the electoral college depends on the likelihood a state and its voters will have a competitive election and be decisive in determining the outcome of the presidential election. Some studies indicate some more populous states are more likely to decide an election under the electoral college and thus have more power. More recent studies, however, indicate either the power of a vote is about the same under the electoral college and the direct vote or that state size has little relationship to actual influence under either system. It is far from clear that most states would enjoy more influence over the presidential election in a direct vote system.

Moving away from the electoral college involves transaction costs and risks. To justify those costs and risks, a state legislator should have clear evidence that its voters will enjoy more influence under direct election than they do under the electoral college. We have seen that more than a few states will do worse under direct election. Several other states by various measures can expect to wield about as much influence under direct election as under the electoral college. Given the costs of moving away from the status quo, these indifferent states have little reason to support NPV. Adding the indifferent states to those who lose from the change may well form a coalition of states who control a majority of electoral votes. The electoral college, not NPV, may be the preference of a majority of states.

Legislators in most states should find it difficult to determine whether their constituents will gain or lose influence over presidential elections by moving away from the electoral college toward direct election. Given that uncertainty, the costs of trying to change the status quo, and the relative apathy of constituents about the way the nation selects the president, it is not surprising that the electoral college has not been seriously challenged within memory.

NPV poses other problems beyond calculations of political advantage. It raises deep questions of legitimacy and institutional change. In this regard, the benefits of the proposal also seem doubtful.

COSTS OF THE NPV PROPOSAL

Legitimacy

The Oxford English Dictionary defines legitimate as "conformable to law or rule; sanctioned or authorized by law or right; lawful; proper." Similarly, the same dictionary defines the noun legitimacy as "the condition of being in accordance with law or principle." The word itself can be traced to a Latin root that means "to be declared lawful." A legitimate government action should conform to the law and ultimately to the fundamental law, the U.S. Constitution. The idea of legitimacy is particularly important for actions that changed the law and especially the fundamental law. If *any* action changing a law could be considered legitimate, the fundamental law would be irrelevant for practical purposes. A second, related meaning of legitimacy may be found in the social sciences: "to ask whether a political system is legitimate or not is to ask whether the state, or government, is entitled to be obeyed." The idea of legitimacy thus links "being in accordance with law" with being worthy of being obeyed. Article V of the U.S. Constitution provides a procedure for amending the fundamental law. It depends on demanding supermajorities; typically, an amendment requires approval by two-thirds of Congress and three-fourths of the states. The supermajority requirement tends to inhibit amendments but does not preclude them. It favors amendments that have broad support. The amendment process thus protects significant (but not quite small) minorities.

Some supporters of NPV concede that their proposal seeks to circumvent the amendment process. The prominent journalist, E. J. Dionne ["Bypassing the Electoral College," *Washington Post,* April 2, 2007] wrote of the NPV plan: "this is an effort to circumvent the cumbersome process of amending the Constitution. That's the only practical way of moving toward a more democratic system. Because three-quarters of the states have to approve an amendment to the Constitution, only 13 sparsely populated states—overrepresented in the electoral college—could block popular election." Some who believe the constitutional method of electing the president should be changed agree that the NPV plan circumvents the Constitution. The editorial board of *The Milwaukee Journal Sentinel* concluded, "The U.S. Constitution, when it comes to the Electoral College, is flawed. However, rather than take the direct route to fix that, amending the Constitution, this proposal simply subverts it. This method complies with the letter of the Constitution but violates the spirit."

NPV advocates argue that their proposal comports with the Constitution and no amendment is necessary. They argue that the states are empowered by the Constitution to appoint electors "in such Manner as the Legislature may direct" which arguably includes assigning electors with regard to the outcome of the national popular vote. They suggest that the power to appoint electors is unconstrained by the Constitution. It is accurate that the Constitution does not explicitly constrain the power of state legislatures in allocating electors. But a brief consideration of the history of the drafting of this part of the Constitution suggests some implicit constraints on state choices.

The Framers considered several ways of electing a president. The three major ways were the current system, direct election by the people, and selection by Congress. On July 17, 1787, the delegates from nine states voted against direct election of the president; the representatives of one state, Pennsylvania, voted for it. The Framers chose an alternative to direct election which is described in Article II, section 1 of the Constitution. Of course, that decision by the framers need not bind Americans for all time. The Constitution also permits overturning the decisions of the framers through amendments to the Constitution. In contrast, NPV proposes that a group of states with a majority of electoral votes should have the power to overturn the explicit decision of the Framers against direct election. Since that power does not conform to the constitutional means of changing the original decisions of the framers, NPV could not be a legitimate innovation.

The authors of NPV strongly suggest that congressional consent to the proposed interstate compact is not necessary. Robert Bennett [*Taming the Electoral College*

(Stanford University Press, 2006)] argues the Supreme Court might not require a compact be approved by Congress if the agreement did not "enhance the political power of the [agreeing] States at the expense of other States or have an 'impact on the federal structure.'" But NPV does not meet these conditions. It harms those states whose citizens benefit from the current system of election. NPV also eliminates all states as electoral districts. Those states that adopt the NPV may see that elimination as a boon; others outside the compact may find the change to be a cost. The elimination of the states as electoral districts surely has "an impact on the federal structure" of presidential elections. For all practical purposes, NPV eliminates the federal character of presidential elections. For these reasons, Congress should have the chance to consent to NPV or to reject it.

E.J. Dionne's comment suggests that the demands of democracy should take precedence over constitutional constraints on the will of the people. The current means of electing the president may slightly reduce the influence of states that comprise a large majority of the eligible voters in the United States. Democracy in this regard may be taken to mean: the majority shall rule. Here again we have a question of legitimacy. The United States was designed to be a republic, "a government which derives all its power directly or indirectly from the great body of the people." It was not designed to be a government ruled by unconstrained majorities.

Would E.J. Dionne agree that the wishes of a majority should trump the Constitution's guarantee that Congress shall make no law abridging freedom of the press? The number of constraints against majority rule could be extended, but the point has been made. Circumvention of the Constitution in the name of majority rule cannot be legitimate in the United States. In sum, the NPV group poses the question whether we wish to have legitimate presidential elections and a constitutional government. If NPV succeeds, we will have less of both, at the margins.

Nationalization

The U.S. Constitution allocates presidential electors according to the federalist principle. Anti-federalists feared the new Constitution would centralize power and threaten liberty as well as subordinate the smaller states to the larger. The founders sought to fashion institutional compromises that responded to the concerns of the states and yet created a more workable government than had existed under the Articles of Confederation. With regard to presidential elections, they pursued a middle course that rejected both election by state legislatures and election by a national popular vote. The constitutional plan instead offers a compound means of election in which the states are considered as both co-equals in an association and as unequal members.

This same balancing of state and national elements may be found elsewhere in the Constitution. This general preference for federalism signaled that the new Constitution would not be wholly national in character and that the national government would be part of a larger design of checks and balances that would temper and restrain political power, a major concern of both the Founders and their Anti-Federalist critics.

These expectations for federalism have not been realized. In the past fifty years, the national government has increasingly treated the states as administrative units for larger national undertakings. Looked at historically, the role of the states in electing a president would be a likely target for elimination as part of these nationalizing trends. The nationalization of the political parties has also vitiated the selection of electors as state representatives; they now are chosen for their loyalty to national parties rather than as citizens of a state.

The realization of the NPV plan would continue this trend toward nationalization and centralized power. The president is the most important elected official in the nation. Under the NPV proposal, he or she will be elected by the nation acting as an electorate. Inevitably, this change will foster the creation of a national consciousness among Americans, a unified and centralized political identity. The president will thus be empowered as the choice of this national electoral district; he or she will speak for a plurality of that nation. As the renowned constitutional scholar Martin Diamond said, direct election of the president will not "increase the democracy of the election or the directness of the election but the pure nationalness of the election. The sole practical effect of [direct election] will be to eliminate the States from their share in the political process." A president so elected may be more likely to pursue national interests at a cost to state or regional concerns because state identities and considerations will no longer matter at all since the states will no longer exist so far as presidential elections go. Such a president "might also be likely to pursue policies that enhance or enlarge the scope and power of the federal government."

While direct election may not have strong partisan effects, the further empowering of the federal government and a subsequent increase in its ambit would run counter to the founding aspirations for limited government and individual liberty. It would be fully in line with the progressive emphasis on the national community, a purely national electorate, and the empowered executive. In other words, if people create institutions, institutions also create people, and the NPV will lead to a more nationalized and progressive electorate. Skeptics might object that the United States has already developed a centralized, national political identity. Few people are said to think of themselves as citizens of a particular state. The same skeptics might also note that the integration of the states into a unified national Leviathan has been a natural development fostered by the preferences of voters. Yet in our lifetime the hope for limited government has proven politically popular, and the states have enjoyed a renaissance based on policy achievements. The possibility of a renewed decentralization of power remains open.

The NPV plan also mistakenly assumes that the people living in the United States are a unified nation that should act as one in selecting their leader. But the United States today is deeply polarized along partisan, ideological, and other dimensions. These differences relate strongly to territorial and regional differences. Rather than forcing all these differences into a single national electoral district, the nation would do better to foster institutions that allow people who deeply disagree to live at some distance from one another in fact and in politics. Instead of further fostering a national identity, we should hold open the possibility of a more decentralized government in which people who profoundly disagree about things can live separately in peace. The NPV proposal would make that decentralization of identity marginally more difficult.

Disputed Outcomes

As in 2000, it is possible that one state will experience an election dispute that could affect the outcome of the presidential race. The struggles associated with such a dispute will be relatively confined. The same would not be true of the NPV alternative. Rational candidates or party leaders would have reason to dispute results throughout the nation to overturn close outcomes. Indeed, what constitutes a close election would become broader since the necessary votes to overturn the result could be found nation-wide. That would be more difficult and more contentious than the current system. As political scientist David Lublin ["Popular Vote? Not Yet. Problems With a Plan to Kill the Electoral College," *Washington Post*, July 16, 2007] has noted, the parties and the media would have difficulty supervising recounts and litigation around the country. As Lublin argues, "We might not even be able to have a national recount. All existing recount laws were designed to address elections within states. Compact states cannot compel other states to participate." NPV's supporters say it tends toward a clear result. But in a close election, the scope of its electoral district might well preclude a settled outcome in a close presidential contest.

PUTATIVE BENEFITS OF THE NPV PLAN

Ignored States

The authors of NPV note that under the current system candidates write off many uncompetitive states, which means those states are ignored by the campaigns. Several political scientists recently wrote that "Presidential campaigns have a clear tendency to concentrate their resources on a relatively small number of competitive states—states that both candidates have some legitimate prospect of carrying—while ignoring states that appear solidly to favor one camp or the other." This is not a new story. Scholars found that candidates in both the 1960 and 1976 campaign concentrated their resources in this manner. In contrast, the NPV advocates argue, a direct popular election would value all votes equally. Candidates would presumably seek votes in all states since they would all count equally toward victory.

The states, and not the Constitution, create the problem complained of by the NPV authors. Currently 48 states allocate their electors according to the winner-take-all standard; the District of Columbia also employs this method. This has been true for some time. By 1824 only six of twenty-four states selected electors by state legislatures. By 1832, all but one chose by popular election. After 1832, selecting electors by popular vote meant popular vote by general ticket which meant "winner take all." This rule offers the dominant party in the state legislature (and thus probably in the presidential contest) more electors than under say, a division of electors along the lines of the popular vote.

Of course, state legislatures need not choose a "winner take all" rule for selecting electors. They could divide electors according to the popular vote if they believed it would attract attention from presidential candidates thereby benefiting their state. But few states do so. That suggests most legislators believe "winner take all" benefits their state more than the candidate attention that might come from a division according to the popular vote. Since these legislators are elected by the people, we have to reason to think the "winner take all" system reflects the popular will.

This judgment by legislators raises another issue. Why should citizens in a state be concerned about being ignored because of a lack of competition? Voters can easily gather sufficient information from the national media to cast their ballot. Businesses in a neglected state may miss the tax receipts generated by the candidate, her entourage, and the media, but such losses do not seem relevant. After all, the nation does not hold presidential elections to foster local economic development. Neglected states may be concerned that if a candidate can take a state for granted during the campaign, he or she will do less for the state once in office, at least compared to what they might have done if the state had been competitive. NPV thus appeals to the material and thus political interests of voters in neglected states.

As a political tactic, the appeal to neglected states seems likely to fail. Imagine that a presidential candidate has the same sum to spend on votes under NPV as he does under the Electoral College. Imagine also, as predicted, the candidate decides to spend more under NPV on formerly neglected states (for example, by budgeting more public works for them once in office). Where would the president find the money for this spending with a fixed budget? It would have to come from states that were competitive under the Electoral College. With a fixed budget, NPV would impose losses on battleground states to benefit previously neglected states. However, individuals and groups tend to value losses more than identical benefits. All things being equal, the voters who lose by moving to NPV would care more than voters who gain from it which suggests the appeal to the material interests of neglected states would fail as a political tactic.

The "neglected state" argument also raises budgetary and moral questions. If a president under NPV simply spends more public money to reward voters in formerly neglected states, competitive states will not face losses, but the federal deficit will rise and will be financed by public borrowing. Future voters will pay higher taxes because of this increased debt. Such voters, however, will have no say about the decision to incur the debt; many of them are either too young to vote or do not exist. NPV aspires to an equality of votes for the current generation. Its political appeal, however, may rely on exploiting an inequality of voting power between the current generation and future voters.

Even if all votes are weighed equally in an election, the cost of attracting a marginal vote for president would vary. For example, it would be less expensive per voter to attract votes in populous states because of the structure of media markets. As noted earlier, there is a relationship between population size and competitiveness in presidential elections. In that respect, the marginal effect of the NPV plan would be to draw candidates toward large, competitive states. The cost of votes also depends on the efficiency of a campaign and party organization. The least costly votes are thus likely to be found in large, competitive states where the organizations have become efficient through competition and in large, non-competitive states where party organizations may have unique advantages in "running up the score." In that way, the NPV plan might bring some candidate attention to states that are now non-competitive and ignored. But running up the score in party strongholds may also increase the regionalization of presidential politics. In general, because of the relative costs of attracting votes, the NPV proposal seems likely at the margin to attract candidate attention to populous states. Many voters outside low-cost media markets may be as ignored under NPV as they are under the status quo.

Certainty of Election

NPV advocates have argued that their compact will create a clear, nationwide winner of the presidential election. Direct election of the president by a plurality or majority would almost certainly lead to a clear winner. But NPV seeks to attain direct election through an interstate compact. The question of certainty turns on whether the interstate compact will work as NPV advocates hope.

State legislatures might have strong incentives to withdraw from the compact if their commitment elects a president opposed by a majority in the legislature. Indeed, the voters who elected the legislature might demand they withdraw from the compact or face the consequences at the next election. The backers of the NPV plan outline a model compact that prevents a state from withdrawing until a president is qualified for office. NPV supporters argue the U.S. Supreme Court would enforce the agreement against a state wishing to withdraw from it; they rely on the Court's decision in *West Virginia ex rel. Dyer v. Sims,* a 1950 case involving the Ohio River Valley Water Sanitation Compact. They also cite the influence of public opinion and "safe harbor" provisions in federal law that give preference to election returns that are in accord with laws enacted prior to election day.

The Constitution empowers states to select presidential electors within the constraints implicit in the work of the Constitutional Convention. It does not say a legislature cannot change its manner of selection or that its choice must be made prior to election day. The significance of this grant of power should not be underestimated; it is one aspect of how the Founders included the states in the new government. The Constitution includes other clauses, of course, including one forbidding states to impair contracts. The Supreme Court might force a state legislature to hold to the terms of the NPV compact, but the issue would certainly be litigated, perhaps between election day and the day when electoral votes are cast. In any case, the compact has no backup provision if a state withdraws. That state's electoral votes would remain in limbo. If a legislature has withdrawn from the compact, we may presume public opinion approves or perhaps even demands a withdrawal. To be sure, a majority outside of a state may disapprove of the withdrawal, but no legislator in the withdrawing state will face those disapproving voters unless he or she runs for president. The "safe harbor" provision, if effective, will simply mean that a state withdraws prior to election day. Modern polling often enables legislators to guess the outcome of a state's presidential election.

The NPV compact may work as advertised in practice. But in a close election legislators will be under tremendous pressure, and many voters may see their states casting electoral votes for a candidate who finished second in their state. It is not clear that outcomes under the NPV compact will be any more certain than under current arrangements.

INCENTIVES FOR HIGHER TURNOUT

NPV advocates argue that the current system depresses voter turnout because voters in non-battleground states doubt their participation matters. If all votes counted equally, so the argument implies, more people would feel their votes mattered and would turn out on election day. Others have suggested that direct election would increase the incentives for a state to increase turnout. It seems unlikely that switching to direct election would actually increase turnout. Several experts on voting behavior have noted: We would expect voter participation among the most informed segments of the electorate to respond positively to the popular election of the president. This effect is probably small if not trivial. The most informed and attentive voters are already predisposed to vote. Replacing the Electoral College with the popular election of the president is not likely to be perceived by inattentive and less informed voters and will have only a trivial influence on the likelihood of voting among the most informed voters.

Should increasing voter turnout be an important goal of the nation? Current levels of turnout do not seriously bias election results; the sample of voters reasonably well represents the partisan and ideological views of the entire population of voters. Voting turnout is highly correlated to education which in turn is the best predictor of economic literacy. As the economist Bryan Caplan [*The Myth of the Rational Voter: Why Democracies Choose Bad Policies* (Princeton University Press, 2007)] discovered, increasing turnout to 100 percent would mean candidates "have to compete for the affection of noticeably more biased voters than they do today." Even lesser increases would be expected, all things being equal, to increase the number of biased (i.e. ill-informed) voters compared to the status quo. Insofar as candidates follow the wishes of voters, increased turnout would mean worse (i.e. more irrational) economic policies.

Increasing voting turnout should not be a high priority for American policymakers and even if it were, moving to direct election, perhaps especially in such a complicated way as NPV, would not bring out more voters.

CONCLUSION

NPV offers a way to institute a means of electing the president that was rejected by the Framers of the Constitution. It does so while circumventing the Constitution's amendment procedures. Implicitly, NPV advocates believe that direct election of the president by the greater number of voters weighs so heavily on the normative scales that bypassing constitutional propriety should be accepted. Yet the U.S. Constitution establishes a liberal republic not a majoritarian democracy. The NPV plan appears unlikely to deliver its promised benefits and likely to impose other costs, not least by throwing into question the legitimacy of our presidential contests. NPV gives the supporters of a losing presidential candidate little reason to accept the outcome. Legitimacy and political obligation are rooted in law, and the NPV plan circumvents our legal procedure for changing presidential elections. That alone should be enough to convince legislators in the various states that this proposal should not be adopted. The fate of NPV will also depend on the play of political interests. Would states controlling a majority of electoral votes benefit from joining NPV? Many people believe small states benefit from the electoral college. Certainly, many small states would do relatively poorly by moving to the NPV. That result does not mean, however, that large states would benefit from direct election of the president. Populous states tend to hold the most actual power over the election of the president under the current system since they tend to be the most competitive and more likely to decide an election. Medium-size states may expect few gains from NPV and losses from the change if they are competitive. It is often assumed that the electoral college persists because of the difficulty of amending the Constitution. But it appears that both small and large states have reasons to support the status quo in electing a president, and other states have good reason to be indifferent toward a change to direct election. The electoral college, though much maligned, may satisfy the interests of more states and voters than any other alternative means of electing the president including NPV.

THE CONTINUING DEBATE:
Electing the President

What Is New

In August 2011, California's governor signed an NPV plan into law. That made California the ninth Electoral College participant to adopt the NPV plan, joining the District of Columbia, Hawaii, Illinois, New Jersey, Maryland, Massachusetts, Vermont, and Washington. These states have a combined 132 electoral votes, or 49% of those needed for the plan to go into effect. Several other states, including New York with 29 electoral votes, appear to be on the verge of also enacting NPV legislation. It has been since 2007 that a national poll has tested public sentiment on using a national popular vote system rather than the Electoral College to elect the president, but that poll showed 72% favoring the popular vote.

Where to Find More

The National Archives at www.archives.gov/federal-register/electoral-college/ has extensive information on the Electoral College. The National Popular Vote organization's Web site is www.nationalpopularvote.com/. Another group opposed to the Electoral College is FairVote, and its Web site has a good discussion of options beyond the NPV. Go to www.fairvote.org/ and choose "Electoral College" in the drop-down issues menu. Additional cri iques of the NPV plan and defenses of the Electoral College are available from Daniel P. Rathbun, "Ideological Endowment: The Staying Power of the Electoral College and the Weaknesses of the National Popular Vote Interstate Compact," *Michigan Law Review* (2008); and Bradley A. Smith, "Vanity of Vanities: National Popular Vote and the Electoral College," *Election Law Journal* (2008). Taking the opposite point of view is Alexander S. Belenky, "The Good, the Bad and the Ugly," *Michigan Law Review* (2008). An edited book in which contributors discuss various alternatives to the Electoral College and the implications of each is Paul D. Schumaker and Burdett A. Loomis, *Choosing a President: The Electoral College and Beyond* (Chatham House, 2002).

What More to Do

Calculate three things: your state's percentage of the national population, its percentage of the electoral vote, and given its turnout in 2008, its percentage of the presidential vote. Keep in mind, your state's seats in the U.S. House of Representatives, and therefore the number of its electoral votes, may have changed on the basis of the 2010 census. These numbers are widely available including www.270towin.com/. Based on these updated calculations, would your state gain or lose political advantage if the Electoral College were to be abolished? Also expand your consideration past just the NPV plan discussed here. Do some research on alternative plans at the FairVote site noted above, and compare all the possibilities before making your decision.

11

CONGRESS

SENATE FILIBUSTERS:
Blocking Majority Rule *or* Preventing Majority Tyranny?

BLOCKING MAJORITY RULE

ADVOCATE: Thomas E. Mann, W. Averell Harriman Chair and Senior Fellow, Brookings Institution

SOURCE: Testimony during hearings on "Examining the Filibuster: Legislative Proposals to Change Senate Procedures" before the Committee on Rules and Administration, U.S. Senate, June 23, 2010

PREVENTING MAJORITY TYRANNY

ADVOCATE: Lee Rawls Faculty Member, National War College and Adjunct Professor, College of William and Mary

SOURCE: Testimony during hearings on "Examining the Filibuster: Legislative Proposals to Change Senate Procedures" before the Committee on Rules and Administration, U.S. Senate, June 23, 2010

James Madison and many of the other delegates to the Philadelphia Constitutional Convention of 1787 were wary of democracy, at least too much of it. One thing they worried about was how to protect minority rights from the tyranny of the majority. As Madison put it, there was a need to ensure that "no common interest or passion will be likely to unite a majority of [Americans] in an unjust pursuit." It should be noted that the delegates did not mean the rights of minority racial and ethnic groups. Instead, they were worried about the rights of the propertied class being threatened by the poor majority. One thing that the delegates did to restrain democracy was to design the U.S. Senate to play something of a "cooling" role, to temper the passions of the democracy manifested in public sentiment and the popularly elected House of Representatives. To accomplish this function, the Constitution as written in 1787 took several steps. First, senators were chosen indirectly by their respective state legislatures instead of directly by popular vote like members of the House. Second, any law passed by the House also had to be agreed to by the Senate. James Madison, the "father" of the Constitution depicted the Senate as "the great anchor of the government" and a "temperate and respectable body of citizens" that would resist public passions "until reason, justice, and truth can regain their authority over the public mind." Third, the Senate, unlike the House, was given two key unilateral legislative powers: ratifying treaties and confirming presidential appointments. Fourth, the Constitution gave senators six-year terms of office, three times longer than those of House members. Madison explained that the longer term of senators would make them less likely than members of the House to yield to the public's "sudden and violent passions."

The smaller number of senators and the sense that the chamber was meant to carefully deliberate on issues—especially anything pushed forward by unstable public passions and the House that might threaten and be adamantly opposed by a minority—led the Senate in 1806 to abolish any method of forcing a vote on a measure before all senators were willing to do so. This set the stage for the first filibuster in 1826. Filibusters are a parliamentary tactic whereby one or more senators continue to speak on a measure in order to prevent it from coming to a vote. This tactic can be used to force a compromise or to even have a measure withdrawn from Senate consideration in order to continue with other, more pressing business. Even the threat of a filibuster can have such an impact.

Prior to 1917 there was no way other than making concessions to end a filibuster, but that year the Senate adopted a rule that allowed it to invoke cloture (end debate) by a vote of two-thirds of all senators present and voting. The vote necessary to invoke cloture was changed in 1975, and Senate Rule 22 now requires a vote of three-fifths of the entire Senate membership, or normally 60 senators, to end debate. The Senate also has a number of other procedures that enable one or a few senators to delay or even prevent final action. A "hold" is one of these tactics. Senate Rule 7, which bars the Senate from floor consideration of any matter without the "unanimous consent of the membership" allows individual senators to put a hold on a measure by refusing to give their consent. Like a filibuster, a hold can be overcome, but it is difficult to do so.

Although the use of filibusters and similar delaying tactics is almost as old as the country, there is growing concern about them because of their increased use. Before the mid-1960s, filibusters were rare. They began to increase as Southern senators used the tactic to block civil rights legislation. That factor has waned, but intensifying partisanship in the Senate has escalated the number of filibusters even more steeply. Among other uses, filibusters have become a much more common method by which the minority can delay or defeat presidential judicial nominations. Indeed, filibuster activity has become nearly routine on the most important votes ("key votes") in Congress. Filibusters occurred, or were threatened on, 50% or more of the key votes since 1990, including more than 80% of these votes in 2008. It is now often reported that passing a piece of legislation will require a "supermajority" of 60 votes, the de facto number given the cloture threshold, instead of 51 votes, the normal majority in the Senate.

The frequent need for a supermajority of 60 is questionable as a matter of democracy and also increases the chances for stalemate in the Senate. Given this and the increase in filibuster activity, Thomas E. Mann, a well know scholar in the area of Congress who is at the Brookings Institution, focuses on the confirmation processes and contends that whatever advantages filibusters may have, their costs outweigh their benefits. Also focusing on the confirmation process, Lee Rawls, who teaches at the National War College, counters that the filibuster should not be abolished because it continues to foster moderation and consensus in the picking the federal judiciary and executive branch officials.

POINTS TO PONDER

➢ What relationship, if any, does the filibuster have to the familiar notion of having "majority rule with respect for minority rights"?

➢ Is the original "cooling" role of the Senate still desirable? Was it ever in a democracy?

➢ Note the suggestions for reform made by Professors Mann and Rawls and think of yet other possibilities.

Senate Filibusters:
Blocking Majority Rule

THOMAS E. MANN

Testimony [already] presented at [these] hearings usefully [has] clarified the origins of unlimited debate in the Senate, circumstances surrounding the adoption of Rule XXII in 1917 and its subsequent amendment, changing norms and practices regarding the use of filibusters, holds, and cloture petitions, and in recent years the extraordinary increase in the frequency of extended-debate-related problems on major measures before the Senate.

I concur with the scholarly consensus that the emergence of an ideologically polarized Senate, with sharp party differences on most important issues, appears to be a major force behind the routinization of the filibuster. The striking unity within each of the party caucuses reflects this ideological separation but also arises from the rough parity between the parties. Control of the Senate is now regularly up for grabs. Both parties have powerful incentives to use the available parliamentary tools to wage a permanent campaign to retain or regain majority status. The resulting procedural arms race has served individual and partisan interests but has diminished the Senate as an institution and weakened the country's capacity to govern.

The focus of my testimony at this hearing is the impact of the increasing use of filibusters and holds on the Senate confirmation of presidential appointees. The Constitution provides that the President "shall nominate, and by and with the Advise and Consent of the Senate, shall appoint Ambassadors, other Public Ministers and Counsels, Judges of the Supreme Court, and all Other Officers of the United States, whose Appointments are not herein otherwise provided for, and which shall be established by Law..." The Framers differed amongst themselves on the proper role of the Senate in the nomination and confirmation process so it is no surprise that this has been a bone of contention between the branches throughout the course of American history. Because it holds the constitutional authority to withhold its approval of presidential appointments, the Senate can wield formidable negative power. How responsibly the Senate exercises that power importantly shapes the performance of the executive and judicial branches.

All presidential appointments subject to Senate confirmation are not equal. Approximately 65,000 military appointments and promotions are routinely confirmed each Congress, with very few (though occasionally prominent) delays or rejections. Many of the roughly 4,000 civilian nominations considered each Congress are handled by the Senate in a similar fashion. These include appointments and promotions in the Foreign Service and Public Health Service as well as many nominations to part-time positions on boards and advisory commissions. In many other cases (U.S. attorneys, U.S. Marshals, and U.S. district judges), a long-standing custom of "senatorial courtesy" gives home-state senators support to object if they are not fully consulted by the White House before nominations are submitted. In addition, a number of fixed-term appointments to commissions, boards, and other multi-member entities are required by their enabling statutes to maintain political balance in some way or to follow an explicit selection procedure. In both cases, these consultations and selection processes go some distance in limiting the potential friction between the branches in resolving their shared responsibility. (Not the entire distance, to be sure. Nominees to the Federal Election Commission have often been subject to prolonged delays, even denying it the ability to have a quorum to conduct business during much of the 2008 election campaign. Similar examples can be found with the Election Assistance Commission and other regulatory bodies and boards.) Consequently, it is no surprise that 99% of presidential appointees are confirmed routinely by the Senate. More problematic are appellate judicial nominations (numbering roughly 25 to 50 per Congress) and the 400 or so Senate-confirmed senior positions in cabinet departments and executive agencies (excluding ambassadors) who serve at the pleasure of the president. In the case of the former, the confirmation process over the last three decades has become increasingly prolonged and contentious. The confirmation rate of presidential circuit court appointments has plummeted from above 90% in the late 1970s and early 1980s to below 50% in recent years. A particularly acrimonious confrontation over the delay of several judicial nominations in 2005 led then Majority Leader Bill Frist (R-TN) to threaten to use the so-called "nuclear option"—a ruling from the chair sustained by a simple majority of senators to establish that the Constitution required the Senate to vote up or down on every judicial nomination (effectively cloture by simple majority). Before Frist's deadline for breaking the impasse arrived, a group of 14 senators (seven Democrats and seven Republicans) reached an informal pact to oppose Frist's "reform-by-ruling" and to deny Democrats the ability to filibuster several of the pending nominations. This diffused the immediate situation but did little to alter the long-run trajectory of the judicial confirmation process. Lifetime appointments and high ideological stakes provided ample incentives for senators whenever feasible to use holds and silent filibusters to prevent a majority of their colleagues from acting on judicial nominations.

These delays in confirming appellate judges have led to increased vacancy rates, which has produced longer case processing times and rising caseloads per judge on federal dockets. Moreover, the conflict over appellate judges is spilling over to the district court appointments, which are beginning to produce similarly low rates of confirmation.

Even more disconcerting has been the impact of the changing confirmation process on the ability of presidents to staff their administrations. My colleague on this [hearing] panel, Cal Mackenzie, this country's preeminent student of the presidential appointments process, has in his prepared testimony made a powerful case that "we have in Washington today a presidential appointment process that is a less efficient and less effective mechanism for staffing the senior levels of government than its counterparts in any other industrialized democracy." Professor Mackenzie summarizes the longstanding flaws in the present system and documents how it has steadily deteriorated over the last several decades. That deterioration has occurred at both ends of Pennsylvania Avenue.

In fact, delays in filling senior executive positions are substantially larger at the nomination than the confirmation stage. This reflects in substantial part a defensive posture by new administrations seeking to reduce or eliminate any possibility of adverse publicity about any of their nominees surfacing after they are chosen. But the trends over the last four administrations place an increasing responsibility for delays with the Senate. As Professor Mackenzie, drawing on important new work on this subject by Professor Anne Joseph O'Connell of the University of California, Berkeley School of Law, notes, the average time taken to confirm nominees in the first year of new administrations has steadily increased (from 51.5 days under George H.W. Bush to 60.8 days under Barack Obama) while the percentage of presidential nominations confirmed by the end of the first year declined (from 80.1% under Bush 41 to 64.4% under Obama).

These discouraging statistics actually understate the problem. Cabinet secretaries are usually confirmed within a couple of weeks while top noncabinet agency officials take on average almost three months. Some nominees have been subject to much more extended delays, putting their personal lives on hold for many months and critical positions unfilled for much or all of a president's first year in office. Some Cabinet secretaries have had to manage with only skeleton senior staffs, with few empowered with the formal authority that is contingent on Senate confirmation. Recent administrations have many horror stories associated with the absence of timely confirmation of its top executives.

The Obama administration is no exception. Indeed, its stories are more numerous and telling than those that came before it. Consider just a few examples. In the midst of a financial meltdown and critical decisions to be made on the implementation of TARP [the Troubled Asset Relief Program enacted in 2008], the Treasury Department had no Senate-confirmed officials in many high-ranking policy positions, including: Deputy Secretary, Undersecretary for International Affairs, Undersecretary for Domestic Finance, Assistant Secretary for Tax Policy, Assistant Secretary for Financial Markets, Assistant Secretary for Financial Stability, and Assistant Secretary for Legislative Affairs. One of those nominees, Lael Brainard, a former colleague of mine at Brookings, was nominated for the key position of Undersecretary for International Affairs on March 23, 2009 but did not get confirmed until April 20, 2010, over a year later. Her problem was tax-related, reportedly over a deduction she claimed on a home office. Yet her husband, Kurt Campbell, was nominated for a post at the State Department and confirmed by the Senate in about two months, even though they filed a joint tax return.

Other critical positions with urgent responsibilities for a Senate-confirmed appointee subject to extended vacancies included Commissioner of U.S. Customs and Border Protection, director of the Transportation Security Administration, head of the National Highway Traffic Safety Administration, and director of the Centers for Medicare and Medicaid Services. To be sure, delays associated with filling these and other senior executive positions often arose during the nominating process and sometimes were associated with genuine concerns about the nominee. But the evidence strongly supports the view that many nominees get caught in ideological and partisan battles in the Senate or become hostages to the personal agendas of individual senators, often unrelated to the nominee or the position to be filled.

Currently, there is no foolproof way of discerning how many nominations are subject to holds by individual senators. The effort to limit secret holds initiated by Senators [Ron] Wyden (D-OR) and [Charles] Grassley (R-IA) as part of the 2007 ethics bill has loopholes that have rendered it largely ineffective. One can, however, examine the list of nominations that have been approved by committees and placed on the Senate executive calendar. One presumes that absent a hold or other signal of a filibuster, the Majority Leader would move expeditiously to call up these nominations. Not that long ago it was rare that nominees would linger on the list of pending confirmation for days, weeks, and months. On Memorial Day 2002, during George W. Bush's administration, 13 nominations were pending on the executive calendar. Eight years later, under

Obama, the number was 108. Senators have long viewed the confirmation process as an opportunity to express their policy views and to get the administration's attention on a matter of importance to them or their constituents. But the culture of today's Senate provides no restraints on the exercise of this potential power and no protection of the country's interest in having a newly-elected president move quickly and effectively to form a government. One telling indicator of the arbitrary and self-indulgent use of holds on nominees is when a successful cloture vote to overcome a longstanding hold is followed by a near-unanimous vote for confirmation. This happens with increasing frequency in the Senate.

In my view and that of virtually the entire policy and scholarly communities, the costs of the serious flaws on our appointment and confirmation process outweigh the benefits. Government agencies are ill-equipped to operate effectively and to be held accountable by Congress; able individuals willing to serve their country are subject to uncertainty and major disruptions in their personal and professional lives; huge amounts of precious time in the White House and Senate are diverted from much more pressing needs.

I understand that subsequent hearings will deal more directly with remedies to the shortcoming of governance associated with obstruction in the Senate. Let me conclude by urging you to consider two proposals: an effective end to anonymous holds on nominations and, more ambitiously, a fast-track system that sets time limits on committee and floor action for the confirmation of senior executive nominations.

Senate Filibusters: Preventing Majority Tyranny

Lee Rawls

"These opposed and conflicting interests which you considered as so great a blemish in your old and present constitution interpose a salutary check to all precipitate resolutions. They render deliberation a matter not of choice, but of necessity."

Edmund Burke

"The disposition of people to impose their own opinions can only be restrained by an opposing power."

John Stuart Mill

"Partisan competition has been at the center of our struggle to advance as a people and as a nation. It has been our most important engine for adaptation and change—one that remains in full motion."

John Hilley (Chief of Staff to Majority Leader Senator Mitchell, and Legislative Affairs Director for President Clinton)

I am here today because of my previous life as Chief of Staff to Senator Frist (R-TN) when he was Senate Majority Leader and also as an Assistant Attorney General for Legislative Affairs at the Department of Justice in the early 1990s. Among my responsibilities at the Department were nominations for the Federal Judiciary, along with nominees for all the senior positions at the Department itself, including that of Attorney General.

I have opened my prepared remarks with several quotes to telegraph my general view of the value of the filibuster, and to preclude me from having to inflict my full philosophical theories of the filibuster on the members. Moreover, my longer musings can be found in my 2009 book *In Praise of Deadlock*—whose title captures much of my thinking.

Instead, I will open with a quote from the famed journalist Eric Sevareid, who wisely noted that "the chief cause of problems is solutions." I have taken a look at the committee's previous hearings on the filibuster which in the aggregate present a thorough review of the filibuster and during which many former members, scholars and practitioners have offered a wide range of possible solutions. My advice to the committee on these proposals comes down to one word: Don't.

At the War College, we train the senior military commanders who attend to ask one question at the start of any discussion on a problem: So What? What is it about a situation that demands a remedy, and what assurances are there that the proposed solution will not make the problem worse?

The filibuster is a perfect candidate for this line of questioning. The Committee has been told that both partisanship and the use of the filibuster are on the rise. You have been told that the American legislative system is "broken," that the nominations process, particularly for the federal judiciary is in disarray, and that strong medicine is necessary to cure the situation.

Let me make 5 points in response, and leave any nuances to questions the members of the Committee may have.

1. Any legislative system that in the face of a deep financial recession and two wars that can enact in the space of two years TARP legislation, $750 billion dollars in stimulus funding, a major overhaul of the world's largest health care system and is preparing to enact a far-reaching reform of its financial system is by definition not broken. Moreover, any nomination process that has not had a single nominee for the federal judiciary rejected as the result of an unsuccessful cloture vote is by definition not in disarray.

2. If rising partisanship is a concern, the sole source in the entire American legislative system of bipartisanship, moderation, continuity and consensus is found in the United States Senate because of the role of the filibuster. The leverage provided to the minority by the filibuster is a two-sided coin. On one side it is the source of bipartisanship throughout the entire legislative process. On the other, it slows down the legislative process that in turn leads to inaccurate cries of "gridlock" which are loudly echoed by the press. In Burke's words, quoted above, the filibuster renders deliberation a "matter of necessity, not choice." This moderating, consensus forming role of the filibuster has been going on for 170 years. As Sarah Binder told the committee, organized use of the filibuster by the political parties started in the 1840s, and as Senator [Robert] Byrd (D-WV) noted in his remarks, "bitter partisan periods in our history are nothing new." In fact, scholars note that parts of the 19th century were clearly more partisan than today.

3. The United States Senate is the most intricate legislative body in the known universe, unique for its permissive rules. At the core of its genius is its ability to moderate a large number of vital political forces all of which have their dark side For example, the filibuster is an essential element in moderating the extremes of our competitive party system. It also moderates the hubris and moral aggression noted by the Mill quote above in those who actually make the rules. Of particular importance it lessens the risks of united government when one party "hijacks" the Constitution's separation of power system and in the name of all Americans exercises power in all branches of government at the same time.

The First amendment explicitly provides for special interests to engage in the political process. These groups range from economic interests to single-interest advocates, all of whom have a narrow focus, and who usually are not interested in compromise. The filibuster, by providing resistance within the legislative system, often smoothes out the worst abuses of this special interest participation. Thus, although the First Amendment guarantees special interest participation, it is often the filibuster that protects the public interest in the legislative process. Professor Smith in his remarks to the Committee lamented the "obstruct and restrict syndrome" that he believes the filibuster has caused. From my vantage point as a practitioner within the system, I believe that the "continuous resistance" that the filibuster provides on a daily basis to these vital, but occasionally dangerous forces, is the essential component in the genius of the United States Senate.

4. The above points lead to the conclusion that if you change the filibuster rule, you unalterably change the nature of the Senate. Chairman [Charles] Schumer (D-NY) has been quite fair-minded in his quest for answers to the filibuster riddle. In particular, because he has been both in the majority and minority, he has asked the right question as to whether one's views of the filibuster are completely dependent on one's political

status of the moment, or whether there are more fundamental issues at stake. I believe such larger issues are at stake. These relate to what it means to have a full and productive Senate career. Such a career requires continuous involvement; namely a full body of legislative work that gives personal satisfaction and contributes to the public needs of the American people. Moreover, such a career requires the full engagement of one's skills whether one is in the majority or minority. A career where minority status means effective banishment falls short of these criteria. In fact, for those who have had acknowledged successful careers, such as the late Senator [Edward] Kennedy (D-MA) or the recently retired Senator [Peter] Domenici (R-NM), the key to their success has often been the important role they played as leaders of the minority skillfully negotiating with the majority.

For the members of the minority, the value of filibuster in achieving a full career is obvious. I believe it is worth noting that the members of the Majority also run some risks if the filibuster were abolished. The first is that the power of the president would be substantially increased, particularly in united government. Given his visibility and power to influence grass roots forces, members of a Senate devoid of a filibuster would be under increased pressure to toe the line of a president of the same party.

Members of the Senate Majority may not appreciate how much they are in control of the entire legislative machine in the American system. The resistance provided by the Minority makes their political judgments the essential ingredient in establishing and implementing legislative strategy. Without such resistance, they will lose their strategic function and their role becomes one of either supporting or opposing the policies of an executive branch of the same party.

The other risk that a Majority party without a filibuster runs is being overwhelmed by the special interests. Every year thousands of bills that reflect strong special interest input are introduced but are not addressed by the Senate because of the filibuster. Absent such a constraint, it is difficult to conceive of the Majority party in the Senate resisting the whole range of special interest legislation that is introduced on an annual basis. For Majority senators who do not conceive of themselves as handmaidens of special interests, this change would be an unwelcome shock.

5. With these first principles in mind, let me make 2 concluding remarks on the nominations process.

   a. The virtues of the filibuster in fostering moderation and consensus are important in picking the federal judiciary. These are lifetime posts vested with immense importance in our system. Trust is perhaps the most important element in the Rule of Law which the federal judiciary oversees. Brilliance and other intellectual virtues are second order virtues, particularly if they come wrapped in strong ideological packaging. Anything that forces matters to the middle is a virtue, and the filibuster certainly does that. Every member here has had discussions as to whether a nominee will face opposition and what a minority armed with a filibuster is likely to do.

In addition, the leverage provided by the filibuster allows for a more thorough examination of candidates for the federal bench. Documents, extensive hearings, additional face-to-face meetings, all these flow form the leverage of a minority armed with the filibuster. As with any tool, or instrument, mistakes and abuses occur. But my view is that in the aggregate, given the importance of the federal judiciary, and their lifetime appointments, the leverage of the filibuster provides for a more thorough vetting process of the federal judiciary than a process without such leverage. As an aside, I also wonder how much of an issue this is at present. During 2003–4 when I was Senator Frist's Chief of Staff, the Senate was split 51–49. We spent a lot of floor time on judicial nominees, winning some and losing some. Today's Majority of 59 votes has a perfect record on judicial cloture votes which leaves me wondering what part of the puzzle I am missing, if any.

b. Some of the same considerations hold for executive branch nominees. Here the problem is numbers. My experience is that the Senate is reasonably prompt in providing the president with his senior Cabinet leadership. With exceptions, usually cases where the nominee has self-inflicted problems, the Senate does a good job on the Cabinet. Where matters get off the rails is the mid-level management of the executive branch on which the Senate insists on providing advice and consent. There are a variety of ways to address this issue, but overall the Senate insists on confirming too many nominees. The problem is not the filibuster; it is the Senate's inability to set priorities. In my own case, I was held up for a period of time with two other nominees after our nominations to the Justice Department. The Senator who held us had a perfectly legitimate beef with the Department, and after some negotiations, the issue was resolved.

Since the post of Assistant Attorney General for Legislative Affairs is really a fancy title for flak-catcher, it seemed to me that the elaborate gyrations surrounding my nomination was wasted effort. In my view, if the nomination is important enough for a Senator to personally meet with the nominee and attend the confirmation hearing then the confirmation process is appropriate. If not, then drop the Senate confirmation requirement. In my case, no courtesy visits were asked for, and one poor junior member of the committee had to be dragooned into chairing the hearing. If following such an effort at establishing priorities to determine which positions actually need confirmation, there is still a substantial problem, then perhaps other measures could be considered.

THE CONTINUING DEBATE:
Senate Filibusters

What Is New

Potential filibusters were a major threat to some key measures in 2010, but most of the important ones moved forward. For example, the Senate leadership used an arcane parliamentary maneuver to avoid a Republican filibuster on the final passage of the reconciled heath care reform legislation early in the year. Also in 2010, the Republicans filibustered financial reform for several days, but they gave way when they concluded that continuing to block the bill would put them in political peril during the impending congressional elections. Still, filibuster remains a potent legislative tactic. One illustration is clear in Debate 13, with Republicans threatening to use the filibuster to block the confirmation of a director for the new Consumer Financial Protection Bureau unless President Obama and congressional Democrats agree to significant changes to the power of the agency and how it is governed. As far as any reform of the Senate's Rule 22 on filibusters, nothing occurred beyond the hearings. For all the criticism of the filibuster, it is hard to change the rules in part because many senators see the filibuster as a valued Senate tradition. Additionally, whichever party is in the majority—and could perhaps change the rules—knows that it will surely someday be the minority party and will then want to use filibusters to gain leverage in the Senate.

Where to Find More

A good place to begin further study is Gregory Koger, *Filibustering: A Political History of Obstruction in the House and Senate* (University of Chicago Press, 2010). The Senate Committee on Rules and Administration held a series of hearings on the filibuster and related procedures. The third hearing was "Examining the Filibuster: Legislative Proposals to Change Senate Procedures." It is available on the committee's Web site at http://rules.senate.gov. Since filibusters are not declared formally, the easiest way of finding and counting them is through is by counting cloture petitions and votes, which are formal procedures. The best source for researching the parliamentary maneuvers is the Historian of the United States Senate on the Web at www.senate.gov/pagelayout/feference/cloture_motions/.

What More to Do

It can be hard to evaluate filibusters in the abstract. So for some applied analysis, go back in history and identify the top ten or so most important filibuster using Gregory Koger's book *Filibustering* mentioned above or other studies such as Gregory J. Wawro and Eric Schickler, *Filibuster: Obstruction and Lawmaking in the U.S. Senate* (Princeton, NJ: Princeton University Press, 2006) and Sarah A. Binder, Eric D. Lawrence, and Steven S. Smith, "Tracking the Filibuster, 1917 to 1996," *American Politics Research* (2002). See what the outcomes were. Did the filibuster defeat the bill at which it was aimed, result in compromise, or fail? For each, was the result one that you think was good or bad? Ask yourself how the outcomes, and your reactions to them, impact your views on filibusters.

12 PRESIDENCY

BARACK OBAMA'S USE OF THE PRESIDENT'S WAR POWERS:
Reasonable *or* Excessive?

REASONABLE

ADVOCATE: Hongju Koh, Legal Adviser, U.S. Department of State

SOURCE: Testimony during hearings on "Libya and War Powers," before the U.S. Senate, Committee on Foreign Relations, June 28, 2011

EXCESSIVE

ADVOCATE: Louis Fisher, Scholar in Residence, Constitution Project

SOURCE: Testimony during hearings on "Libya and War Powers," before the U.S. Senate, Committee on Foreign Relations, June 28, 2011

Among the many ambiguities in the Constitution is what the president may do under the clause in Article II that makes him the "commander in chief of the Army and Navy" in the context of the clause in Article I that gives Congress the authority to "declare War." There is no doubt that the framers wanted the president to be the head general and admiral, so to speak, and to direct the operations of U.S. forces. It is also clear that the framers anticipated that presidents might have to occasionally use U.S. forces without a declaration of war. That authority, according to delegate Roger Sherman, existed when the president needed to "repel and not commence war."

There is a long history of the use of the president's war powers, but the matter became more controversial after World War II when the United States became a superpower that deployed its forces around the world and often used them. Beginning with the Korean War (1950–1953), presidents began to assert unprecedented powers as commander in chief. Without congressional authorization, President Harry Truman committed the country to a full-scale war and justified his unilateral decision on two grounds: that as commander in chief he had "full control" over the use of the military and that North Korea's attack threatened "interest which the president…can protect by [military force]…without [needing] a declaration of war."

This view prevailed unchallenged until the unpopular Vietnam War led Congress to try to reign in the president's war powers by passing the War Powers Resolution (WPR) in 1973. It specifies that the president can only send U.S. forces into action or put them in imminent danger (harm's way) in one of three circumstances: (1) Congress has declared war, (2) Congress has given the president a "a specific statutory authorization" to act, or (3) a "national emergency [has been] created by [an] attack upon the United States, its territories or possessions, or its armed forces." Muddling these clear criteria, the WPR also stipulated that 60 days after ordering action, the president had to terminate it unless Congress had authorized it to continue. Some read this to mean that the president has unilateral authority to take action for 60 days.

Others argue that the 60 days applies only to action begun under the three criteria and that otherwise a president must get prior authority from Congress to act.

President Richard Nixon vetoed the WPR, claiming that it endangered the country and also intruded on his powers as commander in chief. Congress overrode the veto, and the WPR became law. However, its effect has been marginal. In nearly every case since then when presidents have used military force—with or without congressional authorization—they have claimed the unilateral authority to do so as commander in chief.

While running for president, then Senator Barack Obama told the *Boston Globe* in a 2007 interview that, "The president does not have power under the Constitution to unilaterally authorize a military attack in a situation that does not involve stopping an actual or imminent threat to the nation." Less than four years later and without congressional consent, President Obama committed U.S. forces to the effort to unseat Libyan dictator Muammar Qadhafi. In the first reading, Hongju Koh, the chief legal adviser at the U.S. Department of State, argues that the action in Libya do not really constitute "hostilities" within the meaning of the WPR, much less war, and, therefore, the president is on sound legal and constitutional grounds in his use of the military. Louis Fisher, a leading scholar on the war powers, argues the justification of the Obama administration for taking unauthorized action amounts to double talk.

POINTS TO PONDER

➢ It is important to distinguish between your view about whether a particular military action is wise policy or not and the constitutional process by which that decision should be (or should have been) made. Constitutionally, the ends do not justify the means.

➢ Consider how well President Obama's decision about Libya meets with his statement as Senator Obama to the *Boston Globe* quoted above.

➢ Ask yourself under what circumstances presidents should and should not be able to unilaterally commit American forces to combat or put them in harm's way.

Barack Obama's Use of the President's War Powers: Reasonable

Hongju Koh

Thank you for this opportunity to testify before you on Libya and war powers. By so doing, I continue nearly four decades of dialogue between Congress and Legal Advisers of the State Department, since the War Powers Resolution was enacted, regarding the Executive Branch's legal position on war powers.

We believe that the President is acting lawfully in Libya, consistent with both the Constitution and the War Powers Resolution, as well as with international law. Our position is carefully limited to the facts of the present operation, supported by history, and respectful of both the letter of the Resolution and the spirit of consultation and collaboration that underlies it. We recognize that our approach has been a matter of important public debate, and that reasonable minds can disagree. But surely none of us believes that the best result is for [Libya's leader, Colonel Muammar] Qadhafi to wait NATO [North Atlantic Treaty Organization] out, leaving the Libyan people again exposed to his brutality. Given that, we ask that you swiftly approve Senate Joint Resolution 20, the bipartisan measure recently introduced by eleven Senators, including three members of this Committee. The best way to show a united front to Qadhafi, our NATO allies, and the Libyan people is for Congress now to authorize under that Joint Resolution continued, constrained operations in Libya to enforce United Nations Security Council Resolution 1973.

As Secretary [of State Hillary] Clinton testified in March, the United State's engagement in Libya followed the Administration's strategy of "using the combined assets of diplomacy, development, and defense to protect our interests and advance our values." Faced with brutal attacks and explicit threats of further imminent attacks by Muammar Qadhafi against his own people, the United States and its international partners acted with unprecedented speed to secure a mandate, under Resolution 1973, to mobilize a broad coalition to protect civilians against attack by an advancing army and to establish a no-fly zone. In so doing, President Obama helped prevent an imminent massacre in Benghazi, protected critical U.S. interests in the region, and sent a strong message to the people not just of Libya, but of the entire Middle East and North Africa, that America stands with them at this historic moment of transition.

From the start, the Administration made clear its commitment to acting consistently with both the Constitution and the War Powers Resolution. The President submitted a report to Congress, consistent with the War Powers Resolution, within 48 hours of the commencement of operations in Libya. He framed our military mission narrowly, directing, among other things, that no ground troops would be deployed (except for necessary personnel recovery missions), and that U.S. armed forces would transition responsibility for leading and conducting the mission to an integrated NATO command. On April 4, 2011, U.S. forces did just that, shifting to a constrained and supporting role in a multinational civilian protection mission in an action involving no U.S. ground presence or, to this point, U.S. casualties, authorized by a carefully tailored U.N. Security Council Resolution. As the War Powers Resolution contemplates, the Administration has consulted extensively with Congress about these operations, participating in more than ten hearings, thirty briefings, and dozens of additional exchanges since March 1 [2011], an interbranch dialogue that my testimony today continues.

This background underscores the limits to our legal claims. Throughout the Libya episode, the President has never claimed the authority to take the nation to war without Congressional authorization, to violate the War Powers Resolution or any other statute, to violate international law, to use force abroad when doing so would not serve important national interests, or to refuse to consult with Congress on important war powers issues.

The Administration recognizes that Congress has powers to regulate and terminate uses of force, and that the War Powers Resolution plays an important role in promoting interbranch dialogue and deliberation on these critical matters. The President has expressed his strong desire for Congressional support, and we have been working actively with Congress to ensure enactment of appropriate legislation.

Together with our NATO and Arab partners, we have made great progress in protecting Libya's civilian population, and we have isolated Qadhafi and set the stage for his departure. Although since early April we have confined our military involvement in Libya to a supporting role, the limited military assistance that we provide has been critical to the success of the mission, as has our political and diplomatic leadership. If the United States were to drop out of, or curtail its contributions to, this mission, it could not only compromise our international relationships and alliances and threaten regional instability, but also permit an emboldened and vengeful Qadhafi to return to attacking the very civilians whom our intervention has protected.

Where, against this background, does the War Powers Resolution fit in? The legal debate has focused on the Resolution's 60-day clock, which directs the President, absent express Congressional authorization (or the applicability of other limited exceptions) and following an initial 48-hour reporting period, to remove United States Armed Forces within 60 days from "hostilities" or "situations where imminent involvement in hostilities is clearly indicated by the circumstances." But as virtually every lawyer recognizes, the operative term "hostilities" is an ambiguous standard, which is nowhere defined in the statute. Nor has this standard ever been defined by the courts or by Congress in any subsequent war powers legislation. Indeed, the legislative history of the Resolution makes clear there was no fixed view on exactly what the term "hostilities" would encompass. Members of Congress understood that the term was vague, but specifically declined to give it more concrete meaning, in part to avoid unduly hampering future Presidents by making the Resolution a "one size fits all" straightjacket that would operate mechanically, without regard to particular circumstances.

From the start, lawyers and legislators have disagreed about the meaning of this term and the scope of the Resolution's 60-day pullout rule. Application of these provisions often generates difficult issues of interpretation that must be addressed in light of a long history of military actions abroad, without guidance from the courts, involving a Resolution passed by a Congress that could not have envisioned many of the operations in which the United States has since become engaged. Because the War Powers Resolution represented a broad compromise between competing views on the proper division of constitutional authorities, the question whether a particular set of facts constitutes "hostilities" for the purposes of the Resolution has been determined more by interbranch practice than by a narrow parsing of dictionary definitions. Both branches have recognized that different situations may call for different responses, and that an overly mechanical reading of the statute could lead to unintended automatic cutoffs of military involvement in cases where more flexibility is required.

In the nearly forty years since the Resolution's enactment, successive Administrations have thus started from the premise that the term "hostilities" is definable in a meaningful way only in the context of an actual set of facts. And successive Congresses and Presidents have opted for a process through which the political branches have worked together to flesh out the law's meaning over time. By adopting this approach, the two branches have sought to avoid construing the statute mechanically, divorced from the realities that face them.

In this case, leaders of the current Congress have stressed this very concern in indicating that they do not believe that U.S. military operations in Libya amount to the kind of "hostilities" envisioned by the War Powers Resolution's 60-day pullout provision. The historical practice supports this view. In 1975, Congress expressly invited the Executive Branch to provide its best understanding of the term "hostilities." My predecessor Monroe Leigh and Defense Department General Counsel Martin Hoffmann responded that, as a general matter, the Executive Branch understands the term "hostilities" to mean a situation in which units of the U.S. armed forces are actively engaged in exchanges of fire with opposing units of hostile forces. On the other hand, as Leigh and Hoffmann suggested, the term should not necessarily be read to include situations where the nature of the mission is limited (*i.e.,* situations that do not involve the full military engagements with which the Resolution is primarily concerned); where the exposure of U.S. forces is limited (*e.g.,* situations involving sporadic military or paramilitary attacks on our armed forces stationed abroad, in which the overall threat faced by our military is low); and where the risk of escalation is therefore limited. Subsequently, the Executive Branch has reiterated the distinction between full military encounters and more constrained operations, stating that "intermittent military engagements" do not require the withdrawal of forces under the Resolution's 60-day rule. In the thirty-six years since Leigh and Hoffmann provided their analysis, the Executive Branch has repeatedly articulated and applied these foundational understandings. The President was thus operating within this longstanding tradition of Executive Branch interpretation when he relied on these understandings in his legal explanation to Congress on June 15, 2011.

In light of this historical practice, a combination of four factors present in Libya suggests that the current situation does not constitute the kind "hostilities" envisioned by the War Powers Resolution's 60-day automatic pullout provision.

First, the *mission* is limited: By Presidential design, U.S. forces are playing a constrained and supporting role in a NATO-led multinational civilian protection operation, which is implementing a U.N. Security Council Resolution tailored to that limited purpose. This is a very unusual set of circumstances, not found in any of the historic situations in which the "hostilities" question was previously debated, from the deployment of U.S. armed forces to Lebanon, Grenada, and El Salvador in the early 1980s, to the fighting with Iran in the Persian Gulf in the late 1980s, to the use of ground troops in Somalia in 1993. Of course, NATO forces as a whole are more deeply engaged in Libya than are U.S. forces, but the War Powers Resolution's 60-day pullout provision was designed to address the activities of the latter.

Second, the *exposure* of our armed forces is limited: To date, our operations have not involved U.S. casualties or a threat of significant U.S. casualties. Nor do our current operations involve active exchanges of fire with hostile forces, and members of our military have not been involved in significant armed confrontations or sustained confrontations of any kind with hostile forces. Prior administrations have not found the 60-day rule to apply even in situations where significant fighting plainly did occur, as in Lebanon and Grenada in 1983 and Somalia in 1993. By highlighting this point, we in no way advocate a legal theory that is indifferent to the loss of non-American lives. But here, there can be little doubt that the greatest threat to Libyan civilians comes not from NATO or the United States military, but from Qadhafi. The Congress that adopted the War Powers Resolution was principally concerned with the safety of U.S. forces, and with the risk that the President would entangle them in an overseas conflict from which they could not readily be extricated. In this instance, the absence of U.S. ground troops, among other features of the Libya operation significantly reduces both the risk to U.S. forces and the likelihood of a protracted entanglement that Congress may find itself practically powerless to end.

Third, the *risk of escalation* is limited: U.S. military operations have not involved the presence of U.S. ground troops, or any significant chance of escalation into a broader conflict characterized by a large U.S. ground presence, major casualties, sustained active combat, or expanding geographical scope. Contrast this with the 1991 Desert Storm operation, which although also authorized by a United Nations Security Council Resolution, presented over 400,000 [U.S.] troops in the area, the same order of magnitude as Vietnam at its peak, together with concomitant numbers of ships, tanks, and planes. Prior administrations have found an absence of "hostilities" under the War Powers Resolution in situations ranging from Lebanon to Central America to Somalia to the Persian Gulf tanker controversy, although members of the United States Armed Forces were repeatedly engaged by the other side's forces and sustained casualties in volatile geopolitical circumstances, in some cases running a greater risk of possible escalation than here.

Fourth and finally, the *military means* we are using are limited: This situation does not present the kind of "full military engagement" with which the [War Powers] Resolution is primarily concerned. The violence that U.S. armed forces have directly inflicted or facilitated after the handoff to NATO has been modest in terms of its frequency, intensity, and severity. The air-to-ground strikes conducted by the United States in Libya are a far cry from the bombing campaign waged in Kosovo in 1999, which involved much more extensive and aggressive aerial strike operations led by U.S. armed forces. The U.S. contribution to NATO is likewise far smaller than it was in the Balkans in the mid-1990s, where U.S. forces contributed the vast majority of aircraft and air strike sorties to an operation that lasted over two and a half years, featured repeated violations of the no-fly zone and episodic firefights with Serb aircraft and gunners, and paved the way for approximately 20,000 U.S. ground troops. Here, by contrast, the bulk of U.S. contributions to the NATO effort has been providing intelligence capabilities and refueling assets. A very significant majority of the overall sorties [air patrols] are being flown by our coalition partners, and the overwhelming majority of strike sorties are being flown by our partners. American strikes have been confined, on an as-needed basis, to the suppression of enemy air defenses to enforce the no-fly zone, and to limited strikes by Predator unmanned aerial vehicles against discrete targets in support of the civilian protection mission; since the handoff to NATO, the total number of U.S. munitions dropped has been a tiny fraction of the number dropped in

Kosovo. All NATO targets, moreover, have been clearly linked to the Qadhafi regime's systematic attacks on the Libyan population and populated areas, with target sets engaged only when strictly necessary and with maximal precision.

Had any of these elements been absent in Libya, or present in different degrees, a different legal conclusion might have been drawn. But the unusual confluence of these four factors, in an operation that was expressly designed to be limited—limited in mission, exposure of U.S. troops, risk of escalation, and military means employed—led the President to conclude that the Libya operation did not fall within the War Powers Resolution's automatic 60-day pullout rule.

Nor is this action inconsistent with the spirit of the Resolution. Having studied this legislation for many years, I can confidently say that we are far from the core case that most Members of Congress had in mind in 1973. The Congress that passed the Resolution in that year had just been through a long, major, and searing war in Vietnam, with hundreds of thousands of boots on the ground, secret bombing campaigns, international condemnation, massive casualties, and no clear way out. In Libya, by contrast, we have been acting transparently and in close consultation with Congress for a brief period; with no casualties or ground troops; with international approval; and at the express request of and in cooperation with NATO, the Arab League, the Gulf Cooperation Council, and Libya's own Transitional National Council. We should not read into the 1973 Congress' adoption of what many have called a "no more Vietnams" the Resolution's intent to require the premature termination, nearly forty years later, of limited military force in support of an international coalition to prevent the resumption of atrocities in Libya. Given the limited risk of escalation, exchanges of fire, and U.S. casualties, we do not believe that the 1973 Congress intended that its Resolution be given such a rigid construction, absent a clear Congressional stance to stop the President from directing supporting actions in a NATO-led, Security Council-authorized operation, for the narrow purpose of preventing the slaughter of innocent civilians.

Nor are we in a "war" for the purposes of Article I of the Constitution. As the Office of Legal Counsel concluded in its April 1, 2011 opinion, under longstanding precedent the President had the constitutional authority to direct the use of force in Libya, for two main reasons. First, he could reasonably determine that U.S. operations in Libya would serve important national interests in preserving regional stability and supporting the credibility and effectiveness of the U.N. Security Council. Second, the military operations that the President anticipated ordering were not sufficiently extensive in nature, scope, and endurance to constitute a "war" requiring prior specific Congressional approval under the Declaration of War Clause. Although time has passed, the nature and scope of our operations have not evolved in a manner that would alter that conclusion. To the contrary, since the transfer to NATO command, the U.S. role in the mission has become even more limited.

Reasonable minds may read the Constitution and the War Powers Resolution differently, as they have for decades. Scholars will certainly go on debating this issue. But that should not distract those of us in government from the most urgent question now facing us, which is not one of law but of policy: Will Congress provide its support for NATO's mission in Libya at this pivotal juncture, ensuring that Qadhafi does not regain the upper hand against the people of Libya? The President has repeatedly stated that it is better to take military action, even in limited scenarios such as this, with strong Congressional engagement and support. However we construe the War Powers

Resolution, we can all agree that it serves only Qadhafi's interests for the United States to withdraw from this NATO operation before it is finished.

That is why, in closing, we ask all of you to take quick and decisive action to approve S.J. Res. 20, the bipartisan resolution introduced by [eleven senators] to provide express Congressional authorization for continued, constrained operations in Libya to enforce U.N. Security Council Resolution 1973. Only by so doing, can this body affirm that the United States government is united in its commitment to support the NATO alliance, the safety and stability of this pivotal region, and the aspirations of the Libyan people for political reform and self-government.

Barack Obama's Use of the President's War Powers:
Excessive

LOUIS FISHER

Members of the committee, thank you for the invitation to testify on the Obama administration's legal and constitutional justifications for military operations in Libya. I start by examining four claims by the administration: (1) the President may obtain "authorization" not from Congress but from the U.N. Security Council, (2) the President may rely on NATO for additional "authorization," (3) military operations in Libya do not amount to "war," and (4) those operations do not constitute "hostilities" within the meaning of the War Powers Resolution [WPR]. My statement concludes by turning to (5) the administration's reliance on [Senate Resolution] 85 for legislative support, (6) references to "non-kinetic assistance," and (7) the claim that the administration received a "mandate" to act militarily from such sources as the Security Council, the "Libyan people," and a "broad coalition" including the Arab League.

PRESIDENTIAL DOUBLETALK

Fundamental to the Constitution is the framers' determination that Congress alone can initiate and authorize war. To secure the principle of self-government and popular sovereignty, the decision to take the country from a state of peace to a state of war is reserved to the elected members of Congress. The framers recognized that the President could exercise defensive powers "to repel sudden attacks." John Jay expressed the framers' intent with these words: "It is too true, however disgraceful it may be to human nature, that nations in general will make war whenever they have a prospect of getting any thing by it; nay, absolute monarchs will often make war when their nations are to get nothing by it, but for purposes and objects merely personal, such as a thirst for military glory, revenge for personal affronts, ambition, or private compacts to aggrandize or support their particular families or partisans. These and a variety of other motives, which affect only the mind of the sovereign, often lead him to engage in wars not sanctified by justice or the voice and interests of his people."

Professor Michael J. Glennon, who previously served this committee as Legal Counsel, recently underscored that the Constitution "places the decision to go to war in the hands of Congress." From 1789 to 1950, all wars were either authorized or declared by Congress. That pattern of 160 years changed abruptly when President Harry Truman unilaterally took the country to war against North Korea. Unlike all previous Presidents, he did not go to Congress to seek statutory authority. He and his aides did what other Presidents have done to expand their control over the war power. They go to great lengths to explain to Congress and the public that what they are doing is not what they are doing. President Truman was asked at a news conference if the nation was at war. He responded: "We are not at war." A reporter inquired if it would be more correct to call the military operations "a police action under the United Nations."

Truman quickly agreed: "That is exactly what it amounts to."

There are many examples of Presidents and executive officials being duplicitous with words. A price is paid for that conduct, both for the President and the country. Korea became "Truman's War." During Senate hearings in June 1951 on the military conflict in Korea, Secretary of State Dean Acheson conceded the obvious by admitting "in the usual sense of the word there is a war."

What sense of the word had he been using? Federal and state courts had no difficulty in defining the hostilities in Korea as war. They were tasked with interpreting insurance policies that contained the phrase "in time of war." A federal district court noted in 1953: "We doubt very much if there is any question in the minds of the majority of the people of this country that the conflict now raging in Korea can be anything but war." In August 1964, President Lyndon Johnson told the nation about a "second attack" in the Gulf of Tonkin, a claim that was doubted at the time and we now know was false. In 2005, the National Security Council released a study that concluded there was no second attack. What had been reported as a second attack consisted of late signals coming from the first. Johnson used stealth and deception to escalate the war, forever damaging his presidency. He learned that being a War President is not the same as being a Great President.

In 1998, during a visit to Tennessee State University, Secretary of State Madeleine Albright took a question from a student who wanted to know how President Bill Clinton could go to war against Iraq without obtaining authority from Congress. She explained: "We are talking about using military force, but we are not talking about a war. That is an important distinction." Iraqis subjected to repeated and heavy bombings from U.S. cruise missiles understood the military operation as war. These distinctions can be easily manipulated to meet the political needs of the moment. The above examples provide some context for understanding the efforts of the Obama administration to define and redefine such words as "authorization," "war," "hostilities," "non-kinetic," and "mandate."

1. "Authorization" from the Security Council

President Obama and his legal advisers repeatedly state that he received "authorization" from the U.N. Security Council to conduct military operations in Libya. On March 21, he informed Congress that U.S. military forces commenced military initiatives in Libya as "authorized by the United Nations (U.N.) Security Council…" His administration regularly speaks of "authorization" received from the Security Council. As I have explained in earlier studies, it is legally and constitutionally impermissible to transfer the powers of Congress to an international (U.N.) or regional (North Atlantic Treaty Organization, NATO) body. The President and the Senate through the treaty process may not surrender power vested in the House of Representatives and the Senate by Article I. Treaties may not amend the Constitution.

In a May 20 letter to Congress, President [Barack] Obama spoke again about "authorization by the United Nations Security Council." He said that congressional action supporting the military action in Libya "would underline the U.S. commitment to this remarkable international effort." Moreover, a resolution by Congress "is also important in the context of our constitutional framework, as it would demonstrate a unity of purpose among the political branches on this important national security matter. It has always been my view that it is better to take military action, even in limited actions such as this, with Congressional engagement, consultation, and support." If that has always been his view, it was his obligation to come to Congress in February to seek legislative authorization.

2. "Authorization" from NATO

On March 28, in an address to the nation, President Obama announced that after U.S. military operations had been carried out against Libyan troops and air defenses, he would "transfer responsibilities to our allies and partners." NATO "has taken command of the enforcement of the arms embargo and the no-fly zone." Two days earlier, State Department Legal Advisor Harold Koh spoke of this transfer to NATO: "All 28 allies have also now authorized military authorities to develop an operations plan for NATO to take on the broader civilian protection mission under Resolution 1973." The May 20 letter from President Obama to Congress explained that by April 4 "the United States had transferred responsibility for the military operations in Libya to the North Atlantic Treaty Organization (NATO) and the U.S. involvement has assumed a supporting role in the coalition's efforts."

Nothing in these or any other communications from the administration can identify a source of authorization from NATO for military operations. Like the UN Charter, NATO was created by treaty. The President and the Senate through the treaty process may not shift the authorizing function from Congress to outside bodies, whether the Security Council or NATO. Section 8 of the War Powers Resolution specifically states that authority to introduce U.S. armed forces into hostilities or into situations wherein involvement in hostilities is clearly indicated by the circumstances "shall not be inferred…from any treaty heretofore or hereafter ratified unless such treaty is implemented by legislation specifically authorizing the introduction of United States Armed Forces into hostilities or into such situations and stating that it is intended to constitute specific statutory authorization within the meaning of this joint resolution." The authorizing body is always Congress, not the Security Council or NATO.

3. Military Operations in Libya: Not a "War"

The Obama administration has been preoccupied with efforts to interpret words beyond their ordinary and plain meaning. On April 1, the Office of Legal Counsel [OLC] reasoned that "a planned military engagement that constitutes a 'war' within the meaning of the Declaration of War Clause may require prior congressional authorization." But it decided that the existence of "war" is satisfied "only by prolonged and substantial military engagements, typically involving exposure of U.S. military personnel to significant risk over a significant period." Under that analysis, OLC concluded that the operations in Libya did not meet the administration's definition of "war." If U.S. casualties can be kept low, no matter the extent of physical destruction to another nation and loss of life, war to OLC would not exist within the meaning of the Constitution. If another nation bombed the United States without suffering significant casualties, would we call it war? Obviously we would. When Pearl Harbor was attacked on December 7, 1941, the United States immediately knew it was at war regardless of the extent of military losses by Japan.

4. No "Hostilities" Under the WPR

In response to a House resolution passed on June 3, the Obama administration on June 15 submitted a report to Congress. A section on legal analysis determined that the word "hostilities" in the War Powers Resolution should be interpreted to mean that hostilities do not exist with the U.S. military effort in Libya: "U.S. operations do not involve sustained fighting or active exchanges of fire with hostile forces, nor do they involve the presence of U.S. ground troops, U.S. casualties or a serious threat thereof, or any significant chance of escalation into a conflict characterized by those factors."

This interpretation ignores the political context for the War Powers Resolution. Part of the momentum behind passage of the statute concerned the decision by the Nixon administration to bomb Cambodia. The massive air campaign did not involve "sustained fighting or active exchanges of fire with hostile forces," the presence of U.S. ground troops, or substantial U.S. casualties. However, it was understood that the bombing constituted hostilities. According to the administration's June 15 report, if the United States conducted military operations by bombing at 30,000 feet, launching Tomahawk missiles from ships in the Mediterranean, and using armed drones, there would be no "hostilities" in Libya under the terms of the War Powers Resolution, provided that U.S. casualties were minimal or nonexistent. Under the administration's June 15 report, a nation with superior military force could pulverize another country (perhaps with nuclear weapons) and there would be neither hostilities nor war.

The administration advised Speaker John Boehner on June 15 that "the United States supports NATO military operations pursuant to UNSCR [UN Security Council Resolution] 1973." By its own words, the Obama administration is supporting hostilities. Although OLC in its April 1 memo supported President Obama's military actions in Libya, despite the lack of statutory authorization, it did not agree that "hostilities" (as used in the War Powers Resolution) were absent in Libya. Deprived of OLC support, President Obama turned to White House Counsel Robert Bauer and State Department Legal Adviser Harold Koh for supportive legal analysis. It would have been difficult for OLC to credibly offer its legal justification. The April 1 memo defended the "use of force" in Libya because President Obama "could reasonably determine that such use of force was in the national interest." OLC also advised that prior congressional approval was not constitutionally required "to use military force" in the limited operations under consideration. The memo referred to the "destruction of Libyan military assets."

It has been recently reported that the Pentagon is giving extra pay to U.S. troops assisting with military actions in Libya because they are serving in "imminent danger." The Defense Department decided in April to pay an extra $225 a month in "imminent danger pay" to service members who fly planes over Libya or serve on ships within 110 nautical miles of its shores. To authorize such pay, the Pentagon must decide that troops in those places are "subject to the threat of physical harm or imminent danger because of civil insurrection, civil war, terrorism or wartime conditions." Senator Richard Durbin has noted that "hostilities by remote control are still hostilities." The Obama administration chose to kill with armed drones "what we would otherwise be killing with fighter planes." It is interesting that various administrations, eager to press the limits of presidential power, seem to understand that they may not—legally and politically—use the words "war" or "hostilities." Apparently they recognize that using words in their normal sense, particularly as understood by members of Congress, federal judges, and the general public, would acknowledge what the framers believed. Other than repelling sudden attacks and protecting American lives overseas, Presidents may not take the country from a state of peace to a state or war without seeking and obtaining congressional authority.

5. Non-Kinetic Assistance

The Obama administration has distinguished between "kinetic" and "non-kinetic" actions, with "non-kinetic" apparently referring to no military force. The March 21 letter from President Obama to Congress spoke of clearly kinetic activities. U.S. forces had "targeted the Qadhafi regime's air defense systems, command and control structures, and other capabilities of Qadhafi's armed forces used to attack civilians and civilian populated areas." By May 20, in a letter to Congress, President Obama stated: "Since April 4, U.S. participation has consisted of non-kinetic support to the NATO-led operation." Elements not directly using military force were listed: intelligence, logistical support, and search and rescue missions. However, the letter identified these continued applications of military force: "aircraft that have assisted in the suppression and destruction of air defenses in support of the no-fly zone" and "since April 23, precision strikes by unmanned aerial vehicles against a limited set of clearly defined targets in support of the NATO-led coalition's efforts."

6. Support from S. Res. 85

OLC in its April 1 memo relied in part on legislative support from the Senate: "On March 1, 2011, the United States Senate passed by unanimous consent Senate Resolution 85. Among other things, the Resolution 'strongly condemn[ed] the gross and systematic violations of human rights in Libya, including violent attacks on protesters demanding democratic reforms,' 'call[ed] on Muammar Gadhafi to desist from further violence,' and 'urge[d] the United Nations Security Council to take such further action as may be necessary to protect civilians in Libya from attack, including the possible imposition of a no-fly zone over Libyan territory.'" Action by "unanimous consent" suggests strong Senate approval for the resolution, but the legislative record provides no support for that impression. Even if there were evidence of strong involvement by Senators in drafting, debating, and adopting this language, a resolution passed by a single chamber contains no statutory support. In addition, passage of S. Res. 85 reveals little other than marginal involvement by a few Senators.

Resolution 7 of S. Res. 85 urged the Security Council "to take such further action as may be necessary to protect civilians in Libya from attack, including the possible imposition of a no-fly zone over Libyan territory." When was the no-fly language added to the resolution? Were Senators adequately informed of this amendment? There is evidence that they were not. The legislative history of S. Res. 85 is sparse. There were no hearings and no committee report. The resolution was not referred to a particular committee. Sponsors of the resolution included ten Democrats and one Republican.

There was no debate on S. Res. 85. There is no evidence of any Senator on the floor at that time other than Senator Schumer and the presiding officer. Schumer asked for unanimous consent to take up the resolution. No one objected, possibly because there was no one present to object. Senate "deliberation" took less than a minute. When one watches Senate action on C-SPAN, consideration of the resolution began at 4:13:44 and ended at 4:14:19—after 35 seconds. On March 30, Senator John Ensign objected that S. Res. 85 "received the same amount of consideration that a bill to name a post office has. This legislation was hotlined." That is, Senate offices were notified by automated phone calls and e-mails of pending action on the resolution, often late in the evening when few Senators are present. According to some Senate aides, "almost no members knew about the no-fly zone language" that had been added to the resolution.

At 4:03 pm, through the hotlined procedure, Senate offices received S. Res. 85 with the no-fly zone provision but without flagging the significant change. Senator Mike Lee [R-UT] noted: "Clearly, the process was abused. You don't use a hotline to bait and switch the country into a military conflict." Senator Jeff Sessions [R-AL] remarked: "I am also not happy at the way some resolution was passed here that seemed to have authorized force in some way that nobody I know of in the Senate was aware that it was in the resolution when it passed."

7. The "Mandate" for Military Action in Libya

President Obama's speech to the nation on March 28 stated that "the United States has not acted alone. Instead, we have been joined by a strong and growing coalition. This includes our closest allies—nations like the United Kingdom, France, Canada, Denmark, Norway, Italy, Spain, Greece, and Turkey—all of whom have fought by our side for decades. And it includes Arab partners like Qatar and the United Arab Emirates, who have chosen to meet their responsibilities to defend the Libyan people." Over the month of March, "the United States has worked with our international partners to mobilize a broad coalition, secure an international mandate to protect civilians, stop an advancing army, prevent a massacre, and establish a no-fly zone with our allies and partners."

Missing from this coalition and mandate was the institution of Congress. President Obama in this speech spoke of "a plea for help from the Libyan people themselves." He offered his support "for a set of universal rights, including the freedom for people to express themselves" and for governments "that are ultimately responsive to the aspirations of the people." Yet throughout this period there had been no effort by the President or his administration to listen to the American people or secure their support.

On May 20, in a letter to Congress, President Obama said that he acted militarily against Libya "pursuant to a request from the Arab League and authorization by the United Nations Security Council." The administration's June 15 submission to Congress claims that President Obama acted militarily in Libya "with a mandate from the United Nations." There is only one permitted mandate under the U.S. Constitution for the use of military force against another nation that has not attacked or threatened the United States. That mandate must come from Congress.

Senate Joint Resolution 20, introduced on June 21, is designed to authorize the use of U.S. armed force in Libya. In two places the resolution uses the word "mandate." Security Council Resolution 1970 "mandates international economic sanctions and an arms embargo." Security Council Resolution 1973 "mandates 'all necessary measures' to protect civilians in Libya, implement a 'no-fly zone,' and enforce an arms embargo against the Qaddafi regime." The Security Council cannot mandate, order, or command the United States. Under the U.S. Constitution, mandates come from laws enacted by Congress.

THE CONTINUING DEBATE:
Barack Obama's Use of the President's War Powers

What Is New

As has often been the case when Congress thought the president was ignoring it with respect to military action, there was a great deal of congressional rhetoric chastising President Obama for violating the War Powers Resolution. As was also common in such circumstances, criticism mostly came from the opposition party, in this case the Republicans, in Congress. When George W. Bush had been president, the Democrats mostly led the charge. A third common aspect of the controversy is that, as before, nothing much happened. The House did finally pass a resolution sponsored by House Speaker John Boehner that declared, "The President has not sought, and Congress has not provided, authorization for the introduction or continued involvement of the Armed Forces in Libya," and that directed the president not to put ground combat units in Libya. The vote tally was 268 to 145, with 223 Republicans and 55 Democrats voting for it, and 135 Democrats and 10 Republicans voting against it. It meant little. A similar measure in the Senate never came to a vote, and in any case, simple resolutions have no legal impact. All other measures in the House, such as one directing Obama to cease all military action related to Libya failed, in that case by a vote of 148 to 265, with a majority of both parties voting against it.

Where to Find More

For a history of the WPR's impact, see *War Powers Resolution: Presidential Compliance*. Congressional Research Service, Report RL33532, April 12, 2011. Among other places, it is available at http://opencrs.com/document/RL33532/2011-04-12/. For a view that President Obama has adopted the same view of the commander in chief powers held by George Bush and other former presidents, read Ryan C. Hendrickson, "War Powers in the Obama Administration," *Contemporary Security Policy* (August 2010). A good compilation of congressional and other documents related to the WPR has been gathered by Jeremiah E. Sanders in *War Powers Resolution After 34 Years and the Continuing Political Debate (Congressional Policies, Practices and Procedures)*, (Nova Science, 2010).

What More to Do

Clear up more than 200 years of confusion about the authority of the president as commander and chief. Write and debate in class an amendment to the Constitution that will define as precisely as possible when (if ever) presidents can use military force or send U.S. forces into harm's way on their own authority and when (if ever) doing so would require a declaration of war or other form of prior congressional authorization.

13 BUREAUCRACY

THE NEW CONSUMER FINANCIAL PROTECTION BUREAU:
Consumer Guardian *or* Dangerous Bureaucracy?

CONSUMER GUARDIAN

ADVOCATE: Elizabeth Warren, Special Advisor to the Secretary of the Treasury for the Consumer Financial Protection Bureau

SOURCE: Testimony during hearings on "The Rulemaking Process and Unitary Executive Theory" before the U.S. House of Representatives, Committee on the Judiciary, Subcommittee on Commercial and Administrative Law, May 6, 2008

DANGEROUS BUREAUCRACY

ADVOCATE: Todd Zywicki, Foundation Professor of Law, George Mason University

SOURCE: Testimony during hearings on "Who's Watching the Watchmen? Oversight of the Consumer Financial Protection Bureau" before the U.S. House of Representatives, Committee on Oversight and Government Relations, Subcommittee on TARP, Financial Services, and Bailouts of Public and Private Programs, May 24, 2011

On July 17, 2011, the U.S. Consumer Financial Protection Bureau (CFPB) began operations. Its genesis lies in the financial crisis that began in 2007 in the United States, intensified and spread globally, and to a great degree continues as part of the worst economic turmoil since the Great Depression of the 1930s. Prominent among the multiple causes were risky practices by financial institutions including banks and other mortgage lenders and traders in stocks and other financial instruments. Also contributing were such factors as soaring prices for oil and other commodities, the massive U.S. trade deficit, and chronic budget deficits by the United States and other leading economies. In the United States, production and other economic activity declined, unemployment nearly doubled, and the housing market crashed. Many people were unable to meet their mortgage obligations, and foreclosures soared. General Motors and other major U.S. businesses declared bankruptcy, as did Lehman Brothers and other banks and financial institutions. There was fear that the entire U.S. financial structure was in danger.

As one response, Congress enacted the Troubled Assets Relief Program (TARP, 2008) allowing the government to buy up to $700 billion in troubled assets in order to keep General Motors, Chrysler, Citigroup, Bank of America, and other such financial mainstays operating. A second response was to change the operation and regulation of the financial industry to avoid a repeat of the practices that were widely blamed for the crisis. Central to this effort was the Dodd-Frank Act of 2010 [Senator Christopher Dodd (D-CT) and Representative Barney Frank (D MA)]. One part of this massive, 2,319 page piece of legislation was its creation in Title X (itself, 432 pages) of the CFPB. The new law shifted most existing federal consumer protection functions to the CFPB and also gave it significant new oversight, rulemaking, and enforcement authority over many consumer financial products and services (such as mortgages, student loans, credit cards, credit ratings, and debt collection) and over the financial institutions that offer them to the public. Congress also gave the CFPB much greater insulation from political control than most other regulatory agencies. The CFPB is part of the Federal Reserve System, which is itself insulated, but the CFPB is not subject to direction by the Federal Reserved Board. Regulations issued by the CFPB can be delayed by the newly established ten-member Financial Stability Oversight Council made up of the Secretary of the Treasury and other top government financial administrators, but only if by a two-thirds vote if they find that an action by the CFPB "would put the safety and soundness of…[the U.S.] financial system…at risk." The CFPB's director is appointed by the president with confirmation by the Senate, serves a five-year term, and can only be removed for "inefficiency, neglect of duty or malfeasance in office." Further adding to the CFPB's insulation, its budget is pre-set at 12% of the earnings of the Federal Reserve System. This works out currently to about $500 million annually.

The creation of the CFPB did not end the controversy about it. Defenders of the CFPB are represented in the first reading by Elizabeth Warren, a leading advocate of creating the CFPB and appointed to set up its initial operations. She argues that CFPB's authority and structure are needed to carry out its intended goals under the Dodd-Frank Act. Critics including Todd Zywicki in the second reading change that the CFPB's director has too much power, that the bureau is too insulated from the oversight of Congress, and that the bureau may require practices by financial intuitions that could endanger their soundness.

POINTS TO PONDER

➤ Insulating regulatory agencies helps protect them from political manipulation, but also shields them from control by elected officials in a democracy.
➤ The CFPB is even more insulated than most federal agencies. Is that warranted and why?
➤ Can the CFPB be "pro-consumer" without being "anti-business"?

The New Consumer Financial Protection Bureau: Consumer Guardian

Elizabeth Warren

INTRODUCTION

Thank you members of the Subcommittee for inviting me to testify about the work of the Consumer Financial Protection Bureau (CFPB). I appreciate the opportunity to report to Congress about the structure and management of the consumer bureau.

Two and a half years ago, I began my work in Washington as Chair of the Congressional Oversight Panel (COP). The COP produced detailed monthly reports for Congress about the Department of the Treasury's administration of the Troubled Asset Relief Program [TARP]. I came to Capitol Hill on many occasions to testify on behalf of the COP about our oversight efforts. Based on that experience working on behalf of Congress, I became a firm believer in the importance of oversight.

Two months ago, I testified before the House Financial Services Subcommittee on Financial Institutions and Consumer Credit. At that appearance, I provided 34 pages of detailed written testimony on the following topics to shed as much light as possible on the efforts underway to establish the CFPB. It is the hope of those of us working at the consumer bureau that the testimony I provided then and in today's hearing will provide you with the information you are looking for to oversee our efforts.

THE CRISIS OF 2008: WHAT WENT WRONG

Last year, the Dodd-Frank [Senator Christopher Dodd, D-CT and Representative Barney Frank, D-MA] Wall Street Reform and Consumer Protection Act established the CFPB, in part, to increase accountability in government by consolidating consumer financial protection authorities that had existed across seven different federal agencies into one. Consumer financial protection had not been the primary focus of any Federal agency, and no agency had effective tools to set the rules for and oversee the whole market. The result was a system without effective rules or consistent enforcement. We have seen the results, both in the 2008 financial crisis and in its aftermath.

In April, after two years of bipartisan investigation, the U.S. Senate Permanent Subcommittee on Investigations released a 635-page report on the key causes of the financial crisis. The report highlighted several causes of the crisis, including high-risk mortgage lending, inflated credit ratings, structured products sold by investment banks, and repeated failures of regulatory agencies to provide adequate oversight of the financial services industry. Senator Carl Levin, who chaired the committee, said that the report "catalogues conflicts of interest, heedless risk-taking, and failures of federal oversight that helped to push the country into the deepest recession since the Great Depression."

Senator Tom Coburn [R-OK], the committee's ranking member, said that "Blame for this mess lies everywhere from federal regulators who cast a blind eye, Wall Street bankers who let greed run wild, and members of Congress who failed to provide oversight."

The conclusions of the Senate Permanent Subcommittee on Investigations have been echoed elsewhere. During the recent hearing on the CFPB before the House Subcommittee on Financial Institutions and Consumer Credit, Chairman Shelley Moore Capito [R-WV] similarly observed, "I think we could all agree that there were lapses in oversight and inherent problems within the regulatory structure."

Last month, the Chief Executive Officer of one of our nation's largest financial institutions [James Dimon, CEO and chairman of the board of JP Morgan Chase & Co] made a similar point. He wrote to his company's shareholders that, "Indeed, had there been stronger standards in the mortgage markets, one huge cause of the recent crisis might have been avoided....As recently as five years ago, most Americans would have called the U.S. mortgage market one of the best in the world—boy, was that wrong! What happened to our system did not work well for any market participant—lender or borrower—and a careful rewriting of rules would benefit all."

The conclusion is bipartisan and shared by both those in government and those in private industry: Failures of our regulatory system were an important contributor to the country's worst financial disaster since the Great Depression.

CONGRESSIONAL RESPONSE: A NEW CONSUMER BUREAU

To address a root cause of the financial crisis of 2008, Congress established the CFPB: 1) to ensure that consumers have timely and understandable information to make responsible decisions about financial transactions; 2) to protect consumers from unfair, deceptive, or abusive acts or practices, and from discrimination; 3) to reduce outdated, unnecessary, or overly burdensome regulations; 4) to promote fair competition by enforcing the Federal consumer financial laws consistently; and 5) to advance markets for consumer financial products and services that operate transparently and efficiently to facilitate access and innovation.

As Congress recognized in creating the CFPB, every market needs rules. Antitrust rules, for example, ensure that companies don't conspire to fix prices or to squeeze out competitors and lock down a whole market. Those regulations ensure that every business—small, large, established, or start-up—has a chance to compete and to innovate. The rules also guarantee that customers have choices. The ability of customers to choose means that competition works at its best: The best businesses—those that produce goods and services that customers want most at the most affordable price—can flourish while those whose products aren't as good or whose prices are too high do not.

A fair, efficient, and transparent market presupposes that consumers are able to compare the costs and benefits of different products effectively and to use that information to choose the product that is best for them. In the world of consumer financial services today, that is a questionable premise. Fine print and overly long agreements make it difficult for consumers to understand and compare products, and that obstacle to sound markets is not removed by disclosures that are too complicated or that do not focus on the key information consumers need. The principal role of consumer protection regulation in credit markets is to make it easy for consumers to see what they are getting and to make it easy for customers to compare one product with another, so that markets can function effectively.

At the consumer bureau, we believe in markets—markets that make prices and risks clear and that give consumers the basic information they need to determine who is offering the best deals. Our primary goal is to make markets for consumer financial products and services work in a fair, efficient, and transparent manner. That means ensuring that consumers have access to information to help them understand the terms of the deal. Fair and transparent markets encourage personal responsibility and smart decision-making. When consumers are presented with a clearer choice between two financial products and they can easily know the costs, benefits, and risks of those products, they will be better able to make decisions that work for themselves and for their families.

Consumers expect to be held responsible for the financial decisions they make. If they don't keep up with their debt payments, they expect to face the consequences. Personal responsibility is critical. But consumers want to know the costs up-front and don't want to be blindsided by hidden fees, interest rate changes, or payment shocks. Informed decision-making allows consumers to drive the financial marketplace so that providers offer products that meet consumer needs and preferences.

GETTING STARTED: MARKETS THAT WORK

At the CFPB, we believe that a simple and straightforward presentation of key credit terms is the best way to level the playing field between borrowers and lenders and to foster honest competition. Our goal is shorter, clearer forms for the most common credit products, the kind that consumers can read in a few minutes with high levels of understanding. The CFPB is working to give consumers the transparency they deserve to make the choices that work for themselves and their families, while easing unnecessary regulatory burdens for their lenders.

In my first week on the job, the Treasury Department sponsored a symposium that brought together lenders and consumer advocates to discuss how to simplify federal mortgage disclosures. Consumer groups explained that many consumers didn't use current disclosures to assess costs or to compare alternatives because the forms are complicated and hard to use. The forms came under even more intense criticism from those who have to fill them out. Mortgage originators, particularly community banks and credit unions that work closely with their customers, described paperwork that was costly to complete, even as it produced little value for borrowers. Now, after months of consultation with borrower and lender representatives, we have developed prototype short mortgage shopping sheets that will be tested with actual consumers and, eventually, result in a simple, streamlined mortgage disclosure that will replace the two existing, complicated forms.

The new consumer bureau is making the early form drafts publicly available, long in advance of the formal process of notice-and-comment for official rule-making. We are seeking feedback early and often from consumers, lenders, brokers, and others now, and we will continue to do so as we refine the forms. We have posted draft forms online, while they are still in the design phase, and we have asked the public to weigh in. We will share the input we receive with our testers and designers, factoring it into our design process. We hope that these expanded procedures will permit us to engage a broader constituency, helping us deliver on the promise of this agency embodied in the Dodd-Frank Act.

A significant part of our mission will also be to help level the playing field for smaller lenders, such as community banks and credit unions. We recognize that the regulatory pressures on banks have increased substantially over time. While regulatory costs may be manageable on a per-account basis for the largest financial institutions, for smaller businesses, all the complicated rules, extensive paperwork, and expensive compliance reviews can be daunting. If we continue on our current regulatory trajectory, traditional banks and credit unions will be put at a further disadvantage that could push many out of business.

American consumers are best served by a strong and diversified financial services industry. Many community banks and credit unions embrace relationship lending, and they often work in partnership with the families they serve. Some smaller institutions provide a banking presence in otherwise-underserved communities, both in our cities and in rural areas. If community banks and credit unions continue to face competitive pressures triggered by a complex regulatory system, then those institutions will not be as able to serve American families. In that case, not only do the banks lose, but families lose as well.

The CFPB is committed to working with smaller institutions to reduce regulatory costs. We have already begun that work, and we are pleased to report to Congress that the spirit of openness and cooperation expressed by community banks and credit unions has been extraordinary. The mortgage disclosure integration project is one area in which we are seeking to reduce regulatory burdens, and we expect that it will serve as an excellent test case as we design our ongoing processes for how the consumer bureau and smaller institutions can work together to increase the ability of these institutions to spend less time on regulations and more time serving America's families.

STRUCTURE AND MANAGEMENT: ORGANIZING THE CFPB

Under Section 1066 of the Dodd-Frank Act, the Secretary of the Treasury is authorized to perform certain functions of the CFPB. On September 17, 2010, the Secretary appointed me to be his Special Advisor for this role. The President is in the process of considering candidates to nominate as the Bureau's first Director.

One of our main tasks since last September has been to develop an organizational design that will provide the infrastructure the Bureau will need to meet its responsibilities in the months and years ahead. Late last year, the CFPB began providing its draft organizational chart to Members of Congress and the media. In early February, we posted the chart to our newly launched CFPB website. In developing the CFPB's organizational structure, we have asked for comments and critiques from individuals in the private sector, community groups, and academia, as well as from Members of Congress.

Our primary goals in designing the CFPB organizational chart have been: 1) to engage the American public; 2) to ensure that the Federal consumer financial laws will be administered by the Bureau consistently, efficiently, and effectively; 3) to help create a level playing field for community banks and credit unions to compete with large banks and non-depository financial companies, 4) to make the CFPB a data-driven agency by making research and market analysis core to all of its work; 5) to advance financial education opportunities for all Americans; 6) to continue an open and candid dialogue with Members of Congress; and 7) to create accountability within the CFPB.

The CFPB team currently consists of more than 200 members and [its senior mangers] include individuals who have previously serves as: Commissioner of Banks in Massachusetts, Deputy Director of the Federal Reserve Board's Division of Consumer and Community Affairs, Attorney General of Ohio, Managing Director at Deutsche Bank Securities, Chief Investigative Counsel of the Committee on Energy and Commerce of the U.S. House of Representatives, attorney in the Office of White House Counsel, Counselor to the General Counsel in the Treasury Department, Chief Procurement Officer for the District of Columbia, Senior Attorney at the Consumers Union, General Counsel of Sprint Nextel, Director of the University of Connecticut's Insurance Law Center, Director of Strategic Initiatives for the Assistant Secretary of the Army, Associate Director of the Division of Financial Practices at the Federal Trade Commission, and head of the credit card business at Capital One.

As this list shows, the leadership of the CFPB is diverse, with people coming from a variety of backgrounds—public and private, banking and non-banking, large institutions and small institutions. The expertise and diversity represented by our leadership team is extraordinary. There is no single point of view that dominates this group, other than a shared vision to make consumer financial markets work better for all Americans.

PUBLIC ENGAGEMENT: REACHING OUT IN MANY DIRECTIONS

The CFPB is currently a construction site and, like most construction sites, it should be in plain view for anyone who is interested. That is why we launched our website in early February, more than five months ahead of the time the agency would assume many of its powers. We posted our draft organizational chart when we launched, and we have posted additional information about our budget and our progress in standing up the new agency over the time since. We have also consulted with various organizations dedicated to transparency in government to explore how we might add more information to our website or provide other useful data to the public.

We are committed to letting everyone know how we are working for the American people. One way we have sought to accomplish that is through the public release of my calendar. We began to post my calendar to the Treasury website proactively on November 24, 2010, even before we launched our website. We have now posted my calendar online each month and will continue to do so as a commitment to our openness.

The posted schedule gives everyone an opportunity to see who we are meeting with and what perspectives we are hearing. Our hope is that by releasing my schedule, the public will see that the agency is listening to a variety of viewpoints about how the consumer bureau should be shaped and where its efforts should be focused. The calendars show that we have now spoken directly with dozens of executives from large banks and banking trade associations. We have also spoken with leaders of community banks, credit unions, and other small financial services providers from all 50 states. We have met with dozens of consumer advocates, both in Washington and around the country. We have met with service members on visits to military bases. We have spoken with state attorneys general and bank supervisors from across the country, and we have had multiple meetings with other federal regulators. We have also met with entrepreneurs, innovators, retailers, leaders of non-profit organizations, and a wide variety of others both in and outside of the financial services industry.

In addition, since September, I have had more than 90 one-on-one conversations with Members of Congress. We have been in close touch with many who supported the creation of the CFPB and many who opposed it. My presence here today reflects our commitment to working closely with you and your colleagues.

OVERSIGHT: SIGNIFICANT LIMITS ON THE CFPB

In recent weeks, there have been many overblown claims about the nature of the CFPB's power. Critics have claimed that the CFPB is "the most powerful regulatory agency that's ever been put together," that it is "the most powerful agency ever created," and that it "doesn't have to explain what it does to anybody." These claims disregard the limits on the consumer bureau's authorities and the very meaningful oversight that Congress imposed over its functioning—oversight that is consistent with that which exists over other independent agencies.

I have been told that if you say anything in Washington often enough, it is eventually treated as fact—regardless of whether it is true or false. While making baseless claims might be shrewd tactics for those who want to undermine the Bureau's work, they are flatly wrong. The CFPB's jurisdiction is fundamentally limited to consumer financial products and services. Even within the world of consumer finance, huge sectors, including investments and insurance, are explicitly excluded from its jurisdiction, left instead to other state and federal regulators. The scope of the CFPB's authority is carefully limited.

False claims about CFPB's power also ignore the structural oversight and accountability that limit the reach of the CFPB. Like all other agencies in the federal government, the CFPB is subject to the requirements and limitations of the Administrative Procedure Act. We are one of only three agencies anywhere in government (and the only banking regulator) that is required to conduct SBREFA panels, a process to gather input directly from small businesses about the potential impact of proposed rules. And we are also specifically required to consider the benefits and costs of any proposed rules to consumers and providers. The CFPB's activities are subject to judicial review, ensuring that the CFPB operates within the constraints set by Congress and the U.S. Constitution.

In addition to being subject to judicial review, the Bureau is the only bank regulator whose rules can be overruled by a council made up of other federal agencies. In an unprecedented restriction unlike that on the authority of any other Federal financial regulator, Congress determined that a two-thirds majority of the banking regulators and other members of the Financial Stability Oversight Council can veto any rule issued by the consumer bureau if the council determines that it would put the safety and soundness of the banking system or the stability of the financial system at risk. And, of course, like with any federal agency, Congress can always overturn the Bureau's rules if the legislature disagrees with our judgments.

The CFPB is also the only bank regulator that is expressly limited in its ability to determine its own funding levels. If the Office of the Comptroller of the Currency believes it needs more funds to hire more examiners, it can raise more through assessments on the industry. But the consumer agency's independent funding is statutorily capped at a portion of the Federal Reserve System's operating expenses. If the CFPB concludes that it needs additional funding, it must persuade Congress to provide that funding.

Other forms of oversight exist as well:

1. The CFPB must submit annual financial reports to Congress.

2. The CFPB must report to Congress twice each year to justify its budget from the previous year.

3. The Director of the CFPB must testify before and report to Congress twice each year regarding the CFPB's activities.

4. The GAO must conduct an audit each year of the consumer bureau's expenditures and submit a report to Congress.

5. The CFPB must submit its financial operating plans and forecasts and quarterly financial reports to the Office of Management and Budget.

6. The Inspector General of the Federal Reserve Board (and the Inspector General of the Treasury Department, during this interim period) have been charged with reviewing the CFPB's activities to inform Congress and the public about the consumer bureau's work.

The formal restraints over the agency are substantial, but informal restraints are significant as well. The financial services industry has substantial resources to ensure that its views about the CFPB and its work are well known and fully considered.

Recent proposals to alter the CFPB's structure—including those that the House Financial Services Committee recently passed—overlook the many constraints already in place. The work facing the new bureau is very challenging; additional restrictions would undermine the consumer bureau before it even begins its work of protecting American families.

Proposals to change the consumer bureau have been put forward in the name of accountability. But accountability is ultimately about being responsible for getting a job done on behalf of American families. Those families know that they are held accountable every day. They have to pay their credit card bills and student loans. They see money disappear from their checking accounts when they make a mistake. And, as millions of families have witnessed first-hand in the past few years, when they default on mortgages they cannot afford, they lose their homes. American families expect to pay what they owe, but they also want to make sure that the rules are fair and followed. They want an agency that will be accountable for getting that basic job done, and, so long as it has the tools, the CFPB will be that agency.

CONCLUSION

I understand—and greatly appreciate—the important role of oversight. Oversight is a deeply important feature of our democracy that provides for checks and balances and helps prevent overreach, violations of law, and misguided expenditure of public funds. Oversight of the CFPB—during its stand-up and beyond—will build greater confidence in the consumer bureau by the public. That is why I welcome the opportunity to discuss our efforts and to update you on our progress.

The New Consumer Financial Protection Bureau: Dangerous Bureaucracy

Todd Zywicki

It is my pleasure to testify this afternoon on the question of "Who's Watching the Watchmen? Oversight of the Consumer Financial Protection Bureau." This is a crucially important question to ask at a crucially important time in our economic recovery. Economic recovery remains fragile, housing markets are still in flux, and consumer credit markets are still recovering from the credit crisis and the imposition of regulations that have increased the cost and reduced the availability of credit to consumers and small businesses, from credit cards to bank overdraft protection. In addition, the Durbin Amendment [Senator Richard Dubrin D-IL] to the Dodd-Frank [Senator Christopher Dodd D-CT and Representative Barney Frank D-MA] financial reform legislation will take effect this summer, imposing confiscatory and punitive price controls on debit card interchange fees and shifting those costs onto American banking consumers. It is estimated that when the dust settles, these new banking fees will mark the end of free checking for low-income Americans and drive some one million of them out of the mainstream banking system and into the hands of check cashers, pawn shops, and fee-laden prepaid cards.

This constant interference with the ability of lenders to price their risk accurately has resulted in higher interest rates, billions of dollars slashed from consumer credit lines, and record popularity for payday lenders and pawn shops.

But these impositions are just the tip of the iceberg of the possible damage that poorly conceived regulation can do to consumer credit, small business credit, and the overall American economy. Just weeks from now the Consumer Financial Protection Bureau (CFPB) will enter its operative phase. If not subject to effective congressional oversight, the massive, vaguely defined powers and expansive reach of the new consumer credit "super regulator" could prove an economy killer, producing still-higher credit costs for consumers, and accelerating regulatory pressures that drive consumers out of the mainstream financial system and into the alternative, high-cost financial sector. Moreover, because millions of small, independent businesses rely wholly or partly on personal and consumer credit to start and build their businesses, heavy-handed, misguided regulation could strangle job creation and economic dynamism. Indeed, based on standard economic analysis and the history of consumer credit regulation in America, an entirely foreseeable consequence of an unchecked CFPB will be—ironically—to produce higher levels of fraud and abuse of American consumers. This is because oppressive and misguided regulation stifles competition, reduces consumer choice, and drives consumers from the mainstream banking system into non-traditional lending products.

At this point, there seems to be a general consensus that the overall impact of the CFPB will be to increase the cost of, and reduce access to, consumer and small-business credit, and to increase the regulatory burden on financial institutions. Even supporters of the CFPB and its continued insulation from responsible oversight generally acknowledge that this will be the overall impact of the body as a purely descriptive matter—they simply believe that higher cost and reduced credit access to mainstream credit is a good thing in light of the experience of the past decade.

I disagree—economics and history teach that reducing access to credit does not reduce consumer need for credit. Washington bureaucrats cannot wish away the need of American families for credit. If you need $500 to repair your transmission to get to work on Monday, you need that $500—regardless of whether you have a bank account or credit card. If you need $300 to pay your rent or electric bill, then you need that money regardless of whether you have it saved up or not. And if you can't get a credit card because a paternalistic Washington bureaucrat doesn't think you deserve one, then you are simply going to go to a payday lender. And if payday loans are regulated out of existence, you are going to turn to a pawn shop. History teaches the unfortunate lesson that if all else fails, illegal loan sharks stand ready to meet your needs.

Even if one believes that increasing the cost and reducing access to credit is a good thing, there should also be agreement that regulators should not try to increase cost and reduce access unduly. But the current organizational structure and lack of responsible oversight of CFPB creates an extreme danger that the agency will overreach, imposing costs on consumers, small businesses, and the economy that will stifle economic growth and drive vulnerable consumers into the arms of less-savory lenders. My testimony today will focus on some structural reforms that might help to minimize those unintended consequences. At the outset, however, let me add one word—we have seen this movie before and we know how it ends. Beginning with the New Deal, central planners in the United States government created a flotilla of massive, unaccountable bureaucracies dedicated to micro-managing the American economy. And we know what happened: by the 1970s, these unaccountable regulatory behemoths had strangled the life out of the American economy—bringing about stagflation, reduced innovation, and declining American competitiveness—until the deregulation efforts, beginning with the Carter Administration and continuing through the Reagan Administration, restored dynamism to the American economy.

The structure of the CFPB is a throwback to this Nixon-era bureaucracy [Richard M. Nixon, president 1969–1974], from which we learned the following: you cannot give massive discretionary powers to unaccountable Washington bureaucrats, however well-intentioned, and expect they can run the American economy and still preserve innovation, competition, and consumer choice. That idea has been tried and has failed. Since that time, scholars have analyzed that historical experience to distill the general lessons of the pathologies that arise from unaccountable bureaucrats tasked with a narrow tunnel-vision focus. I hope this body will take steps to avert the pain that will come from relearning those lessons.

I will focus on several different areas of possible reform to mitigate the damage that the CFPB will do to the economy: structural changes, increased accountability, and substantive changes to the agency's mission. At the outset, let me emphasize that I agree with the motivation underlying the creation of the CFPB—to create a more modern, coherent, and integrated consumer-protection regime for the regulation of consumer credit. Unfortunately, the CFPB is not likely to bring about this result. Reforming the Bureau's Structure [House of Representatives bill number] H.R. 1121, passed by the House Financial Services Committee, would replace the single-director model of the CFPB with a multi-member commission. This is the most important reform that should be made to the bureau's structure to make it more consumer-friendly. Ideally, the entire bureau would be liquidated and sent to the dust bin of history, and all of its responsibilities sent to the Federal Trade

Commission (FTC), where they belong. Absent that, however, the bureau should be reconstructed along the lines of the FTC as a multi-member commission, or the Board of Governors of the Federal Reserve should be given heightened oversight powers over the bureau.

The bureau's structure itself may be unprecedented in American history: an independent agency within another independent agency. Although headquartered within the Federal Reserve, it is almost completely unaccountable to oversight by the Federal Reserve Board or any other entity except through a cumbersome and limited oversight process by a council of regulators. But even this council can act only if two-thirds agree that a proposed action by the bureau would imperil the safety and soundness of the nation's financial system. Moreover, the bureau is headed by a single chief appointed by the President, rather than a multimember commission, leaving the agency's actions subject to the whims and idiosyncratic views of a single individual.

As an unaccountable bureaucracy with a single head, the bureau will be susceptible to bureaucracy's worst pathologies: a tunnel-vision focus on the agency's regulatory mission, undue risk aversion and agency overreach.

Although a more effective consumer protection system is needed, consumer-protection goals often can conflict with other goals, such as promoting competition, lower prices and expanded choice for consumers; and ensuring safety and soundness of the banking system. Failing to account for the potential negative impact of overzealous regulation enacted in the name of consumer protection can result in greater harm to consumers in terms of higher prices, reduced choice, and lower quality services. For example, the law gives the bureau new authority to regulate mortgage brokers, some of whom undoubtedly contributed to the onset of the financial crisis. Although stricter regulations of mortgage brokers theoretically could reduce fraud (although there is no evidence that this is the case), brokers also provide a salutary competitive check on traditional bank lenders. Research by economists Morris Kleiner and Richard Todd finds that overly restrictive regulation that reduces the number of mortgage brokers in a given market results in higher prices and lower quality for consumers—including a higher level of foreclosures.

An effective consumer-protection regulator must be able to balance consumer protection against other benefits to consumers and the economy of greater competition, lower prices, and enhanced safety and soundness. The current CFPB is not structured to weigh those broader trade-offs. A better model is the Federal Trade Commission, the primary consumer-protection regulator for most of the American economy. At the FTC (where I was director of the Office of Policy Planning from 2003–04), the mission of the Bureau of Consumer Protection is virtually identical to that of the CFPB, focusing particularly on unfair and deceptive marketing. But the final decision on whether to act rests not with the director, but with the five-member bipartisan commission to which the bureau reports. Moreover, by combining under its roof the Bureau of Competition and the Bureau of Economics, the FTC has a broader scope to weigh the consumer protection bureau's narrow focus on consumer protection against the larger impacts on competition and economic efficiency (and vice versa).

Yet no one—least of all those who have worked at the FTC in recent decades—contends that this broader focus, greater accountability and internal checks and balances weaken the FTC's effectiveness as a consumer protection watchdog. Instead, FTC officials uniformly recognize that consumers benefit from lower prices and greater choice as well as consumer protection. I don't know a single FTC veteran who believes consumers would be better off if the director of the Bureau of Consumer Protection were unleashed to litigate and regulate without accountability to the commissioners. Yet that's precisely how the CFPB is structured. More generally, there is simply no good reason why this one agency, of all the similarly empowered agencies in Washington, should not be governed by a commission.

INCREASED EXTERNAL ACCOUNTABILITY

The bureau should also have increased external accountability to Congress and/or the White House. First, it is obvious that a bureaucracy with this huge budget and power should be subject to annual appropriations review and other traditional tools of oversight. There is simply nothing inherent in the functions of this bureau that should shield it from the same degree of transparency and democratic oversight as any other independent agency, such as the FTC or cabinet departments. I won't belabor this point as there is no serious argument against this regular degree of oversight.

Second, H.R. 1315, passed by the Financial Services Committee, would enable the Financial Stability Oversight Council to reverse decisions of the CFPB through a simple majority vote rather than the two-thirds majority needed under the current version of the law. This would provide a useful restraint on the bureau's inevitable tendency toward tunnel vision and mission overreach by providing some modicum of balance in the name of safety and soundness.

Third, the acts of the CFPB should be made subject to Office of Information and Regulatory Affairs (OIRA) or other external review for cost-benefit feasibility. Independent agencies, including the Federal Reserve, traditionally have been exempted from OIRA review of their regulations. But that's because the internal deliberation process of a multi-member commission provides a collegial, deliberative process that ensures that all views are heard and all competing policies weighed. An agency headed by a single person, however, lacks these internal checks and balances. As a result, it is crucial that the decisions of the agency be reviewed by OIRA or some external analysts to ensure that the benefits of those regulations exceed the costs imposed.

RESTRICTIONS ON SUBSTANTIVE POWERS

The substantive powers of the CFPB should also be more sharply constrained than the broad and vaguely defined powers that are granted under its 400-page charter by the Dodd-Frank Act. Two areas are of particular concern. First, the bureau is empowered to regulate and punish not only "unfair" and "deceptive" lending practices, but also "abusive" loans and loan terms. This broad, vague, and retroactive standard will likely harm precisely those consumers it is intended to protect, and could dramatically raise the cost of lending by creating unpredictable retroactive liability. Second, the standard for preemption of contrary state laws should be returned to its prior level.

The CFPB has the power to regulate and punish not only "unfair" and "deceptive" lending practices (the FTC's standard) but also "abusive" loans and loan terms—a legal term that appears to be novel in this context. The contours of this new basis for liability are vague, but most obviously it must mean something different and more than attacking those products that are considered unfair or deceptive. In fact, it seems potentially to hold lenders responsible for a subjective standard of understanding and competency by some subcategories of consumers, or with respect to some subcategory of loan products. For example, this power seemingly could enable the bureau to identify some groups of borrowers based on some crude demographic criteria as being thought too dumb to understand credit products that other consumers can understand and therefore have the option of using.

Alternatively, the new super regulator would seem to have power to ban loan terms and products anytime the bureau chief thinks consumers lack the ability to comprehend the full risks of a product. The bureau chief could effectively ban many nontraditional lending products, such as payday lending, if he or she thinks, for example, that consumers using that form of lending are too dumb to appreciate the full cost and risk of those products—even if the consumers fully understand the risks and even though research shows that consumers overwhelmingly are satisfied with their choices and use payday loans because those loans are superior to other available choices.

Congress also should roll back the heightened standard for federal bank regulators to pre-empt state regulatory and enforcement authority over federally chartered banks. The threat addressed by pre-emption is long standing—the effort of populist state legislatures and politically ambitious prosecutors to score political points by attacking out-of-state federally chartered banks and their subsidiaries. But the consequences are heightened by the national character of the modern banking system, which has grown in large part because of the power of federal regulators to pre-empt parochial state laws. Moreover, if the rationale for heightened pre-emption standards is justified, it was because of a fear of inadequate federal enforcement—but that rationale was eliminated by the creation of the new federal bureau itself. Instead, the weakening of pre-emption threatens a nightmare regulatory dystopia: a new federal regulator that reaches down to the level of local payday lenders and small merchants while simultaneously empowering state regulators to attack national banks.

MARKET-REINFORCING VERSUS MARKET-REPLACING REGULATION

There is a better way forward for consumers and the economy. Rather than a return to heavy-handed 1970s-style regulation, we should be moving in the direction of a new regulatory approach that harnesses the power of competition and technology to expand consumer choice and consumer welfare.

Consumer credit can be regulated in two different ways: either through "market-reinforcing" regulation or "market-replacing" regulation. Market-reinforcing regulation builds on the dynamism of the competitive process and consumer empowerment to make it easier for consumers to shop among competing credit products and choose the ones that are right for them. Without question, America's consumer credit regulatory system is ripe for a comprehensive overhaul. As a result of litigation and regulation, the Truth in Lending Act, for example, has evolved from a simple three-page document to a regulatory monster saddled with thousands of pages of regulation. Clearing away this thicket of regulator and lawyer-imposed costs is necessary in order to make disclosure regulation work better for consumers. Defensive, legalistic disclosures designed to protect lenders from class action litigation based on technicalities rather than real harm has proven to be a major burden on the consumer finance system. Instead, the CFPB legislation unleashes class action lawyers and state attorneys general through its elimination of contracts to arbitrate, its heightened standards for preemption, and its coterminous power of state attorneys general to enforce federal law. This combination of new enforcement, with the vague, expansive sources of liability created by Dodd-Frank, are likely to spawn further regulatory confusion and defensive disclosures.

In addition, as noted, the regulatory process is plagued by redundant and oppressive regulation. The proposal for a single integrated mortgage disclosure form is a useful step in the right direction. Similar opportunities for streamlining and rationalizing the regulatory process could be seized—but are unlikely to emerge from this CFPB. Finally, recent decades have demonstrated the clunkiness of the old-style regulatory process. Today, innovations in consumer credit markets quickly outstrip the New Deal regulatory framework that exists. Once regulations are passed, they are too often set in stone; old regulations are almost never repealed. Instead, new regulations are simply piled atop existing regulation in an ever-mounting pile of incompatible and incoherent regulation. Finally, regulation in recent decades has been plagued by mandates regarding what I have referred to as "normative disclosure"—efforts to use disclosure not to help consumers to find the products that suit their needs, but instead to try to use disclosure to shape consumer preferences. For example, a single, simplified mortgage disclosure form would be of substantial value to consumers—provided, of course, that more simplified consumer disclosure forms is not merely an effort to try to indirectly force more simplified products onto the market or to prefer the flawed idea of "plain vanilla" products to other types of products.

Today, for example, only about half of consumers use credit cards primarily as a credit device—others use it as a transactional device where they pay off their balance at the end of every month. Yet the regulatory framework requires credit card marketing to be focused primarily on the assumption that consumers will use it as a credit device. For the half of consumers who use the card like a debit card, however, this information is largely irrelevant. They care about benefits and other factors and compelled prominent disclosures of terms they don't care about simply makes it more difficult to find the information they do want. Furthermore, once imposed, regulations bear the permanent stamp of the particular issues of the day, which are soon obsolete as markets change.

Instead, CFPB is predicated on the old-style model of market-replacing regulation: the idea that Washington bureaucrats know better than real people what is good for them. Whether concealed under the guise of behavioral economics or "nudges" instead of mandates, the underlying premise is still the same—paternalistic bureaucrats who think they know better as to what credit products consumers should be allowed to buy and the terms under which they should be purchased. Again, we have seen time and time again in history where this path leads: to higher credit prices, reduced choice, and harm to the very consumers that these regulations purportedly are intended to help.

CONCLUSION

The new CFPB promises higher costs and reduced access to credit for American consumers. The only question now is how much of an impact will be felt. Congress should take steps to build greater accountability and mission focus into a new consumer-protection regulator. Or consumers will be the losers in the end.

THE CONTINUING DEBATE:
The New Consumer Financial Protection Bureau

What Is New

As of August 2011, Republican senators were trying to force changes to limit the power of the CFPB director and give Congress greater oversight authority. Even though the Republicans are in a minority, they are using the threat of a filibuster (see Debate 11) and the need to gather 60 votes, not just a majority of 51, in the Senate to pass legislation, confirm appointments, or take a range of other legislative action. The first GOP effort involved who might be director. Elizabeth Warren was one of the initiators of the movement to create the CFPB and she was also appointed to supervise its start-up operation. She seemed a "natural" to become director, but Republicans characterized her as an anti-business crusader and vowed to block her confirmation. Moreover, most Republican senators signed a letter to Obama saying that they would block any nominee, not just Warren, unless the president agreed to changes that would weaken the power of the director by creating an executive board with final decision-making authority much like the one the governs the Securities and Exchange Commission and some other regulatory agencies. In the end, Obama bypassed Warren and nominated former Ohio Attorney General, Richard Cordray as director. Perhaps the president would not have nominated Warren anyway, but most analysts thought that Obama had given way in the hope that someone with a more moderate reputation might get confirmed despite the Republican threat. Whether that is true for Cordray or anyone else without meeting at least some of the Republican's demands to restructure of the CFPB is uncertain.

Where to Find More

An overview of the legislative underpinning of the CFPB is in *The Dodd-Frank Wall Street Reform and Consumer Protection Act: Title X, The Consumer Financial Protection Bureau*, Congressional Research Service Report R41338, July 21, 2010. An analysis of the extensive rule-making authority of the CFPB is contained in *The Dodd-Frank Wall Street Reform and Consumer Protection Act: Regulations to Be Issued by the Consumer Financial Protection Bureau*, Congressional Research Service Report R41380, August 25, 2010, at the Open CRS site, http://opencrs.com/document/R41380/. A report by the new bureau outline of its activities during its nearly yearlong set-up phase, *Building the CFPB: A Progress Report*, is available at http://www.consumerfinance.gov/.

What More to Do

At face value, it is hard to oppose a powerful and active consumer protection agency of any type. However, like most issues, "right" is not all on one side. Go back to the "Points to Ponder" in the introduction and consider what, if any, changes you might make in the structure and authority of the CFPB.

14   JUDICIARY

DECIDING ON THE CONSTITUTION'S MEANING:
Rely on the Original Authors *or* Interpret in Light of Modern Circumstances?

RELY ON THE ORIGINAL AUTHORS

ADVOCATE: Keith E. Whittington, William Nelson Cromwell Professor of Politics, Princeton University

SOURCE: "Originalism Within the Living Constitution," *Advance: The Journal of the American Constitution Society Issues Groups*, Fall 2007

INTERPRET IN LIGHT OF MODERN CIRCUMSTANCES

ADVOCATE: Erwin Chemerinsky, Alston & Bird Professor of Law and Political Science, Duke University

SOURCE: "Constitutional Interpretation for the Twenty-first Century," *Advance: The Journal of the American Constitution Society Issues Groups*, Fall 2007

Age is one remarkable characteristic of the U.S. Constitution. It is older than any other written constitution in the world. Moreover, it has survived for more than two centuries with relatively few written changes, having been amended only 27 times. Moreover, the first ten of these amendments, the Bill of Rights, were drafted in 1789, just two years after the Constitution itself had been written and ratified by the states. By contrast, the country which the Constitution governs and the world in which that country exists have undergone transformations that would leave any of the framers gaping in disbelief.

Brevity is the Constitution's second notable aspect. It is only 7,525 words, making it shorter than any of the 50 state constitutions. The few words with which the Constitution structures the American political system has made the document, as scholar Edwin Corwin has commented correctly, "an invitation to struggle" as judges and politicians clash over its meaning. For example, the Constitution designates the president as "commander in chief." But what does that mean, especially in light of the Constitution's delegation of the power to declare war to Congress? This remains an important controversy, as evident in Debate 12 of this volume.

The often vague wording of the Constitution has made the Supreme Court a more influential institution than the founders would have imagined. This has occurred for three reasons. One is that the Constitution designates itself as the "supreme law of the land." That means the Constitution overrides all other law in the United States.

Second, the Constitution gives the federal courts the right to decide case disputes arising under it. This includes disputes about what the Constitution's clauses mean and what language in the thousands of laws passed by Congress mean. As New York Governor (and later U.S. Supreme Court Chief Justice) Charles Evan Hughes put it in 1907, "We are under a Constitution, but the Constitution is what the judges say it is."

Third, the imprecision of the Constitution has strengthened the courts by giving them considerable latitude to decide cases under their power of "judicial review." This means the authority to decide whether laws passed by Congress and actions taken by the executive violate the Constitution and to strike them down if they do. According to the Supreme Court in *Marbury v. Madison* (1803), the "Constitution…confirms and strengthens the principle…" that law and actions "repugnant to the Constitution [are] void."

Thus the Supreme Court at the apex of the judicial branch has the authority to hear and decide any case involving the Constitution, to decide what the wording of the Constitution means, and to void laws and actions that violate the intent of the Constitution.

The question joined in this debate is how judges decide what the Constitution means. One school of thought called "originalism" or "strict constructionism" is represented by Professor Keith E. Whittington in the first reading. This approach holds that judges should interpret the Constitution by emphasizing its literal text and the original intent of its authors. This intent can be found by looking to the debates and the written commentary at the time of the Constitution and its amendments. The idea, Chief Justice Roger B. Taney wrote long ago in the *Scott v. Sandford* (1857), is that the Constitution should be read with "the same meaning and intent" it had "when it came from the hands of its framers."

The second school of thought contends that judges should consider the Constitution a "living document." This means interpreting it in light of contemporary circumstances. Critics of this approach call it "judicial activism," but advocates such as Erwin Chemerinsky in the second reading might call it "judicial progressivism" or "judicial modernism." Advocates of this approach would say that in deciding what is cruel and unusual punishment, the courts should be less concerned with what that meant in 1787 and more concerned with what modern standards are. From this perspective, Justice Oliver Wendell Holmes noted in *Missouri v. Holland* (1920), the Constitution should be interpreted "in light of our whole experience and not merely in light of what was said a hundred years ago."

POINTS TO PONDER

➤ Think about whether Americans and their courts should be bound in the first decade of the 21st century by what people meant in the last decade of the 18th century when deciding what the Constitution means.

➤ What does Whittington say about how originalists believe that judges should decide issues like abortion, about which the Constitution says nothing, or pornography on the Internet, which did not even exist in the 1789 when the First Amendment was written?

➤ What are the views of the two authors about whether originalism prevents judges from "legislating from the bench," that is, deciding what the Constitution means according to their own policy views rather than the intent of the authors of the constitutional or statutory language?

Deciding the Constitution's Meaning:
Rely on the Original Authors

Keith E. Whittington

The argument that original meaning should guide constitutional interpretation is nearly as old as the Constitution itself. Before there were strict constructionists, before there were judicial activists, there were originalists. In those early days, few seriously objected to the notion that the Constitution should be read in accord with its original meaning, though there were plenty of debates over how best to ascertain that original meaning and what exactly was required to be faithful to the Constitution of the founding.

The modern originalism debates are different. The authority of the original meaning of the Constitution has been routinely challenged in basic ways. The claim that the Constitution should be understood differently—that it is a "living Constitution" that means something different today than it meant when it was adopted, for example—is now itself quite old. It is now thought that adherence to original meaning is one alternative among many, a choice that might be made or that might not. If originalism is not exactly on the defensive, it at least has to be defended.

For judges who wish to exercise the power of judicial review, adherence to the original meaning of the Constitution is the only choice that is justifiable. We might make use of the language of the Constitution to help make sense of and to express our highest political ideals and aspirations. We might borrow from the constitutional text to help remind us of our past political struggles or inspire us to take on new national projects. When judges attempt to set aside the policy decisions of our elected representatives, when they claim that their own constitutional judgments trump those of others, then they cannot rest such claims on mere political idealism couched in a loose constitutional rhetoric. Judges are only entitled to respect when asserting that a law is null and void when they can back up such assertions with a persuasive explanation of how the law violates the meaning of the Constitution as it was framed and ratified.

I. WHY ORIGINALISM?

There are several interrelated justifications for jurisprudence of originalism. Originalism is implicit in the design of a written constitution. The adoption of a written constitution is justified by the desire to fix certain principles and raise them over others as having special weight. The writing of a constitution allows the people to assemble and, in a moment of reflection and deliberation, adopt those specified principles. Originalism makes sense of the fact that it was this text and no other that was adopted and ratified, and it channels the judicial inquiry into discovering what was meant by those who adopted this text. A jurisprudence of originalism recognizes and emphasizes that the Constitution is a communication, an instruction, from an authorized lawgiver, the sovereign people, and that the task of the faithful interpreter is to discover what that instruction was and to apply it as the situation demands.

At heart, all of these justifications are concerned with explaining the basis on which judges can claim the authority to ignore the policies made by elected legislators. Government officials in the United States do not exercise force and power by divine right. Their authority for making legitimate laws that average citizens are expected to obey ultimately comes from their constitutional office. Government officials are chosen to make policy within the limited scope of their predefined legal authority. Legislators are elected to make laws that are intended to serve the public good and operate within constitutional limits. The president is elected to secure the national interest and to insure that those laws are implemented effectively. Judges are not elected for the general purpose of making good policy. Judges are selected to interpret and apply the law in the cases and controversies that arise before them.

The claim to exercise the power of judicial review, the claim to the authority to ignore an otherwise valid law, can only be inferred from the Constitution. The Constitution does not in so many words simply give judges the power to veto laws. The power of judicial review in a particular case is merely an inference from the judicial duty to apply the law—all the law—correctly and appropriately to the case at hand. As Chief Justice John Marshall explained over two centuries ago, if Congress were to instruct the judges that a citizen be convicted of treason on the testimony of only one witness when the Constitution requires two or that a citizen be held criminally liable for actions that were legal when they were committed, then judges would have no choice but to recognize that the superior law of the Constitution would have to govern the case, regardless of the instructions of Congress. A jurisprudence of originalism makes better sense of why John Marshall was correct than does any alternative. Once judges depart from originalism, once they are no longer guided by the original meaning of the Constitution in resolving the cases that come before them, then their very claim to the power of judicial review becomes open to question.

The point of issuing an instruction is to convey the meaning of those authorized to issue them to those obliged to obey them. As James Madison noted, the faithful interpreter must recur to "the sense in which the Constitution was accepted and ratified. In that sense alone it is the legitimate Constitution." It is only by recurring to the original meaning intended by those who created the Constitution that we can make sense of and maintain the notion that we seek to establish, in the words of the Federalist, "good government from reflection and choice." It is only by "carry[ing] ourselves back to the time when the constitution was adopted, recollect[ing] the spirit manifested in the debates," seeking the most "probable [meaning] in which it was passed," rather than by seeing what meaning "may be squeezed out of the text, or invented against it," that we can avoid rendering the Constitution a "blank paper by construction."

For some this may seem to be begging the question: Must even a faithful constitutional interpreter be committed to the language and intent of the founders? The short answer is yes. The implicit link between "language" and "intent" indicates the direction of the interpretive imperative. We readily recognize that we cannot be said to be interpreting the text if we disregard its language. But the language of the text does not emerge from the sea or drop from the sky; it was intentionally written by the authors of the text in order to communicate a message, to convey their thoughts to others. At a minimum, the choice of constitutional language reflects the intentions of the framers that a faithful interpreter is bound to respect. But language is a means, not an end in itself. We use language to convey meaning. We interpret language in order to understand that meaning. If we are free to ignore the meaning that the founders sought to convey in the text, then why are we not equally free to ignore the text itself? Why be bound by the words that they happened to write down if we are not bound by what they meant to say with those words? Why should the language of the Constitution, disassociated from any intended meaning, have any particular authority? If the authority of the Constitution lies in the fact that founders were specially authorized to give instruction, to create supreme law, then the meaning of the law that they laid down must be as authoritative as the particular words they used to convey that meaning.

II. WHAT IS ORIGINALISM?

By the original meaning of the Constitution, I am referring to the meaning that the constitutional text was understood to have at the time it was drafted and ratified. To adopt originalism does not mean that judges must hold a séance to call the spirit of James Madison to ask him what was on his mind in Philadelphia in the summer of 1787 or how he would deal with the tricky constitutional question that is raised by the case before the court. It does mean that judges should not feel free to pour their own political values and ideals into the Constitution. It means that the constant touchstone of constitutional law should be the purposes and values of those who had the authority to make the Constitution—not of those who are charged with governing under it and abiding by it.

One important point should be clarified. The commitment to originalism is not a commitment to the particular practices, plans and expectations of particular framers or of the founding generation. We are bound by the constitutional text that they adopted and by the principles embodied in that text. Their understandings about the practical implications of those principles and the particular applications that they expected to flow from them may be helpful to us as we try to figure out what exactly those constitutional principles were, but those early applications are rarely equivalent to the constitutional requirements themselves. The founders and early government officials who were members of or close to the founding generation may well have fully implemented the principles of the Constitution, but in many cases they did not. Some issues may simply not have arisen at an early date, or the circumstances with which they dealt may not have tested the limits or full extent of those constitutional principles. They may have self-consciously limited themselves, adopting policies that did not test or stretch the limits of the powers that they thought the government possessed or the rights to which they thought individuals were entitled. They could also be wrong about what their own principles required.

The members of the founding generation were as aware as anyone of the limits of human reason and of the temptations of political power. They drafted constitutions precisely because they knew that they and their successors would need constant reminders of the principles that they held dear and the foundational agreements that they had struck. As constitutional interpreters, we are required to reason from the principles that they laid down, not take their word for the particular applications that should be made of those principles. The task of constitutional interpretation requires wisdom, learning and discernment, but it also requires humility and discipline. The operative question for a faithful constitutional interpreter is not what would Madison do in such a situation, or even what did Madison do in such a situation, but what does the principle that Madison and his fellows wrote into the Constitution require in such a situation. Reference to the founders is indispensable to answering such a question, but it remains only a starting point.

This should also caution us against confusing a commitment to originalism with hostility to the full range of methods that judges normally employ to resolve legal problems. A jurisprudence of originalism is entirely consistent with traditional doctrinal analysis, engagement with constitutional text and structure, and attention to constitutional purposes and values. Originalism does not insist that judges eschew doctrinal analysis or that they refuse to draw inferences from the structure of the Construction and the government that it creates ("unwritten" though those structural implications might be). Originalism does insist that such interpretive aids be recognized as the tools that they are. Their value lies in their ability to help us in the process of discovering and applying the original meaning of the Constitution. They become inimical to originalism only when the interpreter forgets that they are mere tools, when the manipulation of precedent becomes an end in itself or when a focus on larger constitutional purposes leads us to ignore the specific ways in which the original Constitution was designed to achieve those purposes.

III. ORIGINALISM AND JUDICIAL ACTIVISM

It should be emphasized that the point of originalist constitutional interpretation is not to clear the way for current legislative majorities. Originalist arguments have frequently been marshaled to criticize what the Supreme Court has done, to show how the Court is guilty of "judicial activism" and of striking down laws without constitutional warrant. In that context, it makes sense to say that the Court was mistaken because it departed from original meaning and that a properly originalist Court would not have taken the same action, that an originalist Court would have upheld rather than struck down a particular statute, that an originalist Court would have left a particular policy choice up to the legislature. But we should not generalize from those particular cases. Originalist judges are not necessarily deferential judges. It may well be the case that the originalist Constitution has little of substance to say about some particular current political controversy. The Constitution may not require anything in particular in regards to euthanasia, abortion, homosexuality, or affirmative action. Deferring to the Constitution in such cases may simply mean holding them open for future political resolution, and the constitutional interpreter should be sensitive to that possibility. The judge should have the humility to recognize that the Constitution may not provide clear answers to all the questions asked of it, that elected officials have the right to make important policy choices without judicial intervention, and that the Constitution may not simply write the judge's own preferred policies into the fundamental law.

Nonetheless, it may also be the case that faithful constitutional interpretation requires turning aside the preferences of current legislative majorities. The Constitution enshrines popular, not legislative, sovereignty. It creates a republic with a limited government, not simply a majoritarian democracy. The goal of a jurisprudence of originalism is to get the Constitution right, to preserve the Constitution inviolable. It denies that judges are freewheeling arbiters of social justice, but it also denies that they are mere window dressing. As Chief Justice William Rehnquist once wrote, "The goal of constitutional adjudication is...to hold true the balance between that which the Constitution puts beyond the reach of the democratic process and that which it does not." The jurisprudence of originalism seeks to hold true that balance, whether that requires upholding the application of a statute in a particular case or striking it down. The issue for originalism is which laws should be struck down, not how many (something which, after all, also depends greatly on the behavior of legislators). Proponents of originalism merely open themselves up to charges of hypocrisy when they approve of instances of judicial review if they do not make plain that it is not deference to politicians that they seek but fidelity to the Constitution.

It is also sometimes contended that the value of originalism lies in its ability to limit the discretion of judges. Originalism, it has been argued, will prevent judges from legislating from the bench or imposing their own value judgments on society. There is something to this argument but it can be overstated. To be sure there was a time in which judges and scholars often thought that the very purpose of courts and the power of judicial review were simply to pursue social justice. Thankfully, such hubris is less common today. But here again, judicial discretion as such is not the issue. The issue is the role of the courts and how the power of judicial review is to be used. Individual judges may well feel little discretion about what they should do in a given case, even if their jurisprudential philosophy is one based on, say, theories of liberal egalitarianism or utilitarian pragmatism. Such judges are in error not because they feel free to do what they personally want in constitutional cases but because they misperceive the basis of their own power and the requirements of constitutional fidelity.

At the same time, proponents of originalism should not delude themselves or others as to the difficulty of the task of identifying and applying the original meaning of the Constitution. It is in no way "mechanical." Disagreement among individuals seeking in good faith to follow a jurisprudence of originalism is entirely possible. The judgment, intelligence, skill, and temperament of the individuals called upon to interpret the Constitution still matter. Judges must still resist the temptation to line up the constitutional founders to agree with their own personal views, just as they must resist the temptation to line up the precedents or the moral philosophies or the policy considerations. A jurisprudence of originalism will at least insure that judges are focused on the right discussion—what the Constitution of the founders requires relative to a given case—even though it cannot insure that everyone will reach the same or the correct conclusion once engaged in that discussion. It is one thing, however, for judges to be open to the criticism that they cut corners in their effort to discover the original meaning of the Constitution. It is quite another for them to be open to the criticism that they are imposing the wrong moral value judgments on the political process. A jurisprudence of originalism insists that judges should strive never to be guilty of the latter criticism, while endeavoring to avoid being guilty of the former.

IV. CONSTITUTIONAL SELF-GOVERNMENT

There are three ways to resolve current political disagreements. We can somehow work them out ourselves, through majority rule, bargaining and compromise, deliberation and debate, and the like. That is, we can make our decisions through normal politics. Alternatively, we can delegate the decision to somebody else. To some degree we almost always delegate anyway, by electing and hiring representatives to hash out the nation's business in the capital while we get on with the more important business of living our lives. But "we" could choose to delegate our controversial political decisions to an even greater degree, throwing the issue into the lap of a "blue-ribbon commission," some executive administrator, or even the courts, perhaps with little or no guidance as to how that issue ought to be resolved by this favored agent. We can simply divest political discretion to some third party and live with the results. We do sometimes use courts in this way. The Sherman Antitrust Act famously handed the problem of identifying monopolies and monopolistic behavior over to the courts, instructing them to do something but not leaving many clues as to what they were to do.

It is possible to use courts in that way, but we should be reluctant to conclude that constitutional judicial review was such a delegation of unfettered policy discretion. Statutory delegations such as those contained in the original Sherman Act are subject to legislative oversight and revision; judges exercise discretion, but only for now and only with implicit or explicit accountability to elected representatives. It is possible that the Constitution contains similar delegations to judges. The founders might have said the equivalent of "protect 'liberty,' whatever that is." Given the general design of the Constitution and the political assumptions on which it was based it would be surprising if they did so, or at least did so very often or in especially important ways. Those who would claim such an authority on the part of judges bear a very high burden not only to show that the founders did not give more substantive content to their constitutional language but also to show that when they left constitutional discretion to later generations that they entrusted that discretion to unelected and largely unaccountable judges rather than to the people and their representatives. Those who would give a freewheeling discretion to judges to develop and enforce "preferred freedoms," "fundamental values," or "active liberty," unconstrained by the value choices that were already made at the time of constitutional drafting, bear a heavy burden to show why it is that judges rather than legislators or citizens should have the ultimate authority to identify "our" favored values and most cherished liberties or what is to be done to best realize our national aspirations.

The other way to resolve our current disagreements is to abide by decisions that have already been made; that is, we can adhere to the existing law. Rather than revisit controversies ourselves or trust the discretion of someone else, we can simply defer to earlier judgments embodied in the law. Having made the decision to keep faith with the law, we may appoint someone to interpret and apply the law for us and keep things on even keel until we are ready to revisit the issue—perhaps recognizing that we ourselves may be too tempted to deviate from the law in particular instances or may be too prone to make unintended or unthoughtful mistakes in applying the law. We should recognize that the interpretive effort will require the exercise of some judgment, but we would, of course, expect the appointed interpreter not to exercise the discretion of a delegated decisionmaker.

The issue is what standard should be used to resolve contemporary political controversies and who should have the authority to make the resolution. Contemporary political actors are displaced by any judicial decision. If judges offer an interpretation of the text in accord with the language and intent of the founders, then those contemporary political actors have only deferred their right to make the choice themselves and remake the law. If judges make constitutional law without offering an interpretation of the original Constitution, then we have simply replaced one relatively democratic set of contemporary policymakers with another much less democratic one. If judges interpret the originalist text, then the people retain their sovereign lawmaking authority to create, amend or replace the higher law. If judges do not, then the legislative power of the sovereign people would have been lost. The basic constitutional choices would be made by judges rather than by those who draft and ratify the constitutional text, whether those drafters and ratifiers did their work two hundred years ago or yesterday. As future Supreme Court justice James Iredell observed even as the federal Constitution was being drafted, there would be no point to assembling and writing a constitution if those charged with interpreting and adhering to it could ignore what was decided in those assemblies and instead chose to follow a different rule. The supreme power would no longer lie with those who write the Constitution but instead would lie with those who write the constitutional law.

We privilege the intentions of the founders out of respect for the role of the constitutional founder, not out of respect for any particular founder. It is commonplace that we distinguish between the office and the officeholder, between institutional and personal authority. We respect the actions of the president and the Congress out of regard for the offices, not out of regard for the individuals who hold those offices. Likewise, those who drafted and ratified our present Constitution occupied a political role. It is a role that we do and should respect, not least because it is a role that we could ourselves play. There is no question that the founding generation was uniquely situated at the historical birth of the new nation and uncommonly blessed with political talent and wisdom, but too much myth-making can also be subversive of consensual constitutional governance and should certainly form no part of our current justification for adhering to the inherited Constitution. We should respect the substance of the constitutional choices of the founding not because the founders were especially smart, because they necessarily got it right or because we happen to agree with them on the merits. Although the founders did create a remarkably flexible and successful constitutional system, there are any number of individuals in our own society who are smart, think they can get it right, or whose values others would likely endorse. If being smart or "right" was the sole lodestar for our judgments about constitutional meaning, then there would be plenty of aspirants who could claim that we should follow them rather than the founders. We should respect the substance of choices of the founders because only they spoke on the basis of the "solemn and authoritative act" of the people. We should respect their choices because we should take seriously the idea of constitutional deliberation and choice through democratic means, of constitutional foundings as conscious, real-time political events. We should act so as to preserve the possibility of constitutional self-governance.

Deciding on the Constitution's Meaning:
Interpret in Light of Modern Circumstances

ERWIN CHEMERINSKY

The goal is to develop an understanding of the Constitution for the 21st century. It makes no sense to find this by looking to the 18th century. Throughout American history, the Supreme Court has decided the meaning of the Constitution by looking to its text, its goals, its structure, precedent, historical practice, and contemporary needs and values. This is what constitutional law always has been about and always should be about. It is misguided and undesirable to search for a theory of constitutional interpretation that will yield determinate results, right and wrong answers, to most constitutional questions. No such theory exists or ever will exist.

Only a few Justices in American history have professed to follow an originalist philosophy and they are originalists only some of the time. For example, Justices [Antonin] Scalia and [Clarence] Thomas, the self-professed originalists on the Court, believe that the meaning of the Constitution was fixed when it was adopted and that constitutional interpretation is the process of finding and following this original meaning. But these Justices did not apply originalism in their Tenth and Eleventh Amendment decisions of the last decade. The Court's decisions prohibiting Congress from commandeering state governments and forcing them to adopt laws or regulations cannot be derived from the text of the Tenth Amendment or its intent or its historical meaning. Nor can originalism explain the Court's expansion of sovereign immunity to bar suits against states by their own citizens in federal courts or in state courts. Perhaps even more profoundly, these Justices pay no attention to originalism in condemning all affirmative action programs despite strong evidence that the original intent of the Fourteenth Amendment was very much to allow such efforts.

Moreover, it must be remembered that on many occasions, the Supreme Court has expressly rejected originalism. *In Home Building & Loan Ass'n v. Blaisdell* [1932], the Court declared:

> If by the statement that what the Constitution meant at the time of its adoption it means today, it is intended to say that the great clauses of the Constitution must be confined to the interpretation which the framers, with the conditions and outlook of their time, would have placed upon them, the statement carries its own refutation.

Most famously, in *Brown v. Board of Education*, Chief Justice Earl Warren, writing for the Court [in 1954], stated: "In approaching the problem, we cannot turn the clock back to 1868 when the [Fourteenth] Amendment was adopted, or even to 1896 when *Plessy v. Ferguson* was written."

For decades, prominent constitutional scholars have advanced devastating critiques of originalism. Yet, over the last few decades, originalism as a philosophy of constitutional interpretation seems to have gained legitimacy and even acceptance.

In this essay, I want to explore why this has happened. My thesis is that the appeal of originalism is that it offers a false promise of constraining judges and of limiting, if not eliminating, value choices by judges. Getting past originalism requires demonstrating that this truly is a false hope; no theory of constitutional interpretation can significantly reduce or eliminate judicial discretion. Progressives need to defend constitutional decision-making as it always has been practiced, by both liberals and conservatives: it is a product of judges considering a myriad of sources, including the Constitution's text, its goals, its structure, precedent, historical practice, and contemporary needs and values. No theory can offer determinacy in constitutional decision-making or avoid the reality that results depend on value choices made by judges in determining the meaning of the Constitution. A John Paul Stevens and an Antonin Scalia will disagree in most important constitutional cases, not because one is smarter or has a better approach to constitutional interpretation. They will come to different results because they have vastly different ideologies and values.

First, there is no doubt that the appeal of originalism is its promise of constraining judges. It is the allure of formalism, of decisions derived deductively from sources external to the judges. Originalists claim that decisions in constitutional cases would be based on seemingly objective sources and not on the ideology of the judges. Justice Scalia, for example, has advanced exactly this defense for his originalist philosophy and declared: "Originalism…establishes a historical criterion that is conceptually quite separate from the preferences of the judge himself." There is an understandable appeal to an approach to constitutional law which provides for decisions that have nothing to do with the identity or values of the individual judges.

Second, it is crucial to recognize and to expose this as a false promise. Originalism, no less than any theory of constitutional interpretation, still involves tremendous judicial discretion and decisions that are very much the result of value choices by the judges. There are many reasons for this. Balancing of competing interests is an inevitable part of constitutional law and inescapably involves judicial discretion, just as much for originalists as for non-originalists. Balancing competing interests is a persistent feature of constitutional decision-making. How should the President's interest in executive privilege and secrecy be balanced against the need for evidence at a criminal trial? How should a defendant's right to a fair trial be balanced against the freedom of the press? How should legitimate, important, and compelling government interests be determined in individual rights and equal protection cases? Levels of scrutiny are, after all, just a tool for arranging the weights in constitutional balancing. Moreover, constitutional law constantly asks, as does so much of law, what is reasonable. Under the Fourth Amendment, courts routinely focus on whether the actions of police officers are reasonable. Under the Takings Clause, courts determine whether there is a public purpose by examining whether the government acted out of a reasonable belief that its action would benefit the public. Such balancing is not an exclusively liberal exercise. In a recent case, Justice Scalia, writing for the Court, stressed that the application of the exclusionary rule depends on a weighing of its costs and benefits.

Moreover, originalism allows tremendous judicial discretion because the intent behind any constitutional provision can be stated at many different levels of abstraction. For example, who was the equal protection clause intended to protect? The intent could have been solely to protect African Americans; to protect all racial minorities; to shelter all groups that have been historically discriminated against; or to defend all individuals from arbitrary treatment by the government. Each of these potential answers is a reasonable way of describing the drafters' intent for the Fourteenth Amendment. Yet a judge must eventually choose among these answers, and a great deal depends on that choice. Whether sex discrimination or affirmative action violates equal protection depends entirely on the choice among levels of abstraction. Here, too, neither formalism nor originalism can provide a discretion-free answer.

Originalism also provides enormous discretion to judges in deciding the original intent. The theory focuses on the Framers, but so many people were involved in drafting and ratifying the Constitution and its amendments that it is possible to find historical quotations supporting either side of almost any argument. The debate over the Second Amendment powerfully illustrates this, as sides make strong arguments based on the original understanding of the provision.

These critiques of originalism, of course, are familiar. Yet, their significance cannot be overstated in formulating an approach to constitutional law for the 21st century. No theory of constitutional interpretation can provide formalism or significantly reduce judicial discretion. Inevitably, judges in interpreting the Constitution must make choices as to the meaning of open-textured constitutional language and in balancing competing interests.

Antonin Scalia purports to have a more objective approach to constitutional law and repeatedly asserts a moral high ground compared to his colleagues. He finds in the Constitution no protection for reproductive choice, a prohibition of affirmative action, permission for prayer in public schools and government aid to religious schools, and no exclusionary rule. His views seem far more similar to the 2004 Republican platform than to anything in the original meaning of the Constitution.

Third, progressives must defend their alternative vision of constitutional law. Originalists try to put progressives on the defensive by asserting that originalists have a theory of constitutional law, but that others don't. But this is based on their claim of a theory which reduces judicial discretion and offers a seemingly objective method of decision-making. Once this is exposed as false it becomes clear that all judges are engaged in the same enterprise and that none have an objective methodology that permits decisions removed from their own values.

Progressives must offer a more complex and realistic description of judging in constitutional cases. Supporters of originalism present the debate as if there are only two choices: discretion-free judging or judging by whim and caprice. Of course, the reality is neither. Judges always have discretion, but the exercise of that discretion is not about what the judge ate for breakfast. Rather, discretion is about how judges look at multiple sources and decide the meaning of the Constitution. An accurate description of judicial review's reality is needed to compete with the value-neutral models and the rhetoric supporting them.

What, then, is the role for fidelity in constitutional interpretation for the 21st century? It all depends on "fidelity" to what. Constitutional interpretation always must show fidelity to the document's text. But all Justices throughout history have done this and have based their decisions on giving meaning to the text of the Constitution. Surely, too, fidelity must be to the goals of the constitutional provision. But the goals are inevitably abstract, not the specific intent of the framers. In deciding what is "cruel and unusual punishment," judges must be guided by the goal of ending degrading and inhumane punishments, not the specific views of the framers as to which punishments are unacceptable. In deciding that segregation violates equal protection, the Court rightly followed the general goal of equal protection, not the specific views of the Congress that both ratified the Fourteenth Amendment and segregated the District of Columbia public schools. Courts also need to consider all that has occurred since the ratification of a constitutional provision, including judicial precedents. Contemporary needs should be taken into account as well; there is no other way to balance.

This, of course, means that judges will have discretion in interpreting the Constitution. But that is how it always has been. *Marbury v. Madison* [1803], establishing the institution of judicial review, was an exercise of judicial discretion because the Constitution is silent about the authority of courts to invalidate statutes or executive actions.

As progressives articulate a vision of constitutional law for the 21st century, it must be one based on the Constitution's commitments to freedom and equality. It must be based on the Constitution's respect for the dignity of each individual. It must be based on the Constitution's mandate for separation of powers and checks and balances.

Progressives must explain in judicial decisions, law review articles, and op-ed pieces why the Constitution includes protection for reproductive choice, why it allows affirmative action to achieve racial equality, why it requires a separation of church and state, why it does not permit indefinite detentions of human beings without judicial review. This is the challenge of a Constitution for the new century.

THE CONTINUING DEBATE:
Deciding on the Constitution's Meaning

What Is New

The battle over originalism continues to play a key role in many Supreme Court decisions. In *District of Columbia v. Heller* (2008), the court for the first time ruled directly that Americans have at least a limited right to "bear arms." In the majority opinion voiding the District of Colombia's strict gun control law, Justice Antonin Scalia focused on original intent—what was said at the time the amendment was written and adopted—and dismissed everything said afterwards as irrelevant "post-ratification commentary." Scalia noted, "Undoubtedly some think that the Second Amendment is outmoded in [modern] society," but rejected that view as sufficient reason "to pronounce the Second Amendment extinct." By contrast, John Paul Stevens writing for the dissenting justices argued that both original intent and the "post-ratification history of the Amendment...makes [it] abundantly clear that [it] should not be interpreted as limiting the authority...to regulate the use or possession of firearms for purely civilian purposes." According to a 2010 poll, 49% of Americans favored interpreting the Constitution according to "original intent only" and thus agreed with Justice Scalia; 42% favored also considering "changing times," as did Stevens; and 9% were unsure.

Where to Find More

For historical background on the debate, read Johnathan George O'Neill, *Originalism in American Law and Politics: A Constitutional History* (Johns Hopkins University Press, 2005) and Lackland H. Bloom, *Methods of Interpretation: How the Supreme Court Reads the Constitution* (Oxford University Press, 2009). A look at what the authors of the Constitution were or were not thinking is Cass R. Sunstein, *A Constitution of Many Minds: Why the Founding Document Doesn't Mean What It Meant Before* (Princeton University Press, 2009). A good source for a range of recent thinking on interpreting the Constitution, the source from which the two articles here were drawn, is *Advance: The Journal of the American Constitution Society Issues Groups* (Fall 2007), which can be found on the Web site of the American Constitution Society for Law and Policy at www.acslaw.org/advance/. The majority and dissenting opinions in *District of Colombia v. Heller* (2008) provide an excellent look at how justices on both sides of a question use history to buttress their views. One of many sources is OYEZ at www.oyez.org/. Keyboard the case name into the search window.

What More to Do

Have a class debate over what standards to use when interpreting the Constitution. If you adopt the "living constitution" view and use contemporary standards, is there really a "bedrock constitution," or are judges really policymakers interpreting constitutional language according to their own views? But originalism has been compared to "ancestor worship," leaving modern society bound by centuries-old norms. Moreover, how does originalism deal with modern technology and contemporary standards that the founders could not foresee? Perhaps most importantly, are you comfortable with the idea that we all live under a Constitution, but that Constitution means what nine, unelected justices with life tenure say it does? How does that square with democracy?

15 STATE AND LOCAL GOVERNMENT

ALLOWING STATES TO COLLECT SALES TAXES ON INTERSTATE COMMERCE:
Leveling the Playing Field *or* A Threat to Electronic Commerce?

LEVELING THE PLAYING FIELD

ADVOCATE: Steven Rauschenberger, past President, National Conference of State Legislatures

SOURCE: Testimony during hearings on "H.R. 3396—The Sales Tax Fairness and Simplification Act" before the House of Representatives, Committee on the Judiciary, Subcommittee on Administrative and Commercial Law, December 6, 2007

A THREAT TO ELECTRONIC COMMERCE

ADVOCATE: George S. Isaacson, Tax Counsel for the Direct Marketing Association

SOURCE: Testimony during hearings on "H.R. 3396—The Sales Tax Fairness and Simplification Act" before the House of Representatives, Committee on the Judiciary, Subcommittee on Administrative and Commercial Law, December 6, 2007

Under the first U.S. Constitution, the Articles of Confederation (in force 1781–1788), the United States was more a league than a country. Those who drafted the Articles were so anxious to avoid the excesses of British rule that they created a document that gave the central government very little power beyond foreign affairs and reserved for the states all other aspects of government power. As a result, the central government could not function effectively. Among other weakness, the central government could not regulate commerce either among the states or between them and foreign countries. As such, the individual states could and did establish and apply tariffs, embargoes, and other trade regulations against each other as well as internationally.

With no central economic authority, the country floundered during the 1780s. Rampant inflation, plummeting foreign and domestic commerce, and other economic hardships burdened the land. Economic woes created turmoil, and it is not too strong to say that the survival of the United States as a united country was in doubt by the mid-1780s.

To meet this peril, delegates from the 13 states met in 1787 at the Constitutional Convention in Philadelphia, drafted a new Constitution, and sent it to the states for ratification. When in June 1788 New Hampshire became the ninth state to ratify the Constitution, it went into force. The new Constitution significantly increased the power of the central government and diminished the power of the states. Two clauses in Article I are particularly important to this debate about states levying a sales tax on items moving between states. The "interstate commerce clause" in section 8 gave Congress the authority to regulate commerce among the states and with foreign countries. And section 9 declared that, "no tax or duty shall be laid on articles exported from any state." "Exported" in the meaning of the time meant sent to another state as well as to another country. For most of U.S. history, cases arising under the interstate commerce clause were the most numerous to reach the Supreme Court. However, the legal battle over whether a state can charge a sales tax on items leaving it or arriving in it is relatively new. One reason is that sales taxes are relatively new. The first enacted was by Alabama in 1921. Currently, 45 of the 50 states have a sales tax. Another reason is that despite the advent of catalog sales in the late 1880s by Richard Sears and Alvah C. Roebuck, the amount of goods being purchased by consumers in one state remotely (by mail, phone, or now the Internet) was limited.

As such interstate sales began to grow, however, the states moved to tax them by requiring that vendors collect taxes on items being sent into the state or to supply to the state records of everyone in a state who had purchased an item out-of-state. Frequently these taxes were called "use taxes" because a state cannot apply a sales tax in another state. The legality of this practice was decided by two Supreme Court cases in the 1960s. The first ruled that a vendor that had a "substantial physical presence" such as a store in a state could be required to collect a sales tax on items shipped into the state even if the items bypassed the store and went directly to the consumer. But in the second case, the Supreme Court denied to states the power to tax remote sales if the only connection is that the vendor had with the buyer was by mail or another form of interstate communications. The court reaffirmed this decision in *Quill v. North Dakota* (1992), specifically noting the burden on interstate commerce of complying with the varying sales taxes that are or could be levied by the more than 29,000 state, country, and local governments. Also in that decision, though, the court noted that Congress has the authority to require vendors to collect sales taxes on goods moving in interstate commerce and to devise a formula for passing those on to the states.

In an effort to persuade Congress to allow the taxation of interstate sales, the states have been working to formulate a common program called the Streamlined Sales and Use Tax Agreement to tax online and other remote sales. Hearings on legislation in Congress to allow that brought the countervailing testimony of Steven Rauschenberger, past President of the National Conference of State Legislatures, and George S. Isaacson, Tax Counsel for the Direct Marketing Association. Rauschenberger argues in the first reading that states are losing over $33 billion in possible revenue from taxes on remote sales. He believes there needs to be a change in a tax system that was designed for an economy that existed almost 80 years ago and that creates tax discrimination depending on where a consumer makes a transaction. Isaacson disagrees, arguing that Congress should avoid removing the constitutional barrier to the tax of interstate sales which, he says, have served the nation well for two centuries and created the largest and most vibrant economy in the history of the world.

POINTS TO PONDER

➤ What is the main issue, whether all states agree to the Streamlined Sales and Use Tax Agreement or whether there should be new tax?

➤ If Congress decides to allow a remote-sales tax, should the revenues be divided among the states or used by the federal government for its own purposes?

➤ Is there a "fairness" issue involved, or is this issue simply a matter of money?

Allowing States to Collect Sales Taxes on Interstate Commerce: Leveling the Playing Field

STEVEN RAUSCHENBERGER

Ever since 2002, state legislators through the National Conference of State Legislatures (NCSL) have adopted resolutions calling upon the Congress of the United States to consider and approve federal legislation that would give a state authority to require all sellers (except those qualifying for the small business exception) to collect the state's sales taxes if that state is in compliance with the Streamlined Sales and Use Tax Agreement. The National Conference of State Legislatures is the bi-partisan national organization representing every state legislator from all fifty states and our nation's commonwealths, territories, possessions and the District of Columbia. Let me make this very clear, state legislators are not advocating any new or discriminatory taxes on electronic commerce. We desire, however, to establish a streamlined sales and use tax collection system that is seamless for sellers in the new economy and respects the sovereignty of state borders. [A use tax is a sales tax applied to something purchased in another state or country.]

The new economy or if you prefer, electronic commerce, which is not bound by state and local borders makes it critical to simplify and reform state and local taxes to ensure a level playing field for all sellers, to enhance economic development, and to avoid discrimination based upon how a sale may be transacted. Government cannot allow a tax system that was designed for an economy that existed almost 80 years ago to be the deciding factor as to where our constituents make a transaction.

SALES TAX POPULARITY

As we all know, taxes are never popular. However, if state and local governments are to provide necessary services, such as education and public safety, then we need to maintain our ability to levy taxes. In surveys of taxpayers as to which tax of all the major federal, state and local taxes they dislike the least, the surprising answer has consistently been the sales tax.

Voters all over the country have approved local sales taxes to pay for sports stadiums, added police protection, land acquisition for open space, and transportation improvements. The taxpayers of the state of Michigan overwhelmingly voted to use the sales tax as opposed to property tax as the major source of revenue for education, and then in following years they have voted to increase the sales tax in order to provide additional funding for education.

The general sales and use tax is the primary consumption tax for state and local governments. In 2005, sales taxes accounted for one-third of state revenues—over $311 billion—with the largest percentage of the funds used to finance K–12 education.

SALES TAX AND ELECTRONIC COMMERCE

The problem states have with the sales tax is that the tax base keeps shrinking. In the 1930s, when the sales tax was first imposed, consumers bought goods from the local merchant and it was not that difficult for the merchant to collect a few cents on the dollar. Also, most Americans spent very little on services—they spent most of their money on taxable goods. And there were very few "remote sellers."

In the 1970s and 1980s, the share of personal consumption expenditures began to shift from taxable goods to services—things like medical care, health clubs, legal and accounting services. So the sales tax was applied on a smaller and smaller share of tangible products. This was compounded on the goods side by mail order outlets selling goods without collecting sales taxes from their customers—a practice sanctioned by the U.S. Supreme Court in the *National Bellas Hess* case in 1967 and reaffirmed in the *Quill* decision in 1992.

Today, states face a new threat to sales tax revenue, electronic commerce, with the potential to dramatically expand the volume of goods sold to customers without collection of a sales or use tax. The combined weight of the shift to a service-based economy and the erosion of sales tax revenues due to electronic commerce threatens the future viability of the sales tax and the ability of state governments to fund essential services such as education, homeland security and public safety.

According to the Center for Business and Economic Research at the University of Tennessee, in 2003, the estimated combined state and local revenue loss due to remote sales was between $15.5 billion and $16.1 billion. [Remote sales would include items purchased out-of-state personally, by mail, or by some other non-electronic means and shipped to one's home or business, thus avoiding the sales tax in either state.] For electronic commerce sales alone, the estimated revenue loss was between $8.2 billion and $8.5 billion. The report from the University of Tennessee further estimates that the revenue loss will grow and that by 2008, the revenue loss for state and local governments could be as high as $33.6 billion, of which it is estimated that $17.8 billion would be from sales over the Internet. (See Table 1.)

TABLE 1
Combined State & Local Revenue Losses from E-Commerce and All Remote Commerce—2008

State	E-Commerce Loss ($ millions)	All Remote Sales ($ millions)
Alabama	238.7	449.7
Arkansas	190.6	359.2
Arizona	435.7	821.1
California	2452.0	4620.4
Colorado	287.8	542.4
Connecticut	266.0	501.2
District of Columbia	48.8	91.9
Florida	1248.2	2351.1
Georgia	600.0	1130.5
Hawaii	130.3	245.5
Iowa	141.4	266.4
Idaho	66.3	125.0
Illinois	582.2	1097.0
Indiana	323.6	609.7
Kansas	178.8	336.9
Kentucky	214.6	404.3
Louisiana	409.8	772.2

TABLE 1 (continued)

Combined State & Local Revenue Losses from E-Commerce
and All Remote Commerce—2008

State	E-Commerce Loss ($ millions)	All Remote Sales ($ millions)
Massachusetts	286.4	539.6
Maryland	265.9	501.1
Maine	67.2	126.6
Michigan	587.3	1106.6
Minnesota	381.2	718.3
Missouri	313.9	591.5
Mississippi	191.9	361.6
North Carolina	405.9	764.9
North Dakota	34.3	64.6
Nebraska	123.4	232.4
New Jersey	469.9	885.5
New Mexico	140.4	264.6
Nevada	186.6	351.5
New York	1288.4	2427.7
Ohio	608.6	1146.8
Oklahoma	185.4	349.3
Pennsylvania	585.6	1103.4
Rhode Island	58.5	110.3
South Carolina	209.4	394.5
South Dakota	47.0	88.6
Tennessee	508.3	957.9
Texas	1634.5	3079.9
Utah	150.7	284.0
Virginia	294.8	555.4
Vermont	29.1	54.8
Washington	574.6	1082.7
Wisconsin	303.4	571.7
West Virginia	86.6	163.2
Wyoming	38.9	73.3
United States	17,872.9	33,677.8

Source: Dr. Donald Bruce & Dr. William Fox, Center for Business & Economic
Research, University of Tennessee

State legislators recognize that they have been part of this problem. Over the last 80 years, state and local policymakers have created a confusing, administratively burdensome tax system with very little regard for the compliance burden placed on multi-state businesses. In 1999, NCSL passed a resolution, written by NCSL's Task Force on State and Local Taxation of Telecommunications and Electronic Commerce that acknowledged that states need to simplify their sales and use taxes and telecommunications taxes for the 21st century. We recognized that we have been a key part of the problem and we accepted the fact that it was our problem to solve.

In our resolution, we formulated a set of seven principles that we used to develop a proposal for simplifying and streamlining state and local sales and use tax collection systems. The overriding theme of those seven principles is competitive neutrality. State legislators from across the country unanimously approved this resolution that declared that "State and local tax systems should treat transactions involving goods and services, including telecommunications and electronic commerce, in a competitively neutral manner." The resolution further stipulated that "a simplified sales and use tax system that treats all transactions in a competitively neutral manner will strengthen and preserve the sales and use tax as vital state and local revenue sources and preserve state fiscal sovereignty."

THE COST OF COLLECTION FOR SELLERS

As you are aware, the sales tax is imposed on the customer, not the seller. Sellers determine the sales tax to be collected, collect the tax and remit the tax collected to the state (in four states, Alabama, Arizona, Colorado and Louisiana, sellers also must remit the local portion of the sales tax directly to the local government). Under the current sales tax system, the seller also is liable for any mistakes that might occur due to misinformation from the buyer or even the state. This means that the seller is liable for any uncollected sales tax plus interest and penalties.

A recent national survey commissioned by the Joint Cost of Collection Study, a public/private sector group, and conducted by PricewaterhouseCoopers LLP, has shown that in fiscal year 2003 the total cost to sellers to collect state and local sales taxes was $6.8 billion. This amount was calculated after subtractions for state vendor discounts and retailer float on the sales tax revenues.

The study showed that for fiscal year 2003, for retailers selling between $150,000 and $1 million, the average cost was 13.47 percent of the sales taxes collected or approximately $2,386; for mid-size retailer, between $1 million and $10 million in sales, the average cost was 5.2 percent or approximately $5,279; and for the larger retailers, over $10 million in sales, the average cost of collection was 2.17 percent or approximately $18,233. It is important to remember that these amounts, including the total cost for all retailers of $6.8 billion, are not reimbursed to the retailer by the state or local government, these costs come out of the retailer's own pocket.

The burden on retailers to comply with 46 different sales tax systems and the monetary cost to retailers for compliance resulted in the two Supreme Court decisions, cited above, that prohibited a state from requiring an out-of-state seller from collecting sales tax on a purchase made by a resident of the state.

SOLUTION: STREAMLINED SALES AND USE TAX AGREEMENT

Beginning in 2000, state legislators, governors and tax administrators, along with representatives of retailers and others in the private sector, started the process to develop a simpler, uniform and fairer system of sales and use taxation, that removes the burden imposed on retailers, preserves state sovereignty, levels the playing field for all retailers, and enhances the ability of U.S. companies to compete in the global economy. The urgency to develop such a system caused NCSL's Executive Committee to set aside NCSL's rule of non-interference in state legislation and to endorse model legislation committing sales tax states to multistate discussions on developing a fairer and simplified system. By 2002, 35 states had enacted this legislation, sending delegations composed of legislators, tax administrators, local government officials and representatives of the private sector to monthly meetings that resulted in the formulation and approval of the Streamlined Sales and Use Tax Agreement. As of today, all of the sales tax states, except for Colorado, are participating in the ongoing process to simplify sales tax collections.

The key features of the agreement are simplification of sales and use tax laws and administration; the use of technology for calculating, collecting, reporting and/or remitting the tax; and, state assumption of the costs of collection for remote sellers. The key simplifications contained in the agreement as adopted by the states are:

- Uniform product definitions, from food and related items to digital products
- Uniform state and local tax base
- Reductions in the number of tax rates
- Requirements for state/central administration
- Central seller registration
- Uniform returns and remittances
- Simplified exemption administration
- Uniform audit procedures/reduction of the number of audits
- Uniform privacy protections
- Notice requirements for rate changes
- Uniform sourcing
- Uniform telecommunications sourcing
- Uniform administrative definitions
- Eliminations of caps and thresholds on rates
- Standardization for sales tax holidays
- Uniform rounding rule

Since the agreement was ratified in November 2002, 22 states have enacted legislation to bring their sales tax statutes and administrative rulings into compliance with the agreement. On October 1, 2005, thirteen states with a population of over 55 million residents were certified to be fully in compliance with the agreement. It is expected that on January 1, 2008, the states of Arkansas, Nevada, Washington and Wyoming will be in full compliance with the agreement as their statutes become effective.

SALES TAX FAIRNESS AND SIMPLIFICATION ACT

The Streamlined Sales and Use Tax Agreement is voluntary for states as well as for remote sellers. Since October 1, 2005, over 1,100 retailers have volunteered to begin collecting sales taxes for the member states, and these states have started to receive previously uncollected revenues for sales tax on transactions made through out-of-state retailers.

I believe that you will agree that this effort to streamline sales tax collection has been unprecedented in our history. In less than six years, the states working together with the support and assistance of the private sector, developed a new sales tax system that was fairer, simpler, more uniform and is technologically applicable; 22 states, almost half of all the states with a sales tax, enacted legislation to comply with these changes; and, the system is working. It is operational! However, our work to establish a truly seamless system is only half done. It is now Congress' turn to act. The states through the Streamlined Sales and Use Tax Agreement have provided Congress with the justification to allow states that have complied with the agreement to require remote sellers to collect those sales taxes as was intended in the Quill decision.

The Sales Tax Fairness and Simplification Act, H.R. 3396 embodies all the simplification requirements of the Streamlined Sales and Use Tax Agreement and provides certainty for taxpayers, retailers and other businesses that the states cannot backtrack on simplifications but if we do, the prohibition of the Quill decision will be reinstated.

NCSL supports H.R. 3396 because the legislation:

- provides for a national small business exception so that sellers with less than $5 million in taxable remote sales would be exempt from collection requirements;
- ensures reasonable and adequate compensation for all sellers for the cost of collection;
- provides certainty to taxpayers and sellers by allowing for an appeals process that includes review of the decisions of the Governing Board of the Streamlined Sales Tax System by the United States Court of Federal Claims;
- ensures that any filings by sellers in the course of registering, calculating, collecting and/or remitting sales and use taxes collected cannot be used as a criterion for determining nexus for any other tax responsibilities, including state business activity taxes; and
- ensures that the agreement simplifications are applied to the administration and collection of transactional taxes on telecommunications services.

MISCONCEPTIONS AND MISSTATEMENTS

Over the last six years, as we have worked to develop a simplified and fairer sales tax system, we have heard criticisms and arguments against streamlining and against Congress setting aside the *Bellas Hess* and *Quill* decisions. I would like to take a few moments to correct some of the misconceptions that our opponents have made, some of which I am sure will be expressed this morning.

Myth: "The Streamlined Sales Tax Agreement does not simplify tax compliance for retailers."

Fact: Even if states did nothing more than adopt the proposed administrative changes contained in the Streamlined Sales and Use Tax Agreement, all retailers will benefit from reduced complexity. Opponents contend that rates are the biggest complication, but even Robert Comfort, Vice President for Tax Policy at Amazon.com, told a congressional hearing in 2001, "...rates are not a problem for Amazon.com." Sellers have testified over and over that the real burdens with collection are not sales tax rates but the different product definitions from state to state, different state and local tax bases and the different rules and administrative procedures for registering, collecting, filing and remittance of sales taxes.

Under the agreement, the certified automated system calculates the sales tax to be collected not the merchant, based upon the delivery address submitted by the consumer. All merchants that collect sales taxes using the state certified automated technology would be held harmless for any miscalculations. The state assumes the liability from the merchant, who under the current collection system bears total liability. The merchant would only be held liable for under-collection, if the merchant tampered with the certified technology or fraudulently failed to remit the sales taxes collected.

Myth: "The agreement will pose a threat to consumer privacy."

Fact: The Streamlined Sales and Use Tax Agreement has strong provisions that will protect the privacy of all consumers. The agreement provides that a certified service provider "shall perform its tax calculation, remittance, and reporting functions without retaining the personally identifiable information of consumers." The only time that a certified service provider is allowed to retain personally identifiable information is if the buyer claims an exemption from taxation.

The agreement requires the certified service providers to retain less information than is currently captured by VISA, MasterCard, American Express, Discover, or any other credit card company when a consumer makes a purchase and these companies can use this information for marketing purposes. If certified providers use or sell any information gathered from calculating sales taxes, they would lose certification to be a collector.

Let me set the record straight; the only information maintained by the vendor or third party collector for sales tax calculation are product, price, zip code, and sales tax collected. Unless the consumer is the only person living in the zip code, no one would know who the consumer is!

Myth: "The agreement will force states to forfeit sovereignty over tax policy to out-of-state bureaucrats."

Fact: No, the Streamlined Sales and Use Tax Agreement does not force any state to forfeit its sovereignty. Compliance to the agreement is always optional for a state. The decision to comply with the agreement can only be made by the state legislature and governor—and they can withdraw at any time.

Each state that complies with the agreement will have one vote on the Governing Board of the agreement. Each state that complies with the agreement can have a delegation of up to four people with the state legislature in each state deciding who represents the state. In many cases, state legislators and tax administrators have been designated to serve on the Governing Board. The agreement protects the sovereignty of each state to decide who represents them.

The agreement also requires a 60-day notice on amendments that must be sent to the governor and the legislative leaders of each member state; the same governor and legislative leaders who have appointed the delegates to the Governing Board. The Streamlined Sales Tax Governing Board cannot change any state's sales tax statute, only the state legislature and the governor have that authority and nothing in the agreement abrogates that authority.

Myth: "The agreement and federal legislation to require remote sales tax collection would violate the Constitutional doctrine of federalism. It would force businesses in states where the legislatures have chosen not to join the system or do not have a sales tax to collect sales taxes for other states."

Fact: The Streamlined Sales and Use Tax Agreement does not in any way violate the Constitution and is actually a vibrant example of federalism. The agreement is voluntary for states and for merchants; this is not a mandatory compact or violation of the Commerce Clause of the Constitution. The states voluntarily participated in the process to formulate the Streamlined Sales and Use Tax Agreement by enacting legislation by the people's elected representatives in each state, signed by the governor. The agreement ratified by the states' delegates, responds to the challenges raised by the Supreme Court in two decisions, *Bellas Hess* and *Quill*, and provides a blueprint for Congress to overturn these decisions.

Should Congress grant states remote sales tax collection authority if they comply with the agreement, then businesses that are located in a state that chooses not to comply with the agreement or that has no sales tax would only be subject to collection requirements under the agreement if that seller chooses to sell into a state in which the legislature has decided to comply with the agreement. Opponents exclaim fear that "This implicates profound practical and theoretical federalism concerns." However, no seller is forced to sell into states that comply with the agreement. Out-of-state sellers make that decision and in doing so, they also make themselves liable to the other state's non-sales taxes statutes and regulations protecting consumers and conducting business. An insurance company domiciled in Illinois must follow New Hampshire's insurance laws when doing business in New Hampshire, the same for banks and many other interstate businesses.

Myth: "The agreement will reduce tax policy competition between the states."

Fact: No. As I have stated many times, the state legislature in each state that complies with the Streamlined Sales and Use Tax Agreement will still decide what is taxed, who is exempt and at what rate it wants to tax transactions. How is tax competition eliminated by simplified administrative efficiency or even uniform product definitions? In fact, the competitive strength of America's businesses would be enhanced by reducing the regulatory complexity, costs and burden of the current state sales tax collection system on businesses. Who could oppose reducing or eliminating the current $6.8 billion a year it costs American retailers to collect our sales taxes?

The Streamlined Sales and Use Tax Agreement is a prime example that states are "laboratories of democracy." States working together have developed a solution to ensure the viability of a major revenue stream while eliminating the burden, complexity and cost on retailers to collect the states' sales taxes and maintain state sovereignty for tax policy. State legislators and governors are finding ways to maintain vital government services such as education, health care, public safety and homeland security while ensuring the viability of America's businesses in a global marketplace.

Myth: "The agreement will impede the success of electronic commerce. Collecting sales taxes on electronic commerce transactions is a new tax."

Fact: Under the Streamlined Sales and Use Tax Agreement, the buyer making a transaction will not need to fill out any additional forms in order for the sales tax to be calculated or collected. The tax is determined by the delivery address, and anyone who is buying a tangible product online wants to make sure that the product is delivered to the right address. The consumer fills out only one address field. In cases of digital products like online books or movies, the online seller wants to be paid and they will not accept a credit card payment without address verification. Once again, no additional tax form would be required.

A study released by Jupiter Research in January 2003, "Sales Tax Avoidance Is Imperative to Few Online Retailers and Ultimately Futile for All," found most people are unaware that they are not paying sales taxes when they make a purchase over the Internet. In the same study by Jupiter, only 4 percent of online buyers said that the collection of sales and use taxes would always affect their decision to buy online.

The effort to streamline sales tax collection is not a new tax on electronic commerce. Online sellers already collect sales taxes where they have nexus. The effort of states to streamline sales tax collection will only remove the burden from all sellers in collecting a tax already levied by state and local governments.

Myth: "The University of Tennessee's study on revenue loss for states due to remote sale transactions is not accurate. The estimates of revenue loss are too high."

Fact: The Business and Research Center at the University of Tennessee issued its first study on potential revenue loss due to transactions that occur through remote sellers, including electronic commerce in 2001. This study was updated in July 2004 at the request of the National Conference of State Legislatures and the National Governors Association. The updated study shows that the estimates of potential revenue loss was not as high as first predicted. The authors of both studies, Dr. Donald Bruce and Dr. William Fox, provided the following explanation for the difference in estimates between 2001 and 2004: "The experience of the last several years indicates that e-commerce has been a less robust channel for transacting goods and services than was anticipated when we prepared the earlier estimates. The findings provided here are based on lower estimates of e-commerce, and the result is a smaller revenue loss than we previously indicated. Our loss estimates are also lower because many more vendors have begun to collect sales and use taxes on their remote sales. Still, the Census Bureau reports a combined $1.6 trillion in 2002 in e-commerce transactions by manufacturers, wholesalers, service providers, and retailers, and Forrester Research, Inc.'s expectations continue to be for a strong growth in e-commerce in coming years. Thus the revenue erosion continues to represent a significant loss to state and local government."

Myth: "The agreement will widen the digital divide, because it will disproportionately impact rural, low income, disabled or even elderly buyers."

Fact: If brick and mortar stores are not as accessible in rural areas as they were say, ten years ago, perhaps they no longer can afford to compete with the price advantage enjoyed by online/remote sellers that do not collect sales taxes. When brick and mortar stores in rural areas are forced out of business that means the rural farmer will have to pay higher property taxes on his farm or increased state income taxes. Higher property or income taxes, just so that one can buy a book or CD on-line sales tax free?

Opponents imply that the streamlined sales tax effort will have the effect of widening the so-called "digital divide." Unfortunately, they fail to show an equal concern for those hard working Americans who may lack the credit or the ability to shop on-line because of a lack of access to the Internet or even a computer. These Americans are paying the sales tax every time they make a purchase in a local brick and mortar store. However, those consumers who have sufficient credit, home computers and access to the Internet are able to avoid the sales tax with almost every online purchase. In truth, if the states fail to simplify their sales tax systems and Congress fails to give states that comply with the agreement remote sales tax collection authority, the consequences will be the greatest for low income Americans who do not have the resources to shop out of state.

Myth: "The agreement is a good concept but it can never really work."

Fact: Since the Streamlined Sales Tax System became operational on October 1, 2005, over 1,100 remote sellers have volunteered to begin collecting sales taxes for those states that have complied with the agreement. The certified service providers were approved in May of 2006 and even before the certified automated system was online and available to sellers, these sellers had started to collect sales tax and remit those taxes to the states. The Streamlined Sales Tax System is so much simpler that without even the software in place, remote sellers could begin collecting sales taxes on transactions made by residents of these states.

CONCLUSION

In closing, I would like to reiterate for the members of this Subcommittee that twenty-two states have enacted compliance legislation and many others have enacted some of the changes needed to comply with the agreement. I believe we are at a point that if Congress fails to act soon on the federal legislation as envisioned in the Sales Tax Fairness and Simplification Act, the momentum in the remaining states will slow. In some of these states, compliance to the agreement may require politically difficult changes to the sales tax statutes. Congressional approval of this legislation will help the legislatures in those states make the necessary changes. As I stated previously, states have made unprecedented progress to eliminate the burdens and costs to retailers that the *Quill* decision outlined. It is now Congress' opportunity to ensure that the simplified system that the states have developed for the seamless collection of transactional taxes in the new economy is not impeded by those who merely are trying to avoid paying legally imposed taxes.

Allowing States to Collect Sales Taxes on Interstate Commerce: A Threat to Electronic Commerce

GEORGE S. ISAACSON

I want to thank you for the opportunity to testify today. The DMA is the largest trade association for businesses interested in direct marketing to consumers and businesses via catalogs and the Internet. Founded in 1917, the DMA today has over 4,700 member companies in the United States and 53 foreign countries.

As both an attorney practicing in the area of sales and use tax law for more than 25 years and an instructor in Constitutional Law at Bowdoin College, I welcome the opportunity to discuss with you the important public policy implications associated with H.R. 3396, the so-called "Sales Tax Fairness and Simplification Act," and the threat it presents to core constitutional principles and America's ability to maintain its preeminent position in the field of electronic commerce.

H.R. 3396 presents a critical policy choice for Congress. Advocates of expanded state tax jurisdiction argue that the need for additional state revenue outweighs the constitutional protections for interstate commerce. Congress should be loathe, however, to set aside these constitutional standards, which have served the nation well for two centuries and created the largest and most vibrant economy in the history of the world. Expanded and overlapping state tax jurisdictions would seriously jeopardize the continued growth of electronic commerce in the United States and it would impede the access of small and medium-sized companies to a nation-wide market. Indeed, the Internet has been an incubator for start-up companies and small businesses that have the entrepreneurial ambition and talent to market their goods and services throughout the country. Erecting a tax compliance barricade across the electronic highway is no way to spur economic growth or encourage small and medium-sized companies to expand their markets.

IF ENACTED, H.R. 3396 WOULD RESULT IN AN UNPRECEDENTED EXPANSION OF STATE TAXING AUTHORITY

The Streamlined Sales and Use Tax Agreement (SSUTA) was drafted by state tax administrators for the express purpose of expanding the jurisdictional reach of state tax systems. H.R. 3396 now seeks congressional complicity in this effort. The peculiar process by which the SSUTA came into being is a troubling one. Unlike the procedure customarily employed for the development of uniform state laws, which follows the time-tested route of hearings, deliberations, and drafting by the Commissioners on Uniform State Laws in the case of the SSUTA, state tax administrators in this instance chose to bypass altogether the Uniform Law Commission, whose membership consists of distinguished jurists, law school professors, government officials, and lawyers. Instead state tax officials chose to confer almost exclusively among themselves, sometimes even in closed sessions, to produce an agreement that contains scant contribution from the academic community and, most significantly, a rejection of almost all of the suggestions from that portion of the business community that would be most affected by the agreement, *i.e.*, the direct marketing industry.

The Commissioners on Uniform State Laws have successfully produced over 200 uniform state laws in addition to their landmark work—the Uniform Commercial Code. A number of these uniform state laws deal with multi-state taxes (such as the Uniform Division of Income for Tax Purposes Act—UDITPA) and with electronic commerce (such as the Uniform Electronic Transactions Act). If state tax officials had truly been interested in streamlining, simplifying, and making more uniform the crazy quilt of existing state and local sales and use tax laws, they would have requested that the Uniform Law Commission develop draft legislation for consideration and adoption by state legislatures. The fact that this traditional approach to developing uniform state laws was not employed is revealing of the true motives of state tax administrators. Their goal was neither simplicity nor uniformity, rather their objective was to obtain authority to export their tax systems across state borders and impose tax obligations on businesses that currently are constitutionally protected from over-reaching state tax laws.

The SSUTA is a document drafted by tax administrators for tax administrators, and, as might be expected, it resulted in little in the way of tax simplification. It has not reduced the number of sales/use tax jurisdictions in the United States, which currently number over 7,500. It has not reduced the number of state and local tax rates; indeed, it has authorized an increase in the number of such rates. It has not reduced the number of audits to which an interstate marketer would be subject (each state revenue department would still conduct its own independent audit). It has not produced a one stop/one form tax return and remittance system. It has not halted the explosion of confusing and totally discrepant sales tax holidays, which create mini-tax systems with separate rules of only several days' length. In fact, in certain respects, the SSUTA makes sales/use tax compliance more complex and confusing for both consumers and retailers.

Put simply, Congress should not endorse this misnamed exercise in state tax reform. Instead, this subcommittee should urge state governors and the direct marketing industry to work together in a genuine and collaborative effort, under the auspices of the Uniform Law Commission, to standardize the administration of state tax laws. The Direct Marketing Association would be a willing and active participant in that process.

STATE TAX ADMINISTRATORS HAVE GROSSLY OVER-ESTIMATED LOST SALES/USE TAX REVENUES

The alleged tax revenue benefits of the SSUTA are illusory. SSUTA advocates have grossly exaggerated, by as much as 400 percent, the revenue "losses" states and localities have incurred as a result of the constitutional limitation on their ability to impose tax collection obligations on catalog companies and electronic merchants beyond their borders. The true figure is, in fact, only a fraction of one percent of total state sales and use tax collections. Recent analysis shows that the "lost" revenue for all current SSUTA full member states for 2006 totals only $145 million, not the billions of dollars claimed by state tax officials.

The claims of state government officials of enormous revenue "losses" because of uncollected sales and use taxes on electronic commerce are simply not supported by currently available data. Advocates of the SSUTA rely almost exclusively on predictions of lost tax revenue reported by two researchers affiliated with the University of Tennessee ("UT Study"). Their report, first issued in 2000, and then updated in 2001 and reviewed in 2004, is based on non-validated data collected by a private research firm. Actual data from the U.S. Department of Commerce Census Bureau's 2007 E-Commerce Report analyzed by DMA Senior Economist Dr. Peter Johnson ("Johnson Study"), however, shows that on-line consumer sales growth has been much more modest than predicted in the UT Study, so that untaxed sales are (and will continue in the foreseeable future to be) much lower than assumed by state tax administrators.

Even more to the point, the UT Study also was founded on a number of faulty assumptions. The Johnson Study is illuminating in this regard. First, the vast majority of e-commerce—well in excess of 90 percent—is comprised of business-to-business ("B-to-B") transactions on which transaction taxes are either collected by vendors or remitted by companies that self-report the use tax. Most B-to-B transactions (88%) are conducted via electronic data interchange ("EDI"), for which the sales/use remittance rate is effectively 100 percent. Even for the much smaller portion of B-to-B sales conducted over the Internet, a recent study by the Department of Revenue for Washington State indicates a sales/use tax remittance rate of 85 percent. Thus, the implication that states are "losing" a substantial portion of their sales tax revenues to electronic commerce is simply false, because the vast majority of e-commerce transactions are not consumer sales.

Furthermore, even as to business-to-consumer ("B-to-C") Internet transactions, state estimates of uncollected tax revenues are grossly inflated. Again, the UT Study over-estimated both total e-commerce growth and B-to-C growth, so state projections of gross revenue potentially subject to tax are far off the mark. Moreover, as the authors of the UT Study conceded in 2004, there are many more multi-channel retailers (*i.e.*, retailers with both retail stores, Internet websites, and, in some cases, catalog operations) that have commenced collection of sales/use tax on their Internet and other remote sales than originally estimated by the UT Study. In this regard, the perceived "problem" of catalog and Internet vendors not collecting use tax has proven to be largely self-correcting. As remote sellers grow, most of them embark on a multi-channel sales strategy, which includes opening retail stores and a corresponding decision to begin collecting state sales/use taxes voluntarily on all sales (including Internet sales) to residents in states where their stores are located.

Correcting for these and other flaws in the UT Study and relying on actual data from the U.S. Commerce Department, the Johnson Study shows that the amount of sales/use tax which remote e-commerce retailers could not be compelled to collect for all states is a mere fraction of the amount predicted in the UT Study. In total, combining B-to-C with B-to-B transaction data, "uncollected" sales and use taxes on on-line sales is best estimated to be only 0.2 percent of all state and local tax revenues for 2006. For the 15 states that are currently full members of the SSUTA, this translates into $145 million in total, not the many billions of dollars claimed by SSUTA advocates. (In fact, SSUTA member states have probably experienced somewhat higher tax collections than indicated above, as a result of voluntary participation in the SSUTA by some retailers that might otherwise not have decided to collect use tax.)

In light of these figures, I would hope that members of this Committee would question whether forsaking long-standing constitutional standards is the proper response to the greatly exaggerated, and largely self-correcting, problem of lost use tax revenue claimed by state tax officials.

JURISDICTIONAL LIMITATIONS ON STATE TAXING AUTHORITY ARE NOT A LEGAL "LOOPHOLE" EXPLOITED BY RETAILERS, BUT RATHER DERIVE FROM CORE CONSTITUTIONAL PRINCIPLES

The stated purpose of H.R. 3396 is to authorize member states of the SSUTA to subject businesses not located within their borders—*i.e.*, companies lacking "nexus"—to tax collection and remittance obligations. This is no trivial matter. Determining the appropriate reach of the sovereign authority of state and local governments is central to the American system of government. Indeed, the Constitutional Convention of 1787 was initially called to address the problem of individual state legislatures imposing taxes and duties on trade with other states, a practice that was pushing the young country into a depression. The solution devised by the Constitution's Framers was a federal system of dual national and state sovereignty, the genius of which is that *each state is sovereign within its own borders* and can adopt those policies that best suit its particular needs and reflect the political preferences of its citizens. Needless to say, this plan has worked remarkably well for more than 200 years.

Of necessity, federalism restricts the ability of a state (or locality) to export its tax system across state borders. Permitting each state to visit its unique tax system on businesses that have no nexus with the taxing state would be chaotic as a matter of both tax administration and compliance (involving fifty state governments, and the more than 7,500 local taxing districts in the United States, imposing their vastly different tax regimes on businesses in each of the forty-nine other states). Moreover, out-of-state companies would have no way to influence the very state tax systems that are newly imposed on them. In the most real sense, allowing the expansion of tax authority beyond state borders is "taxation without representation."

The constitutional limitations on the territorial scope of state and local taxing jurisdiction also has enormous economic importance. The United States Constitution—and the Commerce Clause in particular—has been the guardian of this nation's open market economy. A central purpose of the Commerce Clause was to prevent states from suppressing the free flow of interstate commerce by imposition of taxes, duties, tariffs, and other levies. Indeed, more than two centuries before the establishment of the European Union, the framers of the United States Constitution created a common market on this continent through the Commerce Clause, and their foresight powered the greatest economic engine mankind has ever known.

In this era of electronic commerce and increased international competition, it is imperative that Congress not abandon, or undermine, the core Commerce Clause principle of a single, free-flowing national marketplace. In the last two decades, U.S. companies have been dominant in the field of electronic commerce; but abandoning constitutional ideals in favor of short-sighted efforts to increase state tax revenues could undermine the position of American companies in this crucial, but still fledgling, sector of the world's economy. The vitality of e-commerce should not be curbed by federal legislation that saddles American businesses with the burdens of disparate state tax laws whose authority extends far beyond traditional jurisdictional borders.

With record high energy prices threatening the nation's economy, now is certainly not the time for Congress to abandon the original intent of the Commerce Clause. Moreover, debate over the wisdom of a federal law to expand state and federal tax jurisdiction cannot be divorced from consideration of the impact such legislation would have on the competitiveness of American companies. Forcing new tax collection obligations on U.S.-based companies would have the undesirable (and undoubtedly unintended) effect of advantaging their foreign competitors, on whom state and local tax collection obligations could never be effectively imposed.

Congress should be skeptical of arguments that the Commerce Clause is outdated and its restriction on state taxing authority is nothing more than a constitutional loophole exploited by business. As a professor of constitutional law, I respectfully disagree. In my view, the Supreme Court's consistent application of long-standing constitutional principles should not be viewed as a "problem" in need of correction. Rather, the inter-related ideals of federalism and unfettered interstate commerce have made America both the greatest experiment in representational democracy and the most successful economy the world has ever known.

H.R. 3396 WOULD UNFAIRLY BURDEN BUSINESSES IN A MAJORITY OF STATES TO SATISFY THE DEMANDS OF A MINORITY OF STATES THAT ARE MEMBERS OF THE SSUTA

The proposed legislation being considered by this subcommittee would be unfair to the great majority of states—including California, Texas, New York, Florida, Illinois, Pennsylvania, and Massachusetts—which have elected not to become members of the SSUTA. The burdens of H.R. 3396 would fall primarily on businesses in those states that will realize no reciprocating benefit. The legislation grants favored treatment to the minority of states that are full members of the SSUTA (only 17 states, representing approximately 25 percent of the nation's population). The bill would allow those few states to impose tax collection, reporting and remittance duties on *retailers in every other state in the nation*, regardless of whether a state is a member or not a member of the SSUTA.

Most states that participated in the Streamlined Sales Tax Project have decided not to become members of the Streamlined Sales and Use Tax Agreement for a variety of different reasons. The most common reason is that these states (primarily larger states) do not want to surrender their tax sovereignty to the dictates of the SSUTA Governing Board. Consequently, most states have concluded that membership in the SSUTA would be detrimental to their best interests.

H.R. 3396 would, nonetheless, force non-participating states to tolerate the incongruous situation in which companies headquartered in their states are required to collect sales/use taxes for SSUTA member states, but there would be no similar and reciprocal obligation on the part of retailers located in the SSUTA member states. To put the issue in more specific terms, under this bill, an Internet retailer based solely in California or Massachusetts (neither of which are SSUTA members) would be subject to tax collection, reporting and remittance obligations for its sales to residents of Nebraska, North Carolina, Wyoming, and every other SSUTA state, but neither California nor Massachusetts would receive any additional tax revenue from an Internet retailer with operations solely in any of the SSUTA member states. In this regard, H.R. 3396 is hardly a bill promoting sales tax fairness for retailers, consumers, and states through the country.

Supporters of H.R. 3396 argue that the legislation would encourage additional states to bring their sales/use tax laws into compliance with the SSUTA. But this is faulty and self-flattering reasoning. If the SSUTA were attractive on its own merits, more states would have already joined. Instead, the reality is that the legislatures in the vast majority of states, making up more than 70 percent of the United States population and including each of the six largest states in the nation—California, Texas, New York, Florida, Illinois, Pennsylvania—have chosen not to adopt the SSUTA for good reasons. Legislative leaders in those states have concluded that the SSUTA is simply not consistent with their state's tax scheme (*e.g.*, sourcing requirements) or otherwise is not in the state's best interest. Large states are also skeptical of handing over authority to an SSUTA Governing Board dominated by tax administrators from smaller states. Moreover, because the SSUTA has been so frequently amended by the Governing Board despite the short life of the agreement, these larger states are concerned over what future requirements might be imposed upon them by the Governing Board in the event they were to become full members.

In fact, it is this inherent tension between the insistence of states on maintaining sovereignty, pitted against the desire to expand their taxing jurisdiction, that has made the SSUTA fatally flawed and doomed to fail in achieving real simplification and uniformity in state and local sales and use tax systems.

THE SSUTA ADOPTED "LOW BAR" REFORM FROM THE OUTSET AND HAS PROVEN TO BE A MOVING TARGET OF INCREASING COMPLEXITY AND DECREASING UNIFORMITY

Although nominally a bold reform initiative to simplify, harmonize and modernize state and local sales and use tax laws, the Streamlined Sales Tax Project has never promoted true simplification or uniformity. Instead, state tax administrators, from the outset of the Project, and at every turn since, have sacrificed real reform to accommodate the peculiarities of individual states tax systems. The goal of the Project's organizers was not to maximize uniformity among state laws, but rather to maximize the number of states willing to sign on to SSUTA full membership.

The inevitable result of this recruitment-at-all-costs strategy has been the progressive dilution of the Project's stated uniformity objectives. Successive compromises of the SSUTA's stated principles have produced a lowest-common-denominator standard for sales/use tax reform. Moreover, these on-going revisions have made the SSUTA a moving target for affected businesses, as they confront frequent amendments, illogical interpretive rulings and a burgeoning number of complex rules. Having closely followed and contributed to the SSTP process over the past 7 years, I find the contrast between the SSUTA process and the more conventional drafting process for uniform state legislation developed by the Commission on Uniform States Laws (such as UDITPA) a most striking one.

THE SSUTA FAILED TO ADOPT FUNDAMENTAL REQUIREMENTS OF SIMPLICITY AND UNIFORMITY

To understand the dissolution of the SSUTA process, it is instructive to consider its history. The Streamlined Sales Tax Project was launched in 2000 on the heels of two earlier joint government/industry initiatives (the National Tax Association [NTA] Communications and Electronic Commerce Tax Project, and the congressionally established Advisory Commission on Electronic Commerce), both of which had concluded that the existing state sales and use tax system was one of daunting complexity, and that true simplification would require sweeping reforms. To this end, in August 2000, the Direct Marketing Association set forth in a letter to Streamlined Sales Tax Project leaders a comprehensive list of reform proposals, a copy of which is attached to my written testimony. The fate of DMA's proposals is telling: of more than 30 specific reform recommendations offered by the DMA, the SSUTA fully adopted only two, centralized registration and uniform bad debt provisions, and the latter provision has not been honored by most of the member states.

Perhaps most emblematic of the SSUTA's failure to achieve genuine sales/use tax reform was the early demise of the single most important step toward simplification: the adoption of a single sales and use tax rate per state for all commerce ("one rate per state"), which would have eliminated the problem of merchant compliance with thousands of local tax jurisdictions with different tax rates. The United States is the only economically developed country in the world with a system of sub-state transaction taxes not only for municipalities and counties, but also for school districts, transportation districts, sanitation districts, sports arena districts, and other local tax jurisdictions. In light of this wildly complex system, the adoption of a "one rate per state" standard was the unanimous recommendation of the NTA's E-Commerce Project (which included delegates from the National Conference of State Legislatures, National Governors Association, and the U.S. Conference of Mayors) and was also the majority report recommendation of the Congressional Advisory Commission.

Despite this background, the SSTP abandoned the "one rate per state" standard early in its deliberations, and instead decided to permit (a) two state-level rates (one of which only applies to food, food ingredients, and drugs) and (b) additional separate rates as chosen by each local taxing jurisdiction in the state. The effect of this decision was to allow an increase, rather than require a decrease, in the number of sales/use tax rates to which an interstate merchant might be subject in collecting and remitting taxes.

How could such a fundamental goal of sales/use tax reform be forsaken so early in the SSTP process? State tax administrators associated with the SSUTA now freely admit that the "one rate per state" proposal was dead on arrival, because they quickly were informed that it was unacceptable to most states and localities who clearly prized their unique taxing prerogatives over the uniformity and simplification recommendations of the prior commissions.

I have had the opportunity, in testimony before this subcommittee (in October 2003) and last year (July 2006) before the Senate Finance Committee, to explain in detail numerous other ways that the SSUTA disregarded broadly recognized principles of sales/use tax simplification and standardization, and I would be happy to provide copies of such testimony to the subcommittee members. In brief, a few of these glaring shortcomings include:

- **The failure to establish uniformity in the tax base:** The SSUTA rejected from the outset adopting a uniform tax base, instead insisting that uniform definitions among states for taxable and exempt products would be adequate simplification for retailers. But the number of product definitions in the SSUTA to which member states must adhere is very limited, and states can choose to exempt or tax any product or service not specifically defined. The agreement has no definitions that would cover many everyday consumer items, from cookware to holiday decorations to home and garden items.

- **There is no uniformity in the measure of tax for like transactions:** The SSUTA also does not simplify the way retailers must measure the dollar amount (transaction value) subject to tax. Instead, the SSUTA's definition of "sales price" allows states to include, or exclude, multiple components, resulting in a dizzying array of state-specific alternatives, with no uniform measure of tax among states for identical transactions. In fact, as explained later, the SSUTA has recently made the determination of "sales price" even more complex.

- **There is no meaningful reduction in the burdens of tax collection, reporting, remittance and audits for interstate marketers:** State tax administrators refused to adopt a proposal for joint audits (i.e., one audit for all member states). As a result, the number of tax audits to which an interstate marketer would be subject under H.R. 3396 would substantially increase over current practice, since non-nexus companies would become subject to audit not only by the state revenue department in their home state, but by tax auditors from each of the member states, at considerable additional administrative burden and expense to America's retailers.

- **The SSUTA failed to seek independent testing of tax compliance software:** While SSUTA officials rely heavily on computer technology as the "silver bullet" to address the increased tax compliance burdens that would result from passage of H.R. 3396, the Project never sought independent testing of the software systems put forward by service providers (none of which were originally developed for the purpose of SSUTA compliance), and instead conducted the certification process internally. To date, the SSUTA has certified 3 private companies, but many retailers, after investigating the available providers, have concluded that using their software would be prohibitively expensive without any real guarantee of accuracy. Moreover, despite the fact that private service providers will have access to highly confidential personal consumer information, the SSUTA has no articulated standards for assuring the security and privacy of such information.

- **The failure to guarantee fundamental fairness with respect to vendor compensation for tax collection:** On its face, the SSUTA, since its adoption in 2002, has required states to compensate both third party service providers and self-reporting vendors for the considerable costs of serving as the states' collection agents, but five years later the Governing Board has only approved compensation for the certified providers (who would not, of course, have sought certification otherwise), and has reneged on its promise of compensation to retailers.

THE SSUTA HAS BEEN STEADILY WEAKENED SINCE ITS ADOPTION THROUGH A MYRIAD OF AMENDMENTS AND INTERPRETIVE RULINGS THAT LESSEN ITS UNIFORMITY REQUIREMENTS AND INCREASE ITS COMPLEXITY

Regrettably, the SSUTA has suffered a further "lowering of the bar" since its initial adoption. Again, in stark contrast to a truly Uniform Act, such as the Uniform Division of Income for Tax Purposes Act, which was promulgated 50 years ago and has remained remarkably stable over time, the SSUTA has already been subject to more than 70 amendments during its short life span. Not surprisingly, there are nearly 20 additional proposed amendments on the agenda for the Governing Board's meeting next week. Dozens of the agreement's provisions have been materially modified; whole sections have been repealed or replaced; and new sections have been added. At the same time, the Governing Board has issued numerous interpretive rulings which, rather than requiring member states to conform strictly to the agreement's provisions, have instead tolerated widely disparate practices by member state revenue departments. The result has been to increase, rather than reduce, variations in the administration of state tax laws. In a very real sense, the SSUTA is a moving target, adding new uncertainties for businesses and increasing both their compliance costs and their exposure to unantici-pated tax assessments.

THE SSUTA HAS OPENLY AUTHORIZED STATES TO ADOPT REPLACEMENT TAXES

Many of the recent amendments to the SSUTA, as well as those currently under consid-eration by the Governing Board, represent a further degradation of even the modest uni-formity provisions contained in the agreement when it was first adopted. The enactment by member states of "replacement taxes," and the now infamous example of the "fur clothing tax," has become emblematic of the Governing Board's refusal to stand firm and of member states' refusal to abide by the agreement's requirements. Instead, the Governing Board has tolerated, at times even encouraged, blatant departures from the substance and spirit of the SSUTA on the part of state governments in order to avoid member states from withdrawing, or being disqualified, from membership in the SSUTA.

The replacement tax issue came to the fore in the following way. SSUTA advocates proudly point to the list of product definitions as the Project's central accomplishment in achieving greater uniformity. Member states are required to adopt the definitions, and must then either tax, or exempt, all items that fall within each product definition. Among the defined products is "clothing," defined as "all human wearing apparel suit-able for general use," with a lengthy, non-exclusive list of examples within the defini-tion that includes furs. Observers, I among them, noted that the full member state of Minnesota exempted "clothing" from sales and use tax, but separately imposed an excise tax on fur clothing, in apparent violation of the agreement.

In 2006, I submitted a request to the SSUTA Governing Board for a determination whether the fur clothing tax imposed by Minnesota violated the agreement. In response, the SSUTA's Compliance and Review Committee determined, and the Governing Board agreed, that because the fur clothing tax was denominated in Minnesota's statute as a gross revenues excise tax separate from its general sales and use tax, it was not subject to the agreement's requirements. In other words, simply re-nam-ing a sales tax as an excise tax frees a state from the requirements of the SSUTA. The ruling clearly signaled to all states (current SSUTA members and those states that had reservations about surrendering tax sovereignty to the SSUTA) that they were free to game-the-system simply by re-naming transaction taxes to take them outside the scope of the agreement.

This message was readily received by other states. For example, the legislature in New Jersey, another "Full" SSUTA Member, soon followed suit, enacting in its 2006 legislative session its own version of the fur tax. The New Jersey law creates a new gross receipts tax on fur clothing, despite the fact that New Jersey otherwise exempts "cloth-ing" (as defined in the SSUTA) from its sales tax. Moreover, the New Jersey fur tax applies at a rate of 6 percent, despite the fact that New Jersey in 2006 raised its gener-al sales and use tax rate to 7 percent. As a result, the New Jersey fur tax flaunts not only the definitional requirements of the SSUTA, but also the requirements that members have only one state-level sales tax rate (other than for food and drugs).

Following the enactment of the New Jersey tax, there was an outcry among observers, and even some supporters, of the SSUTA. Such "replacement taxes," *i.e.,* sales and use taxes re-named to avoid the agreement, undermined the integrity of the entire SSUTA process. The SSUTA's Business Advisory Committee, comprised of industry supporters of the agreement, was highly critical of the enactment of replacement taxes. Proposals were presented to the Governing Board to prohibit the practice. To date, however, these proposals have not been acted upon, and the SSUTA Governing Board has failed to pass an amendment, or even a resolution, that would prohibit state legislatures from making an end-run around the SSUTA by adopting replacement taxes.

Rather than punish states that have enacted replacement taxes, the Governing Board has instead chosen the path of least resistance. Its approach has been: "If a state violates the agreement, we will simply change the agreement." With the fur clothing tax, rather than disciplining New Jersey, the SSUTA in December 2006 amended the agreement to remove fur from the general "clothing" definition and approved a new, separate definition of "fur clothing," thus allowing separate tax treatment for fur clothing and glossing over the non-conformity of both New Jersey and Minnesota.

THE SSUTA HAS ELIMINATED UNIFORMITY IN THE TREATMENT OF DELIVERY CHARGES

The SSUTA Governing Board's willingness to bend and amend the agreement to accommodate state-specific tax practices has taken a decidedly disturbing turn in connection with the treatment of delivery charges. Consumers need to know whether sales tax will be computed before or after inclusion of "shipping and handling charges." Early in the streamlining project, the Direct Marketing Association urged uniformity on this subject for the benefit of consumers and retailers alike. Not only did the SSUTA not incorporate DMA's original proposal, but recently it has taken a giant step backward from the position taken at the time of the agreement's original adoption.

A little background on this subject may be useful in understanding direct marketers' concerns. The tax treatment of charges to consumers for delivery of products has long been an area of considerable complexity. Some states impose tax on all delivery charges; others exempt all delivery charges so long as they are separately stated on the invoice; some states tax handling charges, but not common carrier freight charges; most, but not all, states exempt postage charges for direct mail paid to the USPS, even if the state taxes freight charges by a private carrier; some exempt "shipping" charges only if they represent the actual cost of shipping a particular product, but not if the charge is based on average shipping costs; and the list goes on.

Initially, the SSUTA sought to simplify the definition of "delivery charges" to include all charges related to delivery of product to a purchaser, which meant not only shipping costs, but also handling and other charges (including postage, a decision which allowed some member states to impose new taxes on postage they had not previously levied). At the same time, however, the SSUTA protected state tax prerogatives (at the expense of uniformity) by listing delivery charges among those items that a state could elect to include, or exclude, from the taxable "sales price" of the product.

Under political pressure from a number of quarters, including states that previously separated the tax treatment of shipping from other charges, the Governing Board in September 2007 approved an amendment that modifies the definition of "delivery charges" under the agreement to allow member states to treat "shipping" separately from "handling," undoing any simplification that had previously been achieved. Beginning in 2008, SSUTA member states may elect to tax both shipping and handling, may tax neither, may tax only shipping and not handling, or vice-versa. As a result, the number of possible permutations of the taxable "sales price" that consumers and retailers may encounter has greatly increased.

THE SSUTA HAS INTERPRETED SOME DEFINITIONS, IN PARTICULAR "DIRECT MAIL," TO APPLY ONLY FOR ADMINISTRATIVE PURPOSES, LEAVING STATES FREE TO TAX OR EXEMPT MULTIPLE ADDITIONAL PRODUCTS

In addition to amendments to the agreement, the official Interpretations issued by the SSUTA Governing Board and its committees have further degraded any claim to uniformity. For example, the SSUTA contains a definition for "direct mail," *i.e.*, printed material delivered at no charge via U.S. Mail or by another delivery service to a mass audience or persons identified on a mailing list. This is an area of great importance to the direct marketing industry. In October 2006, the SSUTA received a seemingly innocuous request "[w]hether billing invoices, return envelopes and any additional marketing materials are included in the definition" of direct mail. Although on its face this was a question about the definition, the answer had additional significance because member states are authorized to allow a different tax treatment for "delivery charges" on direct mail transactions, *i.e.*, to include or exclude such charges on direct mail in a manner different from the state's treatment of delivery charges for most products.

The SSUTA's Interpretations Committee found that the invoices, envelopes and other items met the SSUTA's definition of direct mail, but then went on to state that the definition of "direct mail" in the agreement applies only for the purpose of determining proper "sourcing" of sales transactions, and *not* for determining whether "delivery charges" are included in the taxable price! The Governing Board subsequently approved the ruling in December 2006.

The direct marketing industry was left totally confused. As a strained rationale, the SSUTA stated that the "direct mail" definition appears in the agreement's "Administrative Definitions" and not its "Product Definitions," so that the agreement does not purport to define, at all, what categories of printed material are subject to tax in a member state, and what categories are not subject to tax. In other words, states could have conflicting definitions and categorization of direct mail for different tax purposes. Indeed, several SSUTA member states have chosen to tax and exempt different categories of printed materials, all of which appear to meet the uniform definition of "direct mail" under the agreement. The result is that even though the SSUTA purports to define "direct mail," sellers and buyers cannot look to the agreement to determine whether their products and services are subject to tax or not, or what taxable measure applies to the transaction.

The Interpretive Ruling that the SSUTA's "Administrative Definitions" cannot be relied upon to determine which types of "direct mail" are taxable and which are not, is disturbing, yet there are now proposed amendments pending before the Governing Board that would formalize and extend that understanding to all Administrative Definitions in the agreement. Currently, the "Administrative Definitions" include such terms as "bundled transaction," "delivery charges," "telecommunications non-recurring charges," none of which apparently can be relied upon anymore by retailers for guidance except in regard to the "administration" of taxes under the agreement. Perhaps most incredibly, the Administrative Definitions include the SSUTA's definition of "tangible personal property," the bedrock definition of every sales and use tax system. On even this point, the SSUTA has implicitly disavowed uniformity among the member states.

SALES TAX HOLIDAYS DEFEAT UNIFORMITY, AND THE SSUTA FAILS TO RESOLVE THIS PROBLEM

One of the myriad ways the SSUTA has bowed to parochial state concerns is through its preservation of sales tax "holidays," the temporary suspension of sales and use taxes on particular products or classes of products, such as clothing, computers or school supplies. Sales tax holidays are increasingly attractive to state legislatures as (a) a form of consumer tax relief, (b) a way to encourage purchases that will promote certain state government policy objectives, and (c) a means of stimulating the economy around specific seasonal events, such as the start of the school year. Although this form of short-term tax incentive is very popular with the public, and always focused around local events, sales tax holidays present enormous complexity to interstate retailers, who need to publish tax instructions on their websites and in their catalogs. The SSUTA currently permits members to implement such tax holidays only with respect to product categories specifically delineated in the agreement (such as clothing or school supplies). The agreement, however, imposes no limit on the duration of such holidays, and allows states to impose eligibility thresholds, so that the temporary exemption applies to purchases only above a minimum dollar amount, increasing the complexity for retailers to administer tax holidays.

The popularity of sales tax holidays among state legislatures means that new proposals for such holidays are frequent. Now before the Governing Board is an amendment proposed by North Carolina, a full member state, to allow a sales tax holiday for all products that qualify for "Energy Star" designation under guidelines set by the U.S. Department of Environmental Protection. According to the EPA, products in more than 50 categories qualify for the Energy Star label. Authorizing a sales tax holiday based on such a designation would have the effect of creating a new mini-tax system of limited duration. Moreover, every SSUTA member state would be free to choose whether, when and for how long to implement such a holiday, imposing enormous burdens on retailers. It is precisely the pursuit of such state-specific tax policy objectives that generate the overwhelming complexity in sales and use tax systems.

Even more complex proposals for sales tax holidays are being considered by state legislatures. This year, the State of Florida (not currently a member of the SSUTA) adopted a "Hurricane Preparedness Sales Tax Holiday" running for 10 days in late May 2007 designed to encourage residents to prepare for the hurricane season. The holiday applied to dozens of types of products in multiple categories, such as candles and flashlights, coolers and ice chests, cell phone batteries, radios, tarpaulins, and window shutter materials. Moreover, the exemptions for different types of products applied only *below* a specified dollar cap, such as $20 for gas-powered lanterns, $50 for bungee cords, and $75 for carbon monoxide detectors. This may be laudable tax policy, but allowing such a system to be exported across state lines would require retailers across the country to comply with the unique policy prerogatives of distant states. Such a system would place crushing burdens on interstate commerce.

THE SSUTA IS POISED TO COMPROMISE ITS ADOPTION OF UNIFORM, DESTINATION-BASED SOURCING

The one rate per state proposal has recently re surfaced in the debate among SSUTA members concerning the "sourcing" of transactions for sales and use tax purposes. "Sourcing" is the term used by tax analysts to describe the mechanism for determining which jurisdiction will have the opportunity to tax a particular transaction. The issue of sourcing would be far less controversial under a "one rate per state" rule, because the absence in variation among tax rates within a state would make sales tax compliance straightforward. However, when local rates differ widely, the issue of which jurisdiction gets to tax the transaction becomes very confusing. Does a merchant who delivers product from one jurisdiction to another charge sales tax at the merchant's home district rate ("origin sourcing") or must the retailer "source" the sale to the location where the product is received and collect tax based on the recipient's jurisdiction ("destination sourcing")?

The SSUTA originally committed itself, for reasons of simplicity and uniformity, to destination sourcing for all transactions. This meant that a retailer would collect tax for the state and local jurisdiction where the consumer—not the retailer—is located. This effort at uniformity has not gone down well, however, with a number of states and localities that permit or require origin sourcing for in-state vendors. Consequently, the SSUTA Governing Board has been asked to abandon its commitment to destination sourcing and accommodate states that want to have destination sourcing at the state level but origin sourcing at the local level. Such a change in the SSUTA would hardly serve the interests of consistency, simplicity, and uniformity. But those concerns have not deterred the Governing Board from amending the agreement in the past.

If a state allows origin sourcing for in-state businesses, while demanding destination sourcing for out-of-state businesses (as some of the proposed amendments would permit), there is an obvious issue of fairness. Moreover, if the combined state and local tax rate applicable to an in-state seller is lower than the combined rate applicable to an out-of-state seller for a comparable transaction, the Supreme Court has ruled that such a tax scheme violates the Commerce Clause and is unconstitutional in *Associated Industries of Missouri, Inc. v. Lohman* (1993).

An obvious question is: "Why would the Governing Board consider abandoning its straightforward commitment to destination sourcing for all transactions and, instead, create a complex set of rules that would differentiate between state and local taxes on the one hand, and in-state and out-of-state sellers on the other hand?" The answer is that the Governing Board is willing to abandon principle to attract new member states.

Instead of insisting on state conformity with the original requirements of the SSUTA as a condition of full membership, the Governing Board is trying to broker a "compromise" that would permit states to retain their origin sourcing rules. Interestingly, Indiana, one of the states represented on the Governing Board, has proposed an amendment that would, in effect, allow a member state to adopt a separate single rate for delivery sales (in contrast to over-the-counter sales). This would have the effect of keeping compliance burdens on in-state sellers light, but it would also eliminate much of the unfairness of disparate sourcing rules for out-of-state sellers. Thus, under the Indiana proposal, states with origin sourcing could join the SSUTA without adopting destination sourcing, if they would adopt one rate per state. Although the Indiana proposal is on the agenda for the meeting of the SSUTA Governing Board next week, and has considerable support among the business community, Governing Board officials have indicated in public meetings that they feel the proposal does not even merit discussion, because states with origin sourcing will never accept the "one rate per state" alternative, showing again that real reform under the auspices of the SSUTA is impossible.

The DMA has expressed its concerns regarding multiple sourcing provisions for a single state in a letter to the Governing Board.

THE SSUTA HAS REPEATEDLY COMPROMISED CONFORMITY STANDARDS IN ORDER TO INCREASE OR MAINTAIN MEMBERSHIP

The SSUTA has repeatedly demonstrated a willingness to descend to the lowest common denominator of uniformity in order to accommodate members and potential members, and it has likewise repeatedly bent and even changed its rules regarding compliance requirements. The purpose behind this progressive lowering of the bar has been to enlist and retain member states that are unable or unwilling to bring their laws in line with the agreement's requirements.

A Weak Compliance Standard. To become and remain a member of the SSUTA, a state must only certify to the Governing Board that the "effect" of its laws, rules, regulations and policies is "substantially compliant" with each of the requirements of the agreement. This weak standard of compliance means that there is no guarantee that any member state's laws are fully compliant with the terms of the agreement to begin with. This is only one way that the SSUTA has enabled states to circumvent its compliance requirements.

The SSUTA Began by Creating a Class of Not Fully Compliant "Associate Members." Initially, the agreement, by its terms, was only to take effect when at least ten states comprising at least twenty percent of the total population of all states imposing a state sales tax were determined to be in conformity. The participating states set a deadline for themselves of October 1, 2005, to achieve this level of conformity.

The SSUTA Governing Board was so concerned, however, in April 2005 that it would not secure the membership of enough states to meet their self-imposed threshold, that it quickly adopted a new provision allowing for so-called "associate" members, which were states that the Project participants acknowledged had not yet conformed their laws to the agreement, but which states would, nonetheless, be counted toward the critical mass necessary for the SSUTA to become effective. State representatives to the SSUTA have publicly acknowledged that the provisions regarding associate members were adopted in haste in 2005, without careful consideration of all of the ramifications of creating this second class of members on other parts of the agreement, in order to "meet the quota" necessary for the SSUTA to take effect.

When this new category of membership was created in April 2005, associate members were given more than three-and-a-half years, until December 31, 2007, to bring their laws into full conformity with the agreement, or they would forfeit their associate membership status. At the time the participating states declared success in meeting the membership threshold on October 1, 2005, there were six states granted associate membership status: Arkansas, Nevada, Ohio, Tennessee, Utah, and Wyoming. Together with the thirteen states granted full membership, the SSUTA claimed to have enlisted states comprising a little more than 29 percent of the population as of October 1, 2005.

The SSUTA Next Refused to Expel Utah After Its Legislature Repealed Conformity Legislation. After creating the associate member category, SSUTA officials have shown themselves ready to take any measures necessary to prolong the membership of associate members. The first such compromise came in 2006, when the legislature in Utah, one of the associate member states, repealed a large number of laws that had originally been enacted to bring the state into SSUTA conformity. There was no question that Utah's tax code was no longer in compliance with multiple SSUTA requirements and that the state did not, after the repeal legislation, meet the standard for associate membership.

Rather than take steps to terminate Utah's SSUTA membership, the Governing Board determined that it was not required to expel Utah on the theory that, under the agreement, the status of associate members did not need to be reviewed until the December 31, 2007 deadline for full conformity. The Governing Board simply declined to take up the matter of Utah's non-compliance and, as of this date, Utah remains an associate member, accepting SSUTA vendor registrations, participating on SSUTA committees, and voting on matters with other associate member states.

The SSUTA Created a New Category of Associate Member to Accommodate Tennessee. While some states originally granted associate member status have subsequently petitioned for and been granted full membership, the two largest of the states initially granted associate member status in 2005, Ohio and Tennessee, have remained associate members. In Tennessee, a number of the changes in its laws that have proven most controversial within the state were adopted with effective dates pushed off well into the future for political reasons. The proposed effective date for many such laws had been July 1, 2007, in time for the December 31, 2007 deadline for associate member states to come into full compliance. But in the 2007 legislative session, the Tennessee legislature pushed back the effective date on many provisions until July 1, 2009, delaying the date for the state's possible conformity until after the SSUTA's previously set deadline.

Rather than Tennessee losing its membership status, the SSUTA in June 2007 promptly enacted an amendment to the agreement which created a new category of associate members, described as states petitioning for membership after January 1, 2007. Such states are qualified for associate membership status if they are found to be in compliance with the agreement's requirements except that the effective date of their conformity is delayed for not more than twelve months, or with Governing Board approval, eighteen months, beyond their proposed entry date into the agreement.

Although Tennessee was already an associate member prior to January 1, 2007, it was nevertheless permitted to petition for associate member status under the new provision for associate members petitioning after January 1, 2007. The Governing Board promptly approved Tennessee's associate member status under the new provision, based on its proposed new conformity date of July 1, 2009. These machinations are little more than smoke and mirrors.

The SSUTA Is Poised to Make Concessions on Origin Sourcing to Extend the Deadline for Ohio. Of considerable concern now to SSUTA officials is the impending failure of Ohio, the largest state with membership status in the SSUTA, to gain full membership status by December 31. For Ohio, the central issue of non-conformity is its system of in-state origin sourcing. With Ohio's deadline to conform to the SSUTA approaching, the Ohio legislature in the 2007 legislative session not only declined to adopt destination sourcing, but affirmed its system of origin sourcing. As a result, Ohio will not meet the December 31, 2007 deadline for conformity, and will be required under the current language of the agreement to forfeit its membership.

SSUTA officials desperately want Ohio to retain its membership and, indeed, to attain full member status. Indeed, the possibility of Ohio falling out of the SSUTA, together with the desire to attract other states that have origin-based sourcing, is driving the Governing Board's push to amend the agreement and depart altogether from a uniform destination-based sourcing standard.

At the same time, separate amendments have been proposed regarding associate member status that would prolong Ohio's membership. One such measure would simply extend the current conformity deadline by an additional six months, to July 1, 2008. Another would allow the Governing Board to approve associate membership for a state whose only area of non-conformity is with SSUTA sourcing rules. The proposed amendments will be voted upon at next week's Governing Board meeting. Given the SSUTA's track record to date, it will come as no surprise if Ohio is granted some form of reprieve and remains an associate member for some additional period of time. When it comes to membership status, SSUTA rules are meant to be waived—not enforced.

The Governing Board Amended the Agreement to Approve New Jersey's Non-Conforming Fur Tax. The SSUTA's weak stance on conformity has also benefited at least one full member state. As I explained earlier, the New Jersey legislature in 2006 enacted a replacement "fur tax" which most observers believed was not in conformity with the agreement's requirement that a state [either] tax or exempt all products for which the agreement has a formal definition. After New Jersey enacted the fur tax, the SSUTA, rather than disciplining or even expelling the state in its annual re-certification process, simply amended the agreement to adopt a definition for fur clothing, thus bringing New Jersey's fur tax into *post-hoc* conformity.

DESPITE REPEATEDLY DILUTING ITS STANDARDS, THE SSUTA HAS NOT ATTRACTED MANY NEW MEMBERS, AND NOW FACES DECLINING MEMBERSHIP

The contortions the Governing Board has gone through to retain members is probably best explained by its inability to attract additional participation by states. The SSUTA has proven unattractive to most states, and the largest states have been most averse to membership. A number of state legislatures, including Florida and Virginia, have outright rejected conformity legislation. Upon the agreement's effective date in October 2005, the SSUTA had 13 full member states; on January 1, 2008, it will have 17. The only states to join as full members in the past three years have been Arkansas, Rhode Island, Vermont and Wyoming. The SSUTA is clearly a minority system.

In fact, the SSUTA is losing membership. With Ohio and Utah due to fall out of the SSUTA, the percentage of population will likely fall below the 29 percent level claimed by the SSUTA in October 2005. In fact, if the SSUTA were vigilant regarding compliance and excluded both Tennessee and New Jersey, the percentage of the population represented by full and associate member states participation would fall dangerously close to the 20 percent threshold necessary for the agreement to remain in effect under its own terms.

It is now time for the Streamlined Sales Tax Project to confront the painful reality that the terms of the SSUTA and its governance procedures are fundamentally flawed, that it has not achieved meaningful sales and use reform, and that is not attractive to the great majority of states. It is time, instead, to re-assess the process that brought the SSUTA to this point and initiate a new process, perhaps through the Commissioners on Uniform State Laws, to craft a truly uniform act whose hallmark is real simplification of state sales and use tax regimes. On behalf of the DMA, I want to thank you again for the opportunity to offer my comments on this important issue.

THE CONTINUING DEBATE:
Allowing States to Collect Sales Taxes on Interstate Commerce

What Is New

The bill, "H.R. 3396, The Sales Tax Fairness and Simplification Act," discussed in the readings, did not make it out of committee and to the floor for debate and a vote. One reason that allowing states to collect sales taxes on remote interstate sales has not received more support in Congress is that 52% of Americans oppose the idea, with only 38% in favor, and 10% unsure. Still, many states continue to find a way to tax remote sales. In 2008, New York State passed legislation to tax the sales of vendors like Amazon whose only physical presence in the state is affiliate vendors that advertise through Amazon. Whether this is sufficient to meet the Supreme Court "substantial physical presence" standard for such taxation remains to be determined by the courts in the suits that have been filed by Amazon and others.

Where to Find More

Congressional Research Service, *State and Local Sales and Use Taxes and Internet Commerce,* Report RL31252 (March 9, 2006). A related CRS report that is helpful is, *The Streamlined Sales and Use Tax Agreement: A Brief Description,* Report RS22387 (February 22, 2006). The University of Tennessee study discussed in the readings with updated data including 2008 is Donald Bruce and William F. Fox, "State and Local Sales Tax Revenue Losses from E-Commerce: Estimates as of July 2004." It is available on the Web site of the university's College for Business Administration at www.cber.utk.edu/ecomm.htm/. U.S. government data on e-commerce can be found at www.census.gov/mrts/www/ecomm.html/. For the Web site of the NCSL's Executive Committee Task Force on State and Local Taxation of Telecommunications and Electronic Commerce go to www.ncsl.org/programs/fiscal/tctelcom.htm/. The opposing view of the Direct Marketing Association is on the Internet at www.the-dma.org/taxation/. An argument opposed to an interstate sales tax on the grounds that sales taxes are regressive and extending them to new areas would compound that problem is made by Christopher G. Reddick in "Electronic Commerce and the State Sales Tax System: An Issue of Tax Fairness," *Journal of Electronic Commerce in Organizations* (2006). The taxation of e-commerce is a global, as well as a U.S. issue, as evident in Subhajit Basu, *Global Perspectives on E-commerce Taxation Law* (Ashgate, 2007).

What More to Do

Formulate a proposal to tax remote sales. Consider letting each state collect the taxes based on its own rates or having a single national tax rate with the federal government distributing the revenue. If each state gets tax from commerce within it, should the sales tax apply to the state where the item is shipped from, where the vendor's corporate headquarters is located, or where the purchaser is located? Would you tax all items sold in interstate commerce or would you exempt some, such as children's clothing and medicine? Should the government compensate vendors for the new burden of tax administration? How would you deal with goods going to/arriving from overseas?

BUDGETARY POLICY

ADDING A BALANCED BUDGET AMENDMENT TO THE CONSTITUTION:
Fiscal Imperative *or* Unnecessary and Unwise

FISCAL IMPERATIVE

ADVOCATE: Andrew Moylan, Vice President of Government Affairs, National Taxpayers Union

SOURCE: Testimony during hearings on "Should the Constitution Be Amended to Address the Federal Deficit" held before U.S. House of Representatives, Committee on the Judiciary, Subcommittee on the Constitution, May 13, 2011

UNNECESSARY AND UNWISE

ADVOCATE: Robert Greenstein, President, Center on Budget and Policy Priorities

SOURCE: Testimony during hearings on "Should the Constitution Be Amended to Address the Federal Deficit" held before U.S. House of Representatives, Committee on the Judiciary, Subcommittee on the Constitution, May 13, 2011

In order to be better prepared to consider this debate over whether to add an amendment to the Constitution that would require a balanced budget, let us begin with a number of general points about the federal budget.

Budget "jargon": Some technical terms are important to understand. The fiscal year (FY) of each annual U.S. budget runs from October 1 through September 30 (FY 2011 ran from October 1, 2010 through September 30, 2011). Thus each fiscal year is referred to by the calendar year in which it ends. In this introduction we will mostly look at data for FY 2011 and for comparative purposes, data for three decades (FY 1981) and six decades (FY 1951) earlier. The budget is divided into two parts: the *discretionary budget* and the *mandatory budget*. The first involves program that receive specific annual appropriations. The second involves "entitlement" programs that are funded by a formula (such as food stamps) and also expenditures that the government is legally obligated to make (such as paying the interest on the national debt). Discretionary spending in FY 2011 was 34% of the total budget, and mandatory spending was 66%. Note that mandatory expenditures (except for interest payments) are not truly mandatory because Congress may change the formula at will. Also, mandatory spending programs are not entitlements in the sense of addressing recognized fundamental rights under the Constitution. The flow of money comes and goes through *on-budget* and *off-budget* receipts and expenditures. On-budget accounts are those that flow through the U.S. Treasury. Off-budget accounts either go through special "trust funds," as does the Social Security funds, or through such corporate-like activities as the U.S. Postal Service. Data here on budget includes both sets of accounts.

The size of the budget: The budget (herein calculated as expenditures) for FY 2011 budget was $3.8 trillion. A trillion is a thousand billion. In FY 1981 the budget was $678 billion, and it was $46 billion in 1951.

The importance of the budget to the U.S. economy: Federal spending is the most important aspect of the economy. The FY 2011 budget accounted for about 25.3% of the U.S. gross domestic product (GDP, the value of wealth produced within a country). That is up from 22.2% in FY 1981 and from 14.2% in 1951).

Budget growth: In "current dollars" (not figuring in inflation), the FY 2011 budget is 5.6 times larger than the FY 1981 budget and 83 times the size of the FY 1951 budget. Even in "real dollars" (or "constant dollars," those controlled for inflation), the FY 2011 is more than twice the size of the FY 1981 budget and almost 8 times larger than the FY 1951 budget.

Revenue sources: Individual income taxes are the biggest source (43% of receipts), followed closely by social insurance and retirement taxes (such as Social Security and Medicare, 37% of receipts). Corporate taxes take in 9% and excise taxes 3% of receipts, with the remaining 8% from miscellaneous sources such as tariffs, fines, and user fees.

Spending categories: Human resources (such as health, welfare, and Social Security) consumed 66% of the FY 2011 budget, national defense accounted for 20%, followed by physical resources (roads, building, etc.) 6%, and 6% to pay interest on the national debt, with the remaining 2% going to miscellaneous costs. The biggest changes in shares of the budget have been increased human resource expenditures (53% in FY 1981, 24% in FY 1951) and lower defense expenditures (24% in 1981, 52% in 1951).

The history of budget surpluses and deficits: There has been a budget deficit more than 70% of the years since 1900, and every year since 1970 except for four years (FY 1998 through FY 2001). The budget deficit for FY 2011 was $1.7 trillion. As a percentage of the budget, the 2011 deficit was 43%, compared to 12% in FY 1981 and 13% in FY 1951.

Funding the deficit: The government makes up the revenue gap by borrowing money. The government borrows some from itself by, for example, dipping into the Social Security trust fund. The rest it borrows by selling bonds to investors. By the end of FY 2011, the national debt will be an estimated $15.5 trillion, compared to $995 billion in FY 1981 and $255 million in 1951. Of the FY 2011 debt, the government owes about a third to itself and the rest (the public debt) to private lenders. The national debt in FY 2011 is equal to about 103% of the U.S. GDP, compared to 33% in 1981 and 80% in 1951. Foreigner investors hold about 47% of the public debt, with Chinese and Japanese investors each holding nearly 10% of the public debt. Interest payment on the debt for FY 2011 came to about $430 billion, an amount kept relatively low by historically low interest rates. An increase in inflation and interest rates could send debt payments soaring.

The history of trying to control the budget: In recent decades, attempts to legislatively control the budget began amid the perennial and mounting deficits between FY 1970 and FY 1997. During these years, Congress passed several budget control acts. Each had some impact on restraining the budget, but none has proven to be a permanent solution. The rare budget surpluses between FY 1998 and FY 2001 were

253

more the result of booming revenues generated by one of the most prosperous times in U.S. history than the result of budget controls. Proposals to amend the Constitution to require a balanced budget are submitted almost every Congress but rarely receive much notice. An exception was in 1997 when the House passed a balanced-budget amendment measure, but the Senate defeated it by one vote.

The soaring budget deficits of the last decade and the associated increase in the strength of the Tea Party movement (see Debate 9) have once again brought the idea of a balanced-budget amendment to the foreground. Andrew Moylan argues in the first reading that the only sure way to control dangerous deficits is to make them unconstitutional without a supermajority vote in Congress to permit deficit spending. Robert Greenstein disagrees in the second reading, contending that such an amendment is not necessary and would be dangerous to national governance and prosperity.

POINTS TO PONDER

➤ Compare the dangers Andrew Moylan project for continuing huge deficits with those Robert Greenstein says will result from a balanced-budget amendment. Which are more likely? Which are worse?

➤ Ask yourself, why does the president and Congress have such a difficult time balancing the budget?

➤ Is balancing the budget an inherently liberal or conservative idea? Why or why not?

Adding a Balanced Budget Amendment to the Constitution: Fiscal Imperative

Andrew Moylan

Distinguished members of the Subcommittee, thank you for the opportunity to testify on behalf of the American Taxpayer regarding the important issue of a constitutional amendment to address the federal deficit. My name is Andrew Moylan, and I am Vice President of Government Affairs for the National Taxpayers Union (NTU), a non-partisan citizen group founded in 1969 to work for lower taxes and smaller government at all levels. NTU is America's oldest non-profit grassroots taxpayer organization, with 362,000 members nationwide. We look forward to this hearing as the beginning, rather than the end, of robust and serious deliberation of constitutional protections for taxpayers.

Few citizen groups in Washington can match NTU's decades-long history of principled advocacy in favor of a Balanced Budget Amendment (BBA), which is why I hope you will find these comments on solutions to our staggering debt problems helpful. NTU has been one of the most powerful voices in support of durable structural reforms to our budget process to protect taxpayers. We were active participants in several major campaigns to enact a BBA in Congress, including the closest-ever effort in the 104th Congress [1995–1996] that saw House passage and fell one vote short in the Senate. During that time and to this day, NTU has additionally sought to propose a BBA for ratification through the limited amendment convention process provided under Article V of the U.S. Constitution. You can also find further research into these topics on our website at http://www.ntu.org.

In pursuit of a sustainable fiscal future, NTU has worked in conjunction with friends and allies as part of the "BBA Now Coalition." The result of these deliberations is a "Common Sense Balanced Budget Amendment" proposal that has attracted the support of more than 90 grassroots and campus groups across the country. Along with NTU, our coalition includes such national groups as the American Civil Rights Union, Americans for a Balanced Budget Amendment, Americans for Tax Reform, American Solutions, Balanced Budget Amendment Now, Contract from America, Institute for Liberty, Let Freedom Ring, National Tax Limitation Committee, ReAL Action, Regular Folks United, 60 Plus Association, Tea Party Express, Young Americans for Freedom, and Young Conservatives Coalition. The proposal details and a full list of supporters can be found at the coalition's website, www.bbanow.org.

In the course of our work with coalitions such as BBA Now, other organizations, and academic experts on public finance, we have received a great deal of advice and consultation on the elements of a successful federal tax and expenditure limitation. Much of that advice and consultation has been informed by experience at the state and local level. For example, Colorado's Taxpayer's Bill of Rights (TABOR) has, since its adoption in 1992, been regarded as one of the most important constitutional mechanisms for state and local fiscal discipline ever devised. TABOR, in turn, can trace its lineage to a wealth of experience in other states.

We were gratified that the three most important components of the BBA Now Coalition's product are reflected in several resolutions under consideration in Congress: a simple balanced budget requirement, a supermajority threshold to enact any tax increase, and a limit to prevent spending from climbing above historical averages. We believe that these three cornerstones, along with greater discipline in the appropriations process, a restructuring of our entitlement programs, and a complete overhaul of our burdensome and loophole-ridden Tax Code would provide a solid foundation for America's future.

THE PROBLEM

In the past decade, under the direction of Presidents and lawmakers from both parties, our federal budget has expanded dramatically no matter what measure one consults. At the dawn of the new millennium in 2001, federal outlays were about $1.8 trillion or 18.2 percent of our Gross Domestic Product (GDP), a level below post-World War II averages. Through the middle of the decade, we saw an explosion in spending driven by such factors as the creation of a new cabinet-level Department of Homeland Security as well as increased expenditures on defense and education. By 2003, the modest spending discipline of the late 1990s had given way to federal outlays that now seem permanently fixed at or above the post-war average of 19.6 percent of GDP. Add in the more recent surge in so-called "crisis response" spending, such as the $700 billion Troubled Asset Relief Program (TARP) of 2008 or the $862 billion "economic stimulus" bill of 2009, and the picture grows even bleaker.

In 2011, our budget is more than twice as large as in 2001, reaching about $3.8 trillion. As a percentage of our economy, 2011 outlays will surpass a level unseen since the era of full-scale war mobilization in the 1940s, at over 25 percent. Perhaps most disturbing, President [Barack] Obama's estimate of our overspending problem, at roughly $1.6 trillion in 2011, is about equal, in inflation-adjusted terms, to the entire federal budget in 1982. Put another way, we will raise through the Tax Code and spend (in real terms) roughly the federal budget of 2003 and borrow an amount approximating the 1982 federal budget just for good measure.

Perhaps even more disturbing, Congress and Presidents alike in recent years have not only failed to grapple with our broken entitlement programs but have actually added to their size and scope. The Medicare prescription drug benefit that passed in 2003, which NTU vigorously opposed, added another layer to the program's liabilities. Just last year, the health care reform bill passed by Congress included large changes to Medicare spending that would lead to significant savings; however, that legislation spends every single dime of the savings (and more than $500 billion raised through higher taxes) on a dramatic expansion of Medicaid and a new regime of health care subsidies. These and other actions have led the nation's finances to the point where if leaders do not take corrective action soon, the United States could face a devastating debt crisis that would likely precipitate not only dramatic spending cuts but also massive tax hikes in very short order.

The federal government has seen deficits during 44 of the last 50 years. This fact ought to give pause even to die-hard Keynesians, who believe surpluses should be the norm in most economic growth cycles. While NTU's dedication to limited government would on its own lead us to conclude that this spending spree is unacceptable, sheer mathematics tell us that it is unsustainable. As of today, we are perilously close to the point where our country's debt exceeds its economic output. This sad statistic places us in rare company—just slightly below countries already staggered by debt crisis (like Ireland) and just above countries thought to be under grave threat of one (like Portugal).

THE SOLUTION

While the causes of the recent spending spree are myriad and complicated, the remedies are relatively straightforward. On the discretionary side, Congress must cancel wasteful programs, root out inefficiencies, and roll back agency spending to pre-bailout, pre-stimulus levels. With mandatory spending, Congress must take hold of the so-called "third rail" of politics with both hands and enact serious entitlement reforms primarily focused on controlling the growth in spending on Medicare and Medicaid and rectifying the terrifying prospect of Social Security operating in deficit from here on out.

Though Congress should aggressively pursue these prudent spending restraints, they will not be enough to rectify the defects of the budget process itself. Thus, Congress must enact with all deliberate speed a robust Balanced Budget Amendment to the Constitution.

As I briefly recounted earlier in this testimony, NTU's most fundamental and enduring goal has been to establish constitutional limits on the size and future growth of government. Throughout the 1970s and 1980s, my organization helped to launch and sustain the movement for a limited Article V amendment convention among the states to propose a Balanced Budget Amendment for ratification, all while pursuing a BBA through Congress. Our members were elated over the passage of S.J. Res. [Senate Joint Resolution] 58 in 1982, and the passage of H.J. Res. [House Joint Resolution] 1 in 1995 through the House of Representatives. In both cases the measures, whose provisions varied somewhat, fell short of enactment in the other chambers of Congress.

This history provides an illustration of how prescient the arguments of BBA advocates have proven to be, and how specious those of opponents have been. For the better part of 40 years, we were told that fiscal discipline would evolve simply by "electing the right people," all while Republican and Democratic Presidents and Congresses abused the nation's good credit. We were told that statutory measures would bring outlays under control, even as laws such as the Gramm-Rudman Hollings Act were trampled underfoot. We were told that our foundational document shouldn't be "cluttered" with mundane matters of budgeting, even as the tax-and-spend culture in Washington eroded the foundations of prosperity for current and future generations.

This is particularly interesting in light of an oft-overlooked portion of our nation's history: the failure of the Articles of Confederation and the drafting of the Constitution. In 1995, NTU's then-Chairman (and current Chairman Emeritus) James Davidson testified before this very Subcommittee about that event's connection to fiscal mismanagement:

> Our Constitution was adopted precisely because of fiscal collapse under the Articles of Confederation. As Sidney Homer wrote in *A History of Interest Rates,* "The finances of the nation were chaotic. Expenditures were authorized without the power to tax. Government credit sank so low that by 1787 certified interest-bearing claims against it were worth less than fifteen cents on the dollar." As Sidney Homer and other historians have documented, the need to balance the budget and restore the good credit of the government led directly to the drafting of the Constitution in the first place. Mr. Homer says, "In spite of the great potential economic strength of the new country, its financial and political system broke down completely in 1786. Credit at home and abroad was no longer avail-

able. The impossibility of government without money, credit, or power led to the Constitutional Convention of 1787 and a new nation in 1789."

It is often said that politicians do not need constitutional help to maintain fiscal responsibility; all they are supposed to need is the "will" to do so. The evidence of our own history says otherwise. No one would argue that the great leaders who brought our country its independence lacked political will. Yet even they could not balance the budget and keep up payments on the national debt under the Articles of Confederation. It took a change in the Constitution to restore sound policy and sound credit.

The notion that limits on taxes and spending are too trivial for the Constitution seems quaint today, as our national debt tests the ominous level of 100 percent of the nation's economic output. As noted earlier, unsustainable entitlement programs, whose dire condition has been known for at least 20 years now, threaten to heap unfathomable burdens on taxpayers. BBA naysayers sought to derail the constitutional budgetary discipline that could have made adjustments to the realities of these programs gradual and bearable, all while they complained that the measure would "take too long to ratify" for it to have any salutary effect. The question now before Congress is, how could our Constitution not be allowed to contribute toward restoring our nation's fiscal stability? The fiscal crisis our government faces overwhelmingly demonstrates the continued relevance of a BBA to curing the maladies that threaten the health of our economy.

CURRENT PROPOSALS

To our members, a BBA would provide the very lifeblood that will restore and sustain the financial health of our Republic. We are therefore encouraged over the intensifying interest among Members of Congress and state legislators in a unified BBA concept. Several iterations of a Balanced Budget Amendment have already been introduced in the 112th Congress. NTU has traditionally supported a range of approaches to a BBA, but several merit specific discussion here.

Perhaps the most prominent proposal is the so-called "Consensus BBA" introduced by Senator [Orrin] Hatch (R-UT) as S.J. Res. 10 and by Representative [Joe] Walsh (R-IL) as H.J. Res. 56. This resolution combines and refines elements from several amendments introduced thus far in Congress. Its structure is relatively simple. First, it directs the President to submit and Congress to enact a balanced budget while allowing for a two-thirds vote to authorize any specific excess. A two-thirds vote would also be required for any tax increase and courts would be prevented from ordering any increase in revenue. It would provide a backstop by requiring a three-fifths vote of Congress in order to approve any increase in the national debt. Further, the resolution carefully spells out how Congress could suspend the provisions of the BBA and authorize specific additional spending to address national security threats: by majority vote in the event of a declared war, and by three-fifths vote in any other type of military conflict. Finally, it enacts a spending limitation that will hold federal spending to 18 percent of GDP.

NTU supports this proposal for its strength and comprehensiveness and its proper focus on the true cause of our fiscal maladies: overspending. By including a strong expenditure limitation, this version of a BBA would provide a vital check on irresponsible budgeting. Although several types of mechanisms could answer to the purpose of controlling growth in expenditures, any such protection incorporating Gross Domestic

Product must pay careful heed to historical experience. In this case, NTU believes that an annual spending cap at 18 percent of GDP is clearly the most prudent choice. Such a level reflects the share of economic output that federal revenues have typically represented since World War II. Given that constitutional amendments should be designed with a long nod to the past and an equally farsighted view to the future, 18 percent is a most stable and logical benchmark.

In addition, setting the expenditure limit at 18 percent would make a valuable contribution toward harmonizing all parts of the amendment so that the whole functions as intended. An assumption that spending should normally be linked to the average and customary federal revenue proportion would, by its very nature, give Congress and the President a starting point that is closer to balance. Indeed, the limit helps to remedy Washington's increasingly metastasized affliction of tax-spend-and-borrow, by elevating the concept of expenditure restraint to its rightful place in policymaking. While the two-thirds "supermajority" override requirement is essential to ensuring this place, so is the 18 percent cap on expenditures. If set too high, the spending limit would merely institutionalize, rather than minimize, deficits. Recent spending-to-GDP ratios in excess of 20 percent—and the resulting pressures to borrow or tax even more—ought to convince fiscal disciplinarians of the need for a carefully-designed limit, given that Washington has only collected more than 20 percent of GDP in revenues three times since 1940.

Another strong BBA proposal is S.J. Res. 5, introduced by Senator Mike Lee (R-UT). This version is similar in structure to the aforementioned "Consensus BBA," with a balanced budget requirement, an 18 percent spending cap, and a supermajority threshold for tax hikes but is stricter in several areas. First, it harmonizes all supermajority requirements at a two-thirds vote of Congress. Second, it contains no specific language authorizing excesses for national security purposes, preferring to allow the supermajority override option to serve that purpose.

Senators [John] Cornyn (R-TX) and Hatch (R-UT) have also introduced a BBA, S.J. Res. 3, which would achieve many of the same goals, though its spending limit is placed at a higher level of 20 percent of GDP, roughly the historical post-war average for outlays. In your chamber, Representative Bob Goodlatte (R-VA) has continued his long history of leadership on this issue by introducing H.J. Res. 1, which incorporates other supermajority requirements and spending limitations, and H.J. Res. 2, which takes a more basic stance. All of these proposals, and perhaps some others yet to be introduced, deserve consideration, but Congress must do so without delay.

In NTU's opinion some particular BBA concepts are worthy of further deliberation, and some should be avoided. While many proposals in Congress achieve a cap on spending by limiting it to a certain percentage of GDP, this is not the only way to achieve such a goal. Basing a limitation on a prior year's revenues, or receipts over a range of years, could achieve similar aims. However, we would strongly urge Members to avoid any provisions to exempt certain portions of the federal budget from a BBA. This policy would provide an enormous loophole through which to drive additional spending and unleash a destructive lobbying war over what programs should receive special status.

REBUTTALS TO COMMON ARGUMENTS AGAINST A BBA

The latter, chilling prospect aside, a legion of BBA opponents has for quite some time waged war against the very notion of a constitutional protection against greater debt.

Some of the arguments they deploy have gained an unwarranted amount of political currency and I'd like to address the more common ones here.

During the BBA debates of the 1980s and 1990s, one familiar refrain from opponents was that an amendment was simply unnecessary to restrain deficits because Congress could do so on its own. If political "will" were enough to protect citizens from unwise or pernicious legislation, then we could likewise do without the all-important First Amendment to the Constitution as well since Congress could simply refrain from passing any laws abridging freedom of speech. But our Founders recognized, and citizens and scholars now universally accept, the need for limitations on the power of government to abridge fundamental rights such as these. So it is that we must limit the power of legislators to imperil our nation's finances and our children's future. Just as our Founders did, Congresses and Presidents both present and future need a credible fiscal structure and reasonable guidelines within which they can operate. A strong BBA would provide exactly that kind of protection. Though prominent in prior debates, this argument ought to have no relevance now that we've had decades of intervening experience with scarcely interrupted (and bipartisan) support for ever-higher debt to the detriment of our fiscal health.

The common refrain heard today is that a BBA would be a "depression-maker" because it would prevent Congress from utilizing fiscal policy to counteract an economic recession. The response to this contention is two-fold: one technical, the other practical. The technical response is that under the "Consensus BBA," Congress can enact whatever kind of spending or tax policies it likes so long as two-thirds of its Members vote in the affirmative. Other proposals include lower thresholds, such as three-fifths, to achieve such an override. These provisions preserve Congressional flexibility by allowing large majorities to act in times of emergency.

The practical response is that despite claims to the contrary, Congress is not only capable of achieving such supermajorities but has done so regularly when faced with truly urgent decision points in recent history. For example, when the financial panic of late 2008 gripped the nation, Congress passed the Troubled Asset Relief Program with strong bipartisan supermajorities in both chambers (including 74 votes in the Senate). Setting aside for a moment whether or not TARP was good policy (for the record, NTU was a staunch opponent), it was clearly advertised as an emergency measure to prevent an economic collapse. For better or worse, Congress took that advice and passed the bill with votes from both parties.

For further evidence, we can look to supplemental appropriations bills. In recent years, these have generally fallen into two categories: spending on wars, or response to natural disasters. Disaster spending tends to draw strong support and pass with huge majorities, but the vigorous public debate surrounding the wars in Iraq and Afghanistan led to much closer votes. NTU took no position on U.S. involvement in these conflicts, but it is clear that policies enjoying widespread public support have no trouble clearing a supermajority hurdle while policies that are controversial have a more uncertain path.

Some opponents of a BBA contend that we have never enshrined any specific economic policy in the Constitution and should not do so now. But the BBA is not an economic policy and it is not a federal budget; it is a set of guidelines within which Congress can create economic policy and a federal budget. It is no more an economic policy than the 21st Amendment, which repealed alcohol prohibition, was a specific regulatory policy for states. Neither of these amendments prescribes the manner in which legislators must incorporate them in daily policy; they simply lay out the ground rules for the debate.

Others argue that a BBA would take too much time and effort to ratify and gain the force of law. While it is true that ratification can be protracted, the process of amending our Constitution is rightly one that involves meeting strict criteria. Nonetheless, the obvious point needs to be made: had the Senate followed the House's lead in 1995 and passed the BBA, the measure could very well have been ratified and operating for the better part of a decade by now. In any case, NTU urges passage of statutory language in pursuit of the same goals expressed in a Balanced Budget Amendment to help bridge the gap. Still, given that statutory measures exist at the whim of Congress, taxpayers can only count on a strong constitutional measure to protect them from fiscal disaster.

There are often questions about how such an amendment would be enforced. Some say that a BBA is essentially unenforceable because there is nothing that will compel Congress to comply with its mandates, but that cynical view could be extended to virtually any policy, whether constitutional or statutory. President Jackson famously said of an 1832 Supreme Court decision, "[Chief Justice] John Marshall has made his decision, now let him enforce it!" Marshall, of course, did not have an army at his disposal and could rely only upon the tensile strength of the fabric of our system of checks and balances and robust public involvement in the federal government. As with essentially every other policy, a BBA would be enforced through these tools if a violation occurred.

BBA opponents argue that it is unwise for it to include a spending limitation since that would necessitate large reductions in expenditures over the coming years. First, it is simply not accurate to characterize a return of spending to post-war revenue averages as any kind of "steep" or "draconian" cut. Further, even the most aggressive budget outline that has been proposed (by the Republican Study Committee, the caucus of House conservatives) would envision outlays hovering around $3.3 trillion (an amount just shy of 2009 expenditures of $3.5 trillion) and then modestly increasing to $4.3 trillion by the end of the decade. This would merely allow for the historical trend for spending increases to catch up with the massive spikes witnessed in 2009 and 2010. But most importantly, these kinds of reductions are absolutely necessary to changing our trajectory of ever-increasing deficits and debt. We must begin to reduce spending now to ward off fiscal catastrophe.

Others argue that a BBA in and of itself does nothing to solve the long-term drivers of our debt: entitlement costs. While technically correct, no single policy is likely to solve those problems and the Constitution would be the wrong place to deal with such details. What a BBA will do is ensure that future leaders do not dig the debt hole any further and that that they do not habitually deviate from historical norms on spending. By establishing those boundaries, the BBA will give Congress the proper incentives to finally grapple with entitlement reform.

CONCLUSION

Thomas Jefferson, a hero to many conservatives, once wrote, "I wish it were possible to obtain a single amendment to our Constitution... [an amendment] taking from the federal government the power of borrowing." Franklin D. Roosevelt, a hero to many liberals, once said, "Let us have the courage to stop borrowing to meet continuing deficits. Revenues must cover expenditures by one means or another. Any government, like any family, can, for a year, spend a little more than it earns. But you and I know that a continuation of that habit means the poorhouse." Though they lived more than a century apart in time and miles apart on the ideological spectrum, both of these titans of American history recognized the threat posed by deficits and expressed support for policies to make them a thing of the past.

No proposal in Congress today would guarantee such an outcome—an end to deficit spending. What a BBA will guarantee is a more deliberative, accountable budgeting process that avoids the rash impulse to tax or borrow and encourages consensus-building toward spending restraint. Constitutions shouldn't make policy, but they should set rules within which policymakers operate and they should safeguard the rights of citizens. If the fundamental right—of every generation—to be free of excessive federal debt cannot be protected by our Constitution, little else in that precious document will matter. Thus, the past, present, and future all speak clearly to us on behalf of this reform.

Adding a Balanced Budget Amendment to the Constitution: Unnecessary and Unwise

ROBERT GREENSTEIN

Thank you for the invitation to testify today. I am Robert Greenstein, president of the Center on Budget and Policy Priorities, a policy institute that focuses both on fiscal policy and on policies affecting low- and moderate-income Americans. We, like most others who analyze fiscal policy developments and trends, believe that the nation's fiscal policy is on an unsustainable course. As part of our work, we have been analyzing proposed changes in budget procedures for more than 20 years. We have conducted extensive analyses of proposals to write a balanced-budget requirement into the Constitution, among other proposals.

The purpose of changing our fiscal policy course is to strengthen our economy over the long term and to prevent the serious economic damage that would likely occur if the debt explodes in future decades as a share of the economy. But we need to choose our fiscal policy instruments carefully. We want to avoid "destroying the village in order to save it."

The goal of a constitutional balanced budget amendment is to address our long-term fiscal imbalance. Unfortunately, a constitutional balanced budget amendment would be a highly ill-advised way to try to do that and likely would cause serious economic damage. It would require a balanced budget every year regardless of the state of the economy, unless a supermajority of both houses overrode that requirement. This is an unwise stricture that many mainstream economists have long counseled against, because it would require the largest budget cuts or tax increases precisely when the economy is weakest. It holds substantial risk of tipping faltering economies into recessions and making recessions longer and deeper. The additional job losses would likely be very large.

When the economy weakens, revenue growth drops and revenues may even contract. And as unemployment rises, expenditures for programs like unemployment insurance—and to a lesser degree, food stamps and Medicaid—increase. These revenue declines and expenditure increases are temporary; they largely disappear as the economy recovers. But they are critical for helping struggling economies to keep from falling into a recession and for moderating the depth and length of recessions that do occur.

When the economy weakens, consumers and businesses spend less, which in turn causes further job loss. The drop in tax collections and increases in unemployment and other benefits that occur automatically when the economy weakens cushions the blow, by keeping purchases of goods and services from falling more. That is why economists use the term "automatic stabilizers" to describe the automatic declines in revenues and automatic increases in UI and other benefits that occur when the economy turns down; these actions help to stabilize the economy.

A constitutional balanced budget amendment, however, effectively suspends the automatic stabilizers. It requires that federal expenditures be cut or taxes increased to offset the effects of the automatic stabilizers and prevent a deficit from occurring—the opposite course from what sound economic policy calls for.

Over the years, leading economists have warned of the adverse effects of a constitutional balanced budget amendment. For example, in Congressional testimony in 1992,

Robert Reischauer—then director of the Congressional Budget Office [CBO] and one of the nation's most respected experts on fiscal policy—explained: "If [a constitutional balanced budget amendment] worked, it would undermine the stabilizing role of the federal government." Reischauer noted that the automatic stabilizing that occurs when the economy is weak "temporarily lowers revenues and increases spending on unemployment insurance and welfare programs. This automatic stabilizing occurs quickly and is self-limiting—it goes away as the economy revives—but it temporarily increases the deficit. It is an important factor that dampens the amplitude of our economic cycles." Under the constitutional amendment, he explained, these stabilizers would no longer operate automatically.

Similarly, when a constitutional balanced budget amendment was under consideration in 1997, more than 1,000 economists including 11 Nobel laureates issued a joint statement that said:

> We condemn the proposed "balanced-budget" amendment to the federal Constitution. It is unsound and unnecessary.... The proposed amendment mandates perverse actions in the face of recessions. In economic downturns, tax revenues fall and some outlays, such as unemployment benefits, rise. These so-called "built-in stabilizers" limit declines of after-tax income and purchasing power. To keep the budget balanced every year would aggravate recessions.

More recently, in January 2011, the current CBO director, Douglas Elmendorf, sounded a similar warning when asked about a constitutional balanced budget amendment at a Senate Budget Committee hearing. Elmendorf observed:

> Amending the Constitution to require this sort of balance raises risks .... [t]he fact that taxes fall when the economy weakens and spending and benefit programs increase when the economy weakens, in an automatic way, under existing law, is an important stabilizing force for the aggregate economy. The fact that state governments need to work... against these effects in their own budgets— need to take action to raise taxes or cut spending in recessions—undoes the automatic stabilizers, essentially, at the state level. Taking those away at the federal level risks making the economy less stable, risks exacerbating the swings in business cycles.

Proponents of a constitutional amendment likely will respond to these admonitions by noting that the proposed constitutional amendment would allow the balanced-budget requirement to be waived by a vote of three-fifths of the House and the Senate. That, however, does not address this problem. It is difficult to secure three-fifths votes for anything; consider the paralysis that marks the work of the Senate. Moreover, it may take months after a downturn begins before sufficient data are available to convince three-fifths of the members of both houses of Congress that a recession is underway. Furthermore, it is all too likely that even after the evidence for a downturn is clear, a minority in the House or Senate would hold a wavier vote hostage to demands for concessions on other matters (such as new, permanent tax cuts). By the time a recession were recognized to be underway and three-fifths votes were secured in both chambers, if such support could be obtained at all, extensive economic damage could have been done and hundreds of thousands or millions of additional jobs unnecessarily lost.

The bottom line is that the automatic stabilizers need to continue to be able to work automatically to protect American businesses and workers. The balanced budget amendment precludes that.

Nor is a recession the only concern. Consider the savings and loan crisis of the 1980s, or the financial meltdown of the fall of 2008. A constitutional balanced budget amendment would have hindered swift federal action to rescue the savings and loan industry or to rapidly put the Troubled Assets Relief Program in place. In both cases, history indicates that federal action helped save the economy from what otherwise likely would have been far more dire problems.

Moreover, the federal government provides deposit insurance for accounts of up to $250,000; this insurance—and the confidence it engenders among depositors—is critical to the sound functioning of our financial system so that we avoid panics involving a run on financial institutions, as occurred in the early 1930s. A constitutional prohibition of any deficit spending (unless and until a supermajority of both houses of Congress voted to authorize it) could seriously weaken the guarantee that federal deposit insurance provides. That is a risk we should not take.

These are illustrations of why fiscal policy should not be written into the Constitution.

A parallel problem is that the proposed constitutional amendment would make it even harder than it already is to raise the debt limit, by requiring a three-fifths vote of both the House and Senate to raise the limit. This is playing with fire. It would heighten the risk of a federal government default. A default would raise our interest costs and could damage the U.S. economy for years to come.

MISTAKEN ANALOGIES TO STATES AND FAMILIES

Proponents of a constitutional amendment sometimes argue that states and families must balance their budgets every year and the federal government should do so, too. But statements that the constitutional amendment would align federal budgeting practices with those of states and families are not accurate.

While states must balance their *operating* budgets, they can borrow to finance their *capital* budgets—to finance roads, schools, and other projects. Most states do so. States also can build reserves during good times and draw on them in bad times *without* counting the drawdown from reserves as new spending that unbalances a budget.

Families follow similar practices. They borrow—they take out mortgages to buy a home or student loans to send a child to college. They also draw down savings when times are tight, with the result that their expenditures in those periods exceed their current incomes.

But the proposed constitutional amendment would bar such practices at the federal level. The *total* federal budget—including capital investments—would have to be balanced every year, with no borrowing allowed for infrastructure or other investments that can boost future economic growth. And if the federal government ran a surplus one year, it could *not* draw it down the next year to help balance the budget.

I would also note that the fact that states must balance their operating budgets even in recessions makes it all the more important from the standpoint of economic policy that the federal government *not* be subject to the same stricture. American Enterprise Institute analyst Norman Ornstein addressed this matter in a recent article, where he wrote:

Few ideas are more seductive on the surface and more destructive in reality than a balanced budget amendment. Here is why: Nearly all our states have balanced budget requirements. That means when the economy slows, states are forced to raise taxes or slash spending at just the wrong time, providing a fiscal drag when what is needed is countercyclical policy to stimulate the economy. In fact, the fiscal drag from the states in 2009–2010 was barely countered by the federal stimulus plan. That meant the federal stimulus provided was nowhere near what was needed but far better than doing nothing. Now imagine that scenario with a federal drag instead.

H.J. RES. 1 RAISES ADDITIONAL ISSUES

The foregoing concerns apply to all versions of the balanced budget amendment that have been introduced. Some versions of the balanced budget amendment, such as H.J. Res [House Joint Resolution] 1, raise additional serious concerns, because they would write into the Constitution new prohibitions against raising any revenues—including closing wasteful tax loopholes—to help balance the budget and also would prohibit federal expenditures in any year from exceeding a figure such as 20 percent of the Gross Domestic Product. These constitutional prohibitions could be overridden only by supermajority votes in both the House and the Senate.

This requirement for a supermajority to raise taxes would be extremely unsound. It would protect what President [Ronald] Reagan's former chief economic advisor, Harvard economist Martin Feldstein, has called the biggest area of wasteful government spending in the federal budget—what economists call "tax expenditures" and Alan Greenspan has called "tax entitlements."

In 2010, tax expenditures amounted to $1.1 trillion, more than the cost of Medicare and Medicaid combined (which was $719 billion), Social Security ($701 billion), defense ($689 billion, including expenditures in Iraq and Afghanistan), or non-defense discretionary spending ($658 billion, including expenditures from the Recovery Act). Many of these tax expenditures are fully the equivalent of government spending.

Let me use child care as an example. If you are low- or moderate-income, you may get a federal subsidy to help cover your child-care costs, and the subsidy is provided through a spending program. If you are higher on the income scale, you still get a government subsidy that reduces your child-care costs, but it is delivered through the tax code, as a tax credit. (Moreover, if you are a low or modest income parent with child-care costs, you likely will miss out because the spending programs that provide child care subsidies are *not* open ended and can only serve as many people as their capped funding allows. By contrast, if you are a higher income household—and there is no limit on how high your income can be—your child-care subsidy is *guaranteed*, because the tax subsidy you get operates as an open-ended entitlement.) It is difficult to justify making the tax-code subsidy sacrosanct and the program subsidy a deficit-reduction target merely because one is delivered through a "spending" program and the other is delivered through the code.

And as the child-care example illustrates, sharply distinguishing between subsidies delivered through the tax code and those delivered through programs on the spending side of the budget also has a "reverse Robin Hood" aspect. Low- and moderate-income households receive most of their government assistance through spending programs;

affluent households receive most of their federal subsidies through tax expenditures. Effectively barring reductions in tax expenditures from contributing to deficit reduction is a prescription for placing the greatest burden of deficit reduction on those who can least afford to bear it.

The problems do not stop there. If it requires a supermajority to raise any revenue, another likely outcome is a proliferation of tax loopholes. New loopholes—including loopholes that Congress *did not* intend but that high-priced tax lawyers and accountants have found ways to create—could become untouchable once they appeared, because it would require a supermajority of the House and Senate to raise any revenue. It would become more difficult to close tax loopholes that opened up, since special-interest lobbyists could seek to block such action by preventing a supermajority in one chamber.

Finally, H.J. Res 1 would bar federal spending from exceeding 20 percent of GDP. To hit that level would require cuts of a draconian nature. This can be seen by examining the austere budget that the House of Representatives passed on April 15, sometimes referred to as the Ryan budget [after Representative Paul Ryan (R-WI), chairman of the House Budget Committee].

Under that budget, Medicare would be converted to a voucher system under which, the Congressional Budget Office [CBO] has said, beneficiaries' out-of-pocket health-care costs would nearly triple by 2030 (relative to what those costs would be that year under the current Medicare program). CBO also has written that under the Ryan budget, federal Medicaid funding in 2030 would be 49 percent lower than it would be if the Affordable Care Act's Medicaid expansion were repealed but Medicaid otherwise was unchanged. And funding for non-security discretionary programs would be cut more than one-third below its real 2010 level. Yet CBO says that under this budget, total federal spending would be *20¾ percent of GDP in 2030*, so it would breach the allowable limit under H.J. Res 1. This illustrates the draconian nature of the proposed 20 percent-of-GDP requirement.

Another way to look at the 20 percent of GDP level is to examine federal expenditures under Ronald Reagan. Under President Reagan, who secured deep budget cuts at the start of his term, federal expenditures averaged 22 percent of GDP. And that was at a time *before* any members of the baby boom generation had retired and when health care expenditures throughout the U.S. health care system (including the private sector) were one-third lower as a share of GDP than they are today. It also was before the September 11 terrorist attacks led policymakers to create a new category of homeland security spending, and before the wars in Iraq and Afghanistan led to increases in veterans' health-care costs that will endure for a number of decades.

CONCLUSION

Policymakers need to begin to change our fiscal trajectory. As various recent commissions have indicated, we need to stabilize the debt as a share of GDP in the coming decade, and to keep it stable after that (allowing for some fluctuation over the business cycle). But establishing a balanced budget amendment in the Constitution would be most unwise. It would likely exact a heavy toll on the economy and on American businesses and workers in the years and decades ahead. It is not the course the nation should follow.

THE CONTINUING DEBATE:
Adding a Balanced Budget Amendment to the Constitution

What Is New

During the first session (2011) of the 112th Congress (2011–2012), 12 proposals to amend the Constitution to require a balance budget were introduced in the House of Representatives and 5 were submitted in the Senate. House Joint Resolution 2 (H.J. Res. 2), the most widely supported of these proposals with 240 cosponsors, directs the president to submit a balanced budget to Congress annually. It also directs Congress to pass a balanced budget (except of interest payments) unless both houses authorize specific nonconforming expenditures by a three-fifths, roll-call vote. The resolution also would require a three-fifths roll-call vote of each chamber to increase the public debt limit. The proposed amendment would also prohibit any bill to increase revenue from becoming law unless approved by a majority of each chamber by a roll-call vote. Finally, the amendment would allow Congress by a majority vote in each chamber to waive the requirements when a declaration of war is in effect or when Congress by majority vote has recognized the existence of a "military conflict which causes an imminent and serious military threat to national security." Other resolutions had proposals such as capping spending at a percentage of the GDP (18% was one level) and requiring supermajorities (two-thirds, three-fifth) to raise taxes. For a time, the Republicans tried to force the president to support a balanced-budget amendment as part of the face off over raising the national debt ceiling in mid 2011. In the end, though, the Republicans did not hold fast on the demand. Moreover, with a two-thirds vote in both houses required to send a proposed amendment on to the states for ratification, it is unlikely any of the resolution will come to fruition.

Where to Find More

A neutral review of the approaches to a balanced budget amend is found in *A Balanced Budget Constitutional Amendment: Background and Congressional Options*, Congressional Research Service Report R41907, July 8, 2011, available at the Federation for American Scientists Web site at www.fas.org/. There are groups such as Americans for a Balanced Budget (www.balanceourbudget.com/) specifically dedicated to supporting a balanced budget amendment. For the opposite stand, visit the Web site of Center on Budget Priorities and Analysis at www.cbpp.org/. Bypassing the difficulty of getting a balanced budget amendment through Congress by calling a constitutional convention is discussed in Michael Stokes Paulsen, "How to Count to Thirty-Four: The Constitutional Case for a Constitutional Convention," *Harvard Journal of Law and Public Policy* (2011)

What More to Do

Debate H.J. Res. 2, including allowing changes to the proposed amendment that members of the class might offer. You can find the text of H.J. Res. 2 by going to Thomas, the Library of Congress Web site for Congress at http://thomas.loc.gov/home/thomas.php. Under "Search Bill Summary & Status" you can choose "bill number" and enter "H.J. Res. 2" or, to get it and other similar proposals, choose "world/phrase" and enter "balanced budget amendment."

17 NATIONAL SECURITY POLICY

TRYING THOSE ACCUSED OF TERRORISM:
Use Civilian Courts *or* Use Military Commissions?

USE CIVILIAN COURTS

ADVOCATE: Stephen A. Saltzburg, Wallace and Beverley Woodbury University Professor, George Washington University Law School

SOURCE: Testimony during hearings on "Justice for America: Using Military Commissions to Try the 9/11 Conspirators" before the U.S. House of Representatives, Committee on the Judiciary, Subcommittee on Crime, Terrorism and Homeland Security, April 5, 2011

USE MILITARY COMMISSIONS

ADVOCATE: Stephanie Hessler, Adjunct Fellow, Manhattan Institute for Policy Studies

SOURCE: Testimony during hearings on "Justice for America: Using Military Commissions to Try the 9/11 Conspirators" before the U.S. House of Representatives, Committee on the Judiciary, Subcommittee on Crime, Terrorism and Homeland Security, April 5, 2011

One aspect of globalization is the increasing prominence of international terrorism as a form of conflict. The 9/11 attacks underline this reality. Dealing with al Qaeda and other such terrorist organizations that operate across borders (transnationally), have a multinational membership, and may even recruit a country's citizens to attack their own country presents new legal uncertainties. One of these is how to treat alleged terrorists connected to international terrorist organizations. The treatment of another country's military prisoners of war (POWs), including captured members of irregular forces such as guerillas, is governed by a series of treaties collectively called the Geneva Conventions (1864, 1906, 1929, and 1949). Generally, POWs may not be tried or punished for the acts they have committed in combat. The treatment of "home-grown" terrorism and terrorists (those who commit terrorist acts in their own country and have no global ties) are subject to their country's laws, and such terrorists are tried in their country's general court system. Captured international terrorists, arguably even including those who commit their acts of terrorist within their own country at the behest of, or through association with, an international terrorist organization, occupy an uncertain status between the clearly defined spheres of prisoners of war and domestic criminals.

The status of alleged terrorists who had been captured came into prominence with regard to al Qaeda members captured by the United States in Afghanistan and others held for the most part at the U.S. naval base at Guantanamo Bay, Cuba. The administration of President George W. Bush argued that these prisoners were not members of an organized military and set up military commissions (tribunals) to try them. Under the rules establish by the Department of Defense, defendants did not have many of the protections available to anyone, not just Americans citizens, tried in U.S. civilian courts or military personnel and POWs tried in military courts martial. The differences in treatment included such matters as whether prisoners had to be charged and brought to a speedy trial, what evidence could be used, and the right to counsel.

When Salim Ahmed Hamdan, an al Qaeda member captured in Afghanistan, challenged the constitutionality of the military commission process created by the Bush administration, the Supreme Court ruled in *Hamden v. Rumsfeld* (2006) that the president had exceeded his authority by unilaterally establishing the military commissions. But the Court also indicated that Congress could legislate special procedures for the treatment of prisoners like Hamden. After considerable debate, Congress did so by passing the Military Commission Act (MCA) in 2006 and amending it in 2009. It authorized the president to set up military commissions to try terrorists, and specified procedures that, overall, give defendants more rights than they had under the Bush plan but fewer protections than prisoners of war, much less U.S. citizens, charged with crimes have in civilian or military courts martial. Among other things, the MCA permitted the use of hearsay evidence and barred defendants and their attorneys from seeing evidence obtained from sensitive intelligence sources. The MCA also expansively applies to those who support as well as engage in terrorism against U.S. targets, but it does specifically rule out U.S. citizens (but not all U.S. residents) from being subject to military commission.

Although the MCA as passed in 2006 and amended in 2009 has brought the rights of accused terrorists closer to the rules applying to civilian courts and courts martial, there are those, including George Washington University law professor Stephen A. Saltzburg in the first reading, who believe that justice will best be served if those accused of participating in 9/11 and other acts of international terrorism are tried in a U.S. district court. Stephanie Hessler of the Manhattan Institute for Policy Studies disagrees. She contends that the 9/11 conspirators should be tried by military commission—not in federal district court.

POINTS TO PONDER

➤ The language in the Bill of Rights related to the investigation of crimes and the prosecution and punishment of accused individuals does not distinguish among individuals based on their citizenship status. Is there difference anyway?

➤ What is the line between foreign combatants, including guerillas and other irregular forces protected by the Geneva Conventions, and terrorists?

➤ Would it give at least a greater appearance of justice if foreign terrorists apprehended abroad where tried in the International Criminal Court?

Trying Those Accused of Terrorism:
Use Civilian Courts

STEPHEN A. SALTZBURG

Members of the Subcommittee, I thank you for inviting me to testify before you on the subject of using military commissions to try the 9/11 conspirators.

REDEFINING THE QUESTION

I begin by noting that the real question is where to try those who are alleged to be conspirators. At the moment the five individuals who may be charged as principal participants in the horrific attacks on America that occurred on September 11, 2001 have not been prosecuted in any tribunal. They remain presumed innocent irrespective of the assumptions that have been made by many as to their responsibility for the hijacking of airplanes and the killing of innocent people.

TRY CASES IN ARTICLE III COURTS

My position on where those charged with the worst act of mass murder on American soil should be tried is clear: IN AN ARTICLE III COURT presided over by a judge appointed by the President and confirmed by the Senate and before a jury of American citizens chosen from a cross-section of the community as juries are chosen in the United States every working day. [An Article III court is one established under that article in the Constitution and, for the most part, includes the Supreme Court, the circuits of the U.S. Court of Appeals, and the federal district courts. There are also so-called legislative courts, and courts martial and related military commissions are examples of this type of court.]

THE REASONS FOR USING ARTICLE III COURTS

Why do I think it is important for the trial to be in an Article III court? There are a number of reasons, many of which have been well articulated by thoughtful people over the years since the 9/11 attacks:

1. Civilian courts are capable of handling complex terrorism and espionage cases. Their track record is strong. Over 400 terrorism-related suspects have been successfully tried in federal courts since 9/11. Only a handful of cases have been handled by military commissions, and the military commission process has been hampered by starts and stops, changes in the rules, and uncertainty about exactly how cases would proceed.

2. The life-tenure provided federal judges [in Article III courts] by the founders of this Nation is one of our fundamental guarantees that justice in federal courts will be impartial and that those who preside over criminal cases will not be beholden to the Executive. The independence of the federal judiciary is one of the factors that inspires confidence in the decisions rendered by federal courts. There is no comparable independence of military judges who preside over commissions.

3. A civilian jury is one of the greatest democratic institutions that we have. It is chosen from throughout the community. It is inclusive. Men and women serve together. People of all races and religions are called to serve together. Individuals with varying education, expertise and experience serve as a unit to assess the strength and weakness of evidence. The jurors are screened for bias, and challenges for cause and peremptory

challenges offer protections against jurors who are partial. The judgment of such jurors—as, for example, those who assessed a fair punishment for Zacarias Moussaoui—benefits from the many different perspectives that jurors bring to their deliberations. [Zacarias Moussaoui, is a citizen of France, pled guilty in a federal district court to being part of the conspiracy leading the 9/11 attacks and was sentenced by a jury to life in prison without the possibility of parole.] Military commission members are not drawn from a similar cross-section of the community, are chosen by the Convening Authority who also brings the charges against an accused, and will never be viewed as being as fair and impartial as a civilian panel.

4. There is enormous skepticism about the fairness of military commissions that is largely explained by the now discredited procedures originally proposed to govern them. Had the procedures now in place as a result of the Military Commission Act of 2009 ("MCA 2009") and improvements made by the Department of Defense been in place from the outset, some of the concerns about commissions would have been eliminated. But, the process has been slow and once doubts about the fairness of a tribunal arise, it is difficult if not impossible to eradicate them.

5. Many public figures have proclaimed that we ought to use military commissions because they provide a greater certainty of conviction. Such comments fuel the perception that the rules governing the commissions are adopted with an eye to increasing the probability of conviction and a severe sentence rather than increasing the likelihood of a fair and just proceeding. Our goal should be to try individuals charged with these acts of mass murder in a manner that convinces our people and those around the world who look to us for leadership in preserving and protecting the rule of law that we are guaranteeing a fair trial for all charged with crimes, even the worst crimes. Our citizens and those of other nations are most likely to be convinced by trials in federal courts.

6. The individuals charged with the 9/11 murders ought not be treated as warriors. We are in a fight against international terrorism. There is no mistake about it. But, terrorists who commit murder in the United States against innocent civilians are criminals who should be prosecuted as such. Those alleged to be responsible for the 9/11 attacks should be tried in civilian courts just as Timothy McVeigh was tried for the Oklahoma City bombing. [He detonated a truck bomb in 1995 that destroyed the federal building and adjacent buildings, killing 168 people and injuring 680 others.] He was proved to have been a murderer, sentenced to death, and executed. The federal court that tried him used the same procedures that govern criminal trials throughout the United States. Those procedures produced a fair trial and a just verdict. Those same procedures can and should be employed in trying those accused of the 9/11 attacks.

7. There is a place for military commissions in the prosecution of terrorists. They are most defensible when employed to prosecute individuals who attack American military targets abroad, where witnesses and evidence may be uniquely available. But, they are not the forum for trying the most serious charges of intentional murder committed on American soil that may ever be brought. That forum is a federal district court.

8. Some of the arguments made in favor of military commissions sound as though we do not trust civilian courts. The case of Ahmed Khalfan Ghailani is cited as an example of why we should avoid civilian courts. Although Ghailani was acquitted on all charges but one, his conviction on a conspiracy charge relating to the 1998 East Africa Embassy bombings led to a life sentence without the possibility of parole. The fact that a civilian jury found the evidence insufficient on the other charges ought to

inspire confidence that the trial was fair, the government was put to its proof as required by the Constitution, and there is no reason to question the integrity of the guilty verdict of conspiracy.

Those that argue that the evidence deemed inadmissible against Ghailani would have been admissible in a military commission may be wrong. Judge [Lewis] Kaplan, the trial judge, stated in a footnote in his ruling that it was far from clear that the witness's testimony would be admissible if Ghailani were being tried in a military commission because the MCA 2009 likely would require exclusion, but even if it did not the Constitution might do so even in a military commission proceeding.

9. Although the rules of evidence that currently govern military commissions are more favorable to the prosecution than either the Federal Rules of Evidence applicable in federal courts or the Military Rules of Evidence applicable in courts-martial, there is uncertainty as to whether the commission's evidence rules will ultimately be held to satisfy the Constitution's guarantee of due process. We can be certain that the Federal Rules of Evidence will pass constitutional muster and that trials under those rules satisfy due process. The uncertainty as to whether the commission rules will ultimately be upheld is genuine and reason to avoid prosecuting the 9/11 cases in any forum other than an Article III court. The Supreme Court's decision in *Hamdan v. Rumsfeld* (2006), stands as a caution not to assume that federal courts that review commission proceedings will find that the procedure and evidence rules are constitutionally adequate. [The Court ruled in *Hamden* that the military commissions established by President George Bush were unconstitutional because they did not comply with the Uniform Code of Military Justice and the Geneva Convention and because such commissions had to be established by Congress. Note the Court did not rule military commissions as such unconstitutional. Hamden, a Yemeni, who was alleged to have been a driver and bodyguard for Osama bin Laden was later tried and convicted by a statutorily authorized military commission and received a 66-month sentence.]

10. A trial in civilian court that results in a conviction could be appealed to a federal circuit court. If the conviction is affirmed, the defendant could seek review in the United States Supreme Court. The appellate process is familiar and can be efficiently employed. Military commissions will employ an appellate process that is less familiar and more cumbersome. First, there is review by the Convening Authority. Second, there is review by the Court of Military Commission Review, a unique tribunal that was created specifically to review commission proceedings whose membership keeps changing. Third, there is review by the United States Court of Appeals for the District of Columbia Circuit. Finally, there is potential review by the United States Supreme Court. There is every reason to believe that the military commission appellate process will be more prolonged than its civilian counterpart.

RESPONSES TO THE ARGUMENTS AGAINST ARTICLE III COURTS

I am not persuaded that there is any insurmountable problem with trying those accused of the 9/11 murders in civilian court. So let me address some of the so-called problems.

1. *Security for the trial will be prohibitively expensive and disruptive.* This could be true if the trial were held in lower Manhattan and the New York Police Department concluded that prudence required a massive security presence and a substantial cordoned-off area. Although some have questioned the need for such security and have pointed to the fact that Ghailani was transferred to New York City from Guantanamo

and was tried without incident, I would not second-guess the NYPD. There is no requirement that the trial be held in New York, however. It could be held in the Eastern District of Virginia, where the Alexandria federal courthouse is already relatively secure.

The case could also be initiated in the Southern District of New York, and either side could move for a change of venue. The case could be tried, for example, in New Jersey where a federal court sits next to a detention facility and defendants may be moved from the facility to the court through an underground tunnel. Such a forum ought to cut security costs and ameliorate threat concerns considerably.

Moreover, if there were reason to believe that a specific threat of retaliation were directed at the location of a trial, an Article III trial could be convened at a military installation in the United States where security would presumably be adequate to thwart any attempt at retaliation.

There is surely good reason to question the assumption that if the trial is held in a military commission in Guantanamo, there will be no attempted retaliation by sympathizers of the defendants. After all, retaliation can be directed at any American facility; it need not be directed at the courthouse where a defendant is tried. The World Trade Center buildings were attacked as symbols. Any terrorist who sought to retaliate against the United States for trying those accused of the 9/11 attacks could choose another symbol far removed from the trial itself. So, no one should be choosing a military commission as a means of avoiding potential retaliation.

2. *Civilian trials put judges and jurors at risk.* It is true that a federal judge who presides over a trial involving any individual associated with a criminal enterprise could be the target of retaliation. The danger is ever present when judges sentence a member of a group that is known to engage in violence. Yet, our federal judges have not hesitated to preside over these trials. Indeed, our judges fully understand that the rule of law would be weakened if they did not meet their responsibilities even at some risk. It is true security may be required for a judge after some cases, but we have provided it in the past and should be prepared to provide it when necessary to enable our judges to do their jobs.

What is true of physical locations is also true of people. One terrorist sympathizer could retaliate against the trial of another terrorist by retaliating against any government officer. There are no rules governing retaliation. A terrorist could retaliate against a military commission proceeding by targeting a judge, a member of Congress, or a civilian who had nothing to do with the proceeding. The fact is that there is no way to guarantee that there will be no retaliation as a result of any trial.

As for jurors, federal courts have considerable experience impaneling anonymous juries and their use has been upheld by appellate courts. As a result, jurors have been willing to serve and have been safe from retaliation. There is no reason to believe that anonymous juries could not be employed in the 9/11 cases or that their use would put jurors at risk.

3. *The prosecution has a better chance of convicting in military commissions than in civilian court.* I agree that this is true, but do not see it as a reason to choose commissions. Quite the contrary, I see it as one of the reasons that there is so much concern and distrust about commissions. Evidence that would never be admitted in a federal trial or a court-martial can be admitted in a commission proceeding. Why? The answer is that the Executive makes the rules. That does not equate with fair and just proceedings in the eyes of many. It also supports the notion that when federal courts finally do get to review commission proceedings they may find the rules favoring the government to deny due process to a defendant, as noted above.

Moreover, the rules that govern military commissions exclude some of the evidence would have been admissible under earlier sets of rules. Opponents of using the traditional criminal justice system claim that involuntary/coerced self-incriminating statements obtained from defendants would be inadmissible in our traditional criminal justice system, but would be admissible in the military commissions. However, Congress limited the admissibility of such statements in the MCA 2009 providing that: "No statement obtained by the use of torture or by cruel, inhuman, or degrading treatment (as defined by section 1003 of the Detainee Treatment Act of 2005), whether or not under color of law, shall be admissible in a military commission under this chapter, except against a person accused of torture or such treatment as evidence that the statement was made."

It is true that exceptions exist: "A statement of the accused may be admitted in evidence in a military commission under this chapter only if the military judge finds— "(1) that the totality of the circumstances renders the statement reliable and possessing sufficient probative value"; and (2) that—"(A) the statement was made incident to lawful conduct during military operations at the point of capture or during closely related active combat engagement, and the interests of justice would best be served by admission of the statement into evidence"; or "(B) the statement was voluntarily given." Exactly what fits under (2)(A) is unclear. But (2)(B) seems to indicate that a coerced confession that would be inadmissible in federal court is equally inadmissible in commission proceedings.

4. *Civilian trials can turn into a circus and provide a forum for defendants to insult and demean the memory of the victims of 9/11.* Civilian trials are among the most formal, controlled proceedings that governments experience because they are controlled by federal judges who have power to assure that litigants, lawyers and observers behave or are removed from the courtroom if they do not behave.

It is true that a defendant who takes the witness stand or who makes a statement during sentencing has the opportunity to say things that are insulting, demeaning, or even threatening. But, this is equally true in civilian trials and in military commissions. More importantly, the defendant does not get the last word. After Zacarias Moussaoui spoke to the court at sentencing, Judge Brinkema had the last word and informed him that he would have 23 hours a day in solitary confinement to contemplate the crimes he committed. She spoke the last words, and they represented the response of a nation. She was not the only federal judge to speak such words. Judge Coughenour of the Western District of Washington has noted the power of words when federal judges let convicted terrorists know that they are nothing more than mere criminals.

5. *There are speedy trial concerns with proceeding in federal court after so much delay.* There are two responses to this concern. Judge Kaplan addressed the speedy trial issue in the Ghailani trial: "Although the delay of this proceeding was long and entirely the product of decisions for which the executive branch of our government is responsible, the decisions that caused the delay were not made for the purpose of gaining any advantage over Ghailani in the prosecution of this indictment. Two years of the delay served compelling interests of national security. None of the five year delay of this prosecution subjected Ghailani to a single day of incarceration that he would not otherwise have suffered. He would have been detained for that entire period as an enemy combatant

regardless of the pendency of this indictment. None of that delay prejudiced any interests protected by the Speedy Trial Clause in any significant degree. In these specific circumstances, Ghailani's right to a speedy trial has not been infringed." The same analysis ought to apply to 9/11 defendants.

But, if there is a speedy trial problem, there is no assurance that it would not be just as much of a problem in a commission proceeding. As I have noted, no one is sure what aspects of constitutional law ultimately will be held binding in commission proceedings. If it is unfair to try a defendant in a civilian court because of undue delay, it may be equally unfair to try that defendant in a military commission.

6. *Classified information can be better handled in military commissions.* I disagree with this argument on the basis of substantial personal experience with classified information in federal criminal cases. During the Iran-Contra prosecutions by Independent Counsel Lawrence Walsh, I handled the classified information issues for the Department of Justice in the prosecution of Lt. Col. Oliver North. As a result, I became extremely familiar with the Classified Information Procedures Act. Dealing with classified information in a federal trial under the Act poses the same problems as dealing with classified privileged information in a court-martial under Military Rule of Evidence 505. Federal courts are as capable as military commissions of preparing "substitutes" for classified information that protect a defendant's right to confront the evidence against him and to offer relevant evidence in support of a defense. The process contemplated by Mil. Comm. R. Evid. 505 is similar to that which would occur in a federal court. Federal courts have demonstrated that they can protect confidential and classified information while moving federal criminal trials to a successful conclusion.

CONCLUSION

For the reasons stated above, I strongly believe that justice is best served by trying those accused of the 9/11 attacks in an Article III court.

Trying Those Accused of Terrorism:
Use Military Commissions

STEPHANIE HESSLER

Members of the Committee: I thank you for the opportunity to express my views about the use of military commissions to prosecute the September 11th plotters and other detainees held at the Guantanamo Bay Detention Camp.

In my view, the 9/11 conspirators should be tried by military commission—not in federal court. I will focus my remarks on the risks of federal criminal prosecutions and the ways in which military commissions may alleviate these risks. I will also comment briefly on the substantial due process that military commissions afford the accused.

I. LEGAL AUTHORITY FOR MILITARY COMMISSIONS

I would like to begin by briefly outlining the legal authority for military commissions. Our founders understood the difference between keeping *internal* order, through the criminal justice system, and protecting against *external* threats from our enemies, through military action. Article I, Section 8, clause 10, of the Constitution gives Congress the power to "define and punish Piracies and Felonies committed on the high Seas, and Offences against the Law of Nations." Congress has repeatedly exercised this power to establish military commissions.

Indeed, the United States has used military tribunals throughout its history, including in the War of 1812, the Mexican-American War, the Civil War and World War II. As the Supreme Court confirmed in *Ex Parte Quirin* [1942], "unlawful combatants are...subject to trial and punishment by military tribunal." [This case involved eight German saboteurs captured in the United States in 1942. On July 2 a secret military court was convened by President Franklin Roosevelt's order. It quickly convicted the eight. The Court ruled on July 31 that the method of trial was constitutional. On August 8, six of the eight saboteurs were executed.]

Shortly after terrorists attacked us on September 11th, President [George W.] Bush established military commissions to try foreign jihadists for war crimes. In 2006, the Supreme Court ruled in *Hamdan v. Rumsfeld* that the Uniform Code of Military Justice required certain procedural protections for military commissions and invited Congress to enact legislation. In reaction to *Hamdan*, bipartisan majorities of Congress passed the Military Commissions Act of 2006, which was amended in 2009 ("the MCA").

II. MILITARY COMMISSIONS ALLEVIATE THE RISKS
INVOLVED WITH FEDERAL CRIMINAL PROSECUTIONS
FOR UNLAWFUL ENEMY COMBATANTS

In the years before the September 11th attacks and the subsequent establishment of military commissions, foreign terrorists were tried in our criminal justice system. But as we learned on 9/11, trying alleged terrorists after an attack does little to prevent the next one. After September 11th, we changed our approach to terrorism—shifting focus from punishment to prevention.

For at least three reasons, prosecuting foreign war criminals in federal court may undermine our counterterrorism goals. Civilian trials may (A) reveal classified and sensitive information to our enemies, (B) hinder intelligence gathering, and (C) burden military operations abroad. The military commissions enacted by Congress are specifically designed to alleviate these risks while granting the accused substantial procedural protections.

A. Protecting Information

i. Classified Intelligence

First and foremost, we need to protect classified information from our enemies. Acquiring intelligence is one of the most crucial means for penetrating and dismantling terror networks and protecting our national security. Obtaining classified communications and operational capabilities of terrorist groups can be a prolonged, painstaking and often very dangerous job for our intelligence agents. Such information—including sources and methods of intelligence gathering—must be vigorously safeguarded.

Criminal trials, however, risk disclosing top-secret information to our enemies. In such a trial, the federal judge has discretion to order classified materials released if it deems substitutes inadequate. And, if the government refuses to disclose classified information, the judge may order the indictment dismissed. This can put the government in a catch-22 of either disclosing classified intelligence or risking dismissal of charges.

Congress sensibly addressed this issue in the Military Commissions Act. In a military trial, the Government cannot be compelled to disclose classified information to anyone who does not have the proper security clearance. If the judge determines that access to the information is necessary, the government may redact portions of the information, submit a summary, or substitute a statement admitting facts that the classified material would tend to prove. Furthermore, such an order by a military judge may not be reconsidered.

ii. Sensitive Information

Likewise, the United States also has an interest in protecting information that may not be classified but could nonetheless aid our enemies in their fight against us. Because criminal court proceedings are required to be public under the Sixth Amendment of the Constitution, sensitive information may freely flow to our enemies. For example, in the trial of Sheikh Omar Abdel-Rahman for the 1993 World Trade Center bombings, the prosecution made a routine disclosure to the defense lawyer of a list of unindicted co-conspirators. According to Andrew McCarthy who prosecuted the case, this valuable list of key terror suspects reached Osama bin Laden, halfway around the world, within ten days.

Likewise, in that case, there was extensive data about the engineering and construction of the World Trade Center building. It is certainly possible that terrorists used this information to design and plot the attacks that destroyed the buildings a few years later.

Congress recognized that the transparency of criminal trials may undermine the goal of protecting our national security. Therefore, the Military Commissions Act provides that while military trials are generally public, the judge is permitted to close proceedings in order to protect national security interests, safeguarding intelligence and law enforcement sources, methods and activities. This flexibility is vital to ensuring that trials do not turn into a feast of national security information for terrorists at-large.

B. Miranda Warnings Impede Intelligence Gathering

Bringing federal criminal actions may not only reveal sensitive information, it may also impede intelligence gathering. The Fifth Amendment of the Constitution protects criminal defendants from self-incrimination. The Supreme Court has held that statements of the accused are not permitted in criminal trials unless the defendant was advised of his rights. FBI and law enforcement generally read Miranda warnings immediately upon arrest so as to preserve evidence for prosecution.

But the U.S. Constitution does not give foreign wartime enemies the privilege to be tried in federal court and thus shielded from self-incrimination. When an alien terrorist is apprehended, our national security interests demand that we acquire as much information as possible to prevent a future attack and neutralize security threats. Any intelligence officer will tell you that starting off with, "you have the right to remain silent..." is not the way to gain counterterrorism data.

Take, for example, the case of Umar Farouk Abdulmutallab, otherwise known as the Christmas Day bomber. The self-professed al Qaeda-trained operative attempted to explode a flight from Amsterdam [in The Netherlands] to Detroit the Christmas before last [in 2009]. Despite the fact that Abdulmutallab is a Nigerian national, with no right under any statute or the Constitution to be tried as a U.S. civilian, the Obama administration immediately decided to grant him the rights of a U.S. citizen. In a first round of questioning, he disclosed his al Qaeda training in Yemen and mentioned additional terrorist plots. But after only 50 minutes of questioning, he was given Miranda warnings and told he had the right to remain silent and the right to obtain a lawyer—compliments of the taxpayers he had just tried to explode. Needless to say, he quickly became reticent after receiving these warnings.

Congress recognized that reading terrorists Miranda warnings would severely hinder intelligence gathering and compromise counterterrorism efforts. Therefore, in military commissions, detainees' statements are admissible if a judge determines that they are reliable, probative and made during lawfully conducted military operations.

C. Federal Prosecutions May Burden Military Operations

Federal prosecutions may also burden military operations abroad. The facts in a transnational terrorism case often include second-hand statements, known as hearsay, which are generally prohibited in federal court. For example, key witnesses in such cases are often the soldiers or CIA agents who captured the defendant overseas. But these officers may still be engaged in combat abroad, and interrupting their counterterrorism mission to testify in federal court could place an undue burden on military efforts.

Given the unique challenge of prosecuting war crimes while hostilities are ongoing, the military commission rules allow the government greater flexibility to introduce second-hand statements. The Military Commissions Act allows hearsay to be admitted if the judge determines that the statement is reliable and probative and the witness is not available. In determining whether to admit second-hand statements, the judge is specifically directed to take into account "the adverse impacts on military or intelligence operations that would likely result from the production of the witness." Just as important, the hearsay rule is reciprocal. So the accused may admit material to prove his defense that would otherwise be excluded under the Federal Rules of Evidence.

III. UNLAWFUL ENEMY COMBATANTS ARE GRANTED SUBSTANTIAL DUE PROCESS

Finally, while the MCA mitigates many of the risks of criminal prosecution, it also affords the accused substantial procedural protections similar to those provided in federal court. In a military commission, (1) the accused is presumed innocent; (2) the

Government must prove guilt beyond a reasonable doubt; (3) the accused has a right to counsel; (4) he is protected from double jeopardy; (5) the government is obligated to disclose exculpatory evidence; and (6) the accused has the right to appeal to a Military Review Court, then the United States Court of Appeals for the DC Circuit and finally petition the U.S. Supreme Court.

V. CONCLUSION

In conclusion, the 9/11 plotters and other inmates held at Guantanamo should be tried in military commissions—not criminal court. Criminal trials may undermine our national security by revealing important information to our enemies, impeding intelligence gathering and placing an undue burden on military operations. There is no reason to gamble with America's security.

THE CONTINUING DEBATE:
Trying Those Accused of Terrorism

What Is New

While still a candidate for president, Senator Barack Obama deplored the use of military commissions as a "dangerously flawed legal approach." He also promised to end the confinement of terrorists at Guantanamo Bay and transfer them to prisons in the United States. On his third day as president, Obama moved to fulfill his campaign pledges. He suspended the use of military commissions and ordered that the Guantanamo Bay prison be closed within 12 months. Soon thereafter, the administration announced that Khalid Sheik Mohammed, the alleged mastermind of the 9/11 attacks, would be tried in federal court in New York City. The move brought a storm of protest, especially from the New Yorkers concerned about security costs and potential danger. Polls showed most Americans agreeing it was a bad idea, and the idea was dropped. The administration did bring a less-noted terrorist and Guantanamo prisoner, Ahmed Ghailani, to trial in a New York City federal district court. He was charged with 280 counts of terrorist activity related to the al-Qaeda bombings in 1998 of the U.S. embassies in Kenya and Tanzania. However, the administration suffered something of another public relations black eye when the presiding judged excluded critical evidence against the defendant on the grounds that it had been obtained by physical coercion from him and, subsequently, the jury found Ghailani not guilty of all but one of the charges. Generally the public has not been behind the president's moves, with only 28 percent agreeing that alleged terrorists should have the same rights as others in court and only 32 percent in favor of transferring the prisoners at Guantanamo to U.S. prisons. Then in 2011, Congress enacted legislation that would bar the use of federal funds to prosecute Guantanamo prisoners in U.S. civilian courts. Obama criticized the law as infringing on his constitutional authority, but he also backed off his earlier plans by keeping Guantanamo open and, in 2011, resurrecting the use of military commissions to try many of them. To explain this change of course, Obama's press secretary told reporters that, "First and foremost, the president of the United States is going to do what he believes is in the best security interest of the people of the United States."

Where to Find More

The 2006 and 2009 versions of the Military Commission Act are on Web site of the Department of Defense at www.defense.gov/news/commissionsacts.html. To compare the rights of defendants in military commissions and civilian courts, read *Comparison of Rights in Military Commission Trials and Trials in Federal Criminal Courts*, Congressional Research Service Report R40932, January 26, 2010, available on Google books at http://books.google.com. A recent overview of the legal status of alleged terrorists is available in Ashley C. Pope, "Note: After Guantanamo: Legal Rights of Foreign Detainees Held in the United States in the 'War On Terror'," *Fordham International Law Journal* (2011).

What More to Do

The dispute over whether to use military commissions or civilian courts to try alleged terrorists is in most ways about what the rights of the defendants will be. Draw up a "bill of defendant rights" for accused foreign terrorists being prosecuted by the

Untied States. Start by reviewing the Fourth, Sixth, Seventh, and Eighth Amendments. They are the ones that govern Americans' civil liberties related to police investigations and trials. Take each of the protections afforded to Americans in these amendments and debate whether, and to what degree, they should also govern the trials of terrorists.

CREDITS

Asian American Legal Foundation. Amicus curiae brief to the U.S. Supreme Court in *Parents Involved in Community Schools v. Seattle School District No. 1* (2007).

Attorneys representing Arizona and its governor, Janice K. Brewer, seeking to block a petition by the U.S. government to enjoin the enforcement of Arizona's S.B. 1070 in *The United States of America, Plaintiff, v. The State of Arizona; and Janice K. Brewer, Governor of the State of Arizona, in her Official Capacity, Defendants*, Case 2:10-cv-01413, U.S. District Court for the District of Arizona, July 6, 2010.

Attorneys representing plaintiffs Kristen M. Perry, et al. seeking to have California's constitutional clause barring gay marriage declared a violation of the U.S. Constitution in *Kristin M. Perry, et al., Plaintiffs, v. Arnold Schwarzenegger, et al., Defendants, and Proposition 8 Official Proponents Dennis Hollingsworth, et al., Defendant-Intervenors*; Case3:09-cv-02292-VRW; U.S. District Court for the Northern District of California; Responses to Court's Questions for Closing Arguments, June 15, 2010.

Attorneys representing Proposition 8 official proponents Dennis Hollingsworth, *et al.*, seeking to have California's constitutional clause barring gay marriage upheld in *Kristin M. Perry, et al., Plaintiffs, v. Arnold Schwarzenegger, et al., Defendants, and Proposition 8 Official Proponents Dennis Hollingsworth, et al., Defendant-Intervenors*; Case3:09-cv-02292-VRW; U.S. District Court for the Northern District of California; Responses to Court's Questions for Closing Arguments, June 15, 2010.

Attorneys representing the U.S. government seeking to enjoin the enforcement of Arizona's S.B. 1070 in *The United States of America, Plaintiff, v. The State of Arizona; and Janice K. Brewer, Governor of the State of Arizona, in her Official Capacity, Defendants*, Case 2:10-cv-01413, U.S. District Court for the District of Arizona, July 6, 2010.

Bright, Stephen B. Testimony during hearings on "An Examination of the Death Penalty in the United States" before the U.S. Senate, Committee on the Judiciary, Subcommittee on the Constitution, February 1, 2006.

Brown, Barbara Berish. Testimony during hearings on the "Paycheck Fairness Act" before the U.S. Senate, Committee on Health, Education, Labor & Pensions, April 12, 2007.

Chemerinsky, Erwin. "Constitutional Interpretation for the Twenty-first Century," *Advance: The Journal of the American Constitution Society Issues Groups*, Fall 2007. Reprinted with permission from The American Constitution Society for Law and Policy, Copyright © The American Constitution Society for Law and Policy, 1333 H St., NW, 11th Floor, Washington, DC 20005. Telephone: (202) 393-6181 Fax: (202) 393-6189. Web site: www.acslaw.org/.

Cuccinelli, Kenneth T. II. Testimony during hearings on "The Constitutionality of the Individual Mandate," before the U.S. House of Representatives, Committee on the Judiciary, February 16, 2011.

Emanuel, Kerry. Testimony on "Climate Change: Examining the Processes Used to Create Science and Policy" during hearings before the U.S. House of Representatives, Committee on Science, Space, and Technology, March 31, 2011.

Fisher, Louis. Testimony during hearings on "Libya and War Powers," before the U.S. Senate, Committee on Foreign Relations, June 28, 2011.

Fonte, John. Testimony during hearings on "Comprehensive Immigration Reform: Becoming Americans—U.S. Immigrant Integration," U.S. House of Representatives, Committee on the Judiciary, Subcommittee on Immigration Citizenship, Refugees, Border Security, and International Law, May 16, 2007.

Gerstle, Gary. Testimony during hearings on "Comprehensive Immigration Reform: Becoming Americans—U.S. Immigrant Integration" before the U.S. House of Representatives, Committee on the Judiciary, Subcommittee on Immigration Citizenship, Refugees, Border Security, and International Law, May 16, 2007.

Greenberger, Marcia. Testimony during hearings on the "Paycheck Fairness Act" before the U.S. House of Representatives, Committee on Education and Labor, Subcommittee on Workforce Protection, July 11, 2007.

Greenstein, Robert. Testimony during hearings on "Should the Constitution Be Amended to Address the Federal Deficit" held before U.S. House of Representatives, Committee on the Judiciary, Subcommittee on the Constitution, May 13, 2011.

Henderson, M. Todd. "*Citizens United*: A Defense," Faculty Blog, University of Chicago Law School. March 12, 2010. Reprinted with permission.

Hessler. Stephanie. Testimony during hearings on "Justice for America: Using Military Commissions to Try the 9/11 Conspirators" before the U.S. House of Representatives, Committee on the Judiciary, Subcommittee on Crime, Terrorism and Homeland Security, April 5, 2011.

Huffington, Arianna. Testimony during hearings on Senate Subcommittee on "The Future of Journalism" before the U.S. Senate, Committee on Commerce, Science, and Transportation; Subcommittee on Communications, Technology, and the Internet, May 6, 2009.

Isaacson, George S. Testimony during hearings on "H.R. 3396—The Sales Tax Fairness and Simplification Act," U.S. House of Representatives, Committee on the Judiciary, Subcommittee on Administrative and Commercial Law, December 6, 2007.

Koh, Hongju. Testimony during hearings on "Libya and War Powers," before the U.S. Senate, Committee on Foreign Relations, June 28, 2011.

Kroger, John. Testimony during hearings on "The Constitutionality of the Affordable Care Act," before the U.S. Senate, Committee on the Judiciary, February 2, 2011.

Lautenberg, Frank. Remarks on the floor of the U.S. Senate, *Congressional Record*, March 10, 2011.

Laycock, Douglas. From a discussion of the topic "Under God? Pledge of Allegiance Constitutionality," sponsored by the Pew Forum on Religion & Public Life, March 19, 2004. Reprinted with the permission of the Pew Forum on Religion & Public Life. For more information on this issue, please visit www.pewforum.org. Copyright © 2006 Pew Research Center.

Lee, Shirley Jackson. Remarks on the floor of the U.S. House of Representatives, *Congressional Record*, July 19, 2011.

McAdams, John. Testimony during hearings on "An Examination of the Death Penalty in the United States" before the U.S. Senate, Committee on the Judiciary, Subcommittee on the Constitution, February 1, 2006.

McConnell, Mitch. Remarks on the floor of the U.S. Senate, *Congressional Record*, March 31, 2011.

Mann, Thomas E. Testimony during hearings on "Examining the Filibuster: Legislative Proposals to Change Senate Procedures" before the Committee on Rules and Administration, U.S. Senate, June 23, 2010.

Montgomery, W. David. Testimony on "Climate Change: Examining the Processes Used to Create Science and Policy" during hearings before the U.S. House of Representatives, Committee on Science, Space, and Technology, March 31, 2011.

Moylan, Andrew. Testimony during hearings on "Should the Constitution Be Amended to Address the Federal Deficit" held before U.S. House of Representatives, Committee on the Judiciary, Subcommittee on the Constitution, May 13, 2011.

National Education Association, et al. Amicus curiae brief to the U.S. Supreme Court in *Parents Involved in Community Schools v. Seattle School District No. 1* (2007).

National Popular Vote. From "Agreement Among the States to Elect the President by National Popular Vote," National Popular Vote, April 29, 2009. Reprinted with permission.

Podesta, John. Testimony during hearings on "Economic Opportunity and Poverty in America" before U.S. House of Representatives, Committee on Ways & Means, Subcommittee on Income Security and Family Support, April 26, 2007.

Rauschenberger, Steven. Testimony during hearings on "H.R. 3396—The Sales Tax Fairness and Simplification Act" before the U.S. House of Representatives, Committee on the Judiciary, Subcommittee on Administrative and Commercial Law, December 6, 2007.

Rawls, Lee. Testimony during hearings on "Examining the Filibuster: Legislative Proposals to Change Senate Procedures" before the Committee on Rules and Administration, U.S. Senate, June 23, 2010.

Rector, Robert. Testimony during hearings on "Economic Opportunity and Poverty in America" before U.S. House of Representatives, Committee on Ways & Means, Subcommittee on Income Security and Family Support, April 26, 2007.

Saltzburg, Stephen A. Testimony during hearings on "Justice for America: Using Military Commissions to Try the 9/11 Conspirators" before the U.S. House of Representatives, Committee on the Judiciary, Subcommittee on Crime, Terrorism and Homeland Security, April 5, 2011.

Samples, John. "A Critique of the National Popular Vote Plan for Electing the President," *Policy Analysis*, No. 622 (October 13, 2008). Reprinted with permission of The Cato Institute.

Sekulow, Jay Alan. From a discussion of the topic "Under God? Pledge of Allegiance Constitutionality," sponsored by the Pew Forum on Religion & Public Life, March 19, 2004. Reprinted with the permission of the Pew Forum on Religion & Public Life. For more information on this issue, please visit www.pewforum.org. Copyright © 2006 Pew Research Center.

Simon, David. Testimony during hearings on Senate Subcommittee on "The Future of Journalism" before the U.S. Senate, Committee on Commerce, Science, and Transportation; Subcommittee on Communications, Technology, and the Internet, May 6, 2009.

von Spakovsky, Hans. "Voter Photo Identification: Protecting the Security of Elections," Legal Memorandum #70, Heritage Foundation, July 13, 2011. Reprinted with permission of The Heritage Foundation.

Warren, Elizabeth. Testimony during hearings on "The Rulemaking Process and Unitary Executive Theory" before the U.S. House of Representatives, Committee on the Judiciary, Subcommittee on Commercial and Administrative Law, May 6, 2008.

Whittington, Keith E. "Originalism Within the Living Constitution," *Advance: The Journal of the American Constitution Society Issues Groups*, Fall 2007. Reprinted with permission from The American Constitution Society for Law and Policy, Copyright © The American Constitution Society for Law and Policy, 1333 H St., NW, 11th Floor Washington, DC 20005. Telephone: (202) 393-6181 Fax: (202) 393-6189. Web site: www.acslaw.org/.

Youn, Monica. Testimony during hearings on the "First Amendment and Campaign Finance Reform After *Citizens United*," before the Committee on the Judiciary, U.S. House of Representatives, February 3, 2010.

Zywicki, Todd. Testimony during hearings on "Who's Watching the Watchmen? Oversight of the Consumer Financial Protection Bureau" before the U.S. House of Representatives, Committee on Oversight and Government Relations, Subcommittee on TARP, Financial Services, and Bailouts of Public and Private Programs, May 24, 2011.